All About **Aussies**

Dusty and Thistle, a golden cross that created a tremendous influence on the breed.   *Photo by Phil Wildhagen*

Cover photo: Courtesy Weaver

*This book is dedicated to the memory of my friend
Hubert Green. It is for my family for without
whom there would be no Australian Shepherd breed
as we know it today.*

Photo by D. MacSpadden

All About **Aussies**

by Jeanne Joy Hartnagle

Alpine Publications
P.O. Box 7027 • Loveland, CO 80537

Acknowledgements

A special thanks to everyone who made this book possible; to Sandy Case for the illustrations in Chapters 20 and 21; to Jan Logan for the drawing on page 22; and to Michael J. Ryan for the "Spider Web" calligraphy; to Lucie deGreen for providing invaluable historical data; to Robert E. Kline D.V.M. for consultation and professional guidance; to Lucia D. Kline D.V.M. for medical research; to Ernest J. Hartnagle for research, design and preparation of the "Spider Web," as well as assistance in other areas of research; to Elaine Hartnagle for historical and related research... a special thank you for all the years of inspiration and support; to Carol Ann Hartnagle for all the hours of laborious typing and for putting up with me; to my brother James (the Harold Angel) for the harassment and feedback; to my brother Joseph for his sense of humor and sparkling conversation; and to Christine and Vincent for their encouragement.

International Standard Book No. 0-931866-18-9

This book is available at special quantity discounts for breeders and for club promotions, premiums, or educational use. Write for details.

Printed in the United States of America.

Table of Contents

Foreword

I've heard people say, "I like him because he is such a character." Some say, "I like him for his beautiful coat." Others say, "It's the way he guards my home—you know?" Or, "I love him because he has these qualities, and he'll take on whatever working task I ask!" The Australian Shepherd, a companion with such a magnitude of abilities, makes a person feel insignificant! We teach these "Aussies" with elementary words and terms, yet they seem like graduates of a much higher school or art form.

The selection, care, and refinement of skills is left to *you* who truly appreciate the Australian Shepherds for what they inherit and may achieve! I hope that *All About Aussies* guides you and your Aussie toward *your* achievements and ultimate goal.

We should think of this book as a salute to the shepherds, herdsmen, and breeders of the Australian Shepherd, for they have put into our hands a truly versatile friend!

Donald W. Donham Jr.
Montana State University
Fort Ellis Experimental Station
Bozeman, Montana

George Washington Bush, founder of Centralia, Washington, is pictured with an Australian Shepherd in approximately 1893.

Courtesy Oregon Historical Society

THOSE LITTLE BLUE DOGS

"No man knows from where he came, but here he is and here he stays." History is never static, and rarely can all the facts be established to determine an accurate accounting. Much is yet to be discovered and understood before the final story can be written about the breed we call the Australian Shepherd.

Although his name suggests that he is a product of the world's largest island, his roots trace much deeper into the pages of history. Along with the plains sheep, longhorn cattle, and the mustang, the Australian Shepherd is a product of Spanish origin. Several factors enabled Spain to dominate the world sheep markets and to conquer vast foreign lands. The extraordinary wool produced from the merino sheep established Spain as a leader in worldwide trade and became the cornerstone of Spain's economy. The formation of the Conjeja de la Mesta, better known as the Honorable Assembly of the Shepherds, contributed strongly to the expansion of the industry. While Spain was rich in cattle, wool was a mainstay of the economy. The Mesta was a powerful association of graziers designed especially to protect the flocks of "white gold" and their dogs and shepherds.

In the early 1600s, the flocks of the Mesta had approximately two million sheep. King Alphonso X—"The Learned"—was an influential figure in medieval Spain, for it was he who formed and upheld the Conjeja de la Mesta.

Each spring and fall, cañadas or sheep walks (migrations) followed defined routes. During the spring, the flocks journeyed from winter pastures (invernaderos) on the Estremadura and Andalusian plains and then were slowly trailed to the plateaus and sierras of Castilla to graze on the agostaderos, or summer pastures, from which they returned each fall. These great cañadas were accompanied by clouds of dust stirred up by the sheep as they slowly travelled the countryside.

The sheep were tended by shepherds and their dogs. It has been recorded that these courageous dogs not only guarded the sheep against predators such as wolves (wild dogs) and thieves, but they were instrumental in keeping the Mesteños' flocks together. Mules and donkeys were used to pack salt for the sheep, cooking utensils, food for the shepherds and dogs, and any lamb born during the cañada who was too young to endure the hardships of migration. This set the scene for life in the New World.

The first sheep were brought to America by Columbus in 1493. In 1540, Pedro de Castañeda chronicled Coronado and his conquistadores as having set out in the New World with 800 Mexicans, shepherds, and Negro servants. Five thousand head of sheep were taken to provide meat. In 1595, Juan de Onate led an expedition that drove 2,500 wool sheep and 400 mutton sheep into the territory along the Rio Grande up to the Chama River country—now called New Mexico. In another account, it is written that Juan de Onate drove 1,000 head of sheep into the Chama River country in 1598. Old mission documents rarely list dogs on their records, as dogs simply accompanied the shepherds and were not considered a commodity.

The flocks not only survived in their new environment, but they flourished and multiplied. The dogs, too, were hardy individuals, toughened by exposure, and they proved to be capable of withstanding many hardships in the rough, dangerous, and uncharted lands of the Southwest.

The thirteen eastern colonies and their expanding settlements along the Atlantic coastline were inhabited by British breeds of stock, shepherds, and dogs. Due to the vastness of the western territory, and the subsequent isolation of sheep operations even between the Spanish settlements, there was little outside contact or influence. The hostilities stemming from the Mexican-American War (1846-1848) maintained this minimal exposure and a low profile for these dogs and their masters. The California Gold Rush was probably one of the most significant events that started immigration from the eastern states.

During the last quarter of the nineteenth century, Basques began to immigrate to the United States, and Australia (which was becoming a leading wool-producing continent) seeking employment, freedom, and wealth. They failed in the pursuit of wealth, but the Basques did become shepherds,—an occupation with which the Basques of France were familiar but not those who lived in the most southerly regions of the Pyrenees. It was during this immigration that the "little blue dogs" began to gain notice.

The dogs that the Basques brought from their homelands were the same type as those that travelled the world with the Spanish sheep. The Basque dogs more closely resembled the present-day Australian Shepherds. These dogs were capable of herding the sheep over the western ranges and protecting the flocks from predators. They possessed an intense herding ability with an avid devotion to their masters. These qualities were highly sought by the sheepmen of other countries. In the course of time, the Basque dogs were bred to other good working dogs of the sheep countries, but they continued to reproduce true to their type, as they had done for generations.

In the early 1900s, the United States began to gain ground in the world sheep industry. Importations of Australian sheep to upgrade American stock further introduced the Basques and their little blue dogs. It was during this time, when American sheepmen were importing Australian sheep, that these dogs were formally introduced into North America.

Primarily, the Australian Shepherd was accepted as a dependable herding dog of superior intelligence and a loyal family companion who would give his life, if the need arose, to protect his master's possessions. The Australian Shepherd at that point in time was

This portrait taken in 1899 is pictured at 12,000 feet above Salt Lake City, Utah where relatives of Charles E. Watson grazed their sheep. There are three Aussies in the photograph.
Donated by Janiece A. Wilson

2

This Australian Shepherd pictured in 1975 resembles the Aussie peering out between the second and third person on the far right of the portrait on page 2.   *Courtesy Kitty*

concentrated in the west and northwest areas of the United States. The type of dog varied in each region. Those in the northwest states of Oregon, Idaho, and Washington were slightly smaller and more compact than those along the west coast of California.

As new ranching and farming areas opened on the western frontier, flocks of sheep, accompanied by the dogs and herders, were moved to bordering states and thus were introduced to the new regions.

THROUGH A CENTURY OF PROGRESS

Jay Sisler of Emmett, Idaho, has done more than anyone else to introduce the Australian Shepherd to the American public with his trick dog acts performed at rodeos throughout the United States and Canada during the 1950s and 1960s.

When the Australian Shepherd Club of America was formed in Tucson, Arizona, in June 1957, the International English Shepherd Registry (IESR), headed by Mr. E.G. Emanual of Butler, Indiana, became the official Registry for Australian Shepherds. In 1958 The Mountains and Plains Blue Australian Shepherd Club was formed in Colorado. Juanita G. Ely, the dean of old-time breeders, was the first president. A number of clubs were also organized in California, including The International Australian Shepherd Club of America.

In 1972 Breed Club Registries were established by both the Australian Shepherd Club of America (ASCA), headquartered in Portland, Oregon, and the International Australian Shepherd Association (IASA) in California. These clubs offered show and obedience programs. ASCA developed a stock-working program that was first introduced to the public in Santa Rosa, California, in July 1974.

In 1976 the Australian Shepherd was recognized in Mexico and Canada. Possibly the greatest steps to unify the breed were the acceptance of one breed standard for all Australian Shepherds in 1976, and in 1980 the unification of both the Australian Shepherd Club of America and the International Australian Shepherd Association under the Australian Shepherd Club of America, Inc. One parent club was formed with a network of affiliate clubs throughout the nation to promote and preserve the breed as we know it today.

Prior to these Australian Shepherd clubs, there are no known records of research having been done regarding the origin of the breed, and to date, no documented records exist to prove a definite country of origin.

During the 1800s, a breed called the German Coolie, very similar to our Australian Shepherd, was reported to have been developed in New South Wales on a very small scale by one Simpson family. They used a blue merle dog of Scottish border ancestry and

Jay Sisler with Sisler's Shorty (Keno ex Blue Star) on the left with littermate brother Sisler's Stub on the right.

a natural bobtailed dog known as the Smithfield. The Basque people have taken their dogs with them wherever they have secured jobs herding sheep. There are a few accounts of people importing dogs from Spain. In Australia, these similar dogs have only begun to be noticed during the last decade, probably because of the isolation of the Australian continent. These dogs were crossed with other good working dogs throughout Australian sheep stations but continued to reproduce true to type, as they have done in the United States. The breed reached its greatest perfection in America during the last 100 years.

In 1928 William Gibson (Elaine Hartnagle's father) a Wyoming rancher had "bob-tailed" Aussies. Here he is pictured with "BOB" acquired from the Vasquez Basque sheepherders in Walden, Colorado.

Although not familiar with the science of genetics the Basque herders often said that the "black took the red away." Due to the dominance of black and the recessive nature of the red gene, very few reds were ever seen and consequently Aussies became recognized as those little blue dogs.

Mrs. Ina Ottinger of Casper, Wyoming, stated that her parents imported two dogs from Spain in 1937. She still has descendants from these two dogs. She also purchased a little red merle male from a Basque sheep shearer at the World's Fair in Seattle, Washington. Dogs very similar in type to our present-day Australian Shepherds were seen in the Basque homelands by a group of geographers, including author Donald Patten of Tallahassee, Florida, in 1980.

The actual origin of the breed cannot be traced through records, because the Basques had no written language. Many could not speak English, and their language was neither French nor Spanish. What sheepmen did know about these dogs is that they accompanied the Basque herders with boatloads of Australian sheep and came to be identified as Australian Shepherds—a name that is still in use today.

Note the strong similarity between the Aussie pictured with George Washington Bush and this one photographed by Patsy Carson (1982).

What is known about these dogs over the years has been passed down mostly by word of mouth and through legends. The most tangible documentation are the photographs taken during the late 1800s and early 1900s. The dogs have also been depicted in some early western paintings. Legend has it that these dogs were held in reverence by the Indians because of the dog's unusual and often blue eyes; therefore, they came to be called the "ghost-eyed ones." The Indians left these sacred (spirit) dogs and their owners unharmed.

Until further research reveals something vastly different, we can only rely on the stories handed down to us from the early settlers and livestock men who had the privilege and opportunity to know the breed long before our time. Regardless of his past wanderings through different countries helping his master tend the flocks, this dog as we know him today is what we have to pass on to our future generations. He is versatile, and super-intelligent and adapts easily to new situations. He is individualistic in his appearance, and, I must conclude, elusive, at least in documentation of his origin. Just about the time we think just one more step will give us the answer, we find that we are another step farther away. Maybe it was meant to be that way.

Swain Finch and his wife Sarah in front of their log house, Custer County, Nebraska. Photograph from "Great American Plains, A Pictoral History." Reprinted by permission from : Solomon D. Butcher Collection, Nebraska State Historical Society.

In 1978 Ch. Copper Canyon's Caligari, CD (George's Red Rustler ex Quaglino's Miss. Pooh) was chosen to represent the "Dog World" ideal of the Australian Shepherd Standard.

2
THE IDEAL AUSTRALIAN SHEPHERD

Judging and breeding dogs is an art, and the tools with which you have to work are few. You have the Breed Standard as your guideline, the breed itself, and your own ability to visualize these written words. To do this, you must be able to recognize the features that enable each individual dog to go out and function in the capacity of an active working dog under the most adverse conditions day after day.

The Breed Standard is the most important document available to breeders and judges. In 1975 the Australian Shepherd Club of America (ASCA) formed a committee to compile a standard of perfection to improve overall breed quality and thereby standardize breed development. The committee, headed by Robert E. Kline, DVM, included some of the nation's prominent breeders, stockmen, judges, and veterinarians. The rough drafts were reviewed and critiqued by many respected and knowledgeable authorities on canine structure and gait, and all comments were carefully considered by the committee. Other experts were consulted to insure anatomical and physiological accuracy. With input also from member affiliate clubs, the Breed Standard was finalized and approved by the board of directors of the ASCA in Phoenix, Arizona, during the November 1975 meeting.

By the request of the general membership, the section on "Color" was rewritten. The present Breed Standard gained unanimous approval and became effective January 15, 1977.

The philosophy underlying the manner in which such a document should be written was best described by Robert E. Kline, DVM:

"Contrary to the beliefs of many, such a standard is not a textbook but rather an outline describing structure, breed characteristics, color, size, uses, etc. put down in as precise and accurate a manner as possible. In order to perfect such a document without in fact ending up with a textbook the size of a physician's anatomy book, it is predisposed that the people using such a standard have a working knowledge of animal traits, vocabulary, and methods used by the industry to enable them to understand and interpret said standard so as to make it a usable instrument. For those not so familiar with these things and wanting to use the standard, such persons owe it to themselves to seek out knowledgeable breeders and judges, texts, etc. to avail themselves of such knowledge. For accuracy's sake, it precludes a standard to be written for the beginner or novice."

This concise blueprint states the ideal for judges to evaluate against and gives breeders a model toward which to strive. The written word, of course, means something slightly different to each person reading it, which is why the same dog does not win each time it is shown. Ideally, temperament, attitude, working ability, and conformation should be taken into account when judging or breeding dogs.

The Australian Shepherd that does not have sound structure will never be able to realize his full potential or function effectively as the working dog he was intended to be. While the original purpose of the Australian Shepherd was to work stock, the qualities that allowed him to perform these skills have also allowed him to adapt to and excel in other areas.

Unfortunately, there is no way for a judge to determine in the show ring the degree of trainability of each dog or whether a dog possesses the herding instinct.

Newcomers have a difficult time comprehending the basis on which a judge evaluates each dog. As previously mentioned, the Australian Shepherd Breed Standard describes an ideal Australian Shepherd in terms familiar to individuals who understand canine terminology, and it assumes a basic knowledge of anatomy and gait. It is not a detailed layout, nor is it a breeding manual for the novice, but it provides guidelines within which breeders can work without compromising with popular fads.

Any characteristic that deviates from the ideal described should be faulted according to the degree of deviation. Points that significantly deviate from breed character or soundness are faulted. Characteristics that entirely detract from both soundness and/or breed character are disqualifications.

Most references toward measurements are made in terms of comparing one part to another, and all parts to the whole individual, rather than by specific numerical increments. By doing so, slight variations in size of respective segments are allowed when comparing several dogs that differ in overall size. This also emphasizes the importance of each point being *in proportion to one another, therefore maintaining balance and symmetry.*

"GENERAL APPEARANCE"

GENERAL APPEARANCE: The Australian Shepherd is a well-balanced dog of medium size and bone. He is attentive and animated, showing strength and stamina combined with unusual agility. Slightly longer than tall, he has a coat of moderate length and coarseness with coloring that offers variety and individuality in each specimen. An identifying characteristic is his natural or docked bobtail. In each sex, masculinity or femininity is well-defined.

The first sentence sets the theme throughout the Standard. This lets us know what we are looking for in a well-proportioned individual. "Medium-size" describes the Australian Shepherd in relation to the entire canine species. He is neither miniaturized nor giantized. As we read on, we get the impression that an ideal Australian Shepherd has neither one outstanding feature nor any glaring faults that would detract from our total picture of symmetry. An ideal specimen will stand out in harmonious balance at rest or while in motion. He blends from one point to another. The Australian Shepherd should convey the impression at a glance that he is capable of enduring long periods of active duty as a working stock dog, which is attributed to strength and stamina. He is light on his feet. As a genuine athlete, he is nimble. He has a lithe sense of power, never cumbersome nor carrying extra timber.

Variety and individuality in color are unique features of the Australian Shepherd. The variance in tail length accommodates the different lengths that occur naturally at birth. The longer natural bobtail (not to exceed four inches) should *NEVER* be penalized over a shorter natural bob or docked tail.

Although never coarse or menacing, the male's boldness and virile strength are easy to distinguish from his distinctly femine counterpart, who possesses structural equality and a definite strength of character.

Although working characteristics such as low-heeling are inherited, structural features enable each individual to do so. Physical traits influence the center of gravity which comes into play in all physical maneuvers including this one by Ch Las Rocosa Little Wolf.

The natural bobtail is characteristic of the Aussie.

A beautiful head showing lovely expression. Definitely femine. Ch Nelson's Phoebe of Gold Nugget CD.　　　　　*Courtesy Norris*

"CHARACTER"

CHARACTER: The Australian Shepherd is intelligent, primarily a working dog of strong herding and guardian instincts. He is an exceptional companion. He is versatile and easily trained, performing his assigned tasks with great style and enthusiasm. He is reserved with strangers but does not exhibit shyness. Although an aggressive, authoritative worker, viciousness toward people or animals is intolerable.

The Australian Shepherd's intelligence is manifested by a keen and eager expression. The look in his eyes should be that of a questioning curiosity that becomes the look of eagles when at work. He is deliberate as a guardian, tenacious if confronted with a threat, but never hostile. Although his avid devotion and guardian instincts assign him as protector of master, stock, and property, viciousness (unprovoked, unwarranted attacks) or an unreliable nature are totally undesirable because they detract from his ability to perform either as a trustworthy companion or dependable working dog. Eager to please, this loyal, responsive companion may be reserved toward strangers but should never cringe, show fear, timidity, nervousness, snappiness, or an ill temper. If a dog has the intelligence and temperament typical of the Australian Shepherd, he should respond to the control of his master.

As a working dog, he is boldly assertive and forward in his approach. The high-spirited Australian Shepherd is courageous. He can be "tough as nails"

with the rankest livestock but immediately softened by a disapproving tone of his master's voice. Because he is alert and quick to learn, he is highly trainable, as exhibited by his desire to please. Some individuals may have more of an independent nature and may "test" their master. The hallmark, however, is the dog's sense of humor, which is ever present.

"HEAD"

"HEAD: Clean-cut, strong, dry and in proportion to the body. The top-skull is flat to slightly rounded, its length and width each equal to the length of the muzzle which is in balance and proportioned to the rest of the head. The muzzle tapers slightly to a rounded tip. The stop is moderate but well-defined."

Perhaps no other single factor sets the Australian Shepherd apart from other breeds and contributes as strongly to breed character as does the head. This feature also distinguishes major bloodlines within the breed. A good head is a mark of quality. It provides a clue as to the overall quality of the rest of the individual. Variations in expression and makeup (head structure, ear set, eye placement, etc.) are slight between bloodlines and are therefore acceptable, providing that the variation is characteristic of the breed.

The head houses the brain, dentition, ears, eyes, and nose (sinus chambers). Its framework protects these structures and minimizes the effects of blows and injury to the special senses, sight, hearing, scent, and the brain. The formation of the sinus chambers adds structural stability to the frame without adding much extra weight, which is important in respiration. These chambers lend moderate width to the head, which is necessary for muscle attachment without altering the correct contour.

"Clean-cut" is a term meaning that the head is clearly outlined, well formed, trim, and neat; free from extra or loose skin, pads of fat, pendulous lips (flews), and/or visible haws (third eyelid). The lips must be snug and not hang below the line of mouth. The skin should fit well around the eye to form a tight, protective covering. This helps prevent debris (dirt, briars, seeds, brush, twigs) from making direct contact with the eyes. Loose-fitting lips are more subject to rips and tears while working if caught up by hoof or horn and can interfere with "gripping."

The head is equidistant from the width of the backskull to the length of the backskull to the length of the muzzle. The aforementioned dimensions emphasize balance, symmetry, and moderation typical of the Australian Shepherd as a whole. These proportions plus a moderate but well-defined stop contribute to the relationship of the bones of the head that

Identical head types—The difference that the variation between ear sets (both accepted by the ASCA Breed Standard) makes can give a different appearance to identical head types with identical markings—even among littermates.

are sufficiently thick and have adequate muscles to absorb concussion. Fundamentally, the head of the Australian Shepherd is the same shape as that of his wild ancestor—the wolf—which would be classified as mesocephalic.

> *"(A) Teeth: A full complement of strong, white teeth meet in a scissors bite. An even bite is a fault. Teeth broken or missing by accident are not penalized. Disqualifications: Undershot bites; Overshot bites exceeding 1/8 inches."*

The scissors bite is indicative of a correct jaw assembly. The correct scissors bite calls for a well-fitted upper and lower jaw, which includes all of the teeth (incisors, canines, premolars, and molars) rather than the incisors independently. The scissors bite lends substance and support to the face and dentition. The

muzzle formation and bite are primary features in a sound working dog.

The Australian Shepherd must be able to move in and "grip" livestock with a pinching effect and be able to withstand the impact should he be kicked while working. The scissors bite is also necessary in removing burrs and the like from foot pads and the coat. The role that the scissors bite plays in reproduction is incalculable. During birth, the female must be able to effectively sever the umbilical cord of each puppy whelped.

Before man came along to care for nature's weaker members, animals that were born with defects such as an undershot assembly or an overshot bite simply fell by the wayside because they were unable to function efficiently. An undershot jaw leaves the mandible more prone to injury because it is less pro-

 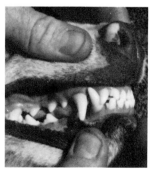 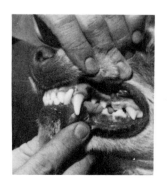 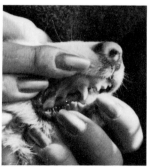

Left to right: SCISSORS. The relationship and alignment of the canine and premolar teeth are correct. UNDERSHOT. The forward shift of the lower jaw creates a space between the upper and lower premolar cusp tips. EVEN. The slight shifting of the lower jaw is evidenced by the positioning of the upper and lower premolars. An OVERSHOT bite is a structural unsoundness.

tected. The mandible is more vulnerable because it attaches to the head in one place only; therefore, the force cannot be dispersed when the mandible is subjected to trauma. On the other hand, an overshot assembly leaves the upper teeth more exposed to trauma.

An even bite is acceptable because it does allow the dog to function. However, because of tendencies toward broken teeth and greater wear on teeth due to constant contact, the even bite is faulted. The typical Australian Shepherd head structure depends on correct underlying skeletal features, including the entire jaw assembly. This is reflected most noticeably in the profile of the muzzle.

To the viewer, teeth can also serve as a window to the quality of bone within the individual. If the teeth appear strong and well textured, there is reason to believe that internal bones are also sound.

Broken teeth or those missing by accident are *NEVER* to be penalized. To do so would place unwarranted precedence on cosmetic features and therefore would discourage the exhibition of active, working stock dogs in the show ring. It would also defeat the original intent of the Australian Shepherd as a versatile breed. The goals of promoting active working stock dogs by denying otherwise exceptional individuals rightful consideration and placement in the show ring would be to deny the fact that the purpose of the breed is first and foremost as a utilitarian. It must be remembered that a mechanical injury of this nature *cannot* be passed on to succeeding generations.

> *"(B) Eyes: Very expressive, showing attentiveness and intelligence. Clear, almond-shaped, and of moderate size, set a little obliquely, neither prominent nor sunken, with pupils dark, well-defined and perfectly positioned. Color is brown, blue, amber, or any variation or combination including flecks and marbling."*

It is often said that the eyes are a window deep into the soul.

The Breed Standard calls for the eye to be clear, or free from (without) cloudiness, which can indicate impaired vision and blindness.

The almond-shaped eye of the Australian Shepherd is created by tissue surrounding the eye, rather than the eye itself, which is round. The correct head structure dictates and allows the eye to be set obliquely, forming the almond-shaped aperture. Faults of round, bulging, and sunken, small eyes result from inadequate and/or incorrect skeletal features and/or head shapes. The relationships of the many contributing bones directly influence the shape of the orbit and the eye set, which afford proper protection to the eye. These bones include the zygomatic

arch, formed by the joining of the zygomatic process of the temporal bone and the temporal process of the zygomatic bone, and the frontal bone (adding protection from above) forming the forehead, inner casing, and top upper portion of each orbit.

Hartnagle's Hud, a male of outstanding head-type. The eyes are well-protected by the moderate, but well-defined head structure and stop. Note the almond-shaped eyes and ideal ear set.

The Australian Shepherd depends upon a moderately curved zygomatic arch, which influences the slightly oblique eye set characteristic of the breed. This allows adequate protection from many factors, including briars, flying hooves, and horns without creating a restricted visual field. The aforementioned characteristics are imperative in the livestock working dog. The flatter the zygomatic arch (lesser degree of curvature), the more obliquely the eyes will be set on the side of the head, and the greater will be the vulnerability of the eyes toward trauma. The more exaggerated (prominent) the curvature of the zygomatic arch, the more frontally the eyes will be positioned. This gives the greatest protection but decreases side vision, which is also important in the herding dog. The necessity of moderation as called for throughout the Breed Standard is readily apparent in compromising the protective properties with the visual characteristics.

Eye defects are known to occur within the breed. One clue visible to the naked eye is an offset pupil. The pupil should not be confused with the marbling (mottled) coloration of the iris, which is a trait of the merling and flecked patterns seen throughout the variety of body color. The pupil should be well-defined by its positioning and darker color.

The eye color offers variety, contributing to the individuality of the breed as a whole. The eyes may be in any combination of blue, brown, and/or amber, depending on coat color. Eye color is influenced by the inherited coat color and pigmentation. No precedence should ever be given to one eye color and/or combination. It must be remembered that the wolf possesses light eyes and has very keen vision. Often, the preference of one eye color over another is generally due to familiarity with one color and a lack of familiarity with another. It takes living with individuals of the various eye colors to learn how to effectively read the eyes, especially blue ones. While

The structural factors that cause the Australian Shepherd's eyes to be set slightly obliquely also indirectly influence ear placement. The temporal bone, whose zygomatic process contributes to the zygomatic arch, also houses the vital structures for hearing. Eyes and ears work as a sensory team. What the eye sees, the ear lifts and focuses on.

Drooping (hound-type) ears lacking "lift" (at or above the base) interfere with keen hearing. In moist climates, hound-type ears hold moisture within the canals that causes severe ear infections.

Unlike scenting breeds, the Australian Shepherd depends upon all of his senses equally. The prick ear is keenest for hearing; however, it lacks the protective hair that prevents burrs and other debris from

Champion Casa Buena Mariquita STD shows the marbled eyes that are characteristic of the merling color patterns.
Courtesy of Weaver

One eye of each color is commonly found in merles. This lends individuality to the breed. Upon retiring, Ch Stonehenge Justin Case of Las Rocosa CD had 40 breed wins.   MacSpadden Photo

it is correct that the lighter-colored eyes possess less pigmentation than the darker eyes, it is *entirely incorrect* to assume that lighter eyes have limited visibility.

> *"(C) Ears: Set on high at the side of the head, triangular and slightly rounded at the tip, of moderate size with length measured by bringing the tip of the ear around to the inside corner of the eye. The ears, at full attention, break slightly forward and over from one-quarter (¼) to one-half (½) above the base. Prick and hound-type ears are severe faults."*

lodging in the ear. Ears that break from one-quarter to one-half above the base allow protection from outside elements without harboring moisture or impairing hearing faculties.

NECK AND BODY

> *"NECK AND BODY: The neck is firm, clean and in proportion to the body. It is of medium length and slightly arched at the crest, setting well into the shoulders. The body is firm and muscular. The topline appears level at a natural four-square stance. The chest is deep and strong with ribs well-sprung. The loin is strong and broad when viewed from the top. The bottom line carries well*

12

back with moderate tuck-up. The croup is moderately sloping, the ideal being thirty (30) degrees from the horizontal. Tail is straight, not to exceed four (4) inches, natural bobtail or docked."

A general rule of thumb states that the length of the neck when measured from the occiput (upper, back point of the skull) to the top of the withers should approximate the length of the head when measured from the occiput to the tip of the nose.

Although described as separate entities in the Breed Standard, the head and neck work together as balancing factors. The head and neck set are thought of as "marks of quality" in many species. They contribute to overall character as well as structural quality. The set of the neck is influenced by and can be used to evaluate the shoulder assembly. In order for the neck to carry back and blend well into the shoulders, the shoulder must have proper angulation (lay-back). The role that the head and neck play in maneuverability is extremely influential in regulating and shifting the center of gravity. By extending the head and neck forward, the dog shifts his center of gravity forward. When negotiating turns, his head and neck shift to one side or the other, and the body follows. When he jumps, the head and neck lift the center of gravity and guide the body while the rear provides the power. When the dog stops, the head and neck lift up to draw the center of gravity back as opposed to propelling it forward.

A neck of moderate length and slightly arched, as called for in the Breed Standard, is most efficient for endurance and contributes to the sense of balance, symmetry, and moderation. The neck is a major influence in supporting the muscles of the front assembly. A short neck, while not lacking in strength, lacks agility and endurance and therefore does not allow maximum flexibility for the body while heeling (gripping) livestock. It is dangerously ineffective in keeping the Australian Shepherd's vulnerable body away from flying hooves. The correct length of neck gives an obedience competitor and all other Australian Shepherd athletes (including Frisbee dogs) the physical capabilities to perform with the greatest amount of ease.

A firm, muscular body is important to the athlete and is reflected in proper conditioning. This feature contributes to overall fitness, balance, and agility and is a prerequisite for the working Australian Shepherd. Muscles play a necessary role in holding the skeletal structure together.

When speaking of the topline— "backbone of the operation"— we are looking for sufficient strength to support the organs that lie beneath. A strong, firm back is ideal. The topline that is firm should appear level and strong. Both the withers and hips should be level. A weak or sagging back tends to break down if it lacks substantial muscle. A roached back, much stronger in design, is also faulted because it deviates from the ideal and is not typical of the Australian

Champion All That Glitters of Gefion CD (Ch Robinson's Bonnie-Blue Yankee CD ex Ch Justa Sample of Sunnybrook CD) exhibits a smooth, free and easy ground-covering stride as described in the Breed Standard.

Shepherd. Any diversion from a strong, firm back leads to undue energy expenditure.

Every aspect must complement the entire network for total efficiency and soundness. This includes the chest. The rib cage should be broad and long, gently arching outward. Ribs should be oblique to the spine and "well laid back," which can be judged by feeling the thirteenth pair of floating ribs. Moderate depth, length, and width give sufficient lung and heart room and help to combat lateral displacement in locomotion. A "slab-sided" body may appear long and flat, but it lacks the spring necessary for lung and heart room, while "barrel-chested" bodies interfere with the elbow in motion and limit the depth necessary for lung and heart room. Both are faults.

Depth of body is measured vertically at the ninth rib, which is where the brisket should sweep gently upward. For the "tuck-up" or bottom line to ascend any sooner than the eighth or ninth rib is to view a restricted diaphragm, limiting lung and heart room, a fault termed "herring-gutted." The bottom line should appear level to the last long rib before tucking up. This gives the Australian Shepherd more stamina in that more room is provided in the cavity for the heart and lungs to work more freely.

The loin serves as the support to the abdominal viscera. The main muscles forming the sling that supports the abdominal organs have their origins in the loin area. Not supported by any other bones of the structure, the loin must therefore be strong and broad. It contains thick telegraphic muscles that surround the lumbar vertebrae and transmit the power from the hindquarter to the shock-absorbing forequarter.

The moderate sloping croup of the Australian Shepherd is most effective for the type of work that is required of him. The croup is the section extending from the loin to the tail above the hind legs and includes the pelvis and associated musculature. The croup pulls the feet and legs under the body, boosts the center of gravity for fast turns during the initial part of the stride, then sends the power and thrust forward by extending the hind leg. This allows the dog to cover endless miles with the greatest amount of ease.

FOREQUARTERS

"FOREQUARTERS: The shoulder blades (scapula) are long and flat, close set at the withers, approximately two fingers width at a natural stance and are well laid back at an angle approximating forty-five (45) degrees to the ground. The upper arm (humerus) is attached at an approximate right angle to the shoulder line with forelegs dropping straight, perpendicular to the ground. The elbow joint is equidistant from

the ground to the withers. The legs are straight and powerful. Pasterns are short, thick and strong, but still flexible, showing a slight angle when viewed from the side. Feet are oval shaped, compact, with close-knit, well-arched toes. Pads are thick and resilient; nails short and strong. Dewclaws may be removed."

The forequarters support over one-half of the entire body weight. They are a shock absorber during movement. They serve to oppose lateral displacement, propel (impel) turns, and control and lift the center of gravity.

The scapula (shoulder blade), often referred to as the cornerstone of the front assembly, is attached to the skeletal structure by muscle and ligament (unlike the hindquarters, which are linked by a ball-and-socket joint).

The well-laid-back shoulder is important for sufficient reach, which allows for shock absorption with the least amount of concussion under actual working conditions. It therefore is also ideal for the Best of Breed winner. Forty-five degrees is an easily estimated point of reference, and shoulders approximating this angle will meet the requirement for sufficient reach of the forelimbs. This angle can be estimated by placing the finger of one hand on the point of the shoulder (shoulder joint). With your second hand, guide your fingers over the cervical angle as it slopes back. The place where it flattens is the crest of the scapula spine. By locating the ridge at the crest of the spine with one hand and the point of the shoulder with the fingers of the other hand, you can get a good estimation.

Ideally, the humerus (upper arm) should intersect at ninety degrees to the shoulder blade. This will

Left: fiddle front, a fault. Right: the correct front. The forelegs are straight, columnar bones for the most effective support.

allow for a longer humerus. If the humerus is of the correct length and is well angled, the front legs will set well beneath the Australian Shepherd for optimal weight-bearing. The attachment of the radius-ulna (forearm) should be straight and vertical when viewed from the front. Ideally, the forearm falls directly beneath the center point of the shoulder, which gives greatest support of the fore assembly.

To enable the pastern to effectively work as a shock absorber, it must be positioned directly under the center of weight-bearing. Sufficient slope provides resiliency for absorbing concussion and greater lift while the dog is in motion. The weak or broken down pasterns do not give adequate support to the rest of the leg. Weak pasterns predispose to hyperextension of the pastern and knee (carples) at fast speeds, inducing injury. Unyielding straight pasterns with no shock-absorbing qualities jar the entire system and lead to early fatigue.

Splayed, flat, or broken down feet are serious faults because they weaken the entire assembly and lead to early breakdown and lameness. Weak feet are more easily affected by rough terrain, rocky surfaces, briars, thorns, etc. The feet support the entire body weight in a small cross-sectional area. Therefore, forces on them are so tremendous that compact feet are essential. The front feet are slightly larger than the back because they support more weight.

Dewclaws on the front legs are a matter of personal preference. Whether or not an individual has front dewclaws should have no bearing whatsoever on judging in the show ring.

HINDQUARTERS

"HINDQUARTERS: Width of hindquarters approximately equal to the width of the forequarters at the shoulders. The angulation of the pelvis and the upper thigh (femur) corresponds to the angulation of the shoulder blade and upper arm forming an approximate right angle. Stifles are clearly defined, hock joints moderately bent. The metatarsi are short, perpendicular to the ground and parallel to each other when viewed from the rear. Feet are oval shaped, compact with close-knit, well-arched toes. Pads are thick and resilient; nails short and strong. Rear dewclaws are removed."

This paragraph of the Breed Standard reemphasizes the concept of balance. The rear assembly must correspond to and be compatible with the front assembly for the individual to function efficiently as a whole. An imbalance occurs when the rear assembly is angulated more than the front assembly, or if the hindquarters are angulated less than the forequarters. Therefore, the two assemblies must compensate

according to the degree of imbalance (also influenced by other factors such as the length of the body in comparison to the height). Lacking necessary synchronization between the support and propelling phases results in faults such as "crabbing," "overdriving" (overreaching), "pounding," "padding," "pacing," etc.

While the rear assembly is not designed to support weight like the fore assembly, it is intended to energize and formulate power. The correct assembly supplies the Australian Shepherd with propelling force and drive.

The "Width of the hindquarters approximately equal to the width of the forequarters at the shoulders... The metatarsi are short, perpendicular to the ground and parallel to each other when viewed from the rear."

The hind legs are secured to the stationary pelvis by an articulated attachment (ball-and-socket joint), just as the humerus and scapula are articulated. From the pelvis, the femur (upper leg) should be attached at ninety degrees to the pelvis in the standing position. Muscle and ligament support is important with this joint, as laxity in them predisposes the dog to hip dysplasia. This angle allows the stifle to assume a moderate bend, which provides greater flexibility to the hind leg and lends sufficient length to both the femur (upper thigh) and the tibia-fibula (lower thigh). This gives a driving stride of sufficient speed and power without wasted energy. The correct angulation also allows the legs to gather adequately under the body. This efficient stride is necessary for maintaining endurance in the working dog.

Short metatarsal bones drop directly beneath the center of weight-bearing, thereby giving maximum support to the rear assembly. Moderate bend to the back, as with the moderately bent stifle, allows maximum flexibility and efficiency.

Since the feet carry the dog over all terrain, they must be as sound as the legs and body they support. The compact foot that is close-knit with well-arched toes gives the greatest amount of strength and spring, allowing for endurance and agility.

COAT

"COAT: Of medium texture, straight to slightly wavy, weather resistant, of moderate length with an undercoat. The quantity of undercoat varies with climate. Hair is short and smooth on the head, ouside of ears, front of forelegs and below the hocks. Backs of forelegs are moderately feathered; breeches are moderately full. There is a moderate mane and frill, more pronounced in dogs than bitches. Non-typical coats are severe faults."

Too often the coat is not thought of, bred for, or judged in the proper perspective. The coat is not simply an item of great beauty, but one of utility. It should not be forgotten that the coat is a protective covering against all elements. Coat texture and its quality are as important as its length and quantity. Although it may seem repetitive, we must never forget "everything in moderation," which serves as a constant reminder that the Australian Shepherd is truly a portrait of symmetry.

The ideal coat is one of low maintenance, due partly to its moderate length, but equally to the

Ch Colorado Sizzlin Sioux (Higgins Fast Buck of Berrycreek ex Colorado Sharade) displays a beautiful coat, ideal for work or show. *Courtesy Linda Wilson*

correct medium texture. When considering environmental conditions on the range such as cockleburs, sandburs, seed pods, mud, rain, snow, and heat, you cannot have a coat that requires tedious grooming. This is not to state that the coat is maintenance free. None are. Debris seems to collect more frequently in wooly, dense, wiry, excessively curly coats or extremely fine coats and is more difficult to remove. Smooth, slick coats are uncharacteristic of the Australian Shepherd and allow direct contact between burrs and the like. A medium-textured, moderate length coat provides insulation against temperature extremes and to a certain degree protects against insect bites and laceration by burrs, and thorns, while affording relatively easy removal due to the proper texture. The undercoat will be commensurate with climatic conditions. An Australian Shepherd working under long hours of Texas sun will not develop the same undercoat as the Australian Shepherd in a Canadian winter. The Australian Shepherd's ability to shed or grow undercoat enhances his utility in a variety of climates.

COLOR

"COLOR: All colors are strong, clear and rich. The recognized colors are blue merle, red (liver) merle, solid black and solid red (liver) all with or without white markings and/or tan (copper) points with no preference. The blue merle and black have black pigmentation on nose, lips and eye-rims; the red (liver) merle and red (liver) have liver pigmentation on nose, lips, and eye-rims. Butterfly nose should not be faulted under one year of age. On all colors, the areas surrounding the ears and eyes are dominated by color other than white. The hairline of a white collar does not exceed the point of withers. Disqualifications: Other than recognized colors. White body splashes. Dudley nose."

None of the accepted colors or patterns is preferred over the others as long as each individual color is within the Standard and is characteristic of the Australian Shepherd. They all receive equal billing and should be bred for and judged as such.

The black color is black. It should be jet black with no sabling to the undercoat. Blue merle is a modification of the basic black body color and is sometimes referrred to as "salt and pepper." It can vary in a striking combination of powder blue, silver blue, steel grey, or blue black. The red color is deep liver, burgundy, shades of rust, or sorrel in hue. The red merle is a variation of the basic red body color and is sometimes called "cinnamon and sugar" with liver skin pigmentation. The colors can be extremely contrasting to evenly blended. The patterns vary from a roan base, flecked, freckle merling (mottling) to marbling, splotches, and bold patches.

An attractive powder blue merle with beige copper trim and white on the front legs.
MacSpadden Photo

An exquisite red-tri against a jet black background.
Courtesy Furnish

An outstanding rich, deep sorrel red merle with light, cream copper trim.
Courtesy Duncan

A black-tri with well-defined rich colors.   Courtesy Rand

Puppies become richer in color as they mature. Often the flecked red merles will look like a blend of cinnamon and sugar which can become a blend of silver and sorrel/liver, similar to that of a red roan. Pictured are three eight-week-old littermates. Left: blue merle. Middle: red merle with predominately liver coloring. Right: red merle with freckled merling.

The variety in color combinations with variations in patterns allow individuality within the breed—an important characteristic of the Australian Shepherd. Each color may be with or without white and/or copper markings. White trim is an acceptable color pattern under the Australian Shepherd Breed Standard. It consists of white appearing in well-defined areas: muzzle, forehead, neck, chest, stomach, feet, and legs. It is not to be confused with other white color patterns that are genetically distinct

converge toward the center line of gravity of the dog, while the topline remains firm and level."

"Gait" is precisely the ideal previously described in motion. The Australian Shepherd must be able to accelerate instantly in order to "get around" (get ahead of) fast-moving livestock. He must also be able to fall in behind a herd or flock and trail it many miles. The correctly built Australian Shepherd will maintain balance and symmetry when set in motion.

Two Track's Terpsichore of Depindet UD displays sheer agility as regulated by total balance and symmetry. Correct angulation is necessary for the thrusting power in a "kick-off," and, when coupled with balance, is also responsible for gathering the legs back under the body for maximum efficiency.
Courtesy of Earnest

and unacceptable under the Breed Standard. White trim can vary from small amounts on the tips of the toes to full blazes, collars, and stockings. (For a more complete discussion on white color patterns, see the coat color section of the genetics chapter). Copper varies from the deep rich color of a new penny to a creamy beige.

Nose leather, eye rims, and lips must correspond to the coat color, such as liver pigmentation on the red and red merle and black pigmentation on the black and blue merle. Deviations from these corresponding colorations—such as black pigmentation on the red, maghogany, pumpkin, beige, and buff—suggest evidence of mongrelization and are uncharacteristic of the Australian Shepherd. It has been suggested that deep, rich pigmentation may help prevent sunburn, especially in reds.

GAIT

"GAIT: Smooth, free and easy; exhibiting agility of movement with a well-balanced, ground-covering stride. Fore and hind legs move straight and parallel with the center line of the body; as speed increases, the feet, both front and rear,

The individual that meets the ideals of structure should also meet the Standard's description of gait, because to move properly he must be built accordingly. The static conformation allows the transformation to proper kinetic conformation. Evaluation of both leads to a total picture of the true properties possessed by the individual.

The Australian Shepherd employs several gaits under actual working conditions but depends primarily on the trot. Therefore, gait is evaluated at a trot. The trot is a natural, two-beat, diagonal gait in which the front foot and the opposite hind foot take off simultaneously, while the hind foot strikes the ground a split second after the fore foot. Timing and coordination must be precise. It is a truly delicate balance. The Australian Shepherd must be able to cover ground in a minimum number of steps without sacrificing the agility necessary for sudden changes of direction. The Breed Standard outlines the ideal gait for all physical demands on the Australian Shepherd in the variety of services he performs for man.

Viewing the Australian Shepherd from the side reveals a smooth, effortless transition between fore and hind assemblies, or it reveals a lack of balance. Regardless of how spectacular the reach and drive (side gait) are, the Australian Shepherd lacking in correctness either coming or going is expending energy unnecessarily, causing early fatigue.

Single tracking, as called for in the Standard, is a natural phenomenon of gravity. The faster the trot, the more distinct the convergence as the Australian Shepherd draws his paws beneath his own center of gravity to minimize side-to-side motion, which wastes energy. This convergence formulates from the shoulder joint (point of shoulder) and from the hip joint to the feet. As the individual moves toward or away from the viewer, the legs appear to form a "V." There must be no deviation from a straight line. The joints must not bend or twist when in motion.

Agility is also dependent on convergence, which enables each individual to swivel (pivot) from the center line, rather than pulling himself around.

SIZE

"SIZE: Preferred height at the withers for males is 20-23 inches; that for females is 18-21 inches, however, quality is not to be sacrificed in favor of size."

The Australian Shepherd is medium-sized in comparison to the entire canine species. When the Breed Standard committee developed the present Australian Shepherd Breed Standard, a great deal of research was done regarding size and efficiency. It was deemed imperative that no superior individual should be lost to the breed because of size. Once all other points are brought into perspective, the importance of the dog's size is minimal against the appearance of the whole individual and the way in which he handles himself in action. There is no sound reasoning for size disqualifications. As is stated in the Australian Shepherd Breed Standard Annotations regarding size limitations: "Disqualifying sizes are believed to be unnecessary, as agility and working efficiency are based more on sound structure than size." Exceptions to the ideal size range should be faulted according to the degree of deviation, as with any other fault. The dog certainly should not be disqualified when there is no similar penalty for unsound structural features that affect the breed's ability as a capable working animal. Contrary to popular belief, size disqualifications easily lead to breed deterioration because you begin to limit available breeding stock. This is quite a sacrifice at the expense of ability. An individual with ideal structure can be disqualified and therefore entirely eliminated from blood stock, while a possibly unsound, inferior individual is left and therefore perpetuated because he is within the limits of an "ideal" size.

Methods of measurement, including the wicket, are questionable in accuracy. Measurements can vary at least one full inch. Variables depend on many factors, including the kind of surface (cement, grass, dirt), grooming techniques, and the way in which an individual holds his head and neck.

OTHER DISQUALIFICATIONS

"OTHER DISQUALIFICATIONS: Monorchidism and cryptorchidism."

Both monorchidism and cryptorchidism are fundamentally serious hereditary faults that affect the reproductive capacity of the animal.

Champion Shanahan's Phantom CDX—a female of excellent type. She typifies balance, symmetry and moderation.

The fluid motion of effortless stride. Champion Tri-Ivory Yankee Dandy CDX. Courtesy Farrington

Champion Tri-Ivory Baked Alaska CDX in a balanced trot displaying good foot-timing. Courtesy Norris

3
THE STANDARD IN MOTION

When we refer to gait, we set the Australian Shepherd Breed Standard in motion. Gait is the study of kinetic structure, or locomotion, as opposed to static (stationary) conformation. Gait and structure are directly related to each other. While in motion, the legs act in unison in either symmetrical or asymmetrical patterns, each of which is labeled gait. In symmetrical gaits, the legs of either side repeat the actions of the other side, but they do so half a stride later. Symmetrical gaits include the walk and trot. A stride is the complete coordinated cycle of action of all four legs, which starts with propulsion and ends with leg stabilization (support). The length of the stride is measured from the place where one paw leaves the ground to the place where that same paw again touches the ground. With each step taken, the dog that is able to cover the greater amount of ground with the least amount of steps while maintaining agility is the most economical with his action. Asymmetrical gaits include variations of the canter and gallop. In asymmetrical gaits, the legs from either side do not repeat the actions of the opposite side.

Each time a pad strikes the ground, it is called a beat. For example, waltz time occurs in the canter (slow gallop), which is a three-beat gait. If each paw strikes the ground separately, the gait has four beats as found in walking. When diagonal legs strike simultaneously, as in the trot, the gait is two-beat, since only two beats occur for each stride.

The Australian Shepherd may have to trail stock for many miles and at any given moment be able to display great bursts of speed to outrun and/or turn a maverick. He often employs many forms of gait during any given day. His ability to maneuver quickly at full speed is referred to as agility.

The Australian Shepherd is slightly longer than tall, which gives him a moderately lower center of gravity that enhances his natural ability to duck and turn at full speed. At a natural stance, the stationary base of support is in the form of a rectangle (not square), formed by the paws on the ground.

SYMMETRICAL GAITS

Walk

At a walk, a triangular outline is formed because one pad is off the ground, and the body weight is supported by the other three legs. The support role is greater for the forequarters, which are placed nearer the center of gravity, while the propulsive role is prominent in the hindquarters.

Trot

Foot timing and leg action between the forequarters and the hindquarters require absolute precision for correctness and efficiency. The trot is a symmetrical gait of medium speed in which the dog is stabilized (supported) by alternating diagonal pairs of limbs. The forequarter legs are off the ground slightly longer (split-second timing) than the legs of the hindquarter to allow the front feet to clear the ground in advance of the placement of the hind legs on the same side. When the front foot leaves the ground, the hind foot takes or "fills" its place.

When the Australian Shepherd shifts from a walk into an easy, slow trot, the gait is then called "collected." in the "extended" trot, the legs reach out to increase stride length and speed. When a period of suspension occurs between the support phases and propulsion, the gait is referred to as a "flying trot" (suspended trot).

ASYMMETRICAL GAITS

Canter (Slow Gallop)

The canter is in essence a slow gallop. It is a three-beat gait (in waltz time). Diagonal pairs of legs hit the ground simultaneously. The pattern is consistent: one hind leg, the other hind leg, and the foreleg diagonal to it simultaneously, followed by the remaining foreleg.

Gallop

As speed increases, the points of support decrease with a corresponding decrease in stability. When a dog is running, his base of support is one point, as compared to the walk that is supported by three points in the form of a triangle. The gallop is an asymmetrical gait of fast speed. The Australian Shepherd is supported by one or more legs or is in suspension during parts of the stride. The support pattern is transferred depending upon the placement of the legs.

ANALYZING STRUCTURE

It can take many years of observation to apply knowledge of gait. The interplay (strengths and weaknesses) between the fore and hind assemblies is more clearly revealed in the trot than in any other gait. Leg action is more readily apparent at the symmetrical trot than in the asymmetrical, faster gaits.

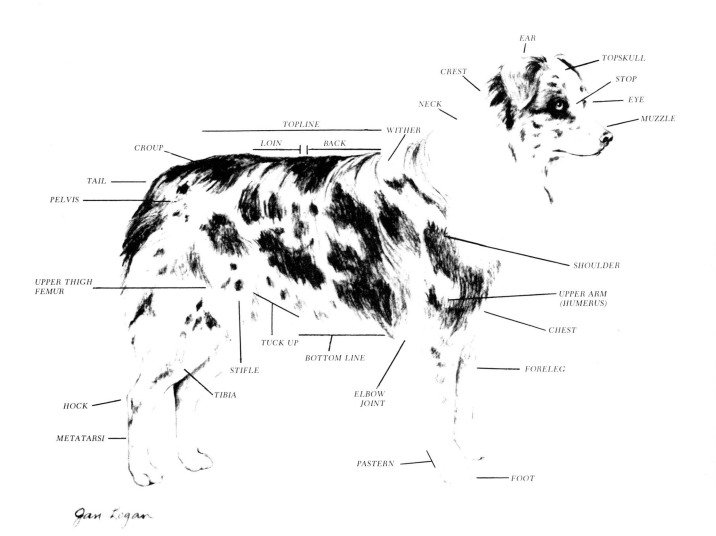

Jan Logan

The "flying trot." Champion Just A Sample of Sunnybrook CD
Courtesy Smith

Sometimes a dog will appear flawless but when set in motion will have some factor that forces him to compensate considerably or "fall apart." Often this is only evident once all of the physical parts react with one another.

Side Movement (Reach and Drive)

When a judge views the Australian Shepherd in action from the side, he is able to study the interaction of the forequarters with the hindquarters. Foot timing is clear and easily accessible to the trained eye. The Australian Shepherd is a confident athlete. When set in motion, his gait suggests endurance. There is an effortless quality in the stride, deliberate without wasted energy. In this sense, the Australian Shepherd is an economist. The most effective movement does not always "stand out" and attract attention. However, its quality is never mistaken, because all parts harmonize without disrupting the interworking of other parts. When viewed from the side, his topline should be strong and appear level between the shoulders and loin. When trotting, there should be no bobbing, as the withers should remain level in motion. Any up-and-down movement wastes energy and indicates another structural inefficiency.

Sometimes while in the working gait, the Australian Shepherd may slightly drop his head. However, when alert or focusing his attention on something, he can lift his head while in motion. The Australian Shepherd is slightly longer than tall. Actual body length determines foot placement, which is specifically governed by angulation. Balance and symmetry are the first and foremost requirements in a working breed such as the Australian Shepherd. This is influenced by correct static conformation but is measured by the yardstick of performance. Correct shoulder angulation that allows maximum reach but that lacks the corresponding angulation of the driv-

ing hindquarters is of little value. This kind of dog cannot "fill" his fore "tracks" (paw prints), so to speak, and ends up wasting energy.

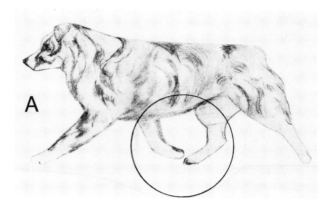

(A) Correct foot timing. Both front feet and hind feet are syncopated so the weight-bearing foot leaves the ground a split-second before the hind foot "fills" the impression.

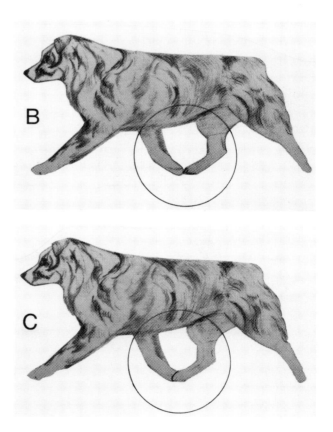

(B,C) Overdriving. In overdriving legs are compensating somewhat due to the weight-bearing front foot which is not out of the way of the approaching hind foot causing the hind paws to over-reach the front ones. Even though crabbing is not occurring and the back is in a straight line with the forward line of travel, feet and legs are forced to compensate to keep from interfering with each other. Instead of the hind foot "filling" the track of the fore print, it creates a new track "side-stepping" the foreprint.

This dog does not display maximum reach and drive, but is in total balance to herself.

THE VIEW GOING AND COMING

The Australian Shepherd is known as a "single-tracking" breed. When engaged in the trot his legs must converge toward a midpoint under his body (his center of gravity) as his movement speeds up. Strengths and weaknesses that are not readily apparent from the side view (presentation) are easily seen as each dog moves away from or toward the viewer. Balance must be constantly maintained. The convergence begins from the point of the shoulder and the hip joint. The "running gear" (legs) consists of strong, straight, columnar limbs. In other words, the joints of the legs should be free from any deviation or twisting actions as the legs converge toward the center line of gravity. An obvious "V" shape occurs as the leg remains steadfast within its position from either the point of the shoulder and the hip joint, but the rest of the leg is drawn inward from the paws rather than from the joints of the pastern or hock, which will remain straight from the paw to their skeletal attachments at either the humerus or the pelvis.

The forequarters of the Australian Shepherd support the dog's weight. The shock caused by the weight being propelled forward by the hindquarters is absorbed by three primary features: the feet, the slope of the pasterns, and the slope of the shoulders. The feet absorb concussion somewhat like an automobile tire does. Soundness and endurance are dependent upon a combination of well-arched toes fitted snugly in a compact oval with thick pads. The toes will withstand more shock and offer more protection to the entire running gear. Flat toes (lacking sufficient arch) or splayed toes (fitted loosely together) are weak and incapable of adequately absorbing concussion. This becomes readily apparent when the dog travels through rocky, brush-covered country. The tight, compact foot does not readily ball up with snow or mud as easily as the splayed foot, and it has better traction on icy surfaces.

Single tracking.

The slope of the pastern acts like the shock-absorbing mechanisms in an automobile. When the foot contacts the ground, the pastern flexes to accommodate the leg and then springs back to absorb the "jar" out of the gait. The absence of sufficient pastern results in constant concussion to the body. Weak or broken-down pasterns lack immediate spring and recovery and can cause a dog to fatigue easily.

The slope of the shoulder (the angle between the scapula and the humerus and between the humerus and forearm) also acts like the springs in an

"Going"   "Coming"

Courtesy Cornwell

Weak pasterns predispose to hyperextension of the pastern and knee (carples) at fast speeds therefore susceptible to injury. The weak or broken down pasterns do not lend adequate support to the rest of the legs.

automobile. Athletes such as skiers know the effect of the "jar" of stiff legs against a rough or hard surface. Try standing stiff-legged in the back of a moving vehicle, then bend your knees slightly. Suddenly your teeth stop being jarred. The angle of your bent legs then act like the pastern and shoulder lay-back of the Australian Shepherd. A sloping shoulder blade and the corresponding hindquarter are conducive toward a smooth passage and transition during the various phases of kinetic balance with little lost motion.

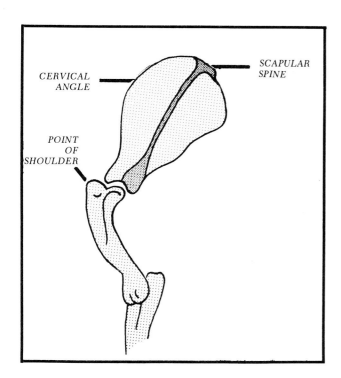

Skeletal structure of forearm.

Perhaps the main contributing factors toward tireless motion (when under working conditions) are the relative proportion and the angulation with the bone assembly of the running gear. The way in which the neck sets into the shoulder indicates the lay-back. The neck should always blend into the shoulders with no pronounced line of anatomical division. Long, sloping shoulders result in a moderately longer neck (relative to the entire length of the top skull, the stop, and the muzzle when measured from the occiput to the tip of the nose and from the occiput to the withers), and the appearance of a short back with a long underline that allows for a smooth, effortless gait when accompanied by corresponding hindquarters.

Short, upright shoulder blades produce a short neck and the appearance of a long back (not to be confused with a long body) and a choppy stride created by the limitations of the upright assembly. The blades should be broad and flat when viewed from the side. Shoulder musculature should be smooth and hard. Muscles firmly attach the shoulders to the body, allowing lateral mobility and a maximum cushioning effect.

Joints such as the elbows and hocks should be adequately broad (in proportion to the bone of each dog) and strong to allow good attachment and placement of muscles and tendons for efficient leverage. The elbows should be neither pinched nor loose. Free action of all joints is essential. The hinge-type joint of the upper arm is able to open enough to aid diagonal extension from the top of the shoulder to the tip of the extended pastern and foot. As the front pad hits the ground at the point of the dog's reach, forward propulsion is maintained. When the leg moves forward, the elbow and pastern bend to allow the leg and foot to move freely without scraping the ground. The hindquarters provide the necessary thrusting action when driving from behind. The well-angulated hindquarter permits the hind legs to extend effectively during motion.

When a judge must decide between two individuals of equal merit, but each has a fault, he must then determine which fault is lesser. To do this, you must first understand what is correct. Then you will be able to figure out what is incorrect, what factor(s) cause the fault, and how it will affect the performance of each individual.

For example, when all else is equal, a fault such as "cow hocks" is more easily recognized and is therefore considered more severe than its counterpart fault—"bowed" or "open" hocks. Yet, it takes relatively little effort to bring the leg under the body for adequate support with "cow hocks" (because it is already there) as opposed to the "open" hocks,

25

which must "twist" inward and also cover a wider distance (because the leg is outside of the center line of gravity) in an attempt to converge. The effect is similar with deviations in the front legs. The individual that slightly "toes out" expends less energy to draw the legs underneath the line of gravity (similar to cow hocks) than an individual that slightly "toes inward" (pigeon toes), because the line of the legs is outside of the supporting feet. Therefore, it will take more distance to draw the legs underneath for sufficient support during movement.

Any deviation from a strong, firm topline requires the body to use additional energy to divert the power sent through the loin from the hindquarters during the transition from the hindquarters to the forequarters. When all other factors are equal, a slightly roached back would be preferable to a slightly dipped topline due to the fact that an arch is structurally stronger. It must be remembered, however, that all factors come into play when a decision is to be made. In other words, when one fault would be considered more detrimental to the individual, the severity of the fault in relation to the individual as a whole and how that fault affects his overall performance must be decided before any generalizations can be made.

When converging toward the center line of gravity, the legs should remain columnar from the point of shoulder to the paws. There should be no twisting at the pastern as the leg is drawn under.

STRIDE VS. SIZE

Size is not applicable when it comes to the science of soundness of gait. The factors that determine soundness, foot timing, and stride are based upon symmetry, balance, and sound structure rather than on size.

CORRECT   BOWED (OPEN) HOCKS   CLOSE BEHIND   COW HOCKS

* CENTER OF GRAVITY (cg)

Often, an untrained eye will interpret that a larger dog is covering more ground than his smaller counterpart. This is especially apparent when comparing a larger dog that naturally "stands over more ground" with a smaller individual with the same angulation. Size has nothing to do with the actual length of stride when placed in proper perspective. This becomes obvious when two individuals of the same size are compared. For example, when a larger dog with straighter angulation is compared with a smaller individual that has greater angulation, the difference may not be that visible to the newcomer.

But when the larger dog is compared to another dog of the same size but that has a greater degree of angulation, the difference becomes more obvious.

The method of evaluating each dog in light of the Breed Standard is far superior to applying numerical increments. Each measurement should take into consideration the relationship of one part to another, and of all parts to the entire individual. This method stresses the importance of breeding well-balanced Australian Shepherds that are capable athletes.

Precision foot-timing is absolutely necessary for the tireless trot. Taylor's Escalante pictured along the historic Outlaw Trail, a remnant of the cattle rustling network that interlaced Utah.

Ready to get out and discover the world.

4
BUYING AND SELLING AUSSIES

Regardless of bloodline (lineage) and specific goals, certain desirable characteristics should be present in all Australian Shepherds. Whether he be chosen for breeding, companionship, obedience, show, or work; temperament, attitude, and physical soundness are necessary.

Theoretically, each individual that closely resembles the ideal described in the Breed Standard should be able to function efficiently as an active working dog. Realistically, this is not always the case. An individual that is totally balanced and sound may lack sufficient angulation to be competitive in the show ring but still be able to function as a capable working dog. Any obedience or companion dog must not only possess the "willing" Aussie attitude, but he must be as sound as the working dog and be able to jump to height specifications (individually determined) to receive a score for qualifying work. Unless injured or ill, the Aussie should be sound enough to get in or out of your vehicle without assistance.

When you consider that an Australian Shepherd will live for about twelve years, it becomes important to choose a dog that has a good attitude and temperament. Environmental factors, management, and handling affect the dog's attitude. Very often, breeders and buyers overemphasize show-ring winnings as a basis of selection. This method is less valuable from a breeding standpoint. It is helpful, however, when evaluating an individual whose performance is reflected in records. When choosing a puppy that does not yet have his own records you must observe for consistency of desirable traits that are found in a specific bloodline and that satisfy your requirements.

CHOOSING THE OBEDIENCE DOG

Remember when choosing a dog for obedience that no two dogs are alike, and no two will respond exactly the same to each person. The puppy that *chooses* to be with you will more than likely be most responsive and willing to perform for you. You must determine what temperament (hard/soft) is best suited to you. Do the parents and grandparents respond with a "what can I do to please you" attitude? The type of dog that will bounce right back from timely corrections when followed by praise is the best choice for competitive obedience. Also, a dog that will perform his exercises with enthusiasm and flair is often the difference between an obedient companion and a High in Trial contender.

Unlike stock work, where the main reward is getting to work in basic obedience, praise and reward come primarily from the handler. Australian Shepherds are very responsive, obedient dogs, and although many are natural retrievers, in advanced obedience work when a dog is trained to retrieve each and every time and only on command, the handler modifies this natural instinct. If this instinct is dominated by the handler, the incentive to respond is somewhat different. In certain phases of obedience work, the motive to perform comes solely from the handler's praise, unlike in play, where the reward comes from getting to retrieve a ball that you have thrown for him in whatever manner comes naturally.

CHOOSING THE STOCKDOG

First you must go to a well-established strain— a bloodline that possesses the working qualities that you desire and that has been bred from a strong line of working ancestors. Line and inbreeding indicate that the offspring will predictably inherit the characteristics of the ancestral lineage.

The rule of thumb to always select the outgoing puppy over one that may be somewhat reserved (don't confuse a quiet, reserved puppy with a shy one) does not always hold true when selecting a dog for herding work. The inherited family traits are all important. Temperament, gathering instincts, fetching versus driving, silence versus barking, wide runners versus close runners, grip versus lack of grip, hardmouthed versus soft-mouthed, degrees of eye, heading versus heeling, type of heeling (whether low or high), degrees of force, and even inherited faults such as tail pulling all must come into consideration.

Once you have located the bloodline or cross that has the desired working characteristics important to your needs, you are ready to inspect the litter for a suitable puppy. Australian Shepherd puppies have an uncanny way of choosing their master, when given the chance to do so. Many times a certain puppy will leave his littermates and keep returning to you for attention, or come and sit by your feet. Do not overlook these actions when looking over a litter. It is generally easy to form a lasting bond with such a puppy. These individuals tend to be very responsive and eager to please you. These qualities are most necessary to acquire a successful and lasting relationship throughout his entire lifetime.

Oftentimes the boldest, most outgoing puppy in the litter may be the most dominant one and not necessarily the most attentive worker. The more dominant puppy could be more difficult for some individuals to train to respond to commands than a slightly reserved one. He may, however, be able to tolerate untimely corrections from a novice, inexperienced trainer without being immediately ruined or cowered (intimidated). Temperament is very important. Try to choose a puppy that will be most complimentary to your own temperament.

Training can alter the natural response or reaction. Because training inhibits approximately 50 percent of the natural instincts, it is far better to choose an enthusiastic working dog. It is far easier to tone down an exuberant dog, but you cannot spiff one up if he doesn't have the "want to."

Basically the Australian Shepherd, when bred from working bloodlines, is born with a tremendous inherited instinct to work. Even in the hands of a rancher or farmer who does not know the fine points in training a dog to herd, the Australian Shepherd will easily learn a routine in daily work schedules.

By the time puppies are between five weeks and twelve weeks, you can observe them around ducks and make note of their reactions. The response will be dynamic, and no two puppies will react the same toward the flock each day. But there are certain traits that, when present, will be consistent. The curiosity or interest may be exhibited by watching and following. Some puppies will move around the ducks toward the head, and some will display the gripping instinct by taking hold of the tail feathers. Puppies cannot express fetching or heading instincts until they have the physical ability and speed to move out and around the stock, especially dogs that are close runners. Many tendencies will become evident later when youngsters are introduced to other types of livestock. Some puppies may not "turn on" until somewhere between four to fourteen months of age. Do not be harsh on the "sleeper." Puppies that are not in actual working homes, or those not exposed to stock until later in life, may not "turn on" immediately when exposed to livestock and will need additional exposure to awaken the natural instinct. Many of these dogs can become successful herders but may never attain the effectiveness of the puppy who has had the opportunity to work at an early age. Also remember that puppies in the presence of their littermates may be under the influence of the pecking order and may not exhibit their full potential until given individual attention.

First encounter.

If you are considering choosing an older dog that has never been exposed to herding livestock, do not be discouraged if it did not immediately arouse its interest on the first introduction to livestock. Australian Shepherds are quick to respond to their natural herding instinct and generally start to take interest after a couple of sessions. If you are in doubt about such a dog, it would be wise to first consult the breeder to get information on the working traits of its ancestors. Such information would be very valuable in determining the working potential before purchasing such an individual.

BLOODLINES AND BREEDERS

Before you choose a particular bloodline and/or breeder, you must decide what bloodline has a consistent reputation for the traits that you most desire in an Australian Shepherd. The decision is yours. The variety offered within the breed is due to the fact that each breeder sets different goals for his breeding program.

Breeders

It is important to buy from a trustworthy breeder. The reputable seller will lend you much assistance in making a decision. Conscientious breeders devote considerable time to studying both the Australian Shepherd and dogs in general. They know all of the distinguishing features of their dogs' bloodline, including temperament and developmental patterns (both mental and physical). Conscientious breeders are aware of current or existing trends and/or problems involved with the Aussie in general. They can inform the buyer if the problems are acquired (congenital) or inherited (genetic). Established breeders are available to answer any questions and lend guidance and expertise (as opposed to the backyard breeder or pet shop owner). The breeder can also give you particulars on the dog's ancestral background. Over the years, the breeder has gained tremendous insight about the breed and can answer many questions concerning training, grooming, and handling by giving actual demonstrations. Reputable breeders have satisfied clients because these breeders will stand behind the quality of their animals.

Often, the pet shop owners and backyard breeders are not familiar with the dog's ancestral background. Registration papers are not always available due to a lapse in record keeping. The pet shop or backyard breeders are more than likely *not* going to take the responsibility and guarantee against genetic defects. They probably won't be around to answer questions or lend expertise when needed. However, conscientious breeders guarantee against genetic defects provided that the owners produce a signed veterinarian statement. If for some reason the dog doesn't work out in your situation (if you have followed the recommendations of the breeder), the breeder is often in a position to either take back the individual, help place it, and/or offer an appropriate solution to the problem(s).

THE RIGHT DOG FOR YOU

Do not ignore your first impressions, because these are instinctive feelings that often guide your judgment. However, do not make a hasty decision.

Sometimes a mature, well-socialized, trained, and even possibly titled dog may become available. For example, an owner or breeder may be limited in facilities, time, or personnel and may cut back on present dogs to make room for up-and-coming individuals and trainees. A champion may even be attainable except that the breeder may want to maintain limited or unlimited breeding rights. The older working dog

Aussies can do it all! Young's Sagebrush of Copper Canyon UD (left) rides in a special box-seat on the back of the motorcycle and (right) outfitted in his own lifevest, has a special place on this 14-foot Omega sailboat.
Courtesy Young

This picture of The Copper Canyon's Wild Bunch displays the very essence of Aussie character.   *Photo by Thom Carter*

may flourish in a slightly different working situation and may even enjoy competition in the trial arena. Likewise, the older obedience dog can make an excellent companion. Due to longevity the mature Australian Shepherd can be a wonderful asset. A special person or family that can devote time and affection will appreciate the honor of owning such a fine dog. This type of opportunity can also help to establish a sincere, dedicated, small-time breeder or newcomer.

Breeders also sometimes have an older puppy or individual that they are willing to sell or place in the right home. For instance, the breeder may not be able to devote the time to properly develop and train another youngster, yet he/she may not want to sell the potential working, show, or breeding prospect outright. As a result, breeders may place the dog with a co-ownership or sell it with the agreement that he/she can exhibit and/or breed the dog.

TEMPERAMENT

Certain features are evident at an early age and will be exhibited throughout adulthood. Environment, socialization, and handling will either enhance or hinder inherited temperament.

When you view dogs and their bloodlines at a show or trial, also make it a point to see these individuals in the natural surroundings of their home environment. The interaction between each dog and his master will help you decide if that type of disposition is right for you.

Typical Australian Shepherd puppies and adults that have been properly socialized, trained, and handled will be reserved with strangers. They will be observant. They probably won't run up and jump into your lap. They will "check you out" and then go off to carry on with their own business. Or they may "show off" and reveal unique personality traits. When allowed to "make up" to strangers on their own accord, Australian Shepherds are much more accepting of the newcomers. Although naturally reserved, it is *not* natural that they should run and hide in the presence of a stranger. They should not have to be coaxed out from behind the sofa when strangers enter the room. "Reserved" denotes a hesitancy with strangers exibited by the look in the dog's eyes and by the way in which he carries his head. The dog should not be flightly, nervous, or snappy. Behind a fenced yard or in a vehicle, he will be very protective, but viciousness is *atypical* of breed character. With his protective nature, the Aussie is willing to accept you into his home, yard, or vehicle with the approval of his master. He will allow you to come into his home or yard *if* his master has invited you. The Australian Shepherd in a kennel may appear overly aggressive, but most individuals with a typical temperament will exhibit the same tendencies as those that are not maintained in the kennel.

After things have settled down, and when you are in the comfort of the home or out in the yard engaged in pleasant conversation, it is unusual that an Australian Shepherd should rush aggressively toward or jump and run away from you just because you shift your weight. The only time that this aggressive behavior would be exhibited in the Aussie would be if you approach the dog's master in a bold aggressive manner. The individual that can be just fine one moment and then for no apparent reason bite out of nervous response is not temperamentally stable.

When choosing the best dog for yourself, much may depend upon your own life-style and disposition. The puppy that exhibits a tremendous amount of enthusiasm will maintain this disposition throughout his life. This temperament may be too exuberant for the average pet owner. However, this type of dog may be an ideal choice for competition. If you spend a lot of active time out-of-doors, a puppy that is constantly on the "go" may match you best. A dog of this nature is always looking for something to do. Unless you are willing to invest a certain amount of time, he may be too demanding, especially if you are looking for a docile, less demanding companion. If you prefer quiet activities, then a milder-mannered dog would better suit your personality.

Champion Twin Oaks Cactus Bud CD (Heard's Cactus of Flintridge ex Klarer's Little Echo) Twin Oaks senior sire.
Courtesy Klarer

Most Aussies exhibit a certain degree of sensitivity. The Australian Shepherd may be reserved with strangers, yet he should never "cower," which should not be confused with shyness or sulking. Nor should the Aussie be overaggressive. Mental soundness is worth a lot when you are speaking of a dependable dog. Aussies are known for their mental stability. The eager-to-please attitude is a hallmark among the bloodlines. Keep in mind that environment, management, and handling can either reinforce temperament or alter it drastically. Courage is ever-important, especially in working dogs, and in order for it to be present, it must be bred into a long line of ancestors.

Hard and soft dispositions combined with dominant and submissive personalities are all to be considered when selecting a dog. Temperament within the breed ranges from those bold as brass to soft as satin. The bold, assertive individuals are dominant. They stem back to the alpha and beta individuals in the pack structure. They are the pack leaders and in training often test the strength or dominance and patience of their handlers. However, rarely will individuals of this nature "quit" when the going gets rough. These individuals do well with a trainer/handler who can be authoritative but kind in his handling. These individuals will accept discipline without falling apart. The more sensitive, mild dispositions do not constantly test their handler. They will often flourish with milder-mannered handlers. This type of individual will more than likely respond most effectively to an authoritative word or tone rather than a heavy hand. A heavy-handed master could easily ruin this type of dog. The soft dog's willingness is often destroyed by a handler who is impatient, loud, harsh, or rough. On the other hand, the soft, gentle owner may lack the necessary authority to gain the respect of a more dominant, headstrong dog. It should be remembered that even the most bold dog can be RUINED in the hands of an incompetent, unkind handler. Ill-tempered trainers should not even have canine companions, but if they feel they must, they should seek individuals of the *toughest* character.

Wilson's Little Annie, UD (Binty's Skeeter Blue ex Binty's Pauper Joy). Judy Wilson William's beginning. "Annie" is also the dam of Blue Heather of Windermere.   Courtesy Williams.

A shy, meek dog takes patient and kind handling. This type of dog may make a suitable companion for a quiet, gentle person or shy child. Sometimes a mature older person or couple gets along well with this type of dog. The shy disposition is not typical Australian Shepherd temperament and should not be confused with reserved or sensitive behavior. The owner has to be willing to coddle and coax the shy dog. Timid dispositions are not recommended for the average dog owner. Nor is the shy dog recommended (suitable) for a competitive or breeding prospect.

Caught napping.

THE NEW BREED

Today, in the Australian Shepherd breed, you will notice two distinct dispositions developing out of various needs of certain breeders. There are several strains of Aussies that are being developed to be docile. These individuals are less demanding than many of their ancestors. They are more capable of withstanding the extreme stress of confinement while in a kennel, an apartment, or small city yards and while being crated when you are away from home. These individuals are more content to lie around the house or yard and are certainly for the person that is not overly active. Although obedient companions, these dogs do not make the top obedience competitor, nor do they make superior working dogs.

The second type of disposition being developed out of certain strains is the more alert, hot-blooded individual. This dog is far too demanding for certain situations and people. He is not content in confinement. You will find this dog waiting at the door anticipating your return. This individual may end up getting into mischief due to boredom. This strain is reflex-responsive. They are ready the moment an event takes place. Many intensely bred working dogs fall into this category and are extremely sensitive and even aware of shadows while they are sleeping. This is what enables these dogs to be superior working dogs. They are able to survive amidst flying hooves and horns.

Your preference depends entirely upon you and your situation. The above types can be best summarized by this scenario: If you had two individuals of these two types lying in the middle of the floor, and a stranger walked into the room and stumbled across the top of them, a dog from the first description would probably look up to see what was happening and then get up and get out of the way, while the dog of the second type would already be on his feet and out of the way. Many intensely bred working dogs, especially those with experience around rough stock, would be scrambling to get out of the way. Keep these facts in mind when considering the purchase of the "New Breed" Aussie.

Kennel Dogs

The older kennel dog may lack confidence when taken from the security of his home. He may not exhibit as much personality as one that has had constant handling. When given special attention however, this type of dog can be a very pleasurable companion. If the kennel dog possesses basic stability and the typical Aussie temperament and has had proper socialization and handling, he should be able to readily adjust to a new home and master. These dogs often flourish when given the chance to become a "special" member of the household and family. Allow the dog to make the initial moves to "make up" to you—don't force yourself upon him.

The conscientious breeder and kennel manager will make every attempt to socialize kennel dogs by allotting special time for them. Regular grooming and handling are necessary for health and welfare. Short trips in the car on errand days add variety and expose kennel dogs to unfamiliar situations, strangers, and children. Mornings, afternoons, or evenings in the house are beneficial in developing stability and personality. Often, breeders will rotate their dogs from the yard to the house so that each has exposure and experience in different situations. Many dogs maintained in the kennels have had former obedience, show, and working careers and therefore are a marvelous introduction to the breed and to the dog world as a whole. Some of the best-behaved dogs are those individuals raised in the kennel that have had proper socialization and handling.

AGE

A "show, breeding, working, obedience, or pet/companion" prospect can be anywhere from an eight-week-old puppy to a mature adult. Australian Shepherds six months and older are more predictable (in lieu of various developmental traits). Between six months to one year of age, the working style, trainability, structure, gait, temperament, and disposition are becoming more apparent, although they are still in various developmental stages. Reflective is the old statement "what you see is what you get." Individuals younger than six months of age are more accurately bought and sold as "potential" show, breeding, working, obedience, or companion dogs.

When a puppy is between eight and twelve weeks of age, he more closely resembles in miniature what he may look like as a mature adult. Sometimes, however, the puppy does not always mature as predicted. You will have to bear with and endure all developmental stages (mentally and physically). The young puppy that is tested on ducks and exposed to stock (such as sheep and ducks) will show certain working characteristics that are indicative of an inherited working style. Some, however, may not "come on" until a little later. You have to rely on the breeder's experience with a certain cross and related bloodlines.

The two-to-four-month-old puppy will easily adjust to a new home and master. After four months of age, the youngster begins to attach himself to someone. It may take slightly longer for an older puppy to become attached to a new owner, but once he becomes fully adjusted to the new life-style and master, he is as happy as the younger puppy. Handling and training help to develop a rapport between dogs and their masters.

Sometimes youngsters between seven and ten months of age will go through a period of insecurity, but they will recover with maturity, proper socialization, and good handling.

When choosing a dog, you will also want to consider your schedule (the time that you have to devote to housebreaking, general handling, and training). Do you have children and/or other animals to consider? If your present situation does not allow adequate time for a puppy, then you may want to consider an older individual. If you have children, you may want a slightly older puppy, three or four months of age or even older. The older puppy may be more sturdy through growth. He may be mentally more adaptable to training and more easily able to cope with children in a family situation. An older puppy from twelve to sixteen weeks does not require such frequent trips out-of-doors and may already be housebroken. Do keep in mind, however, that a certain amount of handling is necessary with any puppy, however young or old.

The temperamentally reliable older individual or adult raised with children might be a superb choice. A reliable, solid (sound) temperament is a primary concern for a family dog, especially around children. An older dog may not take any more time

to adapt to the new situation in comparison to the puppy. Older individuals often flourish in all of the attention and make excellent family companions.

If you already have one or more animals, a puppy may be more easily accepted, adaptable, and less threatening to the resident animal friends. If you have the time to devote to the early stages of puppyhood, a youngster can lend much enjoyment. There will be no habits to correct or reprogram except those that you allow to develop. You can start the puppy out right from the beginning.

MALE, FEMALE, OR ALTERED

Temperamentally, there is little difference between males and females in the Australian Shepherd breed except for those characteristics typical in individuals of certain lineages and crosses. Of course, these traits are further influenced by handling, training, and management.

Both the male and female make excellent obedience competitors, companions, and stock dogs. There are pros and cons to all available options. For training and trialing, the only disadvantage to owning a female is the twice-a-year heat cycles that may interrupt training and/or exhibition schedules, but then males in training for exhibition may be affected by females in heat. If this creates a problem and your only interest is a dog to work or compete in obedience and/or stock trials, then you should consider an altered male or female. However, if you plan to compete in the breed ring, you will have to decide between a male or female, because the breed ring (conformation) is only for individuals capable of reproduction.

If you are prepared to deal with heat cycles twice a year, then the female is an excellent choice. When planning a breeding program or competing in the conformation ring, it is generally advisable to begin with a female. There are usually more quality males available to breed to a top-quality female than vice-versa.

In the conformation ring, males are good choices for show dogs (providing that you are choosing between males and females of equal quality) due to the fact that they are "in coat" for more months throughout the year. Males are often easier to compete with as "Specials," because the frills are more pronounced than in the feminine counterpart. It must be remembered, however, that a superior individual is superior regardless of sex.

Both the male and female can be trained and trialed (in both obedience and working) with equal success. The female will probably be easier to maintain in general than a male because she won't attempt to "lift" her leg on your walls and is less likely to roam.

Cleanliness in the house, however, comes through proper training and management, and either sex can be clean.

YOU THE BUYER

Most breeders/sellers will ask for specific details about your needs and expectations to determine if a suitable dog is available. If one is not, you will more than likely be referred to an appropriate source. It is necessary for breeders/sellers to determine if the potential owner's personality is compatible with that of the Australian Shepherd. They will further need to establish if the potential owner has the proper facilities to care for the dog. Apartment houses are not exactly adequate.

If the breeder/seller is reluctant to allow you to walk through the kennels, respect the wish. Due to bacterial infections and viruses that may be carried on a visitor's shoes and clothing, it may be a health risk to expose the dogs unnecessarily. However, most breeders are delighted to show you their facilities.

As a prospective buyer, you have a right to see at least the dam of the puppy, and if possible, the sire. This will tell you much about what you can or cannot expect. Most breeders will show you other relatives, including the grandparents and littermates.

GUARANTEES

A dog's pedigree and guarantee are only as good as the person who backs them up. Generally, breeders will guarantee individuals to be free from temperament and health irregularities. Often, breeders will place time limits on such guarantees, such as up to

twenty-four hours or perhaps even thirty days after purchase. The reason for such time limits is because exposure to health hazards, injury, disease, parasitic agents, trauma, abuse, neglect, and improper management are all out of the breeders' control.

It is generally understood that the buyer will have the dog examined by a veterinarian. This is done to establish a record of health and to detect any possible or potential problems within the necessary time requirements established by the seller at the time of sale.

Adjustments

Any defects deemed necessary for replacement or adjustment commonly require a veterinarian statement, OFA (Orthopedic Foundation for Animals) evaluation, CERF (Canine Eye Registration Foundation) certification, or Obedience Certificate from an approved training center, whichever is applicable at the time of adjustment or replacement. The breeder/seller has the right to require the necessary documentation at the buyer's expense (unless otherwise specified) to substantiate the claim. This is especially applicable in the case of hereditary defects that are not apparent until later but that affect suitability for the purpose purchased.

If a dog is replaced by the breeder, the breeder may require that the buyer pay shipping expenses for the dog's return. Depending upon the breeder, he will usually pay shipping charges for the replacement. If a replacement or adjustment is necessary, often the breeder will stipulate or offer you a choice of a replacement individual or a total or partial refund.

A costume class at one of the Central Coast Australian Shepherd Fanciers Fun Days.   *Courtesy Young*

36

Some breeders will allow the purchase price or a part of it to be applied to another dog. Sometimes dogs are sold as show and/or breeding quality with the agreement that if the individual does not "develop" as anticipated, the neuter or spay fee will be refunded. Some breeders will refund or apply the purchase price toward a more suitable dog upon proof of alteration.

guarantee that the individual will "win" when entered in competition. Winning is the combination of many variables, including each judge's interpretation of the Breed Standard, condition of the dog, management (care and nutrition), handling, training, and competitive region. Breeding quality may mean that an individual may lack the finer points of

With shoulders braced against the harness, the versatile Australian Shepherd assumes a new sporting role.　　　　*Courtesy Kline*

Often, individuals sold as pet quality will not have papers, or papers will be furnished when proof of alteration is supplied in the form of a signed veterinarian statement. For many reasons, breeders may sell an individual for a pet price but reserve the option (usually at the request of the buyer) to re-evaluate the quality of the dog. This evaluation generally takes place when the dog is between six and twelve months of age to conclude whether or not he is of breeding and/or show quality. If the breeder finds that the dog is, he will issue papers with the difference between a pet quality price and a show/breeding quality price satisfied. If the breeder finds that the individual is not show or breeding quality, then registration papers will be given once there is proof of alteration.

Show and Breeding Guarantees

A dog is usually sold or purchased with the intent that he be able to be bred and/or shown by the new owner. Guarantees for show and breeding animals are similar. The show and breeding animal should be free from any serious or disqualifying features (as listed in the Australian Shepherd Breed Standard), with the exception of those acquired by injury, mismanagement, and/or neglect after sale or purchase is made or while in transit once the dog is placed in the care of his new owner.

The show dog is guaranteed to be a good representative of the breed, but it would be impossible to

showmanship. He may be a superior individual, but due to injury (such as lameness caused by trauma, a working accident, a missing piece of ear from a dog quarrel), the individual may be prevented from being successfully shown. Breeding quality dogs and bitches should be fertile, provided they have not contracted diseases such as brucellosis after leaving the breeder's premises. The individual should be free from hereditary defects that would affect breeding soundness.

Once an individual is used for breeding by the buyer, it is assumed by the breeder/seller that the buyer has given his approval. If the dog is good enough to breed, he is good enough to own.

Working Dog Guarantees

Most breeders will guarantee that the Australian Shepherd (especially in reference to puppies) will have a natural inherited ability (working instinct). However, it is the responsibility of the new owner and handler to provide a suitable environment and proper handling and training. Working dogs should be guaranteed against health or temperamental irregularities. The working Australian Shepherd should be representative of the Australian Shepherd possessing the general appearance, typical Aussie temperament, and personality. He should be free from structural faults and debilitating hereditary defects that would affect soundness in his ability to function as a working dog. There is no guarantee against faults that are acquired by injury or mismanagement.

Obedience Companions and Pet Guarantees

Obedience companions and pets should be guaranteed against health or temperamental irregularities, and/or debilitating hereditary defects. Again, there is no guarantee against faults acquired by injury or mismanagement. The obedience companion and pet should be representative of the breed and possess structural and temperamental features that enable him to function as an obedience companion and/or pet. It is the responsibility of the new owner and handler to provide appropriate environmental conditions, socialization, training, and handling (including a basic obedience class).

Quality

It is usually understood at the time of sale that any individual bought or sold as a working dog, obedience companion, and/or pet may also be show and/or breeding quality, but this is not always the case. Certain individuals may have features such as size, ear set, eye shape and placement, hair texture, and/or color that would affect or prevent serious consideration in the show ring, but that for all practical purposes would not alter the individual in his capacity as a superior working dog, obedience companion, and/or pet.

Too often, buyers will misrepresent their intent to the breeder/seller and will purchase "pet quality" individuals hoping to "get something for nothing." They will then try to breed or show the individual

Luke Skywalker, star of "Real People" and "That's Incredible." Luke hanglides with his owner, Rick Leach as well as works cattle by radio communication from Rick.

Photo by John G. White
Courtesy Leach

without informing the breeder, or they end up changing their minds after the purchase is made. There are usually guidelines that each breeder establishes to determine quality. It is the responsibility of the buyer to honestly clarify his intent for the dog, then rely on the experience of the reputable, established breeder to help him locate such a dog.

MONEY, CONTRACTS, AND REGISTRATION PAPERS

All transactions must be well defined, and the cost and method of payment must be clearly understood by both parties before the closing of the sale. Most breeders/sellers require a deposit. Methods of payment vary with the breeder. Cash and/or money orders with purchase price paid in full are the most widely acceptable methods. Most breeders will accept time installments (to be paid in advance, or a percentage of the total purchase price paid in advance and the remainder to be paid in a manner specified and agreed upon by both parties). Some breeders will accept checks but will keep the paperwork until the check clears. In some cases, they will keep the dog until the check clears. Although not commonly used, some breeders will accept credit cards.

An individual sold with breeding rights, or with part payment to be made in stud rights on a male or with puppies back on a female, are called "breeders terms." Paperwork is generally held by the breeder/seller until all terms are met as agreed upon. With co-ownerships in which two parties own the individual and each handles specific responsibilities and expenses, it must be fully spelled out who is to do what.

Tartaglia's Chocolate (Scaltritti's Dado ex Scaltritti's Stormy) a main foundation sire.
Courtesy McCorkle

In these cases, registration papers may be maintained in both the breeders'/sellers' names and the buyer's name. When all obligations are met, the breeder generally will transfer sole ownership to the buyer.

Although recognized by the American Kennel Club as a purebred breed, the Australian Shepherd CANNOT be registered with the AKC. The Australian Shepherd can be registered with the Australian Shepherd Club of America (ASCA), the National Stock Dog Registry (IESR), and the United Kennel Club (UKC). To participate in Australian Shepherd Club activities (Parent Club) such as working trials, conformation shows, and obedience trials, each Australian Shepherd must be registered with the ASCA. Many individuals are eligible for more than one registry.

Registration papers or applications for individual registration should accompany each individual. If not, proof of registration of both the sire and dam with the Australian Shepherd Club of America should be provided. For the individual to be registered with the ASCA, the breeder must submit a breeder's certificate to the Registry and then be issued a litter

Tutrone's main sire has gained a strong reputation throughout Canada and the United States for his intense working progeny. Las Rocosa Rockin J.R. (Ch Slash V Little Rock ex Ch Las Rocosa Leslie CSD). Courtesy Tutrone.

number. If the breeder has received this paperwork from the Registry (provided he has sent it in after correctly filling it out), he should be able to supply that litter number on the bill of sale along with a brief description of the individual, including sex, date of birth, color (including eye color), registered names and numbers of both the sire and dam, and the name of the breeder (the owner or lessee of the dam).

It should be clearly understood or specified in the contract (if applicable) that registration papers will be provided with the individual or transferred

or forwarded upon receipt from the ASCA if they are still being processed. Papers will be supplied upon fulfillment of "terms" either agreed upon as usually specified in contracts, or will be signed over when proof of alteration is received in the form of a signed veterinary statement in the case of neutering and spaying.

The breeder should also supply a three-, four-, or five-generation pedigree.

Farrington's Buster Ivory UD (Wile's One Too Many ex Wile's Annie Oakley), the foundation sire of Tri-Ivory, pictured at eight and one-half years of age. Courtesy Farrington

5
TAKING HIM HOME

There are many responsibilities that you must assume when you get a dog. It is not a small matter. Puppies are irresistible, but as they grow up into adulthood, they will require daily care (food, water and shelter), housetraining, and practical obedience. You must have appropriate facilities to accommodate your dog. Medical care must be provided. You must assume full responsibility for all of the dog's actions. Each city and county has laws that will affect each dog and his owner. Common sense will guide you.

The first night away from home and the security of his dam and littermates will be a difficult adjustment. Provide a dry, clean, comfortable place for him to sleep that will lend a sense of security. Often, a travel kennel such as an air kennel is quite suitable. Playpens, utility rooms, open baskets, and well-ventilated cardboard boxes have also been used. Care must be taken to place the travel kennel specifically in a draft-free area. Washable materials such as an old blanket or rug (clean) will provide suitable bedding.

Your puppy will more than likely be insecure and lonely. He will probably cry the first night and possibly for several nights until he becomes adjusted. You can use a heavy-duty hot water bottle to provide comforting warmth.

Electric pads or lamps are extremely dangerous, as the puppy can and probably will chew on the cords or pad. Curtains and other items are tempting to the teething puppy. A knuckle or shank bone, as well as chew toys, may provide some entertainment for the puppy, especially those between three and seven months of age. It is best not to give your puppy your old shoes or socks unless you want him to chew your

others as well. If you find your puppy chewing (teething) on your favorite possessions, do not react in anger. Correct him by giving an "ah-ah, no" sound. Tap your index finger on his muzzle. Replace your valuable item with one of his own chew toys.

During the night, an old clock wrapped up in a blanket may simulate the sound of his mother's heartbeat, which lends a sense of companionship. Soft radio music also has a calming effect. If you have to put him to sleep next to your own bed, you can reach down and comfort him during the night with long, reassuring strokes until he settles in. Do not punish the puppy for his insecurity or crying. Go to him and reassure him.

It is especially important to provide the puppy an area that has an even temperature for sufficient warmth. It is not wise to put a new puppy outdoors to sleep until you are reasonably sure that he is conditioned to it and until you can provide shelter with adequate protection from the elements.

HOUSETRAINING

If you feed and exercise on a regular schedule, then housetraining in this sense will be no problem. It must be remembered that a puppy is not physically able to hold his bladder and bowel for long periods until he nears six months of age. By the time your puppy nears five months of age, he should be able to hold himself for a few hours at a time. Whenever your dog is having a problem with clean house manners, it can often be traced to neglect or an inconsistent schedule. Occasionally, there may be some physiological problem. If you suspect this, however, then you should make an appointment with your veterinarian.

As with any type of training, you must first understand and employ knowledge of the dog's natural inclinations. In the wild, young pups are taught at an early age to go far from their den or nest to defecate. If an animal is confined in a small space with no exercise area, then he has no other choice than to soil his area. Often, this individual will use one spot or area to relieve himself. All dogs should be allowed the opportunity to relieve themselves away from their dens but must be taught by you.

To be successful, you must take the youngster out every time he has eaten or consumed water. Before retiring for the evening, and the very first thing in the morning, you must also take the puppy outside. This will establish a pattern for him. Whenever you have been away, or whenever the puppy awakens, take him out immediately. Use the same door each time you take him out to eliminate. Your puppy will soon go to that door to let you know when he needs to go out. If you designate a specific spot to which you take him constantly, he will eventually go there on his own. A specific elimination area is good for many reasons. It allows you to maintain a clean area, which is imperative for sanitation, and it "signals" your dog that it is time to do his business. You can establish some type of a word or command to further signal your dog, which will be invaluable when traveling to unfamiliar places. Praise him for taking care of business and responding to your request.

If left for long periods without a chance to get outdoors, your dog will have no other choice than to disregard his natural inclinations. It is cruel not to be more attentive to the situation. This can cause many complications, including weakening of your dog's bladder through your neglect.

Whenever you are unable to keep an eye on the puppy, confine him to a specific area that you can clean up easily in the event that an accident should occur. Child gates are helpful to use as a divider between rooms. If an accident does occur, DO NOT REACT IN ANGER— simply take the puppy outdoors. Slapping, hitting, or rubbing the puppy's nose in the mess, especially if you do not witness the accident, is ABUSE. If you see the accident take place, give an "ah-ah, no" correction and calmly take the puppy outdoors. Use common sense. Your PATIENCE, and most of all CONSISTENCY, will bring about positive results and help develop a secure, confident puppy. If you develop anxiety through your anger or disgust, the puppy will begin reacting out of fear, which will bring negative results. When you

take your puppy outdoors, allow him ample time to complete his business. If you see your puppy sniffing around, turning in circles, or beginning to squat, take him outdoors, because he is about to eliminate. Do not bring him back in until he does. The best preventative measure is to give your puppy plenty of outdoor exercise.

Sometimes your puppy will be anxious to get back indoors, especially if it is raining or snowing. Even during these times, you must allow ample opportunity for your dog to do his business. Do not bring him back in until he has done so (even if the World Series is on television).

Your dog has a very keen nose. As a matter of fact, he can scent one part of urine in thirty to sixty million parts of water. If he smells urine (as he should when he eliminates in a familiar place), he will instinctively be induced to urinate. If he smells urine on the carpet or the floor, he will more than likely want to use that spot again. A mixture of vinegar and water or odor neutralizers will help eliminate the "urine" odor to prevent him from returning to that same place. Often people will use an ammonia solution, but ammonia is chemically characteristic of urine and very possibly may confuse your puppy's senses. Soap, Clorox®, and water are good basic cleaning agents and should be used frequently.

CRATE TRAINING

If not overused or abused, dog crates, such as air (travel) kennels, can be useful. The crate should be long enough to accommodate the Aussie when stretched out. It should be tall enough to allow him to stand comfortably with his head elevated. For traveling, a crate will safely confine and shelter your dog while offering him a sense of security (a familiar place) and protection. Crates are excellent to initiate housetraining as well as to establish a schedule and introduce a place for sleeping and feeding.

Many crates are designed with rounded or concave angles and corners designed to eliminate places for the accumulation of dirt and dust. This makes them easy to disinfect and clean. Wire crates are excellent, especially for young dogs. The dog is exposed to the normal activities surrounding him, which is ideal for socializing. Individuals needing some special attention can become the center of attention. They will greatly benefit from the constant handling that should occur when frequently released from the confines of the crate.

You must remember that *your dog will be most eager to enter his crate if he knows that he will be getting out again, soon.* Exercise is imperative if your dog is crated overnight. If this is neglected, your dog may develop serious problems, such as bladder failure. If you must crate your dog while away at work, give him plenty of exercise in order to keep him fit. It is then not recommended that he be crated during the evening or night. If he must be crated during the night for sleep, then it is not recommended that he be crated during the daytime hours.

Special care must be taken to place the crate in a cool, shaded area with adequate ventilation during warmer months to prevent heat prostration. Water must be made available at all times. If necessary, a "lick it" type of watering device container can be used.

It must also be remembered that a crate can provide a safe place for your dog, but it can also become a torture chamber if improperly used. If possible, your dog should be crated minimally.

To begin crate training, familiarize your Aussie for short periods, such as for a drive around town, or for feeding. The crate can be a good place to give a knuckle or shank bone.

CHILDREN AND PUPPIES

There is no greater relationship than that of a child with his or her dog. But children and puppies must be guided and supervised. They can be taught to live and play beautifully together. Establish a few rules in the beginning. Puppies and children also need time away from each other. Young children have no comprehension of the damage and serious injury that can occur if they drop, pounce, jump, hit, or step on a puppy. Young children should not be allowed to pick up puppies. Children sometimes get tired of holding the puppy and then throw the puppy down as they would discard a toy or a ball. Puppies do not bounce. Children should *only* be allowed to hold puppies while sitting on the ground or floor, and they should be taught how to properly hold a puppy.

Puppies must be protected from unintentional, unkind, rough, abusive, and even cruel handling (knowingly or unknowingly). Without exception, children must never, never, be allowed to touch or "poke" the eyes. They also must be taught that ears are *not* for pulling or yanking. The puppy must be guarded against such as items as pencils. Young children have been known to poke their fingers, marbles, rocks, dirt, and other foreign objects into the ears. Beware! Children have also been found to place rubberbands over the head and around the neck, and on the legs and tail. They may or may not know better. Age sometimes makes a difference, but you have to be there to teach them those differences.

Kind handling can be taught. Show the children how to pet the puppy in calming strokes. Puppies are easily excitable. They like to play tug-o-war. In the presence of children running, screaming, and yelling, puppies also like to run and play. The needle-sharp teeth can be piercing and easily penetrate skin and clothing. Sometimes the teeth get caught up on a sleeve or pant leg when the puppy jumps up to grab or catch a ball. He can accidentally pinch or bite in the confusion of a keep-away game. Toenails can scratch, too. Toenails must be kept trimmed, and puppies must be taught not to jump up. THIS TASK WILL BE IMPOSSIBLE, HOWEVER, IF YOU ALLOW YOUR CHILDREN TO OVEREXCITE THE PUPPY.

You must not allow children to push the puppy beyond his limitations. The end results are entirely up to you. You cannot scold the puppy for behavior encouraged through improper handling. It is through no fault of your puppy if he jumps on the children, scratches, or grabs them in play unless taught otherwise. This type of play can get rough and easily out of hand. You must be willing to invest time in socialization and training—but you will find that the extra time invested is well worth the effort.

CHOOSING YOUR VETERINARIAN

Above all, you will require a professional in whom you can place your complete confidence. Competence, compassion, and understanding are all features that should accompany veterinarian services. Veterinary Medical Societies can lend you names of qualified veterinarians in your vicinity. Breeders, handlers, trainers, and training centers may be able to make recommendations.

Visit one or two veterinary practices. General cleanliness and proficiency of the staff and facilities should be apparent.

Veterinarians who are members of local, state, and national veterinary medical associations are usually very interested in continuing education. This is important due to rapidly advancing scientific techniques.

Keeping a watchful eye over her master.

Lester Taylor with his dog "Jan" at the end of a long hard day.

6
THE
STOCK DOG

There are far easier ways of making a living than punching cows or herding sheep seven days (and nights) a week, through rain, sleet, or shine, with no guarantee except that your dog will remain faithful to the day he dies.

For centuries, herding and working dogs have served man as faithful companions and as workers with the ability to perform feats that man possibly cannot. A well-bred, well-trained stock dog is one of the highest valued employees in any livestock operation.

With proper care (diet, shelter, grooming), a dog may last as an active working dog for ten to twelve years. Day or night, your dog is willing to serve you, and again the next day. Without complaint, all he asks for is a kind word, to be fed, and to have a warm, dry place to sleep.

WORKING CHARACTERISTICS

As a stock dog, the Australian Shepherd is limited only by his genetic makeup. Certain characteristics must be present, and as the master/handler, you must be able to recognize them in order to bring them to the surface and use them effectively.

There is very little difference between training the Australian Shepherd for trial competition and teaching him to be a useful "hand" on the farm and/or ranch. Relative to all competition, the Aussie (in the trial arena) must exhibit a keener response to his handler but display the same common sense approach appropriate to each class and type of livestock that is expected of him in his everyday work.

The Australian Shepherd can be taught to drop on command, to move directly toward livestock, or to go from one side to the other. The power that these stock dogs have over livestock is inherited, and this instinctive ability is the foundation for their training.

Even though the Aussie has a high degree of trainability (not to be confused with intelligence), he CANNOT be trained HOW TO perform. It is HOW he does these activities that is called STYLE.

Aussies, as with all breeds of working dogs, fall into two main categories: headers and heelers. Headers keep livestock bunched. They consistently go to the head to stop the herd or the flock's flow in motion. These header (or "fetching") dogs gather livestock and very often bring them back to their handler, unlike the heeler (or driving) dogs, which will seek the pressure point (the place or position toward which livestock are influenced to move) to keep their charges moving along. They are characterized by staying behind their stock.

The most versatile Aussie is one that is capable of *both* gathering and driving. A dog can be considered "driving" (regardless if he is a header or heeler) whenever he stays behind livestock. Whenever a dog—either a header or heeler—swings out from behind the flank to the head to change direction and turn stock, he is in essence heading. The term "heeling" is also used to denote gripping, the pinching effect that occurs when a dog "takes hold" or rakes the leg with his mouth.

All of the instinctive working traits and any others possessed by working dogs are derived from the hunting instincts of their remote ancestor, the wolf.

In approaching their prey, the fastest members of the pack come out from behind and run to the lead, cutting off (essentially, heading) their quarry. When the prey would spread or fan out in an attempt to escape, the driving members (heelers), who were generally the slower members of the pack, would move out to the flank to keep their quarry intact and prevent them from escaping. Man was able to take these hunting instincts and eliminate the killing tendencies. Through selective breeding, he cultivated and strengthened the appropriate characteristics for working.

are poor choices for prospective breeding stock.

The Aussie is capable of expertly handling all classes of livestock. This ability, too, comes from his wild ancestry. The wolf does not hunt any two species quite the same, nor does the Australian Shepherd work cattle the same way he works sheep or ducks.

The Aussie has earned his respect among stockmen because he is capable of being many dogs in one. An Australian Shepherd that will not only gather/fetch and drive stock from one point to another, but that will also head and heel when the circumstances call for it will be most effective in his job.

A natural header going to the head to stop the herd's flow of motion. Berkshire's Beau Diddely CDX (Berkshire's Spot of Bar Lazy K ex Stoll's Misty).
Courtesy Pardridge

Now and then you will notice a dog that does not exhibit appropriate herding instincts. These dogs may "throw back" to their wild ancestors more closely, and rather than gathering, driving, and wearing (herding), they simply want to chase stock and deliberately split the bunch by running right through the middle. You will see a dog purposely single out one animal and then "chase" it, preventing it from returning on its own. This stems back to the instinct to cut an animal out to be killed by the pack. Neglectful management and handling can induce or develop these traits, but generally they occur in individuals whose ancestry has not been chosen against the yardstick of performance. A trainer can discourage this from developing. Dogs of this nature can be retrained to be useful individuals. However, these individuals

The split decision.
Courtesy Donham

EYE

"Eye" is of utmost importance in working dogs. Aussies possessing a good amount of eye (concentration) are more successful than those who are less attentive.

FORCE AND STOCK VARIETY

Well-bred Aussies possess an internal power (presence) that allows them to gain the upper hand over their charges. This force is manifested in a deliberate, authoritative manner whenever the dog approaches stock of any class. Force is often asserted in many ways, including bark and grip. Some Aussies will bark, while others are silent. When working with cow/calf herds or ewe/lamb flocks, a barking dog will tend to put the mothers on the fight (due to the mothering instincts). When working livestock in large bunches and/or while working with "blind" stock (i.e., cattle afflicted by pink-eye), a dog that does not bark or growl at a critical point and then if necessary back it up with grip may be totally ineffective. A bark can alert lead cattle, while the grip places pressure upon the immediate stock, which will then push the

"EYE" Appeal. Force is exhibited in a deliberate, authoritive approach. Las Rocosa Lester (Ch Las Rocosa Shiloh ex Ch Las Rocosa Leslie CSD).

An intense approach revealing "EYE" and self-control.

stock ahead. A bark alone may or may not be effective. If a dog is unable to back up the bark with grip, the stock will soon realize that they have the upper hand. Often, when a dog lacks force, he will "yap." Young or inexperienced dogs may also react in this manner until they gain confidence with stock.

Grip is an outward display of force. Often a dog must use a degree of grip even while working sheep. A controlled hit on the nose of a crotchety ram or ewe, or a pinch on the lower leg may be necessary. This should take place when a dog is approached by an individual that is challenging his authority. But biting "here and there" is a serious problem with sheep. Sheep have very thin skin, despite the depth of wool. Any body biting can leave sheep vulnerable to injury. A dog that "grabs"—one that bites and hangs on ver-

Aussies will either grip the hock extended furthest back or the leg with the weight on it. Champion Troy's Gala of Blue Isle.   *Courtesy Wilson*

Taking the Way-te-me command. Goats can also be used instead of sheep.

sus one that pinches and releases immediately—can actually rip the skin. If a dog bites the stomach area unprotected by the ribs, he can possibly even "gut" or expose the intestines in sheep. Once this happens, the sheep can easily die. "Hamstringing" occurs when a dog rips the hamstring (a hind tendon). This is a tactic employed by wild predators that leaves their prey crippled and unable to flee. This will not happen when a dog "heels" the lower leg, rakes, or grips with a pinching effect.

Dairy animals are vulnerable with an udder. Any trauma to the udder is serious. Some dogs will "shoulder" or "bump" the smaller stock (sheep, sometimes calves) with their shoulders or their body. Aussies even "nose" young animals such as lambs, and especially ducks, to persuade them into moving. It is obvious that a bite to a newborn lamb or to a duckling (or duck) could easily maim them.

Some livestock (cattle, sheep, ducks) are gregarious—meaning that they possess bunching or grouping instincts. Some types of stock require that a dog work close in, while other stock—wild and free-moving—are easily handled by a dog that will stay at a distance. Too much pressure on flightly stock by a dog pushing too close or too fast can send them fleeing through a fence, while constant nagging on the heels can put others on the fight. Many times, the mere *presence* of a dog will send them on their way. A soft-mouthed dog may be necessary around sheep and other varieties of stock, where in a different situation, a hard-mouthed dog would be necessary to accomplish the job most effectively.

Generally speaking, a sheep dog must be able to demonstrate the same degree of authority without employing the same techniques imperative with a rough stock dog (cattle). Cattle dogs must be able to demonstrate tremendous force. Although a dog must never lose his head when working cattle, in most instances his degree of control is not placed on such a fine line. However, when working rough stock, there are times when a dog must exhibit an inbred common sense and "read" the situation at hand. When working a cow-calf herd, you need a dog with a quiet nature and calm, deliberate approach. Mother cows with calves at their sides will immediately be prepared to fight, especially if they have been subjected to wild predators. A dog that begins to yap or harass the cow will alert the whole herd to come to the rescue. Some of the grittiest working dogs will learn that when a mother cow turns on them, if they back off to allow some distance, the cow will generally turn back into the herd without incident. If she does not, then he must employ necessary force to gain the upper hand, or the dog will continue to be challenged by his charges.

Each class of livestock offers a challenge of its own, and no two are the same. Some stock, such as

Precise timing displayed by Oliver's Moqui CD, ATD-cs amidst these deadly horns is an inherited, instinctive factor that cannot be trained.   *Photo by Red Oliver*

roping steers, may not budge without a tough, forceful dog convincing them to move. On the other hand, some of the rankest roping steers have been known to move easily from a dog that presents no overall threat. A dog must employ different pressure points with calves as well as a different approach than he would with roping steers or with bulls. Horned stock are obviously more dangerous. A dog must learn to "read" the situation and respond accordingly.

EFFICIENCY

A dog should be efficient and deliberate in all of his moves. If a dog expends all of his energy in the first hour of a twelve-hour day, he may be of little or no value if you need him later that day. Often, at the end of a long, hard day—when stock are tired and have become difficult (sticky)—the dog may have to exert more force. A good stock dog must be able to conserve enough energy for these times. This usually comes with experience in actual working situations.

A WORD OF CAUTION

One word of caution goes to horse owners. Many times dogs are allowed and even encouraged to work horses. This is dangerous and sometimes fatal. Horses are handy with their protective mechanisms and can strike out at any given time with precision and severity. Fatality is more common with horse-induced injuries.

The main reason for not working horses with dogs is because once they are allowed to do so, they will want to keep them bunched with the other classes of livestock. In cattle operations, where it is necessary to ride a horse to gather cattle, you do not need or want your dog heeling your horse every time you send him to "get em up." This habit is not only annoying, but also dangerous.

IT IS NOT RECOMMENDED TO WORK DOGS ON STOCK SUCH AS BUFFALO OR MULES.

As a prospective handler, you must be able to "read" your dog as well as the livestock. It will be beneficial to understand their character and nature of habit and reaction. From time to time, it is good for you to work your stock without the help of your dog. This will lend a greater perspective and increase your own efficiency.

Indian Runners move like a school of fish, with the slightest movement or change of direction. MacSpadden Photo

Rating the sheep well, Green's Boots ATD-cd OTD-s is placing enough pressure to keep them moving without causing confusion. MacSpadden Photo

Sometimes one dog at the head and another at the heels are necessary to convince a bull which way is which. At the head Klarer's Little Concha (Martin's Shadrack ex Klarer's Bug Brush) and her daughter at the heels Champion Twin Oaks Spinner (by Ch Twin Oaks Cactus Bud CD). Courtesy Klarer

Working Indian Runners. Champion Beauwood's Out Rustlin Bear CDX STD-d (George's Red Rustler ex Beauwood's Caligari Bear).

7
TRAINING
THE STOCK DOG

TRAINING

All training and handling time will transfer from one class of livestock to another. However, most trainers agree that it is best to start with the easier types of livestock and then graduate to the more difficult. I believe this to be true in most instances—and especially with puppies—but I also believe that each dog and situation is unique, and that this uniqueness will dictate the type of training that will achieve your desired results.

The fundamental exercises (and puppy training) as described in the chapter on obedience should be taught. Basic obedience will lead toward satisfactory end results. An obedient dog is not only a better companion, but a more effective working dog. Allow your dog ample opportunity to "turn on" to stock before you begin to overemphasize heeling obedience patterns, because some dogs become dependent upon their handler, and until they get the confidence to move away from their handler's side, they may be hindered by this. Generally speaking, many advanced, obedience-titled dogs that have not been started on stock until a later age are at a slight disadvantage, because they keep more of an eye on their handler than on the stock. It will take more time to build this dog's confidence. Once the advanced dog (such as the utility-titled dog) has learned to work away from his handler he is easier to train, because the obedience readily prepares him to accept this type of work away from the handler.

As different as night and day, two dogs of similar abilities may have begun their working careers at two

very different intensities and ages. Most Aussies are early to come on, while others do not show as much interest until later. The foundation of all stock training and handling is based upon inherited characteristics. Usually, puppies are tested from approximately five weeks of age on a small flock of ducks to begin determining their natural tendencies. From the reactions viewed, you can more easily discern which puppies show stronger tendencies for heading or heeling/fetching or driving. These first introductions toward stock provide excellent exposure. Ducks are available for almost any breeder or owner of an Australian Shepherd.

Puppies should first be introduced to ducks because this allows them to exhibit raw instinct, yet sustain no injuries. However, since ducks are unable to properly protect themselves from a dog, puppies or inexperienced dogs should never be left unattended with ducks. Any puppy can and may exhaust the ducks by playing roughly or by trying desperately to herd them. Two or more puppies, when left to their own devices, can begin to pull feathers, play tug-o-war, and even kill a duck unintentionally, no matter how sweet their temperament.

Never work a young dog on anything that he is incapable of outrunning and turning. With flighty sheep, an enthusiastic young dog should always be started in a small enclosure to maintain an initially controlled atmosphere. A young dog should NEVER be worked on rough stock such as cattle until he is *at least six months of age.* The exact age is more specifically designated by the trainee's mental and physical maturity. Ideally, it is best to allow a dog to grow to his approximate adult size before placing him in vulnerable or defensive working circumstances. By the time a youngster is one year of age, he is more than likely "coming together" both mentally and physically. At a year of age, he is still considered a puppy, and by all rights, he is. He is, however, more capable of enduring work and maintaining a longer attention span.

Between ten months to a year of age, I like to begin training a dog on cattle. At this point, he has been worked on sheep to develop his interest but probably knows little of commands except those that are very basic.

If a puppy is bred properly and has been correctly started on sheep, he can easily be taken back to sheep after several months of exposure and work on cattle. He has learned to differentiate between the classes of livestock.

More times than not, it will take a few more months of work on both sheep and cattle for the different manner needed for each to be cemented in the dog's mind.

Too often, if a dog is worked only on sheep or ducks until he matures, and then at maturity, he is used on cattle, he may be hesitant to "get in" and grip/heel, especially if he has been discouraged from gripping while working ducks and/or sheep. This is understandable. Some dogs simply do not have the instinct to grip. However, if a dog is bred for this trait, he will usually display it with time and exposure. These dogs may bark initially, but that will soon diminish with confidence. This is where genetic makeup can lend you a key as to what you can expect from your dog.

Some dogs are trained only on sheep or ducks but are equally effective on the right kind of cattle. Remember—some dogs are specialists, and others are more easily used on all kinds of stock. On the other hand, the finest sheep dog I ever saw was used only on rough stock. The first time that he saw sheep was at a trial, at which point he dazzled spectators with an intricate blend of eye, common sense, and force that allowed him to maneuver his draw with the greatest amount of ease. He never even attempted to dart in and take a hold. This performance can be attributed to the fact that the dog was bred to be a common-sense working dog. Also he was used extensively in a practical operation, which taught him to expend only the necessary amount of energy, and to assert only the *appropriate* force. Even on cattle operations—where plenty of grip (force) is usually necessary under certain circumstances—inappropriate use can be detrimental.

It is far easier to tone down an enthusiastic dog around stock, but to encourage a dog to work that

Using a small flock of goats to train with. The goats gather around the trainer for security while the handler can then teach basic control. Courtesy Warren

A dog must exhibit self-control even while being forceful. Here a black-faced ram is testing the ability of Las Rocosa Charlie Glass ATD. Lawson Photo

does not have the desire is almost next to impossible. And when the going gets rough, he may not have the "heart" when you need him most. Working two dogs together can build confidence by bringing out a pack instinct. Some trainers tie a young or inexperienced dog to an experienced dog. This is very dangerous in rough stock situations where a dog must react at any given moment. The older dog, too, gets a little impatient with playful trainees tugging at his collar and only becomes irritated, which can also inhibit a mild working instinct. It can, however, be beneficial to allow an inexperienced or young dog to follow along until his interest in the stock sparks and he shows that he "wants to work." This is where reading your dog will cue you when he is ready to begin training.

COMMANDS

Basic commands can be taught at almost any age. For detailed information, refer to the chapter on obedience. In addition to the basic commands, the following commands are suggested for stock dogs. Use ones that are comfortable to you, and be consistent so that your dog has the opportunity to learn them:

COME or HERE, or COME HERE—To bring the dog to you, "Phideaux, Come."

COME BEHIND, BEHIND or GET BE-HIND—Come back around, behind the stock in a driving position.

EASY, STEADYON or TAKE TIME—To fluctuate speed or maintain a steady manner; to slow the motion of your dog.

GET AHEAD—Move around to the front (head or lead) of one or more. This command is generally given when one or more are breaking away from the bunch or desired direction of travel.

GET BACK or GET OUT—To move back out away from the stock. Can also be given when you want him to work farther away from the stock.

GO BY or COME BY—Clockwise movement around the stock.

HIT 'EM or HIT-SSS-SKIT—To tell your dog to take hold.

HOLD IT or STOP—To have your dog remain in a stationary position.

LIE DOWN or DOWN—To down or drop your dog in any given place.

THAT'LL DO or THAT'S ENOUGH or O.K.—To let your dog know that the job is finished.

TURN BACK or LOOK BACK—To tell your dog to go back to retrieve missing stock or bunch quitters.

WALK ON or GET 'EM UP or COME UP—To approach the stock directly from any given point; to work.

WAY-TO-ME, AWAY-TO-ME or WAY-TO—Counterclockwise movement around the stock.

WATCH EM—To alert the dog, or to cue him to keep his eye on the stock.

It makes little difference which command(s) you use as long as you are consistent. The flanking or side commands, "go by" and "way-ta-me," have been varied to "by" and "way-to," respectively, by some handlers. Some stockmen prefer "gee" or "go left" for clockwise movement around the stock and "haw" or "go right" for counterclockwise movement around the stock.

Too many commands will confuse your dog, and in a tense situation may even confuse you. For most jobs, five commands will enable you to take stock just about anywhere. You should be able to direct your dog to halt or stop. You must be able to call him off the stock completely. You must be able to send him directly up to the stock from any direction and then be able to tell him to go left or to go right in any given order.

It may sound easy, but a dog that is consistent with five commands may take up to two or three years to become reliable each and every time. This comes with constant handling.

"That'll do" is an important command in working stock, because it communicates that the job is completed. Whenever a job is completed, tell your dog "that'll do" and praise him. To teach your dog

Champion Apache Tears of Timberline UD, ATD fetching sheep to his handler.   *Courtesy Davis*

Experienced, efficient working dogs move in direct lines and move just far enough to check the flock to bring them under control and moving in the desired line of travel.   *Courtesy Donham*

A direct deliberate approach (with the least amount of energy) is necessary especially when working small bunches to prevent zigzagging and weaving all over the area.

First Lessons on Stock

When you take your dog to stock, he may be so intent that he will be aware of nothing else—especially you. Calmly approach your dog, and *use self-control!* Put your lead back on and reinforce the basics. If possible, allow your dog to run off some energy before taking him to the stock. If not possible, put him on a twenty-five-foot lead or longer. Move the stock around your training pen for a few

Moving to the head to stop a single maverick.

the meaning of the command, when your dog is approaching or has his attention fixed on the stock, intervene and tell him "that'll do" then call your dog and walk away. If your dog pays no attention to you, give him a collar correction and praise him for coming away from the stock. Vary this so that he won't anticipate it each and every time. Also you do not want him to begin to watch you more than he does the stock. Overenthusiastic dogs that eagerly charge out to get to the stock are handled differently. Place the lead and collar on and give the command the minute you see your dog "thinking" about taking off. Tell your dog "that'll do." Give him a jerk, release, then walk in the opposite direction. Congratulate your dog each and every time he responds favorably.

Sometimes when your dog is extremely intent on the stock, and you rush in to place him on a down, he may become even more excited. This is why a lead and collar are effective in establishing control. When your dog darts off, step in the opposite direction promptly after giving the command "that'll do." This takes him away from the immediate excitement. Take him from the stock, and give him an opportunity to settle down.

Timing

Correct timing is important in executing an effective correction. The chapter on obedience deals specifically with types of correction. Correct timing is determined when you become aware that your dog is THINKING about doing something—before he is engaged in the act of DOING. It is split-second action that cements each lesson in a dog's mind.

In some instances, if you are able to instill a correction while your dog is in the act, you will have even better success. Correct timing also comes from your ability to read your dog.

Due to the fact hogs are as intelligent as dogs and they can "bite" to defend themselves it takes an especially brilliant dog with sheer courage and necessary force to keep them in line. Green's Boots ATD-cd OTD-s. MacSpadden Photo

minutes, "downing" him every so often in an enthusiastic, authoritative voice. Allow him to approach the stock, and if he gets unruly, step on the rope and walk toward him. Put your hands on him and talk to him until he is relaxed before you let him go again. Tell him "easy" or "steady."

As you work him around the pen, *step on the rope and walk to him many, many times just to say "good dog."* Do this when he is performing well. This will create a very desirable situation between you and your dog.

A pen or arena approximately one hundred and fifty feet in diameter is a good place to put the initial commands on your dog. You can graduate into larger areas and then into the open as you progress in your training. Whenever a dog refuses to take a flanking command, he can be taken back into the enclosure to reinforce the basics. In a smaller enclosure, you can

Pulling at a twelve o'clock balance. J-Bar-D Cimmaron Warrior.
Courtesy Rowe

be on top of most situations, allowing you to develop consistent performance.

Sometimes a dog will not show that much interest. This can be due to age and early handling. If a dog does not see stock until he is four or five years old, it is not his fault. With this type of dog, training may take time. *Be patient!* Do not overemphasize control at this stage. Move the stock yourself, allowing your dog to follow. This type of dog sometimes may benefit from the presence of an experienced dog to "spark" his interest. Puppies get a "spark" from working alongside or with their mothers.

Pulling

A common method of starting a dog on sheep or ducks is "pulling." The handler is situated at the head of the flock, with the dog at the opposite side. Give him your command to "come up." As he starts moving the flock toward you, begin walking backward. When you get to the opposite side of the pen, shift from right to left, or vice-versa. Your dog should position himself directly opposite you and continue moving the stock toward you. The tendency of either the header or heeler is to keep livestock bunched, either when moving them away from or toward you.

A header will go to the head naturally to gain balance. He will keep the leader from breaking away and hold his charges in their immediate position. Without the handler's direction, a green dog showing heading instincts will encircle his flock like a cyclone—an action called "ringing." Teach him to pull and bring them toward you. He will have to wear more with a larger group and much less with a

Going in for a low one. Las Rocosa Christophene, STD-sd, OTD-c (Ch Las Rocosa Shiloh ex Howe's Little Peedee) a multiple High In Trial winner is noted as the top producing dam of the First Australian Shepherd Stock Dog Working Futurity.

smaller bunch. How much he will have to wear also depends upon whether the sheep are sticky or flighty. Check and redirect your dog to the opposite flank with a shepherds' crook or bamboo rod. Tap it on the ground while giving the command to go in the opposite direction. Although he may want to overrun, and go to the head, continue the process. Tap your rod and send him back in the opposite direction. If he ignores being blocked by the use of your rod on the first lessons, drop him as he nears the arc. He will learn that you want him to stay behind. Your shepherds' crook is an extension of your hand. It is used *not* to point the direction you wish him to go, but to *block* the direction of his approach. *The shepherds' crook is never used to punish your dog!*

Occasionally, drop your dog to let him and the stock settle. This allows nature to lay the groundwork. Sheep drift to a point of least resistance. As the flock flows to the other direction, the dog should finish his arc, picking up the opposite flank. Soon, he will be wearing like a pendulum. As his instincts mature and his natural working abilities are cultivated, he should settle in and learn to move more effectively. He will eventually compensate in his movement to keep the flock in a straight line toward you, the handler. Some dogs achieve this naturally. Other individuals have to be corrected from "overrunning" on each flank or side. When this occurs, the dog swings out to the far left, sending the sheep to the far right. When the sheep move to the far right, the dog has to swing out also, sending the sheep to the left, creating a zigzag

pattern all over the training enclosure. If the dog is well bred, he will soon settle in and move more discreetly. This is opposed to the dog that moves more effectively by using less movement to achieve the same line of travel. Instead of swinging out to one side or the other, the more efficient dog moves out only far enough to check the flock from weaving to and fro to bring them to his handler in a direct approach. This often comes with age and handling, but dogs inherit the ability quite naturally.

A dog should never be allowed to come between the handler and the flock. These basic elements teach him appropriate balance. You will gain control of your dog more easily when he has control of the flock. This also puts you, the handler within the flock, which means the dog will never intentionally drive the stock away without you.

The initial stages of the pull are ideal for training most dogs for sheep and duck work, but they are difficult and often dangerous for training dogs to work cattle. This method is sometimes frustrating for stronger "driving" dogs, although in essence they are driving whenever they are behind the livestock. Variations of the pull must then be employed. (This will be discussed later.)

In the case of an unruly, aggressive, overzealous dog that cannot be controlled in the presence of stock, you must create a way to direct his energies as he gains levelheadedness. The best method is to teach your dog to walk up to the flock, put him on a "down," and steady him by placing your hands with soothing

The challenge (A)

strokes. When he has settled down, allow him to walk towards the sheep and move them around the pen. Be sure to drop your dog intermittently to allow him to settle, but do not forget to allow him to move the sheep around the pen. This gives him a feeling of accomplishment!

Some handlers will "put miles" on this type of dog by allowing him to run around the sheep to fabricate the ringing pattern. This exercise is not beneficial to most dogs and could be detrimental. In many cases, it is responsible for winding a dog right out of control. Ideally, you should have a calm group of sheep that will bunch easily and move away from a dog. If the sheep are flighty, any extra pressure added by the closeness of an unsteady dog could send them running to the extreme boundaries of the training enclosure. Stock that is too sticky or stubborn will usually turn back to "fight" a young dog, which can easily destroy his confidence. It depends, of course, on what you can afford to buy and maintain and what your place will accommodate. However, you should have at *least* two head of any stock that you are using for training.

In starting a young dog, do not allow him to come between you and the stock while you are sending him from one side to the other. It can stifle his progress when commanding at greater distances. In later training, it may give him the opportunity to "cross-over," cutting back in front of you and moving in the direction he prefers rather than taking the flanking (side) command that you gave. It is usually

Wearing behind a bunch of cattle to keep them moving. Powder River's Strawboss.   *Courtesy Foster*

a shortcut for the dog to get directly to the stock. If a dog never gets in the habit of coming between you and the stock, he will not inadvertently "cross-over." If an inexperienced dog intentionally moves in the opposite direction from which you commanded, you will be able to step in to "block" from the wrong side and redirect him.

When you have gained basic control of your dog, you are ready to introduce additional commands with your actual everyday work. Use "walk-on" or "get-'em-up" to approach the stock—whatever works best for you. If you do not have regular work for your dog, you can still employ the same methods while trying

The challenge (B)- A controlled grip is sometimes necessary for the dog to gain the upper hand.

to give your dog his "purpose." Even if it is nothing more than penning your stock up at night and bringing them out in the morning, an actual assignment will make your dog want to do it.

If you are gathering or driving stock and your dog leaves some behind or some have split off from the bunch, tell him to "turn back" or "look back."

In training and trialing situations, it may be helpful in building confidence for your dog to move a bunch of stock back to a single that has split away. You can move the bunch back and pick up the stray with the least amount of resistance; however, in a practical situation, it may be unrealistic to move five hundred head to gather only one or two. This is where experience teaches a dog to handle singles under such circumstances.

To teach sides, many different commands can be used by handlers, but basically, one is to send the dog left, or clockwise, and the other is to send the dog to the right, or counterclockwise, The international commands are "go-by" for clockwise (which can easily be remembered as "time goes by—clockwise"), and "way-to-me," which is said "way-ta-me." Being

Gripping—A pinching effect that occurs when the dog takes hold. Ch Windsong's Raisin Cain CD ATD-csd.   *Courtesy Warren*

Generally the experienced Australian Shepherd carefully calculates which leg and where to grip. In this case Windsong's Bell Pepper STD is hitting the leg with the weight placed on it.   *Courtesy Warren*

able to send your dog on a half-flank or completely to the other side of the herd or flock can be a valuable asset when gathering stock from pastures, paddocks, or an arena. Begin sending your dog to a side with a slight motion in the direction that you want him to go. Before giving the flanking command, remember to send him from the same side (of you) to which he will be going. In other words, when you send him to the right he should leave from your right side. Initially, you may even go with him. Repeat the appropriate side command as you go.

As you advance in the training stages, you will be able to give the verbal command without much extra motion. However, it may take considerable repetitive work to cement these commands in the dog's mind. If he begins to take the wrong side (crossover), drop him. Block the dog from continuing in that direction, then re-send him. Allow yourself two years to *perfect* the flanking or side commands.

Never leave *any* dog unattended on the stock, because he will easily pick up bad or uncorrectable habits. For the safety of your dog, never send him to move rough stock where injury is unavoidable. Your situation should be designed or altered to enable him to get away even in closed-in spaces. Whenever you have completed a segment of daily work or training, release your dog with an "o.k!" or "that'll do," and praise him for a job well done!

The previous exercises will allow you to develop a useful hand on any livestock operation. The following exercises will allow you to perfect a proficient working dog that can be used either under actual working conditions or in the trial arena. The biggest difference between training a dog on cattle or sheep involves the gripping factor. If you are going to work your dog on cattle, he will need a lot more grip. On the other hand, the dog will not need as much grip when working sheep, and it should be discouraged. If your dog is a strong driving dog, you may have to make a few variations as when training the fetching dog. It is imperative to begin with the instincts that come natural in each dog for maximum results. This tends to cut down on frustration.

Round Pen

Some trainers will use a small round pen from thirty to sixty feet in diameter, depending on the type of livestock to be used. It should be large enough to allow the ducks or sheep (even calves or hogs) to move freely when a dog approaches them. It should also allow a dog to move freely around his charges without getting out of control. Because he is not being discouraged and restrained, you can then channel him around the flock in a positive manner and at the same time prevent him from upsetting the stock.

You can also drop your dog away from the pen. Let him walk directly up, then send him from one side to the other. Do not allow the dog to become frustrated or sour by overcommanding him at this point. Also, do not encourage him to madly race around the pen in a frenzy. Although it does allow him to release some pent-up energy, it can also wind him up! Remember—these dogs were originally bred to go from sunup to sundown under range conditions.

You can get inside of the round pen with or without a well-trained dog to move the sheep or ducks. The puppy will probably react according to his inherited instincts. If the stock is free-moving, they will more than likely move due to the dog's presence outside of the pen. Do not do this more than several times, and not more than a few minutes each time. If overdone, it will introduce frustration in keen dogs.

Gathering, Casting, Lifting, Bringing

Take your dog quietly into an oval or rectangular enclosure that is between one hundred and two hundred feet in length. If your dog is keen, he may wear your patience with his enthusiasm. If he lacks interest, there is not much that you will be able to do until he "comes on." The extremely keen dog must not be harshly handled. In the long run, you can tone down this enthusiasm without dampening his keenness. If you do not have the patience, give your dog a kind word and excuse yourself for the present.

With your dog at your side, kneel down and allow him to sit, stand, or lie quietly at your side. Give him an opportunity to calm down before you start imposing a lot of control. If he is "biting at the bit," ask him to "lie down." Place your hands on him in long, soothing strokes, and speak to him in even, calming tones. If you are in the center of your enclosure, the sheep are more than likely somewhere along the fence. You can take your dog off the lead, and if he is out of control, place him back on lead for a while. Drop your dog and walk toward the sheep. Place yourself between the flock and the dog—closer to the flock in the beginning. Ask your dog to "come-up." If he tries to race right to them, block his approach. Send him in the opposite direction in a half-circle and work off of the fence. Take your place at the lead or head of the sheep, and allow your dog to approach the open side (the side without pressure). The fence will help break your dog from ringing, if he is inclined to do so.

You As The Handler

You work as a valve. You regulate the flow of motion at the head of the sheep, just slightly off the center. Your dog is at twelve o'clock, and you are somewhere between three, four, or five o'clock,

depending on the nature of your sheep. As the handler, you move away from the lead or head of the flock and out away from the fence, which should give them a place to go. Your dog should be following quietly behind. Before you lose control, drop your dog behind as you step inward toward the fence to "shut off the valve." Give your dog an opportunity to settle down. Continue to let your dog follow the flock a short distance up the fence.

If at any point the situation gets out of hand, you can step on the long line and tell him "that'll do." Let your dog bring the sheep along the fence line while you walk backward in front of the sheep. Let him bring the sheep behind for short distances at first. Drop him and allow him to settle. Use your bamboo pole or shepherds' crook to guide your dog out from behind the flank around to the head—the direction in which they are facing. With natural fetching or heading dogs, this will be a welcome relief. You will step out from in front to the center of the arc that your dog is making as he goes to the head. As your dog approaches the far corner, his presence should turn the stock away. Let your dog follow them a short distance up the fence line, with you working as the valve, regulating the flow of motion, once again at the head of the stock.

This fence work is also the basis for teaching a dog to work on cattle. The main difference is that you will not work directly in front of the cattle but will maintain more of a three, four, or five o'clock position. Again this depends upon the nature of your stock.

If your dog approaches the flock too fast, drop him momentarily at a point of natural balance. Never let the stock get so far away from the dog in this stage that he "feels" he is about to lose control. This is especially true of younger dogs until they are capable of outrunning the class of stock you will be working. This is the main reason why you begin in a smaller enclosure.

When your dog has learned to quietly bring the stock from one end to the other and then back again along the fence line, you will want to teach him to bring the stock away from the fence. If you are using cattle, you must first secure a place where your dog is able to avoid injury. In other words, do not try to teach him to bring stock off of a solid fence that lacks an "escape route."

Teaching your dog to bring the stock off of the fence is not as difficult as it is time-consuming. Keep your dog at the back side, with you at the lead (head). As you are moving back, also move away from the fence. Use your bamboo rod or crook to encourage your dog to swing in behind the stock. If the positioning is right, you may be able to step into your dog

Standing "EYE." Loida's Just Plain Charlie OTD-sc ATD-d demonstrating the intense eye characteristic of his working style.
Courtesy Loida

Mini Acre Peppermint Patti CD OTD-c employing "EYE."
Courtesy Warren

to send him in behind. If you have been working a strong twelve o'clock balance, then your dog will more than likely compensate by cutting behind the stock, in front of the fence. If this isn't effective, send your dog to the head. More than likely, the stock will then turn away from your dog and give him an opportunity to "lift" them away from the fence. If that does not work, step into the stock yourself, bringing your dog in with you, and move the stock out together. Be patient as he will become confident through your consistent, patient handling—he will successfully bring the stock away from the fence and out of corners.

In arena situations and with rough stock, the fence should be designed so that your dog can swing back under the fence if necessary. Much of this depends on your balance. If necessary, walk between the cattle and the fence and call your dog in with you. This same type of work applies to getting stock out of a corner. If your dog has difficulty in getting the stock to move in one direction, then try the other. Stop for a moment and evaluate the situation. See what you can do to lighten up the pressure point. Do not let your dog get into the habit of swinging to the head and pushing the stock back tighter into a corner once you have already brought the stock out of the corner. If you see that your dog is inclined to go to the head, stopping the flow of motion, then drop him while he is still in an effective position to keep them moving. *NEVER drop your dog in a vulnerable position where he can get kicked or hit.* Some dogs lack the confidence to move stock from the fence or corner. If he is reluctant to move in, walk in and guide him.

Allow your dog to bring the sheep behind you as you walk from one end of the pen to the other. If he starts moving them too fast, drop him. When you get to the opposite end of the pen, move back to the other end. Vary the distances that you have him "pull" before you change directions.

Pulling and Overrunning

Your dog will have to constantly be checked from overrunning (moving to the head to stop the flow of motion). To check and redirect this tendency to "ring," you can use a crook or a bamboo pole or even a light fishing pole. Tap it on the ground to block him from continuing around, and send him back in the opposite direction. He will be moving like a pendulum.

The larger the flock or herd, the more your dog will have to "wear," (a pendulum type of motion) to keep them moving. This is undesirable with small bunches. As a dog matures, his approach should become deliberate and exhibit movement that is necessary to get the stock from one point to another. If he is approaching a larger bunch, then it will be necessary for him to wear, but if he has only a few head to work, it is undesirable for him to wear as heavily. This is because with a smaller bunch the pressure point is more sensitive, and this type of movement may send them in the opposite direction. This can also be instilled through improper handling. In the trial arena, this is evident when a dog brings his charges weaving to and fro in a zigzag pattern around the trial field. Discourage the excessive weaving by dropping the dog. Move back to give the stock a place toward which to move, then ask the dog to come up. Do not allow him to go widely from side to side.

Outrun (Casting)

Once your dog is bringing the stock quietly, you can begin the next phase of the gathering exercise. The action consists of your dog moving in an arc from your side to the opposite side of the stock. From the time the dog leaves his handler's side, he should widen out his approach and then move in quietly behind the stock. This is called the outrun, (and the pattern ideally resembles the shape of a half pear). Your dog must be able to get from one side to the other without upsetting the stock and sending them into flight.

The ideal outrun allows the dog to get from one side of his flock to the other without causing a commotion. The outrun sets the stage for the first impression that occurs in the lift and is therefore extremely important.

Some handlers are so intent on teaching a wide outrun that they force a dog to move out wide too soon. Often, when a dog starts out too wide, he will move in too close at the back side of the sheep. A dog should only be forced out wider when he gets close to the sheep. Some dogs naturally work wider than others, but with patience and consistent handling, a good dog can be trained to move effectively.

Teaching Your Dog to Cast for the Outrun - Spend several minutes calming your dog. This will also have a soothing effect on the stock. Leave your dog in a stationary position while you walk around the stock, return to him, and quietly release him. Move the bunch away from the fence to somewhere in the middle. Position the stock in the open, away from obstacles.

Take your dog ten to twenty feet away from the stock. Leave him in a stationary position by either dropping him or placing him in a stand. Walk backwards toward the stock, facing your dog. Allow him to settle a moment, then send him to one side or the other with the use of your flanking (side) commands and bamboo pole to guide him from in front of the sheep to a position on the back side. DO NOT USE THE POLE TO POINT, BUT USE IT TO BLOCK YOUR DOG FROM GOING THE WRONG WAY OR CROSSING OVER BETWEEN YOU AND THE SHEEP.

As he moves from a position in front of you—with you between the stock and the dog—send him to a position directly across from you and the sheep. This is often referred to as the "twelve o'clock balance point." Drop him at the moment he hesitates, which is the natural point of balance. Do not always insist on a perfect "twelve o'clock" stopping point, as it may cause problems of "underrunning" (coming in short) during later stages of the outrun. Your dog should stop when he reaches the twelve o'clock position. If for one reason or another the stock has either drifted or shifted, your dog should not be stopped until he reaches the point of balance to "block" the stock before the lift takes place. During the beginning, you can shift your position to compensate for your dog stopping short or overrunning. When he gets to the back side, then you can move to the point opposite

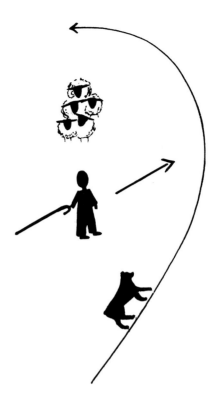

The handler is in a good position to prevent the dog from crossing over and from coming in too tight.

In this illustration the handler is not in position to prevent the dog from crossing between handler and livestock.

your dog at six o'clock. This will help to position him correctly.

Overrunning can shift sheep out of position as well, which forces the dog to reposition before he can complete the lift and start bringing the stock toward you in the fetch.

This is a gradual process. Do not send your dog too far too soon. Slowly and gradually, increase the distance that you send your dog. If at any point he tries to "cut in" and/or cross over on you, drop him immediately! Reposition yourself between the dog and stock, and resend him. This reaction indicates that he wasn't ready for the distance—however short it may seem to you. Shorten it to the place he cut in until he is proficiently taking the outrun at that distance. Gradually, work back up to the distance. When first practicing casting, spend one week sending your dog counterclockwise and the next week sending him clockwise. Vary this so that he will run well to "both hands" or sides.

The time spent solidifying your dog's approach will pay off when you reach the advanced stages of handling. Eventually, you will "inch" nearer to the place where you left your dog when you cast him in an outrun. Remember to acknowledge your dog for his efforts. Initially, if he prefers to take one side over the other, do not be concerned. You can spend more time on the problem or weak side when he has grasped the idea of the outrun.

To teach your dog to move a bit wider, drop him a few yards to your right side, then send him to the left (counterclockwise) or vice-versa. This will teach him to come around you. Increase the distance between you and your dog, and practice the same exercise with the stock farther away. Eventually, your dog will learn to cast out according to the distance. When he is steady at all distances, he will be a big help in bringing in stock that he cannot see. Also, when the dog swings in on the flank (he may hesitate at the place of his natural balance), give a down or steady command, and then redirect him. Step toward him and ask him to "get back" or "get out." As you step toward him, he may try to move past you. Block him from doing so. At first you may need to take hold of his collar and step into him (not on) and encourage him to get back a few steps while you guide him. Let him settle for a moment, then allow him to come up and move the stock a short distance.

Lifting

The lift is what takes place from the moment your dog has reached the opposite side in an outrun or cast. It is a moment of brief hesitation, which is why your dog has learned to stop before he brings in the stock. With full authority, he should move up, the stock should melt away calmly, and the dog should follow quietly behind. This is generally not the case with sticky or stubborn stock. Each situation requires a different approach. He should not rush the stock or exert more power than needed to get them moving. If he is challenged by one of his charges, he should then assert the force necessary to gain the upper hand.

One of the most difficult tasks is training a strict heeler to head, or to grip the head correctly on the nose or foreface when threatened. Where and how a dog "heads" is inherited. A dog must have a tremendous amount of power when he faces his charges, which occurs in the lift. A heeler that is reluctant to head can be worked within a controlled environment. When working with cattle, you can put a cow in a chute or similar device. With an animal in the chute, walk the dog up to the animal and tell him to "hit" or "hit 'em." If necessary, tap the nose of the animal.

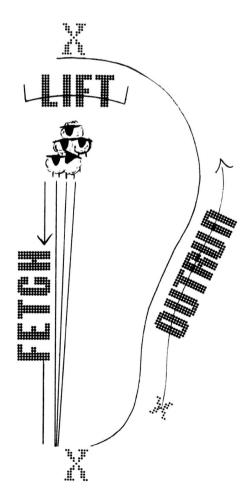

The ideal outrun. Note the half pear shape created when the dog widens his approach around the stock.

(A) *Las Rocosa Maxx CD STD-s moves wide while moving to the head to keep the sheep calm and quiet.*

(B) *At the end of an outrun the dog comes into an appropriate balance point, calculates the sheep and moves deliberately in such a manner to keep from exciting, "blowing" or scattering the sheep.*

(C) *Sticky sheep such as these require a closer working distance between themselves and the dog in order to respond and move away from the dog. Freer moving sheep need less pressure and more distance between themselves and the dog in order to be controlled.*

When the dog hits it, tell him "that'll do," and praise him. Teach your dog to nip the nose or foreface of sheep in a similar manner. Leave your dog in a stationary position, and walk the sheep (guide him with your legs) toward the dog. With a firm grip on the jowls, lower the head, facing the dog. Ask the dog to come up, and give him the same command that you would use in the chute. As soon as the dog hits on the foreface or nose, tell him "that'll do," and praise him. Do this once or twice. Repeat whenever an opportunity arises, such as when an uncooperative animal charges your dog. This will help the dog to understand the lesson. *Never* let your dog hang on or rip. If your dog goes for the throat, immediately cut him off with a "get back." If you have the head lowered, however, the neck will not be readily exposed. Ask him to come back and start over. Sometimes a dog will grip the head in this situation; sometimes he will not.

You can also teach your dog to correctly heel a sheep on command. You can place the sheep in a corner (to help you hold him still) or in the open. Shake the hind leg and give the command to "skit ahold." As soon as he does, praise him and tell him "that'll do." Do this once or twice, then end the train-

ing session. Reinforce this lesson whenever the opportunity calls for your dog to grip, until he understands the lesson and acts on his own from your verbal command.

If the dog lacks confidence and begins barking, take him away. Present him with several situations to build up his confidence. Barking indicates a lack of confidence, although some dogs naturally work with more noise than others. A dog must not be pressured into doing too much at too young of an age, or barking and/or yapping may result.

You must also use a smaller pen and have the dog drive the stock into a corner. When he has them where you want them, tell him "that'll do," and place him a little distance in front of the bunch. Tell him to "watch 'em," and push one head away from the bunch. Ask your dog to come up. If the sheep or cow does not turn back, you can give your dog the command to head. He will be able to apply his previous lesson. He should get the idea if he is keen and mature enough to understand what you want.

Maturity and experience will teach a good dog to be firm and to display full authority in his approach. As the handler, you must not allow stock to "bully" an inexperienced dog. Go to his aid and help build a positive situation. The lift is a crucial time. The momentary pause is a time in which the dog makes a "stand" and the stock know instantly if he has the power to back up his position. The dog is able to discern if the stock will test him. Most all types of livestock know when a dog lacks confidence and power, because the message is conveyed through his approach. To the onlooker, a dog that possesses power may "appear" to have little influence in the movement of his charges, while another dog cannot get to first base. To the novice, this type of work is not "impressive." However, a dog does not have to be right on the heels of his charges. Rather, he can be further behind, calmly and deliberately influencing the direction of travel.

his "draw" and moves the stock effortlessly from one point to another, the inexperienced think that the dog "didn't do anything." This is opposed to the entry that wildly takes his charges running from one point to another, racing them through each obstacle. The novice will applaud this type of action. It takes a better dog—one with more experience—to keep the situation under control and, with ease, complete a course.

Drive

In essence, a dog is driving when he is behind the stock. He has been practicing "driving" in bringing (while fetching) the stock to you, but now you will teach him to take his charges away from you and drive them to your right and left at varying lengths

A trio of dogs moving young bulls to winter range.

The experienced handler and judge are the ones who can determine if the stock is moving by the dog's influence under both actual working conditions and trial situations. They can also tell if the stock is uncooperative due to the dog's lack of experience and methods of approach or if it is the nature of the livestock.

At a trial, spectators are usually impressed if there is a lot of action—whether it is necessary or not. When a dog has complete control and authority over

and distances. The natural fetching dog will easily become frustrated by driving, just as a driving dog could become frustrated when you ask him to go to the head. Of course, a well-balanced dog will fall somewhere in between, generally accepting his lessons as they are presented to him.

A dog can be taught to stay behind his stock, regardless of where you are. Attach a long cord or light line to him, and work a small bunch up an alley, corral, or training pen along the fence line. Each time

Driving along a fence line.

that he extends his movement from behind the stock to the head, check him with your cord and tell him "get behind" or "come behind." If you are working out in the open and he constantly overruns the head, drop him before he moves out of position and tell him to "get behind."

As with "pulling," you can initially position yourself toward the front and more frequently step off to the side. Your dog should be used to this "off-balance" work at this point and begin to accept it in stride. *Remember—if your dog becomes frustrated at any point in his training, go back to the basics!* Ask your dog to drive a few yards. Drop him and allow him to lift and fetch the stock to you. Increase the distances that you ask your dog to drive over a long period of time. The gradual introduction will be rewarding if you do not rush your dog.

Some dogs will fall quite naturally into driving, but due to continual practice with the fetch, he may or may not immediately "pick up" on the exercise. It is also beneficial to put a word with the action (such as get back, come behind, etc). Use your training area and step off to the side so that the dog is in essence "bringing" the stock to you. Soon you will be able to stand in the middle with the dog moving the stock in a perimeter around you (as in the training pen or trial arena).

When you begin to drive, especially away from yourself, your dog may dash over to the head to turn them and bring them back, as he's been taught. Do not scold him for it, but prevent him from going to the head and bringing them back until commanded to do so. Simply bring him back around behind and tell him "walk on." Have him do this for a short distance, and praise him for doing well!

Do not ask too much of him too soon. Go back to the training enclosure until he seems to understand,

and then move into larger areas for practice. Each stage of training, if executed to a degree of perfection, will only lend to the stability of your dog. Exercises go hand in hand. Learn to read your dog as well as the stock. Do not impair your dog's ability as a self-thinker. His instinctive nature and ability to read livestock are probably much keener than yours. Do not make him so dependent on your command that at a critical moment, if a ewe or cow were to break off, your dog would wait for the o.k. or command to bring it back. More than likely, if he were allowed his own decision in those situations, he would have already been there cutting her off.

The Sheep and Cattle Dog

One problem that many handlers have with an Australian Shepherd is that they work him diligently on sheep, and if he has the tendency to "grip," he is

Working as a team. When working sticky stock such as these roping steers one dog places direct pressure on the heels while another works slightly farther back to check any that should turn back.

seriously punished. This also discourages the dog from gripping cattle. If you plan to use a dog on both types of stock, I suggest working him on the two as much as possible. I have several dogs that I use on both classes of stock in the same day. They learn the difference easily. If this is not possible, then at the exact moment when you see your dog moving in to grip a sheep, drop him. If your dog does not act immediately or goes on in and grips, you can correct him for disobeying rather than for gripping. With plenty of work, your dog will learn that he does not need to grip unnecessarily to move the sheep. If your sheep are sticky, you must teach your dog to grip discriminately to gain the upper hand. Once sheep are moving, then your dog should back off. This is where your discretion as the handler is so vital. You must try to prevent situations where this type of dog becomes frustrated and must resort to the initial instinct—which is to grip. If a dog is handled properly, he will be able to be equally effective and assert this force on the cattle.

A natural header can be used effectively to gather stock. This type of dog will not run livestock through a fence because of his instinct to stop the flow of motion. When driving, if he extends himself past the point of moving an animal back into the herd or flock, and if he circles around the stock, drop the dog and send him behind the cattle. As in teaching "sides," position yourself so that you are able to block his flow of motion, then send him back behind. Many of these dogs will grip the heels of rough stock when sent behind.

Dogs often learn a job as they go along. Give him lessons that he can relate to his everyday work. For example, never send your dog to blindly gather stock if you know there are none to be gathered. In the event you must send him to search for missing or lost stock he will work harder knowing there is a task to be performed, rather than "thinking" it is another game to "go out," with no specific goal in mind. The reaction would be similar to the boy who cried wolf. Never send your dog so far away that you are unable to correct mistakes before they become bad habits in the early stages of training. If you take the time to build a strong foundation, there will be less opportunity for it to crumble. *Take your time—TRAINING IS NEVER AN OVERNIGHT SUCCESS!!* Persistence and patience along with common sense will reward you for your extra effort. Always treat your dog kindly. Considering that a good dog takes the place of several men, training is a worthwhile investment. REMEMBER - A DOG MUST BE IN CONTROL OF THE STOCK BEFORE THE HANDLER CAN BE IN CONTROL OF THE DOG.

A good dog may cover double or triple the distance and territory as a rider on horseback. This is due to such factors as the size ratio difference and working style. Balance and symmetry are absolutely necessary to enable each dog to perform his duties with the greatest amount of ease. Las Rocosa Charlie Glass ATD.
Lawson Photograph

A well-trained stock dog relaxes with his flock at the end of the day.

"Capriole" captures Taylor's Escalante effortlessly gliding over a four-foot fence.

8

WORKING TRIALS

by Ernest J. Hartnagle

In 1974, the Australian Shepherd Club of America (ASCA) formed a committee to design a stock dog program that would promote and preserve the natural, inherited working ability of the Australian Shepherd. The initial program included a trial course with a related score card, ranch dog certification, and a simple set of rules. The program has since been amended to include a miniature course for fowl, but the basic concept has remained the same.

In the trial section, a dog is graded on the manner and degree of efficiency that he displays as he herds a small group of three to five head of livestock through a set of obstacles and back into a holding pen. The time allotted to complete the course is ten minutes with a two-minute warning period and seven minutes for fowl and a two-minute warning period.

Each dog must begin in the started division for each class of livestock—fowl, sheep (or goats), hogs, or cattle—to gain that degree before going to the open division and finally into the advanced classes.

TYPES OF TRIALS

Three types of trials are recognized by the Australian Shepherd Club of America.

Training Trials

Training trials are designed to give both the handler and his dog exposure to livestock in the trial arena. There are no specific requirements regarding the type of livestock used, the trial course, or judges and their method of judging. These trials are often held in conjunction with training clinics and seminars.

Fun Trials

The fun trial is not limited to judges approved by the ASCA, but everything else must be held according to the requirements of a Sanctioned Trial, except that no individual is eligible to earn legs towards certification. The Fun Trial is designed to give handlers and their dogs experience on the ASCA Stock Dog Course in preparation for a sanctioned event.

Sanctioned Trials

The Sanctioned Trial must meet the requirements set forth by the ASCA. The criteria include approved judges, judging score cards, trial course layout, and livestock. This is the only type of trial at which dogs are eligible to earn qualifying legs toward certification.

TRIAL DIVISIONS

The Started Dog

The Started Dog is a dog that is at least six months of age or older and that has started to work off lead. He should be able to do a respectable job with the aid of his handler. The handler should have enough control and be able to stop and call the dog back to him on command. The Started Dog is not expected to take side directions or perform intricate maneuvers at this level of work. He is, however, expected to display his natural herding ability and show interest and concentration on the livestock. To gain certification in the Started classes, a dog must acquire two qualifying scores of at least sixty-nine points (60 percent) of 115 available points to be earned under two different judges in the same livestock category. Each individual must be certified in the Started classes before entering in the Open division.

The Open Dog

Any individual that has progressed to the Open classes should show a greater degree of experience and efficiency in his maneuvers and receive much less help from his handler. Certification in the Open classes requires a minimum score of eighty-seven and one-half (70 percent) of 125 available points, out of which 40 percent of the points must be earned by going through the obstacles on the course. Each dog must receive certification by two different judges in the Open class before entering Advanced classes.

The Australian Shepherd Club of America's First Approved Stock Dog Judges who drafted the original Stock Dog Program and Working Trial Score Card. Standing from left to right: Carol Schmutz, Molalla OR, Walter Lamar, O'Keene, OK, Robert Carrillo, Sebastopol, CA. Kneeling: Ernest Hartnagle, Boulder, CO with Champion Las Rocosa Leslie CSD.

Rowe's Commanche Warrior (Sorensen's Gunsmoke ex Van Gordon's Blue Asta), one of the original Invitational Santa Rosa competitors. *Courtesy Rowe*

The Advanced Dog

Certification in the Advanced classes is much more difficult to achieve. Dogs that qualify in these classes are considered to be the elite in the trial divisions. In these classes, it is imperative that the dog have a definite knowledge of direction and be able to respond immediately to commands from his handler. The Advanced dog should also be able to handle situations in which he has to think for himself. In these classes, the handler is not allowed to proceed beyond the center chute obstacle without receiving a 50 percent penalty on the total score earned.

THE TRIAL

Obtaining livestock for trials is a constant problem, because ranchers and farmers are reluctant to lease their sheep and cattle for fear of weight loss through stress or possible injury in transit. Consequently, many of the animals are not uniform or accustomed to dogs prior to the trial. It is the judge's responsibility to recognize the livestock situations and evaluate each dog accordingly. He must know whether a situation, good or bad, is happening because of or in spite of the efforts of the dog.

When a handler opens the gate to begin his run, the dog should enter quietly along one side of the stock until he gets behind them and slowly eases them out. With such an approach, the stock will usually come out without any problem. The manner in which a dog brings the stock out of the pen often determines his success on the rest of the course. A dog that charges in barking will scare the stock or put them on the defensive, setting the stage for problems. Once livestock are on flight, or if they bunch and stick, it is almost impossible to proceed with any degree of success. I would advise a handler who has such a dog to put some definite control on the dog before attempting the trial again. The old adage "experience is the best teacher" certainly holds true in the trial arena. As a dog gains experience with handling livestock, these preliminary situations of charging, barking, and overdriving disappear.

Barking is one trait that needs clarification. An authoritative bark is very effective in moving cattle, especially when it is followed by a quick nip on the heels. It also lets the lead cattle know of the dog's presence. In my opinion, such a bark should never be penalized on the score card. The score card lists five points for bark. To subtract even one point is actually taking away 20 percent in that category. However, continual barking is very detrimental when working sheep in a trial situation. There is nothing that will put sheep on the defensive or cause them to stick any quicker than to be approached by a barking dog.

The Australian Shepherd is naturally a close-working, forceful dog. Most Aussies work no more than ten feet away from their livestock. Working livestock too close with too much force on an open drive will cause them to split into different directions or even turn back over the dog and run back toward the pen area. When this happens, the handler has to give excessive commands, and in a much louder tone of voice. Such situations result in a loss of points in a number of categories when it obviously is the faulty work of the dog that caused the turmoil.

A good, steady drive with the dog in complete control of his livestock, working at his own distance and in contact with their movement on through the first panel, should permit the maximum amount of points. Many handlers make the mistake of giving a "down" command on the dog as the livestock are approaching the first panel, letting the livestock drift through. Such a maneuver causes a break in contact that has to be reestablished before the next obstacle can be negotiated. This may cause the stock to break pace or even stop, which invites a loss of points.

Before scoring on the course can begin, the dog must drive one or more head of livestock through the right side of the first panel. Many times it is difficult to start a good drive, especially with flighty stock that charge up through the middle or on the left side of the arena. If this situation occurs, the dog can only continue to bring them around from the back side (left side) of the first panel, "daylighting" his stock. At least one head of livestock must go through the first panel or completely across the face of it before attempting to turn the stock around to make a correct approach from the right side through the panel. Even in this situation, a dog handling the livestock well may not lose style points; however, he may not earn the maximum amount of course points. The matter rests entirely on how the judge evaluates the dog's work. Less points would be given if the handler allowed only one head to daylight and immediately sent his dog around to head it back than if he let the entire bunch daylight before resuming the drive and approach to the first panel.

Pineridge has based their breeding program on Las Rocosa Hecke's Burgandy STD-csd here pictured at a working trial in Michigan.
Courtesy Blount

Champion Flashback of Windermere CD is in control of his flock. The sheep are moving in a calm manner.
Courtesy Williams

GUIDELINES FOR PUTTING ON AN AUSSIE WORKING TRIAL

PERSONNEL NEEDED:

A. Announcer - 1 +
B. Arena Crew*
C. Award Chairperson - 1
D. Course Director
E. Entry Clerk(s)*
F. Equipment Director - 1
G. Hospitality Chairperson - 1
H. Judges - 1 per division or *
I. Livestock Handler(s)*

J. Photographer - 1
K. Ring Steward(s) - 2 or *
L. Scorekeepers - 2/each judge
M. Scorerunners - 1/each judge
N. Set-Up Crew*
O. Take-Down Crew*
P. Timekeepers - 2/each judge
Q. Veterinarian - On-call

EQUIPMENT NEEDED:

A. Armbands - both blank & printed
B. Calculators - 1/each scorekeeper
C. Canopy or Canvas* - (to shade personnel)
D. Cash Box - 1 at entry location
E. Chairs - 1 at each judging location or *
F. Clip Boards - 1/each staff member & judge
G. First-Aid Kit
H. Pens/Pencils/Paper*

I. Sanolets - proper Restroom Facilities
J. Score Sheets*
K. Signs* - (in vicinity of Trial)
L. Stop Watches - 1/each Scorekeeper
M. Table(s)*
N. Tools* - i.e. wire, rope, tape, tarp or canvas, nails, 2 × 4's, pliers, hammers, cardboard, screwdriver, screws, etc.
O. Miscellaneous Office Supplies* - i.e. rubberbands, paperclips, stapler, scissors, tape, erasers, trash bags, etc.

EQUIPMENT NEEDED FOR STOCK:

A. Feed for the Stock - as much as needed per class of stock/length of stay, etc.
B. Fence Posts - 8 for each arena
C. Gates - (if none are attached)
D. Hoses* - in case trial site does not have any

E. Panels*
F. Water Buckets - 2 per class of stock or *
G. Water Tanks - at least 1 per class of stock
H. Transportation for Stock - to & from Trial Site
I. Tarp or Canvas - to protect stock from elements

AWARDS:

A. All-Around Award + - 1/for all-around dog
B. High Scoring Award + - 1/for highest scoring dog

C. Ribbons - 1st thru 4th for each class, each division or *
D. Trophies*

* - As many as necessary
+ - Optional

A steady, controlled drive through the second panel would be the next maneuver, followed by negotiation of the center chute. No points can be awarded for the center chute until the second panel has been completed. The approach to the center chute is very important, because it determines whether or not the stock will be in a position to go through it. Numerous attempts may be made to negotiate this obstacle; however, the first time that one or more head go through, the score is marked for that portion of the course. The stock are then ready to be taken back to the pen. When the handler opens the gate to pen the stock, he has forfeited any chances to gain more points on the course for any of the obstacles through which he has failed to go. Time for the run is tallied when he closes the gate on the pen.

The ideal run is when the dog handles his livestock in a slow, steady manner. He is alert and in contact with their every move and is able to handle situations where he has to think for himself. He will take commands from his handler and complete the task with a minimum of effort or wasted motion. To the novice, it would seem that very little is being accomplished. Such a run should score very high. On the other hand, with all other factors (including livestock) being equal, there is the flashy run, with excess wearing, too many commands, and possible overdriving and repositioning. These runs are often very exciting, but they are not nearly as efficient and are much more stressful to the livestock being herded. Such a performance should be penalized accordingly. The marketplace does not pay for pounds lost in handling and shipping, and neither should the trial judge give credit for motion wasted and undue stress imposed upon the livestock in the trial arena.

THE SCORE CARD

The score card is designed for use on the trial course for all classes and divisions. It is divided into

INTERPRETING THE SCORE CARD IN PERCENTAGES

COURSE

Points awarded on the course are determined by the manner in which the dog negotiates each obstacle with his livestock.

	100%	70%	60%	50%	40%
Taking From Pen	5	3.5	3	2.5	2
Drive	5	3.5	3	2.5	2
Obstacle # 1	5	3.5	3	2.5	2
Obstacle # 2	5	3.5	3	2.5	2
Chute	10	7	6	5	4
Repenning	5	3.5	3	2.5	2
Total Course Score	35	24.5	21	17.5	14

STYLE

Style is a combination of inherited characteristics, training and experience.

Each line item represents 100% of itself. Each line item represents it's given value of the total 100% of the 90 points obtainable. A line item with a 20 point value, each point represents 5% of that value. Line items with a 10 point value, each point represents 10% of that value. Line items with a 5 point value, each point represents 20% of that value.

	100%	70%	60%
Natural Working Style	20	14	12
Handler Assistance	10	7	6
Dog's Attitude	10	7	6
Dog's Obedience	10	7	6
Degree of Training	10	7	6
Dog's Stock Savvy	10	7	6
Bark	5	3.5	3
Grip	5	3.5	3
Workability of Stock	10	7	6
Total Style Score	90	63	54

To qualify for certification started dogs must earn 2 scores of 60% of a total available 115 points. Open and advanced dogs must earn 2 scores of at least 70% of a total 125 available points that include 40% and 50% of the total course points respectively.

two parts, the course score and the style score. The course score is determined by how the dog negotiates each obstacle, and the style score shows the characteristics and manner in which the trial dog applies himself to the task.

In the Ranch Dog section of the stock dog program, a working dog is able to gain certification for doing daily routine ranch and farmwork. Specialized situations (such as handling livestock in sales yards, rodeo stock, etc.) in which the dog is an integral part of the operation also qualify for certification under this heading. Again, a special score card is used to measure his ability and effectiveness. The working dog does not usually have the directional command polish that is exhibited in his trial counterpart. Nonetheless, he is very efficient and knowledgeable in his work. He has learned his daily chores through constant repetition and experience. Consequently, he needs very few commands and is a valuable asset to his owner.

THE FIRST AUSTRALIAN SHEPHERD STOCK DOG FUTURITY

On September 15 1983, The First Stock Dog Futurity was held in conjunction with ASCA's National Specialty in Fort Worth, Texas. Contestants voted for a panel of three judges, which consisted of Oby Blanchard from San Marcos, California, Joan Campidonica from Sebastopol, California and Walter Lamar from Okeena, Oklahoma. Contestants elected to throw out the low and high score, and the middle score was recorded.

With over 32 original entries, 16 dogs and owners from seven states and Canada went the distance, competing for $6,000 in prize money divided among the top four finalists. Competition was tight. After the scores were posted from the first go, Las Rocosa Bonny Kyle was standing in first position with a score of 88. Las Rocosa Basque, Champion Las Rocosa Little Wolf, and Zephyr's Crimson King were tied for second place with 74 points each.

After scores from the second go were tallied and added to those from the first, Las Rocosa Bonny Kyle (Las Rocosa Lester ex Las Rocosa Christophene STD-sd, OTD-c) owned by Kerry Russell, Edmonton, Alberta, Canada held the top position earning $2,420.60 in prize money. Bonny Kyle was then presented with an engraved gold plate in memory of Champion Las Rocosa Leslie CSD. Las Rocosa Basque (a littermate to Bonny Kyle) owned by Don Donham from Bozeman, Montana garnered second place ($1,815.45). Basque was followed by Zephyr's Crimson King also owned by Don Donham. (Las Rocosa Merlin Hart STD-cs, ATD-d, RDX-s ex

Hobok in Rose) took third place for $1,210.30. Slash V Spirit of Aggieland (Champion Slash V Little Rock CD ex Slash V Semi Sweet STD-d) owned by Russ and Lisa Ford, College Station, Texas moved into fourth place with a $605.15 cash prize.

Out of the five sires nominated, Leo Fourre and Jeanne Joy Hartnagle captured the Winning Sire Award for producing the top entry with Las Rocosa Lester (Champion Las Rocosa Shiloh ex Champion Las Rocosa Leslie CSD).

You can see the trial course obstacles in the background while the dog fetches the stock to her handler.

Ridgetops English Tuppens taking them through the center chute.
Courtesy Pierson

AUSTRALIAN SHEPHERD CLUB OF AMERICA
Stock Dog Trial Program Official Judging Score Sheet

Started _____   Cattle _____
Open   _____   Sheep _____
Advanced _____   Ducks _____

Entry # _____ Aussie _____ Other breed _____   Time _____

Judge's Comments: _____

_____

_____

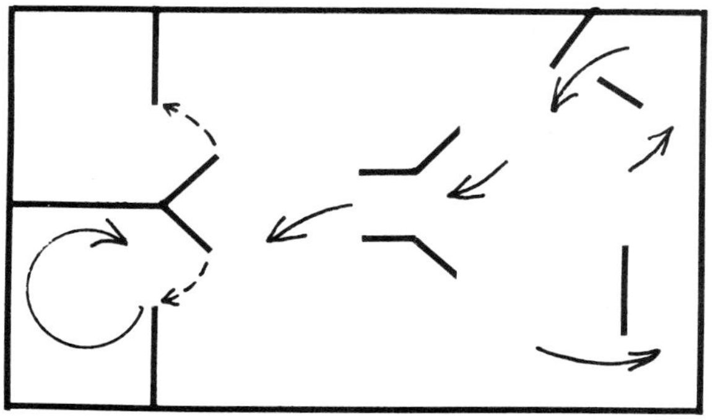

Fill in every blank or write NO in the space

DISQUALIFICATION — MAULING!!

		Advanced class handler passed center chute (deduct 50% of total score)
Course		
Taking from pen	(5)_____	
Drive	(5)_____	
Obstacle #1	(5)_____	
Obstacle #2	(5)_____	
Chute	(10)_____	
Repenning	(5)_____	
Total Course Score	(35)_____	

Natural Working Style	(20)_____	("Eye," Wear, Herding, or Gathering instinct, etc.)
Handler Assistance	(10)_____	(Points lowered for assisting dog or excessive commands)
Dog's Attitude	(10)_____	(Degree of Interest & Concentration on Stock)
Dog's Obedience	(10)_____	(How well Dog responds to commands)
Degree of Training	(10)_____	(Degree of direction Dog has)
Dog's Stock Savvy	(10)_____	(How Dog handles situations where he has to "think" for himself)
Bark	(5)_____	(Quiet workers being marked highest)
Grip	(5)_____	(Where dog grips and how)
Workability of Stock	(10)_____	(Easy cooperative stock scored lower than more uncontrollable stock)
Total Style Score	(90)_____	

Course Score _____

Style Score _____
LESS 50% Penalty
(Advanced) _____

_____
Judge's Signature

Total
(out of 125) _____

_____/_____
Location   Date

A Produce of Dam class win. On the left Champion Shanks' Ginks CD (Heard's Proud Buck of Flintridge ex Iacovetta's Shasta) is pictured with three of her progeny. (Left to Right) Hawk of Flintridge (by The Herdsman of Flintridge), Champion Ginger Blue of Coppertone (by The Herdsman of Flintridge), Champion Kline's Blue Heather of Coppertone CD (by Heard's Salt of Flintridge).

Courtesy Kline

CONFORMATION SHOWS

Conformation shows are based on the process of elimination. The procedure, although seemingly complicated, is quite orderly. Each individual is evaluated against the Australian Shepherd Breed Standard and then compared to other entries within each class. This is a place where the newcomer can view the Australian Shepherd and gain knowledge about the breed.

TYPES OF SHOWS

Three types of shows are recognized by the Australian Shepherd Club of America (ASCA).

Specialty Shows

Specialty shows are organized by either an affiliate club of the ASCA or an approved association recognized for the promotion and improvement of the Australian Shepherd. Championship points are awarded. A Specialty show includes either an Obedience Trial and/or a Working Trial.

Member Shows

A Member show is a competition through which championship points may be garnered. Member shows are hosted by any member club or association of the ASCA.

Licensed Shows

Licensed shows are hosted by any association, individual, or club that is not a member of the ASCA. Championship points can be earned through Licensed shows.

Matches

Sanctioned and Fun matches are generally informal shows put on for the purpose of exposure, experience, and training for handlers, dogs, and judges. Championship points may *not* be garnered at a match; however, Member and/or Licensed shows may be held in conjunction with other breed and All-Breed matches, in which case Championship points will be awarded for the Australian Shepherd.

DOG SHOW CLASSES

Regular Classes

Regular classes are first divided by sex (males and females) and are then judged consecutively beginning with puppy classes and proceeding through the Open classes. Males, or "dogs," are judged in this sequence first, followed by the female, or "bitch," classes.

Six to Twelve Months - To be eligible for this class, puppies must be at least six months of age by the first day of the show but not more than twelve months of age, and they cannot be Champions of Record. This class is generally divided into age categories of six to nine months and nine to twelve months.

Twelve to Eighteen Months - This class is for individuals that are *not* Champions of Record but that are at least twelve months of age and not over eighteen months. As in the six-to-twelve-month puppy classes, the *age is determined up to and includes the day of the show.*

Novice - The Novice class is for any individual six months of age and older. To be eligible to compete in the Novice class, individuals must *not* have garnered either three first place wins in the Novice class or one first place win in any one of the following regular classes (excluding the aged puppy classes): Bred By Exhibitor, American Bred, or any Open class, nor can the individual have earned either one or more points toward an ASCA Championship.

Bred By Exhibitor - The Bred by Exhibitor class is for any individual that is six months of age and older but that is *not* a Champion of Record. To be eligible to compete in this class, the dog (male or female) must be owned and handled by a breeder of record, or by an immediate family member, including a spouse (husband or wife), father, mother, son, daughter, brother, sister, or by an immediate household member of a breeder of record.

American Bred - To be eligible, individuals must be at least six months of age. This category includes all dogs except Champions of Record that are bred and whelped in the United States (which includes all territories and possessions of the United States and vessels sailing under the American flag).

Open - Open classes are designed for individuals six months of age and older and exclude any Champions of Record. The classes are usually divided into four categories: Open Black, Open Red, Open Blue Merle, and Open Red Merle. This gives equal consideration to all of the acceptable color combinations; however, the Open classes may be offered in any combination.

Winners Class - Only undefeated dogs (or bitches) of the same sex which are first place winners from any of the Regular classes the same day are eligible to compete in the Winners class at any given show. No entry fee is charged. After the Winners (Dog or Bitch) has been awarded in either of the sex divisions (male or female classes), the individual placing second to the Winners Dog (or Bitch), only if undefeated by all except the Winner in his or her sex, shall compete with the other eligible individuals for Reserve Winners Dog (or Reserve Winners Bitch). No qualified individual will be withheld from competition.

Best of Breed - Both the Winners Dog and the Winners Bitch become eligible to compete for Best of Breed along with ASCA Champions of Record "Specials."

If either the Winners Dog or Winners Bitch garners Best of Breed, then he or she automatically assumes the Best of Winners award. If a Champion (Special) wins Best of Breed instead of the Winners Dog or Winners Bitch, the judge will award Best of Winners following the Best of Breed placement and

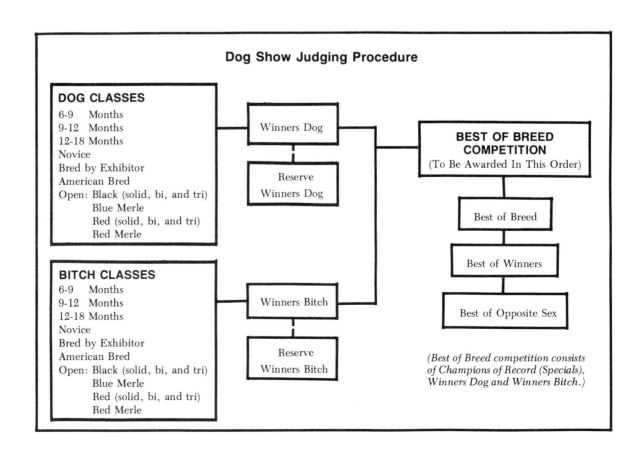

prior to awarding Best of Opposite Sex. The dog or bitch awarded Best of Winners shall receive the greater number of points based on the number of competing dogs or bitches in the regular classes, while the other of the two Winners maintains the amount of points awarded for his or her sex. If either the Winners Dog or Winners Bitch garners Best of Breed, the Champions that have been entered and that have been defeated (for his or her respective sex) are then counted in addition to the nonchampions that competed in the regular classes when calculating points.

After the points have been calculated for Winners Dog and Winners Bitch in accordance with the above procedure, the individual awarded Best of Winners is also credited with the greater number of points awarded to either Winners Dog (WD) or Winners Bitch (WB). In the event that Winners is awarded to only one sex, there shall be no Best of Winners awarded. After the BOB and Best of Winners (BOW) have been awarded, then the judge will award Best of Opposite Sex (BOS) of the Best of Breed. The individuals that are eligible for BOS are those dogs (or bitches) that have been entered for BOB competition, including either the WD, or WB, or the BOW that is opposite of the sex chosen for Best of Breed.

What Class is Best?

The Age classes are ideal for developing youngsters. This lets the judge know that if he likes what he sees now, imagine how good the dog will be when he fully matures.

Novice classes are often a good choice for the newcomer to the breed and to the sport of dog showing. Generally speaking, many beginning handlers and "green" dogs are competing against the like, but Novice is not limited to the newcomer. Often handlers with several dogs may enter Novice. Newcomers should never feel compelled or limited to compete in Novice. There are usually fewer entries in Novice, which means that you may have a better opportunity of getting noticed.

If your Aussie is in optimum condition, it may be better to enter him (or her) in either the American-Bred class or Open. American Bred also gives the handler of several dogs an option of another class in which to compete. This may be a good class for the young dog just out of the Age classes. It may also be a good class for the puppy that has matured more quickly than other individuals of his own age but that may not be quite as mature as the Open class entries.

Bred By Exhibitor is a class designed specifically for the breeder. It is certainly an honor to be eligible to compete with a home-bred individual.

Champion Briarbrook's Donna Summer (Ch Rising Sun of Windermere ex Ch Windsong's Foggi Notion) is free-stacked in a natural four-square stance.   Courtesy Wilson

Open classes are generally for individuals in optimum condition and usually contain the more mature and Championship pointed individuals; however, Open is not limited to these entries.

Nonregular Classes

Nonregular classes are generally more commonly seen at Specialties but may be offered at any Member or Licensed Show. No Championship points can be garnered or awarded for Nonregular classes.

Two- to Six-Month Puppy Classes - This is divided into Two- to Four-Month Puppy class and Four- to Six-Month Puppy class. The age of each individual is tallied up to and includes the first day of the show, as in Regular classes. Nonregular puppy classes may be divided by color. The winners of this class shall compete for Best of Breed Puppy, Best Opposite Sex Puppy, or Best Puppy Dog (male) and Best Puppy Bitch (female). Puppies competing in the Nonregular classes are not eligible to compete further for Championship points.

Stud Dog and Brood Bitch Classes - Each sire (or brood bitch) entered in the Stud Dog (or Brood Bitch) class must be accompanied by two to four of his (or her) offspring. Two of the progeny must be at least six months old and also entered in a Regular class. If any of the progeny chosen are between two to six months of age, they must be entered in a Nonregular puppy class, respectively, if offered at the show. Any individuals competing as a unit for either the sire or dam shall not be allowed to compete as a separate entry with their own progeny.

Brace Class - The Brace class comprises two individuals that look similar in markings, coloration, type, and size.

State Bred - The State Bred class comprises individuals that are either bred and/or whelped in any given state.

Veteran's Class - To be eligible for the Veteran's class, competing individuals must have attained their seventh birthday. This class is generally divided by sex. Veterans ideally exhibit the desired longevity of the Australian Shepherd breed. Champions may compete, as well as any other individual eligible by the age requirement.

Futurities - The requirements for eligibility in a Futurity can vary with the type of competition offered, but generally speaking, Futurities are for puppies that are nominated at or prior to birth. Nomination fees are renewed at designated dates before the actual competition. By entering a Futurity, the breeder of the litter is projecting that the puppies will develop as predicted.

HOW CHAMPIONSHIPS ARE ATTAINED

To attain an ASCA Championship, each individual must win a total of fifteen points. Nine or more of these points must be attained at three separate shows with each major win (between three to five points) garnered under three different judges. The remaining points may be attained in any combination, including minor wins (one to two points). Championship points recorded for both Winners Dog and Winners Bitch are determined by the number of eligible entries *competing* in the regular classes for each sex. The points awarded are predetermined by a point schedule which varies from region to region. Points for any individual that is excused, disqualified, or dismissed, or from which any award is withheld by the judge, are never counted.

Once the requirements are met and officially confirmed with the Australian Shepherd Club of America, then a Championship certificate is issued for the individual.

JUNIOR SHOWMANSHIP

Junior Showmanship is a competition designed for handlers, breeders, and judges of the future. It teaches the art of fine handling as well as sportsmanship (the art of winning and losing). Ideally, it teaches youth to be competent handlers and fair competitors.

Although the actual quality of the dog is never considered by the judge, each handler's ability to "present" his/her Aussie is considered. Junior Show-

manship is a team effort between each youth and his dog; therefore, there must be a rapport between them. Although the Aussie that is used for showmanship need not be of top quality, he must possess the typical Aussie appearance.

There are certain differences between Showmanship and the regular Breed ring. In Showmanship it is the handler's ability that is judged with only the dog's cooperation. In the breed competition it is the quality and soundness of the dog that is judged and the only role that the handler plays is through his or her ability to make the best presentation. Ring procedure is the same, and the patterns are identical, but the Junior Showman must learn to execute them slightly differently. In showing, there is a golden rule that handlers must keep their dog between themselves and the judge at all times. Some judges "overwork" this aspect, causing handlers to frantically move to and fro. In an odd sense, it sometimes defeats the purpose. Nevertheless, each handler will develop his/her own style. Regardless how elaborate or basic the style, the finest handlers master an economy of motion.

The Australian Shepherd is generally shown on a loose lead. The Aussie can either be "hand-stacked"

Old stuff by now. Meg Kimbler pictured winning a Pee Wee Junior Showmanship competition with Champion Potter's Whiteoak Razzle Dazzle CDX, STD-dc (George's Red Rustler ex Dakota Blue Tassativio).
Courtesy Potter

The Junior Handlers of today are the future of the Australian Shepherd Breed.

or "free-stacked." Free-stacking means to position your dog by walking him into a show pose, which is a natural four-square stance, whereas hand-stacking is placing your dog in a four-square stance by manually positioning his legs and feet. Free-stacking is commonly seen because the balance and symmetry typical of the Australian Shepherd also enable him to easily assume the natural four-square stance without a lot of assistance from his handler. When taught to bait, he will stand quietly or vibrantly animated while you simply "show." To add variety, Juniors can reposition themselves down by their dog's side during the individual examination. On occasion, some judges will ask each handler to move out and set up his (or her) dog. Remember—if you are hand-stacking, first set up the front legs, beginning with the one closest to the judge, and then set up the hind legs. Do not nitpick—it will only make your dog nervous. Draw positive attention to your entry by being efficient and then ready. The individual examination is your time to shine. Use it wisely. When the judge is going over the group as a whole, be alert. Keep an eye on the judge. Learn to easily determine the entire picture. If your entry is looking good, but one foot is only slightly out of position, you must know when to change it and when to leave good enough alone. If

you need to move it, first look to see where the judge is. If he has his eye on your entry, don't start fidgeting. Show your dog for all you're worth. Wait for an opportunity and then smoothly correct the problem. Practice makes perfect!

Junior handlers are not required to change their dog with any other handler in the ring.

Junior Showmanship Classes

Showmanship classes are divided into Novice and Open Competition. Classes may further be divided into Junior and Senior divisions.

Novice - Novice is for boys and girls, who at the time entries are taken and/or closed, have not earned three first places at Sanctioned ASCA events.

The third time winner of a Novice class is automatically eligible to enter and compete in the Open division on the same day as long as there are one or more entries in the division. However, if he/she is defeated in the Open division, even though he/she has just earned first place in Novice, that person is not eligible to compete for Best Junior Handler at that show.

Open - Open is for boys and girls who have garnered three or more first place wins at Sanctioned ASCA events.

Junior - To be eligible for Junior competition, boys and girls must be at least ten years but less than thirteen years of age. Age is determined up to and includes the day of the show.

Senior - Boys and girls must be at least thirteen years but less than seventeen years of age. Once a Junior Handler has attained his/her seventeenth birthday, he/she is no longer eligible to compete in showmanship competition, with one exception. Any handler who has qualified for the Junior Handling finals may compete at that particular event even though he/she has turned seventeen since qualifying.

ENTERING A SHOW

To find out about when and where shows are going to be held, contact and/or join a local kennel club and an area ASCA affiliate club. Training classes where trainers and breeders often gather are good sources of information and guidance. Subscribe to the *Aussie Times*, the official publication of the ASCA, and ASCA affiliate newsletters to gain specific information on area activities. You can also subscribe to any of the dog magazines that are informative about dogs in general.

Get on pertinent mailing lists for shows, clinics, and seminars. Entry blanks can generally be obtained from the ASCA show secretary's office or from the club sponsoring the show. Entries are attached to the premium list, which provides information about the show, location, accommodations, judges, etc.

All entry forms must be filled out completely and accurately where applicable and returned within the time limit, accompanied by the appropriate entry fees. Some shows are more informal and entries may be accepted on the day of the show.

Send to the ASCA for a copy of the current show rules and regulations and become familiar with them.

LOOK LIKE A WINNER

Your personal appearance will play a big role in your attitude, which in turn will not only set your dog off, but will make a statement about you and your self-confidence. Your choice should be sporty and comfortable but not so casual that you look as if you just came in from cleaning kennels. Take pride in your appearance, because it reflects the entire sport of dog showing.

You don't need to invest a lot of money in elaborate show outfits. Have a pair of comfortable, basic shoes that you can "run" in. Keep them polished or cleaned and in good repair. A wise selection of a few well-made, well-tailored sport clothes will take you anywhere in style. Choose items that may be blended together to give the impression of different outfits made out of fabrics that will wash and wear well. Coordinate pieces and colors that are becoming to you and that compliment your dog(s). The best-dressed people are those who stay away from "trendy" items and who stick to the basics.

Blouses, shirts, vests, sweaters, ties, scarves, and belts can add variety to any outfit. Basic colors such as gray, navy, beige, brown, and black can be harmonized with light blue, beige, lavender, turquoise, mint, kelly green, pale yellow, lemon, burgundy, rust, poppy red—the color wheel is endless to give you a large selection. Make basic items such as slacks, skirts, jackets, and sometimes vests in neutral colors, while the other items can accent the basic colors.

Above all, be neat, clean, and well-groomed. If you have only one good outfit, do not feel apprehensive about being seen in it time and again. Some of the top showmen (handlers) have an outfit that harmonizes and/or compliments so well that they wear it almost every time they enter the show ring.

Once you look like a winner, it will be easier for you to assume the role of positive handling when you enter the ring. Just don't forget to top off the appearance with a courteous manner.

GET READY, GET SET, GO!

If the show is pre-entry, then you will want to take along your receipt of entry. You will need to take a nonoriginal copy of the registration papers for each dog. Take appropriate collars and leads (including an obedience collar and a show lead). Grooming tools, including a brush and a pair of scissors, may be needed for pre-show preparations. A damp washcloth (or towelettes) and a dry towel may be necessary for emergency cleanup. Bait (such as liver) is another item, or a squeaky toy that you may want to use in the show ring to get "animation." You may also want to take along some kind of "doggie" treats. A travel crate is handy to safely confine your dog in the midst of confusion. Take plenty of newspapers to line the bottom of the crate. If the show is held out-of-doors, you will want to provide some type of shade if it is not readily available for your dog. Nursery net (available at tree nurseries) can be purchased in many sizes for ventilated shade. If you are travelling a long distance, you may want to take along an exercise pen that will allow your dog to move freely about, yet remain under close supervision. Take along cleanup equipment to "pick up" after your dog. Include some smaller plastic sacks and a trash sack. Take along beverages and a snack for yourself. A blanket is another handy item. You may welcome the relief of an umbrella for rain or shine. Some sort of folding or lawn chairs are nice when none are provided at the show site.

You will want to arrive at the show site at least an hour prior to the listed judging time. In Sanctioned events, the judging may take place right at that time or after the advertised time, but it is never to take place before the scheduled time. Inquire at either the entry table or the show secretary's table as to which "ring" you will be exhibiting in. This way you will have the opportunity for last-minute preparation before entering the ring.

After checking in, you will want to take your dog out for exercise. This will let you and your dog relax a bit. Besides being an enjoyable outlet, it will lend a positive outlook toward the show.

IN THE RING

Here is where all your previous handling will pay off. Your dog has been taught to lead by your side and to stand while being groomed and handled on a regular basis. The show ring may bring out foreign reactions, but remember that you are in a new environment. If your dog's behavior is less than becoming, it is a sure sign that you need to get him out and handle him in many new situations and unfamiliar surroundings. It takes a lot of effort to develop a confident attitude in your dog, especially if you are extremely unsure. This nervousness may transfer easily to your dog. However, practice makes perfect, so don't give up. Just make it a point to "haul" your dog more.

Ninety-nine percent of all movement in the ring will be viewed by the judge with the dogs at a trot. You will need to teach your dog to "gait" in a trot at your side, while you learn to step in time with his stride.

You can either "free-stack" or "hand-stack" your dog in the ring. See the section on Junior Showmanship in this chapter for further information.

Speed Stacking

Speed stacking is an acquired skill. It is the ability of the handler to determine with a glance exactly which legs are and which are not out of position—when to leave good enough alone and when to concentrate on simply showing your dog as the judge is making a final selection. Speed stacking means being ready.

If a leg is out of position, you will want to first place the legs in the front, beginning with the leg in the judge's line of vision, since the greatest percentage of weight is carried by the forequarters. Then place the hind legs, beginning with the leg that is in the judge's line of vision (the leg closest to the judge). Sometimes speed stacking means that only one foot needs to be placed before you quickly resume "showing" your dog.

Gaiting

In gaiting around the ring, it is more desirable to show on a loose lead as opposed to a tight one. When the lead is loose, it means that you are not placing any unnecessary strain on the lead that may interfere with your dog's ability to move freely. A tight lead can interfere with your dog's natural gait.

Once Around the Ring

When you enter the ring, you will be identified by an entry number. This number is to be placed on your left arm. In North America, handlers enter the ring counterclockwise with their dogs on their left side. Generally, most judges will first view the entire class while in a single line together stacked in a natural four-square stance. Often he/she will then ask the exhibitors to take their dogs around the ring once or twice before making individual examinations and gaiting. First, the ring steward will ask the exhibitors to enter the ring either in catalog order, which is the specific order in which each entry was accepted and/or listed in the catalog, or the steward will allow them to enter as they choose. At the judge's request, the steward will direct the exhibitors to either line up or to proceed gaiting around the ring. At this point, the judge will take over and command his ring.

Individual gaiting is designed to allow each entry an opportunity to be viewed without distraction of the other entries. This is the time to really "show your dog."

Individual Examination

Each judge has a slightly different approach to "going over" the dogs. Most often, judges will methodically begin at the head and work their way down. A look at the eye will reveal the size, shape, placement, and color as called for in the Breed Standard. Sometimes the judge will gently lift the ear forward toward the inside corner of the eye to check relativity of size. Sometimes the judge will lift the lips back to view the bite and teeth. However, it is most appreciated and accepted that the handler will show the bite and teeth for the judge due to the possibility of transmission of disease.

If your dog appears to be unsteady, it is best that you kneel by his side during the entire examination. Never scold or hit your dog in the ring. If necessary, be firm but never ruthless. You want to create a positive response for your dog. Too often, handlers will expect perfection from their dog without the necessary homework. Stay out of the judge's road, but be there to assist by taking hold of the head and/or collar to steady your dog and to hold him quietly.

The judge will proceed from the head down the neck to check "layback" (see "The Ideal" chapter). The judge's hands will reveal muscle tone, depth and spring of rib cage, width of loin, presence of testicles (in the case of males), etc. A good judge will never have to prod and poke, but will smoothly and effectively go from one point to another.

You may talk to your dog in quiet tones, but do not try to strike up a conversation with the judge. Be polite and courteous. If you are unable to understand or hear a particular directive of the judge, ask him to repeat or explain it. Other than that, ask the ring steward to relay the information to the judge. It is acceptable to present the judge with a copy of a verification certificate from your veterinarian to document accidental missing or broken teeth (when the judge examines the mouth).

Individual Gaiting

Playful youngsters may want to frolic and show off even more while gaiting than during the individual examination. They may want to take hold of the lead and play tug-o-war or balk or slink along at your side. For the time being, make the best of the situation, but plan on putting in a few more hours of homework. At any time during your dog's life, he may act totally opposite to what is normal. However, with proper handling and socialization, this should be the exception rather than the rule.

Generally, after the individual examination, while each dog is fresh in the judge's mind, he/she will want to see the dog move. There are several familiar standard "ring patterns" that judges will use to assess each individual's side gait and front and hind movement.

Be sure to move your dog at a steady, consistent speed and in straight lines in the pattern requested. Occasionally there are variations, but usually you will be asked to move in a straight line away from and back into the judge. You may be asked to move around the ring ("O" shape), in a triangle, or in an "L"-shaped pattern. Rarely will judges ask to see the dog exhibited in the "T" pattern, except perhaps in Junior Showmanship competition.

Remember to keep the dog between yourself and the judge, but USE AN ECONOMY OF MOTION while showing. Too often handlers end up frantically switching from side to side and hand to hand, moving about their dog so much that they cause him to break gait or interfere with the judge's view. When moving from the pattern back into the judge, try to stop approximately five or six feet away (the estimated height of your judge) to allow a full view. As you

move back gradually, quickly adjust your pace until your dog is into the desired stance. With the use of bait (ball, squeak toy, keys), you can cue your dog to animate to show expression.

If you drop bait in the ring, make it a point to pick up after yourself. Toys are to be used discriminately. Do not distract another dog when the judge is going over each individual. Use these items while the judge is comparing your dog to another or while he is viewing the entire group from a visual standpoint.

Be as courteous to others as you would have them be to you. Occasionally, another handler (either very innocently or quite deliberately) will run up on the heels of an exhibitor, possibly block the judge's full view of your dog, or crowd you in a tight space. In this case, firmly but politely request the other handler to either give you more room if that is the case, or to move back. If this occurs several times with the same handler and you feel that the situation is deliberate, seek out the ring steward. If necessary, you may have to file a complaint. Do not involve the judge, as this is part of the steward's responsibility.

The judge may compare several individuals together and ask each handler to move the dog several times, but a conclusion will be made. You may or may not agree with the judge on any given day, but remember that is just another day at the show!

THE ART OF WINNING AND LOSING

As a contestant, you must learn that there are honest differences of opinion. You must learn to take all wins and losses in stride. Try to be objective about yourself, about the performance of your dogs, and about your competition. Graciously accept losses, and be able to win without boasting. Take each accomplishment with a sense of modesty. Congratulate the winners and allow them their own time to shine, because you, too, will have your day in the barrel.

Winning is a state of mind. The truly great individual (either winning or losing) looks more like the winner in defeat than the winner does in winning. Never stop trying. Set goals for yourself. Strive for that incomparable performance rather than the blue ribbon, as you will find that the blue ribbon often accompanies the great performance. What the superior person seeks is in himself. What the small-minded person seeks is in others. It takes a good loser to be a winner.

Theodore Roosevelt once said:

> *It is not the critic who counts; not the man who points out how the strong man stumbled or where the doer of deeds could have done them better. The credit belongs to the man who is actually in the arena; whose face is marred by dust*

CONFORMATION GAITING PATTERNS

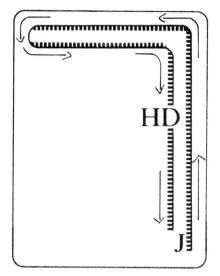

'L' PATTERN

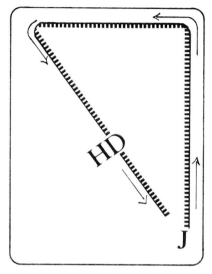

TRIANGLE PATTERN

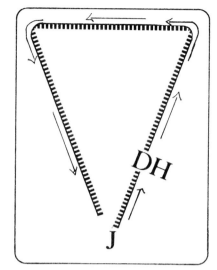

MODIFIED TRIANGLE PATTERN

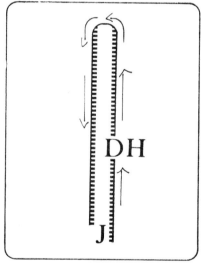

'I' PATTERN
(STRAIGHT OUT AND BACK)

'T' PATTERN

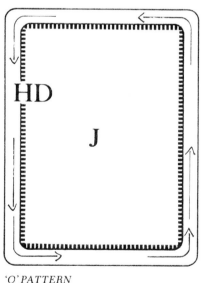

'O' PATTERN
(MOVING AROUND THE JUDGE)

J - Judge   DH - Dog/Handler   HD - Handler/Dog   All Patterns can be reversed as per the Judge's request.

---

and sweat and blood; who strives valiantly; who errs and comes short again and again; who knows the great enthusiasms, the great devotions, and spends himself in a worthy cause; who, at the best, knows the triumph of high achievement; and who, at the worst, if he fails, at least fails while daring greatly, so that his place shall never be with those cold and timid souls who knew neither victory nor defeat.

In his renowned column "Winning," from the

PRCA Pro Rodeo Sports News, Lyle Sankey once wrote:

> I'd like to tell you about two frogs who jumped into a bucket of cream on a dairy farm in Wisconsin. (Now you might wonder what two frogs and a bucket of cream have to do with the exciting world of prorodeo, but if you will just bear with me, I believe you will get the idea.)
>
> "May as well give up," croaked one frog after trying to get out without success. "We're gonners!"

"Keep on paddling," said the other frog. "We'll get out of this mess somehow!"

"It's no use," said the first. "Too thick to swim. Too thin to jump. Too slippery to crawl. We're bound to die sometime anyway, so it may as well be tonight." He sank to the bottom of the bucket and died.

His friend just kept on paddling, and paddling, and paddling. And by morning he was perched on a mess of butter which he churned all by himself. There he was, with a grin on his face, eating the flies that came swarming from every direction.

The little frog had discovered what most people choose to ignore: If you stick with a task long enough, you're going to be a winner. That little frog discovered the secret ingredient - persistence.

It is important that you never let your dream die. Don't give up on your goals. Often, with just a little more effort, you would be there. One more mile. One more minute. Just one more inch to that sought-after victory.

Just because you get off to a poor start, don't quit the race. Life isn't a 100-yard dash—it's a marathon. You have plenty of time to recover from any obstacle.

The winners in life are where they are because they chose a goal, became committed to the challenge, and gave it everything they had. And those same qualities will produce winners in every possible situation.

Everyone has the energy to get things started. But it takes determination to keep things going. It is the finish, not the start, that counts.

Obviously, the more you invest, the better your chances of great return. Make sure that the odds are in your favor. It is possible to increase your chances of success. It's up to you to start today.

Nothing is easy, and it isn't supposed to be. Persistence means hard work. Anything worth achieving is also worth your sacrifice. It's going to take a dedicated effort and untold hours of hard work.

GUIDELINES FOR PUTTING ON AN AUSSIE CONFORMATION SHOW

PERSONNEL NEEDED:

A. Announcer - 1 +
B. Award Chairperson - 1
C. Entry Clerk(s)*
D. Equipment Director - 1
E. Hospitality Chairperson - 1
F. Judges - 1 per division or *
G. Photographer - 1

H. Ring Steward(s) - 1 per ring
I. Set-Up Crew*
J. Show Secretary - 1
K. Take-Down Crew*
L. Veterinarian - On-Call
M. Clean-Up Crew*

EQUIPMENT NEEDED:

A. Armbands - both blank & printed
B. Calculators*
C. Canopy/Canvas* (to shade personnel)
D. Cash Box - 1 at entry location or *
E. Chairs* (for personnel/audience)
F. Clip Boards*
G. First-Aid Kit
H. Mats-Runners* (if showing on cement)
I. Pen/Pencils/Paper*

J. Restroom Facilities
K. Signs/Maps* - (in vicinity)
L. Tables*
M. Miscellaneous Tools*
N. Clean-Up Equipment*
O. Ring Ropes*
P. Ring Posts - 4/ring or *
Q. Miscellaneous Office Supplies*
R. Wicket - (for measuring dogs)

AWARDS:

A. Ribbons - 1st thru 4th for each class offered or *
B. Trophies - 1 for each class offered: Best Puppy; Best Puppy Opposite Sex; Winners' Dog, Winners' Bitch; Best of Breed; Best of Opposite Sex; Best of Winners; and Optional - Reserve Winners' Dog and Reserve Winners' Bitch. Other trophies may be offered.

* - As many as necessary
+ - Optional

Champion Sun's Mark of Windermere CD (Ch Windermere's Sunshine of Bonnie-Blu ex Blue Heather of Windermere) a multiple BOB winner.   *Courtesy Williams*

Champion Copper Wiggles of Somercrest CD STD-ds (Ch Little Abner of Flintridge ex Midnight Lady of Somercrest) was BOB winner at the 1979 ASCofA Specialty.   *Courtesy Cole*

Although markings vary slightly this pair of females makes an attractive brace. Left: Champion Kline's Blue Heather of Coppertone CD (Heard's Salt of Flintridge ex Ch Shank's Ginks CD), Right: Champion Shanks' Ginger Blue of Coppertone (The Herdsman of Flintridge ex Ch Shanks' Ginks CD).
Courtesy Kline

Hyper Hank, World Class Frisbee Disc Star, soars skyward to snare a flying disc thrown by owner-trainer Eldon McIntire.

Photo Courtesy: Eldon McIntire, Irv Lander, Alex Stein, and Cycle Dog Food.

10
FRISBEE CONTESTS

Perhaps you have been fortunate enough to see one of the K-9 Catch and Fetch® contests cosponsored by participating parks and recreation departments, Cycle® Dog Food, and the Wham-O Manufacturing Company. These contests are held throughout the country and lead to the world championships in Los Angeles, where nine regional finalists compete against the current world champions Catch and Fetch titleholder.

Even if you are not interested in Catch and Fetch as a competitive sport, this game is a lot of fun and is good exercise for both you and your dog.

The following suggestions will help you get the most enjoyment from this new sport.

YOUR DOG AS A DISC PLAYER

Although there will be little physical stress on your dog in the initial stages of training, owners of breeds predisposed to joint or disc problems should discuss the effects on their pet with their veterinarian. It is a good idea for your dog to have regular checkups by a veterinarian. This will assure you that your dog is in the best of shape for the more strenuous jumping and running that he will do as he becomes more proficient.

RESPONSIBILITIES AS A DOG OWNER

Since at least part of the training time may occur in areas used by the general public, we urge you as a responsible dog owner to carry cleanup equipment.

From *How to Teach Your dog to Catch a Frisbee* by Gaines Cycle Dog Food Company

It also is your responsibility to make sure that your dog is not a nuisance to other people enjoying the area with their dogs. Because Catch and Fetch necessitates your dog being in public areas, off-leash control is both wise and essential.

FRISBEE THROWING

Learning to throw a Frisbee with a degree of accuracy is essential to the dog's learning to catch!

The backhand grip is the most popular, but any grip with which you feel comfortable is fine. Hold the Frisbee slightly tilted, with your thumb on top, your forefinger along the rim, and the other fingers curled under the rim. Bring your arm back toward the rear shoulder (as you would with a backhand grip with a tennis racket) with your wrist cocked. As you bring your arm forward in the throwing motion, uncock the wrist and release the disc with a snap. This gives the disc the spin that is necessary for stability in flight. Remember—the snap of the wrist as you release the disc is what counts most. You don't have to throw hard.

STEPS IN TRAINING YOUR DOG TO CATCH A FRISBEE

A Reminder

Don't forget that this can be strenuous activity. Short sessions at first are advisable, especially during hot weather. To keep your dog at peak enthusiasm, do not repeat the exercise more than two or three times a day. It is advisable that workouts be at least an hour prior to or following mealtimes. Give your dog small quantities of water for the first half hour after the training session. Make sure that your dog has resumed a normal respiratory rate (not panting heavily) before allowing him normal food and water intake.

Introducing the Frisbee

Most dogs will naturally chase after a Frisbee, but there are certain games that help develop their enthusiasm and the control necessary for the sport. Using the Frisbee as an object for games such as tug-o-war and hide and seek will arouse interest in his new special toy. Another game is keep-away. Hold the Frisbee in your hand and throw it back and forth with short, fast motions. Encourage the dog to snatch it from you, and let him win this game often, with lots of praise. We cannot stress strongly enough during these stages of Catch and Fetch training the importance of profuse praise for any attempt to catch and fetch—whether successful or not.

Step One

Once the dog's interest in and enthusiasm for the disc has been aroused, you are ready to put movement into the game. Roll the disc on its edge, urging the dog to pursue and catch it. It now becomes equally important that the dog not only catch the disc, but that he fetch it back promptly to the thrower! When the dog is enthusiastically chasing the rolling disc and returning it to the thrower, you are ready for the next step.

Step Two

From now on, the game becomes more active, which means that the area in which you train your dog should be larger. It should be open—not congested with people and other activities—and there should be no danger from passing cars. The surface should be soft—preferably grass—enabling the dog to have secure footing. Hard surfaces like concrete and asphalt are never advisable.

The next two exercises can be alternated during Step Two.

Crouching down at the dog's level, with the dog beside you, throw the disc in a straight line, encouraging the dog to catch and fetch it.

To teach the dog to jump for the disc, use another version of keep-away, this time starting with the disc in your hand at least a foot over his head. Encourage the dog to jump up and snatch it. Over a period of time, as your dog's muscles strengthen, you can increase the height at which you are challenging the dog to jump and snatch.

Frisbee is an excellent play time recreation for the Aussie and his owner. Champion Raisin Cain ATD-csd.

Step Three

The third keep-away exercise that builds enthusiasm and teaches your dog Catch and Fetch skills involves a companion. Show the dog the Frisbee, and throw it to your partner, who should be standing five to ten yards away. Throw the disc back and forth slowly and at a low level at first. Encourage the dog to catch it in midflight—the slow, low-level flight will help ensure his success. Make sure that the dog succeeds often enough to encourage him, and when he does, praise him profusely. (When you first started training your dog in Catch and Fetch, it was important to praise him for every attempt to catch the disc, whether successful or not. Now you are trying to impart a little discrimination—catching is better than missing!) After each catch, of course, make sure that the dog brings the disc back to the thrower. When he is successful at slow, short flights, gradually increase the distance and speed of the throw.

Step Four

Now the learning process is in its final stages and the real fun can begin. But before you start, remember to treat your dog like the athlete he is. Make sure that his muscles are properly warmed up before starting a vigorous training session. A few short throws and low jumps to catch the disc will arouse his enthusiasm and help limber him up.

Throw the disc only as far as you have control over it; a short, good throw is better than a longer one that the dog has difficulty in catching. The more success your dog has, the more enthusiastic he will become.

As his prowess increases, give the dog some variety by throwing occasional rollers, slow throws, and fast throws. Teach him to develop a sense for speed and wind direction and an eye for height and the angle of the Frisbee's descent. At this point, you can be inventive in your play and challenge the dog by throwing the disc at varying heights and angles.

By now you may realize that your dog has a flair for certain types of catches, probably to some extent depending on his physical characteristics. Build on the dog's natural talent and style by adding variety to your throws. Develop YOUR skill in throwing to complement your dog's style of catching.

Stop if your dog becomes overtired or bored with the game.

Hyper Hank watches his K-9 pal Ashley Whippet soar for Frisbee disc.

Photo Courtesy: Eldon McIntire, Irv Lander, Alex Stein, and Cycle Dog Food

THE CYCLE® CATCH AND FETCH CONTEST

Each year the makers of Cycle® dog food sponsor the World Championship Cycle Catch and Fetch® contest. It is open to all dogs and is free of charge.

In the first level of competition, the dog/thrower teams compete in the compulsory events. Points are acquired by the skill with which the dog catches the Frisbee and lands fifteen yards from the center of the circle in which the thrower stands. If the dog catches the Frisbee with all paws off the ground, he scores two points, and with any one paw touching the ground, he receives one point. Each time the dog catches the Frisbee, he returns it to the thrower and the procedure is repeated. The team with the highest score in the two-minute time limit wins the title of Local Champion. All teams scoring the minimum required points in the local compulsory event are eligible to compete in one of fifteen Sectional contests. The same event is repeated in the Sectional contest, and the winner goes on to compete in one of three Regional contests.

At the Regional level of competition, the teams are again scored in the compulsory event. In addition, they are required to compete in a timed freestyle event and are judged by the following: style, which includes the dog's judgment of the Frisbee's flight; leaping ability; body control; determination; quickness; teamwork with the thrower; and variety, which includes variation of the throws (distance, angle, spin, and speed) the types of catches (novelty catches involving multiple Frisbee discs and acrobatics).

Prizes are awarded to winners at all levels of competition. Winners and runners-up of the Regional competition are given an all-expense-paid trip to California, where they compete for the title of World Champion and a grand prize of a $1,000 U.S. savings bond.

For more information, contact:
Irv Lander and Associates
Van Nuys Center Building
5430 Van Nuys Boulevard
Van Nuys, California 91401
Telephone (213) 995-1325

Without soundness your dog would be unable to perform simple tasks you ask of him, such as clearing a jump in Obedience or catching a frisbee by leaping in mid-air, or even jumping up in the truck to go for a ride. Thompson's Perky Blue Pebbles CD (Parr's Little Bit ex Young's Calico Cody).

Courtesy Thompson

11
OBEDIENCE

Obedience: (1) the state or quality of being obedient; (2) the act or practice of obeying.

In reality, all forms of training are obedience. The principles of training are easily written on paper, but the success lies in your ability to bring the most out in your dog.

Many training techniques can be observed and developed by reinforcing and applying the "natural pack theory." The most effective reprimands are directly related to the mother-litter relationship—the foundation for all training. In the wild as well as domestic state, mothers warn their pups with a growl. Pups that choose to disregard or challenge their mother's authority are sharply snapped at. Puppies can be reprimanded by warning with a growling sound such as a deep "ah-ah." A puppy will remember his own mother's warning growl. This should get an instant response. When the puppy looks up in surprise, tell him that he is a "good dog—that's a good boy." Instances when he decides to ignore the warning completely, or to test you, you will need to reinforce the command in such a manner that he will relate again to his mother. Place an immediate firm hand around the entire muzzle. Apply firm, but gentle pressure and use eye contact. You may also incorporate another method of correction if you choose. When your puppy ignores your first warning of "ah-ah," you can follow through by shaking the scruff of his neck—just as the mother bitch would do to her puppies. He will also relate this back to his mother. You may tell him "that'll do," "no," or whatever command you will use most comfortably and consistently.

The time that it takes you to give the command and the correction is how long the correction should last. *DO NOT PICK!* Be firm and direct as the canine mother would be—never ruthless, abusive, or nagging. Later, the correction can be amended to a sharp rap of the index finger across the bridge of the nose (muzzle), combined with eye contact and "that'll do." This consistency from mother and pup—to you and your dog—will establish you as "pack leader." It will produce the most effective response. It is the basis of pack behavior, through which all phases of dog handling can be directly influenced. This becomes clear as you observe the social structure of the pack and the mothers with their pups.

The pack system is dynamic—it is always subject to change. Within a litter, puppies also develop a social arrangement—the "pecking order." This early ranking has nothing to do with sex. As the youngsters mature, they eventually become intertwined in the pack. In the "pecking order," there is always a dominant male and a dominant female usually known as the "alpha" pair. The next in line are submissive to the alpha but are dominant to the subservients and are called "beta," and so on down the line. As Barry Holstun Lopez points out in his book "*Of Wolves and Men,*" the social order may be completely reversed from times of mating to times of play and hunting. However, the alpha individuals are not always the ones to lead the hunt, break trails in snow, or eat before others. The intricate working of the dynamic balance and teamwork are the basis for survival of the wolf pack.

Training comes naturally to some, while others must develop the skill. Spending time with your dog will tell you more about his character than any book can ever hope to. You will learn to recognize his natural traits and to discern which ones are induced through your handling. Training is similar to a savings account. The percentage of interest that is paid is reflected by the total investment. You reap from your companion exactly what you invest in time and handling.

Exactly what does it take to make your dog respond? You must use good judgment to discern the degrees of sensitivity. One Aussie may respond to a firmer hand, while another may be destroyed with stern handling. Some may be corrected simply with a vocal correction.

One effective correction is worth ten thousand ineffective ones. An ineffective correction is no better than "nagging." Nagging produces little or no results except resentment and perhaps a dull, next-to-nothing performance. Timing is the key to effective, efficient handling—the time that it takes you to recognize when an incorrect move is about to take place and the point at which you intervene to initiate a correction. Poorly timed corrections produce bewilderment. Improper, harsh, and even injurious corrections are *ABUSE!* Abuse only produces fear, which is quite the opposite of respect.

You should NEVER be stingy with your praise. Companionship and your praise are the only rewards that your Aussie asks for, so be generous. Praise is the element that makes a correction work in actuality. There are many forms of praise. Some Aussies will need considerable recognition, while another may overreact with too much exuberance. This individual will flourish with a simple scratch under the chin or behind the ears, combined with a calming, "good dog." This is where good judgment and knowing your dog really come into play.

Practice makes perfect. This perfection matures in phases over a period of time. Teach only one thing at a time. To add variety to training, work on previous lessons.

Aussies that are labeled "untrainable" are unfortunate individuals in the hands of uneducated handlers. These dogs will remain "untrainable" until they are handled in another, more appropriate manner. A reluctant performer is often force-trained. The mechanical-working Aussie is one created not from repetition, but through drilling, with no room allowed for the AUSSIE to shine through. A well-trained Australian Shepherd is an eager and willing performer. The well-educated trainer is the individual who has the flair to capture his dog's attention and the skill and ability to hold it!

Commands should be given in an authoritative intonation. If you teach him to obey commands in a harsh, raised voice, then it will be that type of command he will listen for before responding. On the other hand, if he is taught to listen for distinct, moderate tones, he will certainly take notice if you ever raise your voice.

CORRECTION

A "collar correction," properly given, will get your dog's attention and guide him in the proper direction. If the correction is executed well, it is given with a quick snap (or jerk) and is immediately released. It is not a pull, but a "snap." If you snap your fingers together, you will get the idea. With some dogs, you may need to give one hefty snap. Another may need two in a row - jerk and release, jerk and release. ALWAYS FOLLOW *ANY* CORRECTION WITH PLENTY OF PRAISE. Praise is the secret ingredient that makes any correction effective, *not* the severity of the correction. Don't neglect to remember that some individuals will respond beautifully with a *light* jerk and release.

Youngsters that have been brought along correctly through proper handling will look forward to the next phase. If your dog slinks away when you get out the lead, something is drastically *wrong!* Analyze your approach. Are you demanding too much at one time? If so, it is time to use a new approach.

PUPPY TRAINING

Regardless of age, any dog is a youngster in the beginning. You cannot expect your dog to know something if it has never been taught to him. When used and introduced properly, the lead and collar are tools that reinforce verbal commands. Many training techniques will depend on the lead and collar during all phases of handling.

The first lessons should be with a medium size collar or a nylon web collar and a six-foot leather lead. A "training collar" (or "choke collar") is far too severe on puppies and should not be used until they are at least six months of age. The collar must fit loosely enough to allow proper air intake and be tight enough so that it will not slip off at the first act of resistance. Once the collar is on the neck, you should be able to slip two fingers comfortably underneath it.

The first lessons should take place at home. This familiar surrounding will give your dog the needed confidence during the introductory stages of handling. It will set an impression in his mind to last a lifetime. Place the collar and lead on while you are around the house or out in the yard. Tell your puppy that he's a "good dog!" Direct your attention to a point to which you will walk (i.e., from one side of the yard to the other). Make the distance short for the first few times, then praise your puppy for responding. At first he may balk at the end of the lead or wildly jump around when he comes to realize that he is "on lead." When and if he panics, DO NOT JERK OR PULL ON HIM. This will only cause chaos. Allow the lead to go slightly slack. He will probably let up when he realizes that he is only fighting himself. A devastating experience will create a negative response and association for the lead or any other lessons that you may want to introduce later. NEVER leave your dog unattended with anything attached to his neck. To do so makes him susceptible to "hanging up" and choking to death.

While you are walking with your puppy on lead, do not keep looking back at or focus your attention on him. Rather, act as if it is not a big deal and take a few steps. Always stop and give the puppy an opportunity to compose himself, then take a few more steps. Always speak positively to the puppy, as this will build a positive association to the lead and to you.

Simple exercises can be taught while doing daily chores. Five or ten minutes spent once or twice a day will bring many progressive results. Kerry Russell from Edmonton, Alberta, Canada is teaching his puppy Las Rocosa Bonnie Kyle to keep an eye on him with the command "Watch Me." Courtesy Russell

If after your lesson around the yard the puppy seems to be panting, offer him a drink of water. Only work for approximately five minutes for the first few times. Remember - you are dealing with a puppy and a very immature mind with a small attention span. Pet your puppy and let him know that he is a *good dog!*

Do not scold during the introductory stages. Practice the above for five or ten minutes twice a day. In the next several days, while you are going about your daily chores, let the youngster trail along. Every so often, step on the lead and call him to you. You will have control should he decide to take off or to not respond. Take the lead in hand. Allow it to go slack, then call your dog and give the lead a light tug and release. Then draw him to you. Always use praise when he responds to your command. Every now and then, pick up the lead and call your dog to you. Praise him for coming, and take a few steps with him. Then go about your business.

Come

Ultimately, all exercises are relative to one another. You begin training your dog to come at a very early age. Call him by name and when he reaches you, praise him. Always praise him for coming to you. You can reinforce this as he gets older with a few lessons on lead. Once you have properly leash-trained your dog, you have also laid a very strong foundation for him to COME WHEN CALLED. All exercises and phases of training and handling are dependent on this strong foundation. These practical handling techniques are easily transformed to formal and required (in competition) obedience exercises.

Never give your dog a command that you cannot enforce, or you will only encourage him to disobey you. Many young dogs will "test" their handlers when they are out of arm's reach or off-lead. The only way to gain reliability is to be consistent and persistent in practicing this exercise at unexpected times in a wide variety of situations. Continue your training by allowing him to accompany you during chores around the house or yard. Let him drag a light line on his leather or nylon web collar (only while you are with him). When he least expects it, step on the lead and call him to you—this will teach him to respond to you each and every time when called; or as you are walking along, call your dog. Switch your direction and begin walking backwards. If he does not respond, take the lead in hand and simply draw him to you. With puppies, you will want to proceed with a gentle tug and release, while with older dogs, you will need to give a correction (a jerk and immediate release) to bring them to you. Praise him warmly for coming. Let him go while you go about your business. By varying the times and places that you teach him the "come" command, he soon will learn to come at anytime and place.

The lead is important in establishing consistency. Some people choose to beg their dogs to come to them. The chase is usually on! This type of handling invites disobedience and gives your dog the impression that you are playing a game with him. Give the command, preceded by your dog's name. "Phideaux, Come." His name gets his attention and the command means come now! Always speak in authoritative, inviting tones. Follow through with a correction if he fails to respond immediately (don't forget the praise). While off-lead, it will be quite a temptation to ignore you when he is out of your reach. When this occurs, *calmly*—no matter how angry you may be—put on his lead and collar. Call his name in the same authoritative, moderate tone. Say it in such a manner that he won't want to be left behind. Give a correction (a jerk and immediate release) to reinforce the command. Take several quick steps backwards to further encourage him. Whenever reinforcing a command, use finesse and discretion. Dogs can easily sense anger in your voice. NEVER CALL YOUR DOG TO PUNISH HIM! This is applying common sense. To do so will teach your intelligent Australian Shepherd to run fast in the opposite direction, and your dog will quickly lose his confidence in you. If you *witness* your dog doing something wrong, you must catch him "in the act" for him to relate the correction to the incident, thus reinforcing the fact that what he is doing is wrong. This will make him relate the correction to the offense—*not* to you or to the command "come!"

STAY

To stay when and where commanded is another cardinal exercise. This exercise will be the basis for many future exercises. As with teaching your dog to come, the stay can be taught while doing daily chores. You have already taught him to respond positively to the lead. He now is coming when called. The stay can easily be taught with the same leather or nylon web collar. While your youngster is dragging the lead about, call him to you as before. After you praise him for coming, slip the end of the lead (the loop) under the leg of a table, a sturdy chair or over a post. As you walk away, he will surely want to follow. Give the comand "stay" in a moderate, firm tone. The split second before he reaches the end of the lead, just as the slack in the lead jerks tight, repeat the stay command. Timing is the key. Go only a few feet away and remain within sight. Leave him only for a few seconds. Return to him and give praise. As with teaching the come exercise, teach him to stay at different unexpected times. When he learns to stay patiently for short periods, you can begin to leave him for longer periods.

During this training stage, the only thing that you have requested from your dog is that he stay. As long as he does, it should make no difference if he chooses to stand quietly and watch or if he chooses to sit or lie down. Young dogs that have not yet mentally matured do not have the capacity to retain a great deal of information. This method of introducing the stay is not so restricting as to frustrate a young dog. The advantage to this type of situation is that when you give the command to stay, it is reinforced through your dog's own weight as the slack in the lead plays out. When he reaches the end, it will check him. Since you have already laid a good foundation with the lead, he will not resent or be frightened by this. He will soon realize that if he stops straining on the lead, there will be no tension. He is also in his own familiar surroundings, which will give him confidence. At this stage in handling, the familiarity of your home is quite beneficial, but do not forget to expose your dog to many new and unfamiliar surroundings and situations, because they will be instrumental in building his confidence.

You've already developed a positive association with the command to "stay." Between six and twelve months at approximately nine months of age you will be getting into stock work and/or formal obedience. You will need to be able to give the "stay" command with complete assurance that your dog will obey. This phase of teaching the stay command is most effectively taught in conjunction with three other familiar exercises: the sit, the down and the stand. Any of these positions can be used when working stock and all of them will be used in formal obedience.

The stay in any position is a *stationary* command, therefore DO NOT use your dog's name when you give the command to stay. To do so will grab his attention. His name should be used in conjunction with a command to alert your dog to be "ready to run." When leaving your dog in a stay, simply use the command "stay" in a firm tone.

Sit and Down Stay - Guide your dog into a sitting position or drop (down) him at your side. For obedience dogs practice this at your left side. Stock dogs should learn this at both your left and right side. Give the command "stay." When you give the command, accompany it with a hand signal by sweeping the open palm of your right hand toward the dog just in front of his nose. The secondary cue to your dog is given by leaving on the foot opposite the side your dog is positioned. In other words, if your dog is on your left side leave on your RIGHT rather than your left one. Leave on your LEFT foot when your dog is on your right.

Step around in front of your dog, facing him. If he moves or starts forward with you, give a collar correction -upward and back. If he gets up, make him sit or put him down again where you first left him. Let him stay for a few, short moments and return to him. The first few times you return to him you can place your hand on his shoulder to keep him steady. After the first week eliminate putting your hand on the dog as you return. Return to him and let him wait a few seconds before you release him. Release him by saying his name and "that'll do" "good boy." When you return in formal obedience you will return counter-clockwise around him to the heeling position. Heel him forward a couple of steps. Halt, and then release him.

Each day, move a bit farther from your dog. Six to twelve inches at a time until you reach the end of your six foot lead. Do this until you can walk to the end of the lead, turn and face him and return without him breaking the stay position.

If your Aussie has progressed well each day by the time you reach the end of your lead, you may try dropping it in place and walking backward - increasing the distance between you and him. If he breaks, you can reach down and get the lead to reinforce the stay.

Always calmly approach your dog. Use deliberate and consistant movements. Do not delay giving a correction, but never should you rush at or "grab" your dog. Always release your dog from a stationary position. Vary the amount of time that you leave your dog at the various distances. Go three feet away for two minutes - and the next time go six feet for one minute.

Stand-Stay - Do not expect your dog to stabilize the stand-stay as rapidly as he will progress with the sit or down stay. It may take several weeks of consistant practice before your dog is steady with this exercise. In the sit and down your dog is in a stationary, immobile position. When standing, your dog is able and ready to move in any direction.

Never rush your Aussie in any stage of his training. If you do not have the time to train him the right way now, when will you have time to retrain him? There are no shortcuts. Young dogs do not have a long attention span. You must always keep them interested in what you are teaching. A few minutes twice a day will develop a keen and eager performer. Always end on a happy note. If your dog's interest begins to wander, end the training session. Sometimes one of the most important things is overlooked—puppies are only babies. A certain amount of training is important, but don't push them. Take your time, young dogs become old dogs all too soon.

As your youngster matures mentally, he will be able to take on more exercises. If you try to teach too much at one time or in a short time, he will only rebel. He may simply stop doing anything that you ask him to do. If you notice that his willing attitude has become dull or lacks attentiveness, back off. Allow your dog a break. Do not always trick your dog to make mistakes so that you may correct him. Proper correction and timing enforces a lesson; HOWEVER if you take the time to guide your dog and allow him to perform correctly, he will actually learn faster and be more willing. While you are teaching new exercises, do not forget the old ones. Familiar lessons are a good way to end a training session, because he can receive your praise for doing it right. *Positive reinforcement!*

The "Stand-Stay." Build up the distance until you can leave your dog, walk to the end of the lead and eventually drop it.

Sit

All of these introductory exercises can be taught at any age, and all can be transferred to formal obedience exercises when your pup matures.

The sit can easily be taught by calling your dog to you. Praise him for coming. While at your dog's side, place your right hand on his collar. Place your left hand just above the dog's hocks. Give the command to "sit." With your right hand, pull the collar back, while your left hand and arm tuck the hind legs under the dog to a sitting position. Praise him when he sits. This method is successful because there is little or no opportunity to resist. The action is very similar to someone walking up behind you and bumping you directly behind the knees.

The first couple of lessons, give the command to "sit." Repeat the above motions. Do not be concerned if he sits, then immediately pops up; however, stop

Teaching the "Sit."

Teaching the "Down."

your praise when he does so. As he begins to understand what you want from him, then you can work toward perfecting the action. Soon you can combine the sit with the stay. Many other lessons will be introduced from the sitting position.

Down

To familiarize your puppy with the down, place him in the sitting position. From this position, place your left hand gently over the shoulders. Give the command to "down" or "lie down," or whatever command you choose, but be consistent in your use of words. Your right hand should be positioned just behind the forelegs. Gently sweep your arm forward, in the same direction in which he is facing. With one continuous motion, your puppy should be lying on the ground with little or no resistance. Use the left hand over the shoulder to guide the body down, but do not apply any pressure. The trick is to give the command and then sweep his legs out from under him—*before* he has a chance to brace them against you.

Down in motion - Teaching the down in motion produces an immediate response necessary for stock work. The trick is to use your dog's own momentum to propel him into a down position with the least amount of resistance. This can best be taught while your dog is walking briskly or trotting by your side. While your dog is in a forward line of travel at your

side, tell him to "down" or "lie down." The split second following the time that you give the verbal command, reach down and place your hand on the lead next to his collar. Without hesitation push down, while at the same time, push forward toward the ground. It is a complete action done in one continuous motion. When done correctly, your dog is on the ground before he knows what happened. If you are too slow in executing the maneuver properly, you will find your dog is able to get his front legs under his body and brace himself against you. Do not struggle with him. Offer some vocal encouragement. Move forward and try again. Take as many steps as you need to get him at a normal pace either at a fast walk or at a trot. Do not interrupt or throw your dog out of balance by pulling backwards on the lead. It is the forward momentum that propells him into position. If he does not remain lying down in the beginning, do not be concerned as long as he drops initially. Offer lavish praise when he succeeds.

Stand

The stand can also be taught from the sitting position. It works in reverse. While your puppy is sitting, place your right hand on the collar. Place your left hand underneath his body next to his stifle. Give the command to "stand." With your right hand, pull forward on the collar. As you are pulling him forward, push the hind legs back by extending your left arm underneath, and in one motion, sweep them back. Praise him for responding to the command.

The stand can also be practiced while grooming your dog. In the beginning, do not expect precision. All of the previous lessons can be taught at any age. Practice these for five minutes once or twice a day.

BAD HABITS AND HOW TO CURE THEM

Biting

If your Aussie bites or snaps at you especially after you have corrected him you need to assert your dominance over him. He may be testing your authority but you need to re-establish yourself as the pack leader. Firmly take ahold of his muzzle with one hand. Sharply rap your index finger across his muzzle with the other hand and give a vocal correction (an ah-ah growling sound, no!). This may be sufficient, but if not, you will need to give him several hefty collar corrections. Call him to you and let him know that he is still your friend.

A dog that has been injured or in shock may bite unintentionally. This is not a situation for correction, however he should be restrained so that he doesn't hurt anyone or himself. If he needs medical attention, an emergency muzzle may be necessary.

If your dog seems just fine, but sensitive or reacts when you take ahold of his collar or elsewhere, take him to your veterinarian to determine that he does not have some factor causing the irritation.

Curbing Aggression

Aggressive behavior can stem from many factors including inherited temperament, environmental influences, handling and management. Over aggressiveness to people can be curbed through proper and consistent handling. Where do you keep him when you're gone? Does anyone have access to his yard, kennel or back porch that may be teasing or harrassing him without you being aware of it? Do children passing by throw rocks and sticks? Does he display this behavior with some people and not others?

Have your leash available to snap on your dog whenever someone arrives on your premises. When he shows tendencies toward aggressive behavior, you can immediately correct the situation. Tell your dog "that'll do," and call him to you. If he doesn't respond immediately to your call, go to him. Several hefty collar corrections given with a vocal correction (an ah-ah growling sound, no!) given each and every time will curb the situation. If you are unable to be in a position to make appropriate corrections, don't leave your dog unsupervised when you are not sure how he will react. Instead, place your dog safely in his outdoor kennel run, fenced-in yard or in another room away from the source of irritation.

Teaching the "Stand."

Teaching Pivot turns.

Jumping Up

Never invite your dog to jump up on you to receive praise and never pet him when he does. Your dog cannot tell the difference between when you're in old clothes or when you're dressed up in your Sunday best. The worst problem with jumping up is that company will usually violate your training by letting your dog climb up in their lap or by inviting them to jump up.

Each and every time your dog does jump up, draw your knee up into the dog's chest with a vocal correction. If that is ineffective, take his front feet in your hands and run towards him backwards. Flip him over backward accompanied with lots of praise. After several times he will probably hesitantly approach you. Pet him and give lots of attention when he is sitting or standing in front of you. Whenever company arrives you can put on his collar. Whenever he attempts to jump up on strangers give him a hefty collar correction downwards, accompanied with vocal disapproval. When he responds, give lavish praise.

Basic obedience will further develop the bond between you and your dog, which will help you gain reliable control over him. Enroll in an obedience class. The contact with other people and dogs will be ideal. It's an opportunity to socialize as well as teach your dog with the guidance of a professional trainer/handler. It is more beneficial for you to learn to train and handle your own dog than to have someone else do the training.

FORMAL TRAINING

When your puppy matures (is at least six months of age), he is ready for more formal training. You will need a "training" or "choke collar." When used in the correct manner, it can be very humane and effective. Used incorrectly, it can be too severe for a training tool.

The training collar must be the correct length for proper response. Timing is of extreme importance. An improperly fitting collar (one that is too long) initiates a delayed signal, which obtains a delayed response from your dog. By the time the signaled correction actually reaches your dog, it is usually too late to do any good. If your dog cannot associate the correction with the incident for which he is being corrected, it is useless.

A collar that is too small (short in length) will restrict air intake and be uncomfortable. Once the collar is on the neck, you should be able to comfortably fit two fingers underneath it. When pulled taut, there should be about three inches of length "not in contact." The collar should NEVER be left on while

your dog is not under your supervision, because the collar can easily snag and subject your dog to strangulation.

Establishing "eye contact" while in the heeling position.

Heeling

Heeling is necessary if you are to enter competitive obedience. It is also a very practical lesson to teach your dog to stay by your side. It will allow you to take your Aussie for a walk rather than allowing him to drag you.

First, check your training collar. It must be on properly so that your corrections will be effective. Sit your dog on your left side. The area from his shoulders to his head should be parallel to your left leg. Your dog should only be inches away, but not touching. Slip the end of the lead (the loop) over your right thumb, and ribbon the remaining length in your palm. The lead should have a small loop at the point where it attaches to the training collar, but it should not be so loose that it interferes with, or gets tangled up in, the front legs. It should be loose enough so that when you give a collar correction, the slack is drawn up sharply and is able to be released immediately.

Heeling is a combination of any of the following motions. The forward and halt is where you walk briskly forward and then stop, at which point your dog sits by your side. You eventually incorporate a right turn, a left turn, and an about-turn. The about-turn is simply a turn 180 degrees in the opposite direction. The about-turn can be to the inside or the outside. In competition, however, it is always done to the outside (to the right). Heeling also includes a change of pace from slow to fast, back to a brisk walk.

ALWAYS leave your dog by traveling with your *right* leg first. ALWAYS leave on your *left* leg when you want your dog heeling at your side.

Whenever you practice heeling, keep your sessions short and interesting. Practice the heeling while your dog is energetic to keep him from getting bored. Eye contact and verbal praise will hold most Aussies' attention.

Say your dog's name, then give the command "heel." Say it in a "let's go," uplifting tone! Step forward on your left foot. The slower you move, the slower your dog will move. Do not adapt to his pace, but establish your own pace. When you step out in a lively manner, it encourages your dog to do the same. Your lively pace should be brisk, but smooth and *never* choppy.

After several days of heeling forward to establish "heel" and "sit," you will want to incorporate some turns. Enthusiastic students will forge ahead of you. Do not jerk him back, but instead change your direction using the about turn. Give him a quick jerk and release the training collar and praise him warmly.

It is recommended that you enroll in an obedience course with a local training class or club. They will be able to demonstrate the correct techniques and socialization necessary for a competitive edge.

OBEDIENCE TRIALS

Like many forms of horsemanship, obedience was created for war and stemmed from the battlefields. Any Australian Shepherd registered with the Australian Shepherd Club of America (ASCA), or Australian Shepherds possessing the LEP number (limited exhibition privilege) with the ASCA, are eligible to compete in ASCA-sanctioned obedience trials, which are often held in conjunction with sanctioned conformation shows.

The obedience rules of the Australian Shepherd Club are adopted from the American Kennel Club (AKC).

Obedience Regulations

Purpose - Obedience Trials are a sport, and all participants should be guided by the principles of good sportsmanship, both in and outside of the ring. The purpose of Obedience Trials is to demonstrate the usefulness of the pure-bred Aussie as a companion of man, not merely the dog's ability to follow specified routines in the obedience ring.

THE CLASSES

Novice

Novice "A" Class - The Novice A class shall be for dogs not less than six months of age that have not won the title C.D. A dog that is owned or co-owned by a person who has previously handled or regularly trained a dog that has won a C.D. title may not be entered in the Novice A class, nor may a dog be handled in this class by such person.

Novice "B" Class - The Novice B class shall be for dogs not less than six months of age that have not won the title C.D. and that are handled by the owner or any other person.

Novice Exercises and Scores - The exercises and maximum scores in the Novice classes are:

1. Heel on Leash and Figure Eight .. 40 points
2. Stand for Examination .... 30 points
3. Heel Free .... 40 points
4. Recall .... 30 points
5. Long Sit .... 30 points
6. Long Down .... 30 points
Maximum Total Score .... 200 points

C.D. Title - The Australian Shepherd Club of America will issue a Companion Dog certificate for each registered dog and will permit the use of the letters "C.D." after the name of each dog that has been certified by three different judges to have received Qualifying scores in Novice classes at three Licensed or Member Obedience Trials, provided the sum total of dogs that actually competed in the Regular Novice classes at each trial is not less than six.

Open

Open A Class - The Open A class shall be for dogs that have won the C.D. title but have not won the title C.D.X. Obedience judges may not enter or handle dogs in this class.

Open B Class - The Open B class will be for dogs that have won the title C.D. or C.D.X. A dog may continue to compete in this class after he has won the title U.D. Dogs in this class may be handled by the owner or any other person.

Open Exercises and Scores - The exercises and maximum scores in the Open classes are:

1. Heel Free and Figure Eight . . . . . . 40 points
2. Drop on Recall . . . . 30 points
3. Retrieve on Flat . . . . 20 points
4. Retrieve over High Jump . . . . 30 points
5. Broad Jump . . . . 20 points
6. Long Sit . . . . 30 points
7. Long Down . . . . 30 points

Maximum Total Score . . . . .200 points

C.D.X. Title - The Australian Shepherd Club of America will issue a Companion Dog Excellent certificate for each registered dog and will permit the use of the letters "C.D.X." after the name of each dog that has been certified by three different judges of Obedience Trials to have received Qualifying scores in Open Classes at three Licensed or Member Obedience Trials, provided the sum total of dogs that actually competed in the Regular Open classes at each trial is not less than six.

Utility

Utility Class - The Utility class shall be for dogs that have won the title C.D.X. Dogs that have won the title U.D. may continue to compete in this class. Dogs in this class may be handled by the owner or any other person. Owners may enter more than one dog in this class, but each dog must have a separate handler for the Group Examination when judged in the Group Exercises.

Division of Utility Class - A club may choose to divide the Utility class into Utility A and Utility B classes, provided such division is approved by the ASCA and is announced in the premium list. When this is done, the Utility A class shall be for dogs that have won the title C.D.X. and have not won the title U.D. Obedience judges may not enter or handle dogs in this class.

Utility Exercises and Scores - The exercises, maximum scores, and order of judging in the Utility classes are:

1. Signal Exercise . . . . 40 points
2. Scent Discrimination-Article #1 . . . 30 points
3. Scent Discrimination-Ariticle #2 . . 30 points
4. Directed Retrieve . . . . 30 points
5. Directed Jumping . . . . 40 points
6. Group Examination . . . . 30 points

Maximum Total Score . . . . .200 points

Teaching the "Swing-Finish" (#1)

"Swing-Finish" (#2)

U.D. Title - The Australian Shepherd Club of America will issue a Utility Dog certificate for each registered dog and will permit the use of the letters "U.D." after the name of each dog that has been certified by three different judges of Obedience Trials to have received Qualifying scores in Utility classes at three Licensed or Member Obedience Trials in each of which three or more dogs actually competed in the Utility class or classes.

TRACKING

In tracking, your dog learns to follow the scent of something or someone often unknown to the dog. A dog must be trained to work under all weather conditions and in all kinds of terrain. When once trained the handler depends solely on his/her ability to discern the correct track. The handler therefore needs to be able to "read" his dog to determine when he is "on."

Any dog of any age can be encouraged to track. The Australian Shepherd is superior when it comes to tracking. His inborn abilities enable him to excel in practical situations as well as competitively. Tracking is unique in that no obedience is required or employed. Tracking is totally an incentive/reward association for the dog.

The talents of the Australian Shepherd have been employed throughout the country in search and rescue work. In 1971 Ruth McGuires' Se Me Go Hemi was accredited with many successful "finds" while on the Colorado Canine Search and Rescue Team. Blue Lad's Mulberry Muffin owned and handled by Rose Spicuzza has been employed by Michigan farmers, to search for lost livestock. To the delight of the farmers "Muffin" not only locates the missing stock, but she gathers them up and brings them back. Blue Lad's Coppercast Russet owned by Bob Spicuzza and Nick Davis' Apache Tears of Timberline are also among the best known tracking dogs in the country.

Tracking tests are designed to accredit a dog's ability to work under the variety of scenting conditions. First however, the dog must be certified by a licensed Tracking judge to determine whether or not the dog is qualified to compete. Tracking judges must be thoroughly familiar with the various conditions that may exist when a dog is required to work a scent trail. The actual tracking test is somewhat more difficult than the preliminary certification. Once a dog has passed an accredited tracking test he is permitted to use the letters T.D. following his name. If the

"Swing-Finish" (#3)

"Swing-Finish" (#4)

Colorado's Ravishing Ruby CDX is shown taking the broad jump.
Courtesy Foster

dog has a U.D. (Utility Dog Title) he may use the letters U.D.T.

Once a dog has earned a T.D. he can work toward the Tracking Dog Excellent. The degree of difficulty is increased. In the first test for the T.D., the track is between 440 and 500 yards on a trail that is between ½ an hour to two hours old, which also involves turns (change of direction). The Tracking Dog Excellent test is laid out between 800 and 1000 yards following a scent that is between three and five hours old with newer distracting tracks somewhere in between. A dog that passes this test is permitted to use the letters T.D.X. behind his name. The U.T.D. titled dog may use U.T.D.X. following their name.

Arrowhead's Homeward Bound owned by Jacquie Hartford was the first T.D.X. Australian Shepherd followed by High Wind's Shawnee, owned by James and Susan Bosse.

TRACKING TRAINING   by Rose Spicuzza

Tracking with Australian Shepherds is one of the most exciting and enjoyable experiences imaginable. As with obedience and stock work, it is a team effort. And, as with stock work, the dog knows far more than the handler.

Aussies can be started at a very young age—six to seven weeks if possible. Beginning with the puppy on a nonrestrictive lead, one person hides behind a tree or any other barrier that conceals him, about twenty-five feet away. The puppy should see him leave. The person calls to the pup, but stays hidden. Most pups will "air scent" at first, but with practice, that little nose soon scoots right along the ground. When the person is "located," a BIG fuss should be made over the puppy!

Start early to use certain words such as "find it" or "track it," and as the pup progesses, start pulling back just a bit so that he has to drive into the leash or harness. He should get used to pulling strongly.

An older dog can be started without the benefit of puppy training. Use a toy or other favorite object. The tracklayer dangles it enticingly above the dog's head, while the handler holds on tightly to the lead. The dog should be wearing a nonrestrictive harness or collar. The tracklayer walks off in a straight line away from the dog, about twenty-five feet. Calling the dog's name to attract his attention, he drops the article *away* from his body about eighteen inches and to the side, so that the dog sees it fall. He then moves away from the article. The handler points to the ground to get the dog's attention to the spot where the tracklayer has begun walking. Encouraging him on, the handler and dog move to the spot where the article has been dropped. Again, make a big fuss— throw the article in the air to get the dog excited. Not too much encouragement is needed to put Aussies on the tracking high! Lay two to five tracks a day, always in a fresh and unused area. If the dog gets tired or bored, QUIT. This is a fun sport, and there is no way anyone can FORCE that nose to quiver along the ground unless the dog enjoys what he is doing.

Over the weeks (two to three weeks are good), make the tracks longer, add a corner or two, and then "age" the tracks gradually up to an hour or so before running them. Do this until the dog is tracking over 600 to 800 yards in length and an hour-old track with four or five corners. Now you are ready to try for your "T." Good luck!

Two Track's Terpisichore of Depindet CDX chooses the correct
utility article during the Scent Discrimination exercise
Courtesy Earnest

GUIDELINES FOR PUTTING ON AN AUSSIE OBEDIENCE COMPETITION/TRIAL

PERSONNEL NEEDED:

A. Announcer - 1 +
B. Award Chairperson - 1
C. Entry Clerk(s)*
D. Equipment Director - 1
E. Hospitality Chairperson - 1
F. Judges - 1 per division or *
G. Photographer - 1

H. Ring Steward(s) - 1 per ring
I. Posts - Human - for Fig. 8 exercise
J. Set-Up Crew*
K. Show Secretary - 1
L. Take-Down Crew*
M. Veterinarian - On-Call
N. Clean-Up Crew*

EQUIPMENT NEEDED:

A. Armbands - both blank & printed
B. Calculators - 1/scorekeeper or *
C. Canopy/Canvas* (to shade personnel)
D. Cash Box - 1 at entry location or *
E. Chairs* (for personnel/audience)
F. Clip Boards*
G. First-Aid Kit
H. Jumps - Board & High 1 set/per each obedience ring used.
I. Mats/Runners* (If competing on cement)
J. Pens/Pencils/Paper*
K. Restroom Facilities

L. Signs/Maps* (in vicinity)
M. Score Sheets* (for each division)
N. Tables*
O. Miscellaneous Tools*
P. Clean-Up Equipment*
Q. Ring Ropes*
R. Ring Posts - 4/ring or *
S. Miscellaneous Office Supplies*
T. Wicket - (for measuring dogs)
U. Yard Stick (for measuring jumps)
V. Stopwatch (for timing long sits & downs) - 1/ring

AWARDS:

A. Ribbons - 1st thru 4th for each class offered or *
B. Trophies - 1 for each class offered

C. Highest Scoring Award - + for highest score awarded
D. Highest Scoring Jr. Handler - youth (handler) award

* - As many as necessary
\+ - Optional

Champion Sadie J of Coppertone CDX, STD-d pictured in training for a TD.
Photo Courtesy of Lorna Ludwig

Champion Shanks' Ginks CD (Heard's Proud Buck of Flintridge ex Iacovetta's Shasta), foundation bitch of the Coppertone line. "Ginks" is pictured with Lucia Kline DVM, author of this chapter, and breeder judge, Walter Lamar.

12

GENETICS OF THE AUSTRALIAN SHEPHERD

By Lucia D. Kline D.V.M.

Genetics is the study of inheritance. Inheritance is responsible for the form and function of the individual, although these can be modified to some extent by environmental and developmental factors. A basic understanding of genetics can be used to advantage not only by the breeder, who can apply genetic principles in selecting sires and dams in an effort to produce superior quality progeny, but also by the fancier when selecting a pet.

The general mechanisms by which traits are passed down from parents to offspring have been fairly well elucidated and appear to be rather constant in most living organisms. However, with regard to the inheritance patterns of specific traits within certain species and breeds of animals, much remains to be studied. This is particularly true of the Australian Shepherd because it is of fairly recent origin as a pure breed and is, therefore, without the benefit of many years accumulation of breeder's records, nor have there been many genetic studies of the breed performed by the scientific community. Therefore, much of the information about the inheritance of traits in the Aussie is based on breeders' observations, accurate and complete record keeping, and cooperation among breeders. With more scientific studies, our knowledge of the genetics of the Australian Shepherd will be enhanced.

FUNDAMENTAL PRINCIPLES OF GENETICS

Deoxyribonucleic Acid (*DNA*) is the chemical molecule that is the genetic material. It is in every nucleated cell of the body and carries coded specifications for growth, differentiation, and functioning of the organism. It can also replicate itself so that when a cell divides (*mitosis*), the two daughter cells contain exactly the same code (except for the egg and sperm cells, which will be discussed later).

Each molecule of DNA, along with other associated molecules, make up a *chromosome*. The number of chromosomes in each cell varies with the species of the animal. The dog has seventy-eight chromosomes that occur in pairs which are generally similar in size and shape (*homologous chromosomes*), one of each pair having come from the male parent and the other from the female parent. One pair of chromosomes—the sex chromosomes—determine the sex of the individual. The other thirty-eight pairs are called autosomes.

In the sexual organs, a special form of cell division (*meiosis*) occurs in which the homologous pairs of chromosomes are separated. The resulting egg and sperm cells contain only one chromosome of each pair. This is called *the principle of segregation*. Whether an egg or sperm cell receives a maternal or paternal chromosome of a given pair is strictly random.

Each pair of chromosomes divides independently of all other pairs so that the egg and sperm cell may each contain one of a great many possible combinations of maternal and paternal chromosomes. This is called *the principle of independent assortment*. These two principles form the basis of what is called Mendelian genetics, named after discoverer Gregor Mendel.

At fertilization, one sperm cell unites with the egg cell to restore the full number of chromosomes. One chromosome of each pair is contributed by the sperm cell, the other by the egg cell. Fertilization is also random such that any one of many sperm cells containing a great many possible combinations of maternal and paternal chromosomes has an equal chance of fertilizing the egg cell. This randomness in the recombination of chromosomes already present in a breeding population explains much of the variation in the population. After fertilization, the egg cell goes through a complex series of mitotic cell divisions to produce the many thousands of cells of the body, and each of these cells contains exact copies of all the chromosomes of the original fertilized egg.

The DNA molecule is functionally subdivided into *genes*, which are considered to be the smallest units of inheritance. Each gene is a code for a specific protein or protein subunit. These proteins may serve either as structural proteins, which contribute to the form of the individual, or as enzymes, which catalyze cellular biochemical reactions that contribute to the functioning of the body. The same genes are present in all nucleated cells of the body, although different genes may be active in different cells—leading to the variation in the tissues of the body—or they may be active at different times during development. Each chromosome contains thousands of genes along its length and has been described as being similar to a string of beads, with each bead being a gene. All the genes on one chromosome have a linear order and tend to be inherited together; therefore, they are said to be *linked*.

Champion Windermere's Sunshine of Bonnie-Blu, CDX (Ch. Wildhagen's Dutchman of Flintridge CDX ex Wildhagen's Thistle of Flintridge), one of the well known "Dusty X Thistle" offspring. The foundation sire of Windermere.   *Courtesy Williams*

A gene governing a given trait has a specific site, called a *locus*, on a specific chromosome. Homologous chromosomes contain genes that govern the same traits; therefore, an individual has two genes—one from its father and one from its mother—that govern the same trait. The gene governing the trait on one of the homologous chromosomes is in exactly the same locus as its partner on the other homologous chromosome. However, these paired genes may not be exactly alike even though they influence the same trait.

Alternate forms of paired genes are called *alleles*. These are the result of mutations and are responsible for the variations within the Australian Shepherd breed. There may be more than two alternate forms of a gene within a breed or species, called *multiple alleles*, but a given individual can only have one pair of these. When an individual has two identical alleles for a certain trait, he is said to be *homozygous* for that particular trait. When an individual has two different alleles as the pair, he is said to be *heterozygous* for the trait.

The kinds of alleles that an individual carries for each of the different gene pairs make up what is called the *genotype*, which is the actual genetic construction of the individual. The visible expression of these alleles, or what we observe, is called the *phenotype*. The phenotypic expression of any given allele depends on its interaction with its paired allele, and in some cases with other gene pairs and with the environment. The major form of interaction between alleles of a gene pair is called *dominance*. A dominant allele will be expressed regardless of whether it is paired with the same (*homozygous*) or a different (*heterozygous*) allele. If it is paired with a different allele, it will completely mask the effects of the other allele. In this instance, the other allele is called *recessive*. Recessive alleles for a trait are only expressed phenotypically when the individual is homozygous.

Which alleles for a given trait are recessive and which are dominant is determined by observing the frequency of the appearance of the phenotype dictated by the alleles in the offspring. Conversely, once the dominance pattern of the alleles is known, the probabilities of the appearance of phenotypes in the offspring of parents of known genotypes can be predicted on the basis of statistics. This is made simple by the use of a shorthand device in which a given trait or gene is assigned a letter. A capital letter is assigned to represent the *dominant* allele, while a lowercase letter represents the *recessive* allele. A geometrical device called the *Punnett Square* is used to visualize all of the possible combinations of alleles. As an example, in the Australian Shepherd, the basic coat color is determined by one pair of genes and is either red or black. The allele for black is dominant to the allele for red. The letter "B" has been assigned to this gene pair, and since black is dominant, it is represented by a capital "B" and red by a lowercase "b."

If an individual that is homozygous for black is bred to an individual that is homozygous for red, the Punnett Square can be utilized to determine the probabilities of the colors appearing in the offspring. The two alleles of one parent are placed across the top of the chart, with the two alleles of the other parent placed on the left side. Then all possible combinations of parental genes and their frequency of occurrence in the offspring can be predicted. Each allele of one parent has an equal chance of pairing up with either of the two alleles of the other parent. This pairing is represented by the boxes of the Punnett Square (Figure 1). Thus, it can be seen that all offspring of homozygous parents, one for red, the other for black, will themselves be black in phenotype but will carry the allele for red in their genotype and possess the potential to pass it to their offspring. Punnett Squares can be constructed for all the possible genotypes for the trait in the parents and for the probabilities of the genotypes and phenotypes of the offspring determined (Figures 2, 3, 4, and 5).

Figure 1   Black parent
homozygous for black

	B	B
b	Bb	Bb
b	Bb	Bb

Red parent homozygous for red

All progeny are heterozygous Bb and will be black in color.

Figure 2   Heterozygous black parent

	B	b
B	BB	Bb
b	Bb	bb

Heterozygous black parent

Genotypic frequency of
the progeny:
25% BB
50% Bb
25% bb

Phenotypic frequency
of the progeny:
75% black
25% red

Figure 3   Homozygous black parent

	B	B
B	BB	BB
b	Bb	Bb

Heterozygous black parent

Genotypic frequency of
the progeny:
50% BB
50% Bb

Phenotypic frequency
of the progeny:
100% black

Figure 4   Heterozygous black parent

	B	b
b	Bb	bb
b	Bb	bb

Homozygous red parent

Genotypic frequency of
the progeny:
50% Bb
50% bb

Phenotypic frequency
of the progeny:
50% black
50% red

Figure 5   Homozygous red parent

	b	b
b	bb	bb
b	bb	bb

Homozygous red parent

All progeny are homozygous bb and red in color.

This device can also be used when more than one trait is being considered, as long as the gene pairs for each trait are found on different sets of homologous chromosomes and are therefore inherited independently of each other. It must be remembered that these are statistical probabilities based on random recombination at fertilization. The statistical probabilites are reflected when large numbers of breedings produce large numbers of offspring. In a given litter, however, where only a relatively small number of offspring are produced, the probable statistical distribution of genotypic and phenotypic frequencies may not be reflected. Nevertheless, the chances of their occurrence at the time of breeding follow the laws of statistical probability.

Unfortunately, genetics is made much more complex by the fact that not every trait is determined by only one pair of genes whose alleles follow strict dominance-recessive relationships. As was stated earlier, the phenotypic expression of a trait may depend not only on the interaction between alleles, but also on the interaction with other gene pairs and the interaction of the individual with the environment. For example, it has been determined that at least ten

both dominant and recessive alleles are expressed in the individual that carries both. Matings between heterozygotes for a given trait produce a phenotypic ratio in the offspring of 1:2:1 for that trait instead of 3:1.

Semi- or Incomplete Dominance—There are many genes whose alleles do not have strongly dominant or recessive relationships. Therefore, when these alleles come together in one individual in the heterozygous condition, they produce an *intermediate, but similar effect*. Semidominant alleles often code for the same genetic product, but in unequal quantity, leading to a heterozygote phenotype that is intermedi-

Taylor's Buena (Sniff's Dandy Danny ex Petramala's Tate), a foundation matron of the breed owned by Joe D. Taylor of Moab, Utah.

gene pairs, with each pair on a different set of homologous chromosomes, influence coat color in the dog. The nine other pairs of genes have altering effects on coat color (black or red) to produce the wide variation seen in the canine species. The inheritance of the coat color patterns seen in the Australian Shepherd will be described in more detail later. The more important types of interactions that affect the phenotypic expression of the individual are as follows:

Codominance—This action occurs when both alleles of a pair are expressed and each allele *produces an independent effect in the offspring*. The phenotype of the heterozygote is *qualitatively different* in character from either homozygote, and the effects of

ate between that of the two homozygous parents. When two heterozygotes are mated, the alleles segregate and resort independently so that homozygous offspring for each allele resemble the extremes of the grandparents homozygous for the same alleles. Heterozygous offspring are intermediate like their parents.

Complementary Genes—These are genes belonging to different gene pairs that are similar in phenotypic effect when present separately in individuals. However, when present together in the same individual, they interact to produce a different trait. If two such genes are complementary for a dominant effect, the phenotypic ratio in the offspring resulting from two individuals heterozygous for both traits is

9:1; if complementary for a recessive effect, a phenotypic ratio of 15:1 results.

Modifier Genes—These are genes that act as enhancers or inhibitors of a trait determined by another gene pair. They cause a range of expression of the trait but seldom entirely obliterate it, and their effects are only evident in a suitable genotype. They are considered to be multiple factors whose members are generally unknown but that are amenable to selection in either direction by their visible effects on traits.

Epistasis—In this type of interaction, a gene or gene pair masks the expression of another non-allelic gene pair. The gene pair that is suppressed is said to be *hypostatic*. The *epistatic* pair blocks the biochemical reactions determined by the hypostatic pair to mask the effect. Epistasis is distinguished from dominance in which the masking effect occurs between genes of an allelic pair. Through epistatic effects and other gene interactions, traits may remain hidden for generations. This is called *atavism.*

Pleiotrophy—This is a situation in which a gene influences the expression of more than one trait. A gene has only one function—coding for the production of a single protein. However, this protein may play several different roles in the body, giving rise to the expressions of several traits at the phenotypic level. Certain pleiotropic genes may influence both qualitative and quantitative traits.

Penetrance and Expressivity—Some traits are manifested in varying degrees in different individuals possessing the genotype for expression of the trait. Certain individuals, although possessing the genotype, fail to exhibit the characteristic at all. *Penetrance* is a measure of the population that both possesses the genotype and expresses the trait. When a trait is not expressed in all individuals that possess the proper genotype, the trait is said to have incomplete penetrance. *Expressivity* is the range of expression of a gene in different individuals. The reason for incomplete penetrance and variable expressivity is not completely understood but is usually explained on the basis of modifiers that influence the action of a given gene or environmental variation. In such cases, breeding tests are used to prove genotype.

Polygenes—This concept was developed to explain the variation along a continuous range of quantitative traits such as size, conformation, viability, rate of growth, and time to reach maturity. Most traits of domestic animals are thought to be quantitative. Traits that segregate into distinct forms, such as with dominant/recessive gene interactions, are called qualitative traits and are said to have discontinuous variation. The concept of polygenes implies that quantitative traits are governed by a number of genes at different locia on many chromosomes. An individ-

Champion Slash V (George's) Buckeye Bobby (Tartaglia's Chocolate ex Caligari's Lady) a prominent sire of the Slash V Line.
Courtesy Martin

ual gene exerts a slight effect on phenotype, but in conjunction with a few or many other genes, a gradual series extends from one parental extreme to the other. The greater the number of genes involved, the more continuous the variation. The contribution of a particular gene varies in accordance with the rest of the genotype—the effects of the various genes involved are not simply additive or equal, but are influenced by other types of gene interactions (linkage, epistasis, modifiers, etc.). One feature of polygenic traits is that their degree of expression can usually be influenced by the environment. Therefore, it is important to distinguish the genetic component from environmental effects. The degree to which a given trait is controlled by inheritance is called *heritability.* It is possible through selective breeding to manipulate traits influenced by polygenic inheritance to produce relatively pure-breeding lines. However, at this time it is not possible to individually recognize the genes involved.

Phenocopies—These are alterations in a phenotypic trait induced by the environment but that resemble those caused by genetic factors. To distinguish hereditary traits from those caused by the environment, appropriate test matings are sometimes conducted. Traits of a hereditary nature will be passed to the progeny, while those caused by the environment will not.

Sex Linkage—This is the association of a hereditary trait with the sex of the individual because the gene for the trait is located on a sex chromosome. Females are homozygous for the X chromosome. Males are heterozygous, carrying both X and Y chromosomes. Unlike the somatic homologous chromosome pairs, the X and Y chromosomes do not have completely corresponding pairs of genes. A portion of the X chromosome has no corresponding counterpart on the Y chromosome, although most but not all of the genes of the Y chromosome do have corresponding genes on the X chromosome. A recessive allele occurring on the nonhomologous part of the X chromosome can therefore come to expression in a male because there is no corresponding dominant allele to suppress it. A female must be homozygous for the recessive allele in order for it to be expressed phenotypically. Sex of the offspring is determined by the chromosomes of the father. The mother can only pass an X chromosome to the offspring; however, the father can pass an X chromosome—in which case the offspring will be female—or a Y chromosome—in which case the offspring will be male. If the father is expressing a sex-linked trait, he can only pass the trait to his daughters, who will all be carriers of the trait. The daughters may or may not pass the trait down to be expressed in their sons depending on whether they are homozygous or heterozygous for the trait. If they are homozygous, having received an identical allele from their mother, all their sons will be affected, and all their daughters will be carriers of the trait. If they are heterozygous, half their sons will express the trait and half their daughters will be carriers.

Sex-Limited Gene Expression—This is the expression of a trait carried on autosomal chromosomes by only one sex. Although an individual of the other sex may carry homozygous alleles for the trait, it cannot be expressed in the individual because the individ-

ual's sex does not allow it. Sex hormones interact to limit the expression of the trait to a given sex.

USING GENETICS IN A BREEDING PROGRAM

From the above discussion, it may appear impossible to master enough genetics in order to plan matings that will result in offspring with the desired characteristics. It may seem even more futile in light of the fact that our knowledge of the inheritance patterns of many traits is limited. However, the knowledge of Mendel's laws and a recognition of the complexity of the behavior of genes are prerequisites to the intelligent breeding of dogs. With an understanding of these, you can also understand methods of selection and systems of breeding that can make the plan-

Ch. Cornwell's Cody CDX STD-c (Tegmeyers Ringo ex Tegmeyers Bronz Lady). "Cody," an exceptional High in Trial Obedience competitor went on to throw these winning traits to his progeny as a main sire of Fairoaks. Courtesy Cornwell

ning of matings much simpler. It must be emphasized, however, that success in breeding also requires you to be a good judge—to be able to recognize traits of soundness as well as faults. Any application of scientific knowledge involves a certain amount of individual judgment, leading some to describe the breeding of animals as an art. Breeding is the process of choosing the genes most likely to produce the ideal Aussie.

The selection process is a major tool available to the animal breeder. Basically, it is an attempt to shift the traits of the population in a desired direction by retaining desirable individuals and excluding those with less desirable characteristics. Selection does not create new traits, but merely changes the proportion of desired and undesired phenotypes. Three basic

Champion Las Rocosa Leslie CSD (Ch Las Rocosa Shiloh ex Hartnagle's Fritzie Taylor), a product of the famous "Fritzie X Shiloh" cross pictured against the image of her renowned son Champion Chulo Rojo (sired by Taylor's Whiskey). "Chulo" is the foundation sire of the Fairoaks line. Courtesy Cornwell

methods of selection are available to the breeder on a practical basis:

(1) Phenotypic Selection
(2) Pedigree Selection
(3) Selection on the Basis of Progeny

The simplest method of selection is *phenotypic* or *individual selection*. This is the systematic choosing of sires and dams in which the desired traits are most strongly visible in the hope that their traits will be passed onto the offspring. The effectiveness of selecting an individual on phenotype is influenced by the relative importance of heredity or environment in the development of the trait. Heritability is a measure of the extent to which a trait is influenced by heredity—the higher the heritability, the more the agreement between phenotype and genotype. Obviously, phenotypic selection is most effective when heritability is high. It is also most effective for simple dominant and recessive traits, which limit its use.

Pedigree selection requires detailed knowledge of the traits possessed by the ancestors of the individual under consideration. Knowledge of the phenotypes of the ancestors provides information as to what traits are genetically available in the descendant. The closer the relationship, the more useful the information; therefore, usually only the first four generations are considered. Pedigree selection is based on the principle that the average phenotypic value for the family is a good indication of the mean genotypic value. It is useful for quantitative traits. If desired traits are seen consistently down through the generations, presumably the descendant will have the genes needed for the trait and have them in greater numbers. Study of the pedigree can also give some indication of the mode of inheritance of the trait, particularly if information on the phenotypes of the siblings (indirect relatives) to the ancestors in the pedigree (direct relatives) is also known.

Selection on the basis of progeny, called progeny testing, is based on the principle that progeny reveal the genotypes of their sires and dams. With this method, you examine the phenotypes of the offspring produced by the individual in question to determine if the expected desired traits are being expressed in the offspring with minimal undesirable traits. Validity of the progeny test increases directly with the number of offspring available for examination. It must be remembered that traits of offspring are the result of the combined effect of the genes of both parents. Progeny testing can be useful to determine if the parents carry recessive genes for either desirable or undesirable traits. If traits not revealed by the phenotype of the parents show up in the offspring, and if these traits are influenced by heredity rather than the environment, it can be assumed that the parents carry the genes for these traits. On the basis of this new information as to the genotypes of the parents, the breeder can decide whether to continue to use these animals in his breeding program, depending on whether he wishes to perpetuate or extinguish these particular traits.

The wise breeder will apply all three of these methods of selection whenever possible. Selection is not simply a one-time matter, but rather an ongoing process of analysis and evaluation. The most common difficulty is that you must select for many traits at the same time, including physical attributes, behavior, fertility, and vitality. The results of selection depend on the heritability of the trait, its mode of inheritance, and the intensity of selection. Obviously, traits of higher heritability are more responsive to selection than those governed by many genes with complex interactions. Selection for a trait produced by a single recessive allele can produce maximum effects in one generation. The intensity of selection, called the *selection pressure*, is measured by the difference in phenotype of the individuals chosen for mating from that of the average of the entire population—in other words—the degree of superiority of those selected. It also implies that fewer individuals of one generation are used to produce the next, because as you move farther from the mean, the individuals available with the desired traits become fewer in number. The greater the selection pressure, the greater the response to selection.

To be a successful breeder, it is not enough to be able to select superior individuals capable of passing the desired characteristics down to their offspring. You must also understand the genetic principles underlying the various systems of breeding and apply these systems in planned matings. With purebred animals, three systems of breeding are used:

(1) Inbreeding
(2) Linebreeding
(3) Outbreeding

Inbreeding is the production of offspring by mating individuals more closely related to each other than the average population. It has been used, together with principles of selection, to produce almost every valuable breed of domestic animal and to develop recognizable strains within breeds. Genetically, inbreeding increases the homozygosity of individuals for the genes that they carry. Since related individuals are more likely to carry the same alleles for a given trait by descent from a common ancestor, the chances of an offspring acquiring identical alleles of a gene pair are increased. As succeeding generations become more homozygous for various traits, the probability that all offspring will receive the same inheritance from their inbred parents is increased, and the population becomes more uniform. Statistics have been used to quantify the degree of genetic relationships and the effect that these relationships have on increasing homozygosity. Homozygosity increases with more intense inbreeding regardless of how the genes interact and express themselves phenotypically. Inbreeding is the method that most easily and rapidly establishes a population that breeds true to type.

Increased homozygosity occurs for defective traits as well as for desirable ones. Therefore, it is imperative that the foundation sires and dams in inbreeding programs be *superior* individuals, as free from faults as possible, and that inbreeding be accompanied by ongoing selection. Many defects affecting the vitality and functioning of the animal are recessive, since defects due to dominant genes are expressed phenotypically and carriers of the defect then are more easily recognized and eliminated. The increased homozygosity from inbreeding can result in the expression of these recessives, leading some to criticize inbreeding for creating defects. However, inbreeding does not create any traits, either good or bad. It merely allows them to appear if they were carried in the original breeding stock. This fact can be used to advantage in breed improvement, because once the presence of recessive genes for a defect is known, selection can take place to eliminate them from the gene pool. Conversely, if after several generations of close inbreeding, no recessive defects appear, it is unlikely that these recessives were present in the original breeding stock. Individuals from the line can then be utilized in the breeding programs of those wishing to avoid those traits. (It must be emphasized here that not all recessive alleles result in a defective trait, and not all defective traits are the result of recessive alleles.) Inbreeding involves some risk and does require you to understand the traits of your line. But it enables the breeder to identify and sort the desirable and undesirable traits in order to produce animals of consistent quality.

Linebreeding is a breeding system that is actually a form of inbreeding. It is the selection of sires and dams both related to some unusually desirable individual in order to keep the relationship of individuals in the kennel as close as possible to the desired ancestor. Ordinary inbreeding is the mating of relatives, but there is no attempt to keep a high relationship to any particular individual. Linebreeding is indicated when some truly outstanding individual has been identifed on both the basis of phenotype and progeny testing and has the objectives of perpetuating this individual's qualities and concentrating them as much as possible. Father X daughter, half-brother X half-sister, and grandson X grandmother crosses are examples of linebreeding.

Outbreeding, or outcrossing, is the mating of unrelated dogs, or at least dogs that are not related in the most recent four or five generations. It tends to produce effects opposite those of inbreeding and linebreeding, namely, it increases heterozygosity and tends to camouflage recessive traits. It does not eliminate them, however, and they may reappear in later generations. Because of increased heterozygosity, the resulting progeny do not tend to produce as true in perpetuating their own characteristics as consistently as inbred animals.

Outbreeding is useful, however, as a means of introducing new genetic material into a population. It allows the breeder to manipulate genes in new com-

Peas in a pod...Champion Sweet Seasons of Heatherhill (Ch Wildhagen's Dutchman of Flintridge, CDX ex McCorkle's Blue Tule Fog) on the left with progeny sired by one-half brother Ch Windermere's Sunshine of Bonnie-Blu CDX. Left to right: "Seasons," Sunsweet of Heatherhill, Heavenly Sunshine of Heatherhill, Sweet 'n Sassy of Heatherhill, and Heaven Sent of Heatherhill.   *Photo by Dai*

binations, then repeat those matings which appear most successful in producing the most desirable traits. It is probably most effective when you wish to improve your line with regard to only one or a few traits, and the sires and dams chosen for the outcross matings are from inbred lines very similar to each other in all respects other than the traits to be changed. This type of outcrossing, between inbred lines that possess similar traits, is termed *positive assortative mating*. It increases the chances that genes for these similar traits will be preserved in the homozygous state, while introducing new genes for the trait to be changed. In this way, the advances made by inbreeding are less likely to be lost.

The use of the above tools will depend upon the objectives and resources of each breeder. With them, the breeder can modify the frequency of expression of traits in all sorts of combinations within the limits of the genetic material available, except those incompatible with life and reproduction. The complexity, manifested by the various forms of gene interaction and the interaction of the genotype with the environment, works to slow the breeder's attempt to shift gene frequency and produce animals most nearly approximating his view of the ideal Australian Shepherd. But it also increases the challenge of breeding improved dogs to perform major services, which, when successful, is very rewarding.

ELIMINATING HERITABLE DEFECTS

Heritable defects occur in every breed and species of animal. The abnormalities can be either structural alterations or defects in metabolism resulting from alterations in biochemical pathways. Part of the process of selection in breeding programs is eliminating genes with undesirable effects. The heritability of many abnormalities has not been demonstrated, nor has the mode of inheritance for many of them. Complicating the issue is the fact that defects resulting from external or environmental conditions often mimic those of genetic origin. Toxins, chemicals, and trauma can disrupt structural development and biochemical pathways in much the same way that faulty gene products do. However, the high recurring incidence of an abnormality within certain breeds or strains is strong evidence for its heritability.

Defects may be *congenital* (meaning present at birth) or *acquired* (meaning that they are not manifested until later in life). Congenital defects result from arrested or defective prenatal development and may be either genetic in origin or the result of external factors that cross the placental barrier. If the defect is incompatible with life, it may be manifested only as reduced litter size. In an attempt to differen-

tiate whether the defect could be the result of genetic or environmental factors, the following should be determined: (1) if any puppies from previous litters of the same parents were affected with the trait; (2) if any ancestors of the litter were affected with a similar condition; (3) the number of affected individuals in the current or previous litters or in the pedigree; and (4) the possibility of exposure of the dam to diseases, drugs, toxins, or chemicals during pregnancy. Acquired defects may likewise be genetic in origin or the result of external factors, and a similar line of questioning can help to distinguish between the two. The heritability of acquired defects is often more difficult to determine because information on siblings and ancestors may be more difficult to obtain. Another disturbing feature of some acquired heritable defects is that they may not become evident until after the individual has reached breeding age and his genes for the defective trait have already been distributed among his offspring. Most breeders find it desirable to consult a geneticist if they suspect a heritable problem.

The method of genetic management of a given defect depends on its mode on inheritance, the frequency with which it occurs, its effect of viability and fertility, and its relative importance to the breeder. All forms of gene interaction have been found to occur among the various heritable defects. The control of any hereditary abnormality is enhanced by accurate detection of the defect as early in the animal's life as possible, and especially prior to breeding age, so that

The proud pop: American Revolution CD (Sorensen's Red Man ex Taylor's Blue Prissy) and his pup Sakonnet Times (out of Beauwood's Whispering Pine). Photo by L.M. Gray

the individual exhibiting the defect can be selected against inbreeding. In addition, family studies and breeding tests are necessary to identify normal-appearing individuals carrying the genes for the trait.

Defects due to simple dominant genes are usually acquired and often do not become evident until after the individual has reached breeding age. Presumably, this is because defects due to a dominant gene are quite evident when expressed early in life, so breeders are more likely to eliminate such individuals from

results in considerable wastage, however, because if the affected parent is heterozygous for the trait, only half of its offspring will receive the gene for the trait, while the other half will be normal.

The majority of documented hereditary abnormalities are autosomal recessive, resulting in homozygous, genetically normal individuals, normal-appearing heterozygous carriers, and homozygous recessive, affected individuals. The latter group, while capable of distributing the deleterious gene to

Taylor's Whiskey (Mansker's (Lamar's) Turk ex Mansker's Anna Lee), a foundation sire known for his working progeny, owned by Joe D. Taylor of Moab, Utah.

their breeding programs, thus extinguishing the trait. Eliminating a dominant gene is simple: merely do not use individuals who exhibit that trait for breeding. For abnormalities that are not grossly evident until after an individual is old enough to breed, studies are underway to develop techniques for detecting biochemical markers that could identify the susceptible individuals at an earlier age. Two other alternatives may not be acceptable to many breeders. The first is to delay breeding the questionable individual until after the age at which the defect becomes apparent. The second is to eliminate any offspring of an individual who later develops the trait. This method

all their offspring, are obviously affected and easily eliminated from breeding programs. In addition, both parents of an affected animal, while normal themselves in appearance, are carriers of the trait, and they, too, can be eliminated for breeding purposes. The problem is in distinguishing normal-appearing, homozygous dominant animals from the normal-appearing, heterozygous carriers when the genotype is unknown. *Test crosses* are used in an attempt to determine the genotype. This is progeny testing in its simplest form. With any of the methods of test-crossing, the production of a single affected offspring is evidence that the suspect individual carries the trait.

The production of no affected offspring is *not* absolute evidence that the individual does not carry the trait but merely increases the *probability* that he doesn't, and the greater the number of unaffected offspring produced, the greater the likelihood that the suspect individual is not a carrier. Statistics have been applied by geneticists to calculate the probabilities associated with the number of unaffected offspring in the various types of test crosses.

The simplest method for detecting a normal heterozygous carrier of a recessive trait is to breed the suspect animal to one affected with the trait and whose genotype is therefore known to be homozygous for the defective recessive gene. The production of a single affected offspring proves that the suspect animal is a carrier. The chance that the suspect could be a carrier, even though no affected offspring result, is reduced to 3 in 100 when five normal progeny are produced; 1 in 100 with seven normal progeny; and 1 in 1,000 with ten normal progeny. It must be recognized, however, that all resulting progeny will themselves be carriers for the defect, so the breeder must be prepared to eliminate these from future breeding programs. Other methods of test-crossing for unknown carriers are to mate the unknown with known heterozygous carriers or to mate the unknown with its own progeny. The latter method requires crossing the unknown with multiple mates and producing large numbers of offspring and is therefore somewhat impractical. The resulting probabilities of the various methods are outlined in the table as illustrated below:

The genes for some abnormalities are found on the sex chromosomes, most commonly the X chromosome, although these traits may have nothing to do with sex determination. They are termed sex-linked. Sex-linked dominant defects are rare because they are grossly evident in both sexes and are easily eliminated. The problem arises with sex-linked recessives because they can be perpetuated by generations of females in the heterozygous state. All males who receive the allele for the trait on the X chromosome from their mothers will be affected because there is no corresponding allele on the Y chromosome to mask its effect. Fortunately, the detection of carrier females is relatively simple. If a female produces any affected progeny, she must be a carrier. There are two methods of test-crossing to detect carrier females: (1) breeding the suspect female to a known affected male; or (2) breeding the suspect female to an unaffected male. How these test-crosses function is best illustrated by the use of Punnett Squares.

The mode of inheritance of some abnormalities is thought to involve multiple sets of genes in complex interactions. These traits are generally those relating to conformation and tend to be expressed in a range of types from worse to better rather than segregated into groups of distinctly normal and distinctly abnormal. These polygenic traits do not respond to selection as rapidly as do simple dominant and recessive ones and are further complicated by the fact that their degree of expression is more subject to environmental influences. The genetic management of multiple-factor defects is basically an attempt to accumu-

Methods of Test-Crossing to Detect Heterozygous Carriers of a Simple Autosomal Recessive Trait

METHOD	NUMBER OF NORMAL PROGENY WITH NONE AFFECTED	PROBABILITY OF CARRIER STATE	COMMENTS
Unknown and Known Homozygous Recessive	5 7 10	3 in 100 1 in 100 1 in 1000	All of the progeny will be carriers of the trait.
Unknown and Known Heterozygous Carriers	11 16	5 in 100 1 in 100	Fifty percent will be carriers of the trait.
Unknown Parent and Five Unselected Unknown Progeny	11 per cross	5 in 100	The probability of the trait existing in the entire family is reduced to some extent by successful test-crossing of this type.
Unknown Parent and Seven Unselected Unknown Progeny	16 per cross	1 in 100	The probability of the trait existing in the entire family is reduced to some extent by successful test-crossing of this type.

late in the progeny more effective genes by selecting those from the upper range of the distribution for mating. Conversely, it is avoiding the use of those individuals at the poorer end of the range in the hope of decreasing the frequency of those genes leading to the less functional forms of the trait. With polygenic traits, it is usually impossible to identify all of the genes involved and the nature of all of their interactions. Thus, the usefulness of test-crosses to determine genotypes is limited. The basic principles, then, are to breed the best individuals available and those from lines in which the defect rarely appears.

Because polygenically influenced traits tend to fall along a gradient for better or worse rather than into distinct groups, it is often necessary for the breeder or breed clubs to arbitrarily assign a point in the gradient to be used as a cutoff for distinguishing acceptable versus unacceptable ranges of expression. Once this decision is made, the following recommendations for genetic management can be applied: (1) select for breeding only those individuals who fall into the acceptable range; (2) do not use for breeding those individuals who themselves are acceptable but whose

parents or siblings or progeny exhibit unacceptable expressions of the trait; or (3) give preference to those acceptable individuals from pedigrees with several generations of acceptable ancestors. Through the use of these guidelines, the incidence of certain polygenically influenced defects has been greatly reduced in certain species of animals. It logically follows that for continued improvement, once the incidence of the defective range has been reduced, the standards for determining acceptable expression of the trait should be raised.

Another tool useful in the management of traits susceptible to environmental influence is to test the individuals under conditions of stress. It has been suggested that some individuals inherit a genetic predisposition to develop an abnormality, but that the trait will not come to full expression in the individual without conducive environmental influences. Environment may determine whether the individual is acceptable or unacceptable if that individual falls in the midrange of expression of a polygenic trait. Testing under stressful conditions requires the influencing environmental factors to be identified. Once this is done,

---

UNKNOWN FEMALE X AFFECTED MALE: Punnett Squares illustrating test crosses for a sex-linked recessive trait.

If dam is a heterozygous carrier

	X^+	$X^=$
X^+	$X^+ X^+$	$X^+ X^=$
Y	$X^+ Y$	$X^= Y$

Affected Sire

Progeny: Half the daughters affected ($X^+ X^+$), half unaffected but carriers ($X^+ X^=$). Half the sons affected ($X^+ Y$), half unaffected ($X^= Y$).

If dam is homozygous noncarrier

	$X^=$	$X^=$
X^+	$X^+ X^=$	$X^+ X^=$
Y	$X^= Y$	$X^= Y$

Affected Sire

Progeny: All daughters unaffected by carriers. ($X^+ X^=$). All sons unaffected ($X^= Y$).

The statistical probabilities, that an unknown female bred to an affected male is a carrier of the defect, are measured by the number of unaffected sons produced and are similar to those for crosses between an individual of unknown genotype and a known homozygous recessive for autosomal recessive defects.

UNKNOWN FEMALE X UNAFFECTED MALE

If dam is a heterozygous carrier

	X^+	$X^=$
$X^=$	$X^+ X^=$	$X^= X^=$
Y	$X^+ Y$	$X^= Y$

Unaffected Sire

Progeny: All daughters unaffected, but half will be carriers ($\frac{1}{2} X^= X^=$ $\frac{1}{2} X^+ X^=$). Half of sons affected ($X^+ Y$), half unaffected ($X^= Y$).

If dam is a homozygous noncarrier

	$X^=$	$X^=$
$X^=$	$X^= X^=$	$X^= X^=$
Y	$X^= Y$	$X^= Y$

Unaffected Sire

Progeny: All are unaffected and none of the daughters are carriers.

The probabilities that the dam is a carrier are based on the number of unaffected sons produced and are similar to those for crosses between an individual of unknown genotype and a known heterozygous carrier for autosomal recessive defects.

McCorkles Blueberry Muffin of Coppercast CD STD-D, the foundation brood bitch for Blue Lad is with some of her offspring from the left to right: Blue Lad Ballintober (by Ch Blue Lad Texas Ranger CD, TD), Ch Blue Lad Mulberry Muffin CDX, TD, OTD-ds (by Oso Rojo of Coppercast), Maranatha Silver Trinket (by Georges Red Rustler), Ch Blue Lad Texas Ranger CD, TD (by Ch Peace Pipe Birch Bark), Blue Lad Roxanna (by Ch Peace Pipe Birch Bark), Blue Lad Checkmate (by Blue Lad Rocky Road), and "Old Muffin" herself.   *Courtesy Spicuzza*

the breeder must be willing to provide the environment conducive to expression of the trait. Individuals who do not exhibit the trait under adverse conditions are considered less likely to possess the genes for the trait, and presumably their selection for breeding purposes will lead to an even greater decreased incidence of the trait under desirable conditions. Unfortunately, many breeders attempt to provide the environment that will least cause the trait to be expressed. This is understandable but leads to the defect being masked and, therefore, the genes for it to be retained in the population.

SOME TRAITS OF KNOWN OR PROBABLE INHERITANCE

For many traits—often those of most concern to the breeder—the heritability and mode of inheritance have not been determined. Many, including refinements of conformation, fertility, vitality, size, and maturity, are thought to involve so many gene pairs in such complex interactions that it is virtually beyond our present state of knowledge to identify all of the factors involved. The challenge, then, is to intelligently apply basic genetic principles in breeding programs in an effort to achieve the desired results. Other traits of relatively simple inheritance or those having a drastic impact on a species have been sufficiently studied. Described below are a few traits that may be of interest to the breeder or fancier of the Australian Shepherd.

Coat Color

Ten different loci have been identified as determiners of coat color in canines. These loci are believed to reside on different pairs of homologous chromosomes and are therefore inherited independently. Multiple alleles have been identified for each locus,

and the expression of many alleles over certain ranges suggests the existence of as yet unidentified modifiers. The ten loci for coat color are believed to be constant between all the breeds of the canine species, with selection pressure having resulted in the concentration of certain alleles within breeds to produce consistent color characteristics.

Eye Color

The mode of inheritance of eye color has not been clearly elucidated. It probably involves interaction between coat color and eye color genes. An allelic series of genes for eye color has been postulated. Some authors suggest that the series contains three alleles; others, two. Whether dominance is partial or complete among the alleles is a matter of debate, although most agree that darker eyes tend to be more dominant. Most believe that dogs of liver base coat color will express their genotype for the eye color locus as a lighter shade than their black counterparts, even though they may have identical genotypes at the eye color locus. The interaction of genes for eye and coat color is a reasonable assumption, because the pigments for both are similar in embryologic tissue origin and are produced by the same metabolic pathways. The scientific community is in agreement that the partially or completely blue eyes seen in merled breeds relates in some way to the coat color gene for merling, as it is not normally seen in the solid body color pattern for these breeds. The varying shades of blue and combinations with brown or amber are explained on the basis of unknown modifiers affecting the penetrance of the blue trait. In fact, it is not uncommon for merles to have eyes that are completely brown or amber, although ophthalmic examination of portions of the eye other than the iris usually reveals a decrease in pigmentation brought on by the merle gene.

Known Genes for Coat Color

LOCUS	ALLELE	EFFECT	COMMENTS
B		Determines basic background color.	Dominance is complete among alleles of this locus.
	B	Produces black pigment.	Acceptable under the ASCA Breed Standard.
	b	Produces red pigment.	Acceptable under the ASCA Breed Standard.
C		Determines depth of pigmentation.	Dominance is thought to be complete among alleles.
	C	Allows full depth of pigmentation.	
	c^{ch}	Chinchilla; produces lighter shades by reducing the number and size of pigment granules, but does not affect black pigment; may play a role in lightening eye color.	Probably results in paling of copper trim; may play a role, together with modifiers, in producing the various shades of red.
	c^e	Existence of this allele not definite; hypothesized to produce extreme dilution of liver to cream with little effect on black.	Cream is not an acceptable color under the ASCA Breed Standard.
	c^a	In the homozygous state produces complete albinism, resulting in a white animal with pink eyes.	Rare in dogs; albinos are not acceptable under the ASCA Breed Standard.
A		Modifies the basic pigments (black and liver) to produce tan (copper) by restricting an enzyme necessary for their full production; alleles of this series determine the regions of the body or hair shaft in which these modifiers occur.	Dominance among alleles of this series is thought to be mostly complete.
	A^s	Distributes base pigment over the entire body.	Occurs in those Australian Shepherds without copper trim; acceptable under the ASCA Breed Standard.
	a^y	Restricts the areas of base pigment in the individual hairs to produce sable or, in its most extreme, a uniform tan color.	Not acceptable colors under the ASCA Breed Standard.
	a^w	Existence of this allele not definitely established, nor has its position of dominance; hypothesized to produce the banded hairs of wild canidae.	Not acceptable under the ASCA Breed Standard.
	a^t	Restricts pigment in the following areas to produce the typical "tan point" pattern: sides of muzzle, throat, chest and belly line, over each eye, on feet and part of legs, around the anus.	Occurs in those Australian Shepherds with "copper trim"; an acceptable color pattern under the ASCA Breed Standard.
D		Determines intensity of base pigments.	Dominance among alleles is complete.
	D	Causes normal intense pigmentation.	All purebred Australian Shepherds are DD.
	d	Causes the flat, uniform bluish color "Maltese dilution" (not to be confused with the blue of blue merles).	Not acceptable under the ASCA Breed Standard.

LOCUS	ALLELE	EFFECT	COMMENTS
E		A complicated group of alleles which modify basic pigments in varying ways.	Dominance is usually complete, although E may be incompletely dominant to e^{br}.
	E^m	Induces "black mask" pattern; displaces tan points, when present, on the head.	Not known to be present in pure-bred Australian Shepherds.
	E	No effect if base pigment is black; changes liver pigment to brown.	Brown is not an acceptable color under the ASCA Breed Standard.
	e^{br}	Produces "brindling" (dark mottling) of base coat color.	Not known to occur in purebred Australian Shepherds; not an acceptable pattern under the ASCA Breed Standard.
G		Determines intensity of pigment with age.	Dominance is partial.
	G	Produces progressive, uniform graying from birth to old age in dogs born uniform color (not to be confused with graying of old age, which occurs mainly around the head in geriatric individuals).	Not known to occur in purebred Australian Shepherds
	g	Produces no such graying.	Probably all purebred Australian Shepherds are gg.
M		Responsible for the two basic patterns (solid and merle) recognized by the ASCA Breed Standard.	Dominance is incomplete.
	M	Produces irregular patches of dilution of base coat color over the body; in the heterozygous state (Mm) it results in the typical merle color pattern; the homozygous state (MM) produces excessive dilution, resulting in nearly completely white individuals often accompanied by eye and ear defects probably as the result of pleiotropic effects of the gene.	Merling (the heterozygous state) is an acceptable pattern under the ASCA Breed Standard; the mostly white coloration resulting from the homozygous state is not acceptable due to the frequency of associated eye and ear defects; merle and merle crosses result in one-fourth of the offspring being homozygous merles, and recommendations are that these individuals be euthanatized at birth.
	m	Produces uniform, undiluted ("solid") base coat color in the homozygous state.	An acceptable color pattern under the ASCA Breed Standard; solids are often crossed with merles to avoid producing defective white puppies for the merle gene.
S		Produces white in various distributions over the body.	Dominance of alleles of this series is complete, although modifiers may result in overlapping expression of the alleles; alleles of this series are inherited independently of the white resulting from the homozygous merle gene.
	S	Results in coat with no white trim or with very minute spots on the toes and chest.	An acceptable color pattern under ASCA Breed Standard.
	s^i	Produces white trim on one or more of the following areas: muzzle, forehead, feet and legs, chest, belly, or neck.	An acceptable color pattern under the ASCA Breed Standard.

LOCUS	ALLELE	EFFECT	COMMENTS
	s^p	Produces a variable amount of white over the body, ranging from an amount similar to the white trim produced by s^i to 85 percent white; the white produced by this allele is more irregular in location and distribution than that produced by s^i.	Not an acceptable color pattern under the ASCA Breed Standard, although it is known to occur in purebred Australian Shepherds; it may phenotypically resemble the white caused by the homozygous merle condition, potentially causing confusion in culling practices were it not for the fact that both patterns are unacceptable.
	s^w	Produces white in an extreme distribution, limiting dark color to only an ear, eye, or tail patch.	Not an acceptable color pattern under the ASCA Breed Standard for s^p.
T		Determines whether dark spots will appear in white areas.	Dominance is complete; no preference is given to either allele over the other by the ASCA Breed Standard.
	T	Produces "ticking," flecks of color, on areas of white determined by genes at other loci.	
	t	No ticking produced; white areas are clear.	
P		Deals with a very rare dilution caused by the recessive allele (pp).	Only the dominant normal allele (P) of this series occurs in purebred Australian Shepherds, so this loci is of little significance.

Tail Length

The mode of inheritance for bobtails has not been established, although most geneticists have concluded that it is due to multiple factors. Breeding tests and family studies among various breeds suggest that shorter tails tend to be dominant over longer tails, although usually not completely so. There is also evidence that the factors affecting tail length are probably polygenic, because tails of varying lengths have been observed in single litters among matings of sires and dams born with various phenotypes. It is worthy of mention that among other breeds of dogs and species of animals, selection for naturally occurring bobtails has been accompanied by an increased incidence of malformation of the posterior vertebrae and spinal cord, resulting in neurologic deficits such as fecal and urinary incontinence and abnormalities of gait or stance in the rear limbs. It should be noted that the ASCA Breed Standard accepts either naturally occurring bobtails or docked tails with no order of preference. Its only stipulation is that tails are to be four inches or under in length regardless of whether this length is achieved naturally or by surgical intervention.

Relationship of the Jaws

The attention paid to the relationship between the upper and lower jaws, or "bite" as it is termed, by the breed standards of many breeds, including the Aussie, reflects the importance of this trait to the well-being and functioning of the animal. Under many breed standards, abnormality in the relationship is cause for disqualification of the animal from the show ring. Much to the frustration of the conscientious breeder, the number of genes involved and their mode of inheritance are by no means completely understood. There is general agreement that multiple factors are involved and that they are inherited independently for each jaw. The common abnormalities—"overshot" and "undershot" bites—are the result of disproportionate growth between the upper and lower jaws due to their genetic independence. Different factors may act at different stages of growth, resulting in abnormal bites appearing at various ages during the growth period.

Due to their vulnerable position on the body, the jaws and teeth are highly susceptible to trauma. A traumatic accident in the growing individual may result in a defect in the relationship of the teeth, which mimics a genetic abnormality of the jaw assembly. It is of utmost importance in selecting individuals for breeding to be able to distinguish between abnormalities of genetic origin and those due to external factors. The incisor teeth, by virtue of their position and less secure attachment by a single root, are most susceptible to modifications in direction to growth as the result of injury. Thus, the common practice of determining bite by the relationship of the upper and lower incisors is less than reliable. (This relationship in the "scissors" bite is one of the upper incisors overlapping the lower incisors, with their opposing surfaces touching.) Evaluation of bite is more accurately accomplished by examining the relationship of the canine and premolar teeth. The correct bite requires the lower canine tooth to interlock between the outermost upper incisor and the upper canine, and for the premolars to intermesh with each other, with the lower premolars in front of their upper counterparts. Once individuals have been properly evaluated for correct jaw assembly, selection for this trait can take place as for any trait of polygenic inheritance.

Hip Dysplasia

Hip dysplasia is a defect in the conformation of the hip joint and is known to occur in most breeds of dogs. It is of concern to the breeder and fancier alike because it can result in severe pain and crippling of the dog. It is an inherited trait with a polygenic mode of inheritance. The basic defect appears to be an acetabulum (hip socket) that is more shallow than normal. This results in excessive laxity in the hip joint, which over time produces secondary changes in the

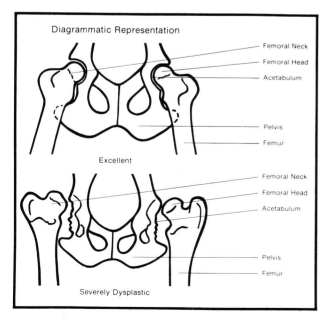

Artwork courtesy of "Purina Kennel News"

shapes of the bones composing the joint in the body's effort to compensate. Diagnosis of hip dysplasia is made by radiographs which are best taken between two and five years of age. In a younger animal, the secondary bony changes may not yet be evident, and defects in the acetabulum may be so slight as to be difficult to detect. Normal wear and tear of aging may make it difficult to distinguish such changes from those due to the heritable defect in aged individuals. There is often poor correlation between the occurrence of hip dysplasia and outward symptoms in individual animals, so freedom from pain and lameness is no guarantee that the animal is free of the defect.

The Orthopedic Foundation for Animals (OFA) was established to encourage breeders to have their dogs' hips radiographed and evaluated by providing a program in which dogs proven phenotypically free of hip dysplasia can be certified as such. In addition, the OFA established guidelines for rating the quality of hip joint conformation in normal animals and the severity of hip dysplasia in affected ones. Like all polygenic traits, hip dysplasia is manifested by a range of expression which is partially influenced by environmental factors. Diet, growth rate, and level of activity in growing puppies have been implicated. Some misguided breeders have attempted to lower the incidence and severity of dysplasia in their kennels by providing an artificially favorable environment. However it must be remembered that this does not alter the basic genotype and only serves to perpetuate the genes for dysplasia. Breeding recommendations for decreasing the genetic incidence of hip dyplasia are the same as for any trait of suspected polygenic origin. Breeding studies, using only nondysplastic individuals from dysplasia-free families, have proven the effectiveness of this method in lowering the incidence of hip dysplasia. There is no evidence proving that "excellent" hip joint conformation ratings are significantly better in lowering the incidence of development of hip dysplasia in subsequent progeny than "good" ratings. Perhaps this is because differences in conformation at this refined level are due to factors other than those influencing hip dysplasia or to environmental influences. For the purposes of decreasing the incidence of hip dysplasia, selection simply on the basis of freedom from dysplasia without regard to hip joint conformation ratings appears to be sufficient.

Ocular Dysgenesis with Variable Deafness

A complex of eye defects accompanied by variable degrees of deafness is seen in excessively white Australian Shepherds believed to be homozygous for the merling gene. These defects occur in varying degrees and combinations and include the following:

(1) reduced size of the entire eye (microphthalmia); (2) incomplete development, fissuring, and outpocketing of tissues in various parts of the eye; (3) detachment of the retina (the layer of tissue in the back of the eye responsible for receiving and transmitting light impulses to the brain) from underlying supporting structures; (4) abnormal shape and position of the pupils; and (5) incomplete development of the optic nerve and blood vessels supplying the eye. This complex is inherited as an autosomal recessive trait with incomplete penetrance, and whether it is the result of pleiotropic effects of the merle gene or of a separate gene positioned on the same chromosome (linked) at a locus close to the merle gene has not been definitely established. However, breeding studies tend to support the former. Pigments are thought to play an essential role in the embryologic development of vital structures in the eye and ear. Apparently, a certain threshold level of pigments is required for the normal and complete development of these structures. It has been theorized that the merle gene, when present in the homozygous state, inhibits pigment production to a quantity below the threshold level required for normal development. Because these are defects in embryologic development, this complex is considered a congenital abnormality detectable grossly or by ophthalmic examination in early life.

Merling is valued as a unique contributor to the characteristics of the Australian Shepherd breed. The retention of this trait in heterozygous individuals will probably prevent the ocular dysgenesis complex from ever being completely eliminated. However, genetic principles of selection and a willingness on the part of breeders to destroy affected individuals at a young age can greatly reduce its significance. When *normal merled* individuals are mated, approximately 25 percent of the resulting progeny can be expected to be of solid base coat color (mm), 50 percent merles of heterozygous constitution (Mm), and 25 percent excessively white homozygous merles (MM). Recognizing the association of the homozygous condition for merling with the ocular dysgenesis complex while desiring to retain the merle trait, conscientious breeders have adopted the practice of euthanatizing excessively white puppies at birth. Others, seeking to avoid this necessary task, have preferred to avoid merle matings. Matings of merles to solid individuals or solids to solids should produce no excessively white homozygous puppies, providing the phenotypes of the mates accurately represent their genotypes. It is important to distinguish the excessive white of the homozygous merle condition from white occurring as the result of other independently inherited genes, such as those for white markings.

Ocular defects, other than the ocular dysgenesis complex, have also been reported in the Australian Shepherd. Some of these defects are believed to be genetically influenced, but their modes of inheritance

Punnett Square illustrating the probabilities associated with merle X solid matings.

Merled parent

		M	m
Solid parent	m	Mm	mm
	m	Mm	mm

Progeny: 50% heterozygous merles (Mm), 50% homozygous nonmerles (mm). None of the progeny express the ocular dysgenesis complex.

Punnett Square illustrating the probabilities associated with solid X solid matings.

Solid parent

		m	m
Solid parent	m	mm	mm
	m	mm	mm

Progeny: 100% homozygous nonmerled (solid) individuals with none of the progeny expressing or carrying the gene for the ocular dysgenesis complex.

Punnett Square illustrating the probabilities associated with merle X merle matings.

Merled parent

		M	m
Merled Parent	M	MM	Mm
	m	Mm	mm

Progeny:

¼ homozygous nonmerles (mm): These individuals are solid in base coat color and have normal eyes.

½ heterozygous merles (Mm): These individuals are of the typical merle pattern and have normal eyes.

¼ homozygous merles (MM): These individuals are excessively white and express the ocular dysgenesis complex.

have not been definitely established. The defects reported include retinal dysplasia and cataracts. Retinal dysplasia is abnormal development of the retina, resulting in its folding and detachment. Detachment may sometimes progress with the age of the animal and result in complete blindness. Retinal dysplasia is a congenital defect and can be detected by ophthalmic examination early in life. A cataract is any opacity of the lens. Cataracts can be congenital or acquired, and either form may be the result of either hereditary or environmental factors. Family studies and a detailed history of the potential exposure of an affected individual to inducing environmental factors may be necessary to determine whether a cataract is the result of inheritance of extrinsic factors in a given individual.

The Canine Eye Registration Foundation (CERF) has been established to study the incidence and inheritance patterns of eye defects in dogs. Like the OFA with hip dysplasia, CERF has developed a certification program for animals ophthalmically examined and determined to be phenotypically free of inheritable ocular defects. It has been recommended that puppies be examined at eight weeks of age to detect congenital heritable defects. In all domestic species, the eye undergoes some further maturation in the first few weeks of life. By eight weeks of age in the dog, congenital eye defects have usually reached fuller expression, resulting in more accurate detection. Because other inherited ocular abnormalities are acquired and, therefore, may not be detectable until late in life, CERF recommends annual reexamination of apparently normal animals, especially through five years of age. Since the modes of inheritance of many heritable ocular defects have not been established, specific breeding recommendations cannot be provided. However, it is generally advised not to breed any animals that are affected with potentially heritable ocular defects nor their close relatives.

Champion Las Rocosa Shiloh (Boehmer's Four Man ex Hosmer's Jill), one of the nation's leading sires of Certified Working Dogs and Champions of Record noted for their intense working style.

Behavior

Dogs, like human beings, exhibit different personalities. Genetic mechanisms associated with structural characteristics have been studied much more thoroughly and successfully than those of behavior. This is due to the complexity of behavior and to the fact that behavior is developed under the combined influences of both heredity and the environment. Detailed breeding studies have shown that different genes become active at different developmental stages the differences in social responses to man—trainability. On the other hand, the inheritance of such traits as the ability to perform well in particular situations and problem-solving capabilities tends to be very complex, mediated by numerous independent genetic factors. As a result, these traits exhibit broader ranges of expression that are more susceptible to the influences of environment. It is of interest to note that no correlation was found between behavioral patterns and conformational "type" within breeds, except where the expression of a behavioral trait was limited

George's Red Rustler (Ginther's Rusty ex Ginther's Red Velvet), recipient of "Dog World" Award of Canine Distinction. "Red Rustler" is the foundation sire of Copper Canyon.

Photo by Thom Carter

and that their expression during periods of activity may be modified by earlier environmental experience. The modes of inheritance of some behavioral traits, however, have been found to be rather simple, depending on only a few genes. These traits are modifiable only by experience within a limited range. These traits include differences in emotional reactions, such as gregariousness versus shyness, inquisitiveness versus reticence, and passiveness versus aggression, and by physical capacities. Despite the complex nature of behavior, it is possible to alter behavioral traits, within certain ranges, by the process of selection. By identifying individuals that exhibit the most favorable behavioral traits and selecting them for use in breeding programs, the genetic factors responsible for the desired traits will tend to be concentrated in succeeding generations. In this way, individuals capable of providing major services to man, probably the most important of which is companionship, are more likely to be consistently produced.

The list of traits described above is far from exhaustive. Readers are encouraged to consult the various texts available on canine genetics for information on other traits. As stated previously, the information on heritability and modes of inheritance for traits specific to the Australian Shepherd is limited. The genetics of certain, but not all, traits is similar among breeds. However, for other traits, different modes of inheritance have been determined for different breeds. Therefore, you must not be too hasty in drawing conclusions from other breeds with regard to the inheritance of traits in the Australian Shepherd. Likewise, it is important to try to differentiate whether a trait is governed more by genetics or by the environment. This is sometimes difficult because some traits, resulting mainly from the animal's genetic constitution, can appear similar or even identical to ones caused mainly by extrinsic factors. Only extensive family studies and breeding trials can prove the tendency for a trait to be inherited, and even then the results may be inconclusive. By increasing the scope of scientific inquiry and applying good judgement and basic genetic principles, our understanding of the Australian Shepherd and progress in breed development can be greatly enhanced.

Blue Heather of Windermere (George's Red Rustler ex Wilson's Little Annie UD), the foundation dam of Windermere, produced numerous breed greats.
Courtesy Williams

Hartnagle's Hud (Taylor's Whiskey ex Taylor's Buena).

Type setting is accomplished through a well-planned breeding program. Line and in-breeding can be valuable tools. Las Rocosa Rowdear CD (Las Rocosa Sydney by Taylor's Whiskey, ex Coffee's Fancy, a Hartnagle's Hud granddaughter) shows strong family resemblance to Hartnagle's Hud.
Courtesy Bunten

13
BREEDING CONCEPTS

Breeding the Australian Shepherd is not quite as simple as breeding a flock of sheep or dairy and beef cattle. In the latter, you are breeding for a known, concrete factor: mutton or wool, beef or butterfat. Unlike breeding livestock, in which you are reproducing a visible, concrete factor, breeding dogs is trying to reproduce and improve a less tangible quality: PERFORMANCE. Performance stems from physical ability and "want to" and is closely tied to general conformation. No matter how much "want to " a dog may possess, it is of little value if he does not have the physical ability to allow him to perform. On the other hand, if a dog is extremely capable of performing and does not "want to," it is of equally little value.

The capable breeder aims not simply for type and conformation, but also for style, temperament, and "heart" or endurance, since those are the qualities that determine superior performance. It is clear that breeding for qualities such as desire, style, and temperament is not an easy task, especially when those qualities must be accompanied by the ability to perform.

An Aussie's temperament is an essential ingredient for performance. The need for disposition is equal to that for conformation. Temperament is closely associated with "trainability" and with the desire to execute tasks when called on. "Heart" is endurance. It is the ability to work when tired and to give that extra effort. Conformation is the freedom of movement that makes the task easier to accomplish.

Pedigrees are a key to the background and help indicate consistency for certain traits that have been passed on through the generations.

PEDIGREES

The pedigree is a family tree. It is the record of an individual's sire and dam in both name and performance, and it reflects the performance of the ancestry as far back as permits.

To some, the pedigree is a myriad of names with little or no meaning. The pedigree is no guarantee that the subject of the pedigree is any better or worse for having the document. For the future breeder, it is an indispensable point of reference. It establishes the strain (or strains) from which the individual has descended, and in this way, the breeder or owner may be able to determine the possible and probable tendencies of the sire and dam. It also gives the breeder the opportunity to delve into the history of his (or her) Aussie and to help him find suitable, appropriate mates for the future.

BREED STANDARD

The Breed Standard will help you more closely determine an ideal specimen. (See also "Interpreting the Breed Standard.") The Breed Standard must be utmost and unaltered in the breeder's mind.

SETTING GOALS

A breeding program must have the proper correlation of conformation, bloodlines, and performance as represented by individuals which, when crossed will produce with all consistency possible an ideal. The program can, will, and should vary if results are not forthcoming, but the ideal or goal cannot be altered if permanent improvement is to be achieved. Only failure awaits the breeder who does not know what he desires, as every breeder has the option to vary his program. Every successful breeder is always constant in his goals.

Breeders need to study family characteristics—the good points as well as the undesirable ones. Being aware of any possible weakness as well as the strengths leads to an intelligent breeding program.

Any progressive breeder must have an ideal in mind. The constructive breeder should always try to be an impartial judge of his own product and of the products of other lines. If he loses the ability to look with an impartial eye and an open mind at both the virtues and faults of his own Aussies, the chances of realizing a goal and improvement are very slim.

THE BROOD BITCH

The value of a good brood bitch is considerable, and the value of a great one is incalculable. Not only does 50 percent of all hereditary material go into the offspring from the bitch, but according to her desirable matronly qualities, she is largely responsible for the puppies getting off to a good start.

Taylor's Lola (Taylor's Whiskey ex Taylor's Buena) with a litter sired by Champion Stonehenge Justin Case of Las Rocosa, a blue merle. The resulting litter from a merle to a solid (with or without white and/or copper trim) can consist of both merle and solid progeny.

The brood bitch is the cornerstone of a bloodline for generations. Care in selecting a foundation female will influence the strength of your bloodline and the future of the breed. If you are someday fortunate enough or wise enough to possess a truly great brood bitch—one that is a pleasure to work, a joy to be around, that possesses ideal characteristics, and that also has the ability to transmit them—do not part with her! If she transmits those great qualities, you will someday develop pleasing uniformity of type, dis-

position, soundness, and working qualities that establish a bloodline and make breed improvement possible.

For those who are trying to establish a breeding program, it is best to acquire a *proven* brood bitch. Her progeny serve as a valuable evaluation for consistency in type and quality. Although most breeders cannot and/or will not part with a bitch of this caliber, sometimes circumstances make a foundation bitch available to discriminate buyers. The good, proven bitch also has unlimited access to good studs.

If a proven bitch is not available, an excellent option would be to obtain a top-quality daughter of the bitch. A strong lineage should be considered. The visible characteristics possessed by the bitch, also known as the phenotype, play a role in choosing future breeding stock. A top-winning bitch does not always have the ability to throw "top-winning" traits to the offspring, but the chances of reproducing quality from a strong, quality lineage is far greater than producing quality from a superior-quality specimen with an inferior ancestry. Always remember that a title bestowed upon any individual Aussie is *no* guarantee of her ability to produce. Ancestry should be considered, especially in unproven bitches. The conformation must be good, and her dam must be a good individual. These bitches are then considered as prospective breeding stock. However, if their progeny do not measure up, the sire's quality should be considered, as he contributes the other 50 percent. If a certain cross does not produce a greater portion of offspring that are at least as good as the dam, then she should be bred to a different stud. After breeding her to three or more studs with no luck, then it is wise to eliminate her from the breeding program as a brood bitch. A bitch of this nature can still make an excellent performance animal.

For proven bitches, the performance, conformation, and background all come into play. When judging the progeny to determine the quality of a proven brood bitch, there must be a determining factor, such as an overall impression for the consistency of quality or the lack of it.

A strong ancestry of top-producing bitches is exceptional to a lineage with a solid background of top-producing sires, because a superior stud can be found or can appear in a greater number of pedigrees since he can be bred to a larger number of females in a lifetime. For example, if a sire breeds a different female for each month in a year, he is capable of siring twelve litters. If the average litter consists of six puppies, then he has sired seventy-two offspring. By comparison, the offspring of a superior foundation bitch is limited to the litters that she may have in the same lifetime. A female that is bred twice in one year is capable of having two litters. By relative comparison of the average litter size being six puppies, then this bitch has produced twelve puppies in the same given period.

However, it must not be misinterpreted that the sire is of less importance, since the consistency in quality of any individual is equally dependent on both the sire and dam, who each contribute 50 percent.

The general health and reproductive soundness in the ancestors are especially important in the brood bitch. Any reproductive weakness and/or ill health harbored in a bitch will carry through to the offspring. Before you have control over it, you have instilled a weakness that makes breeding the finest individuals next to impossible. This also limits the gene pool. It is not only expensive to "baby" such inadequacy, but detrimental to the health and soundness of the breed in general.

In the wild, reproductive problems are unaided by man's devices and are therefore eliminated. Usually, if a bitch has a difficult time during mating, she may have a problem whelping. It is nature's way of preventing a fault from passing on.

For all practical purposes, it is of little value to place a great deal of emphasis on ancestry beyond the fourth generation. The greatest genetic contribution is attained from the sire, the dam, the grandparents, and the great-grandparents. Although a bloodline is well established with the stability of sixty-two ancestors in the fifth generation, it is highly unlikely that any generations beyond the fifth and sixth have a great deal of influence on the offspring.

THE STUD DOG

The selection of a potential sire is a grave responsibility. Any sire offered "at stud" can serve many bitches and therefore have a large number of offspring. Because of this, his quality—either good or bad—leaves its mark on the breed.

Champion Coppertone's Cactus of Bonnie-Blu CD (Ch Wildhagen's Dutchman of Flintridge CDX ex Wildhagen's Thistle of Flintridge) with Champion Kline's Blue Heather of Coppertone CD (Heard's Salt of Flintridge ex Ch Shank's Ginks CD) are two of the foundation dogs for the Coppertone line.

Courtesy Kline

A sire must have all-around excellence through his ancestry. A male himself should have a strong constitution combined with charisma, desire, trainability, temperament, and heart packaged in a well-balanced, sound structure. He must, beyond question, be able to transmit his phenotype to his progeny—prepotent—for said characteristics.

In selecting a sire, the criteria is exactly the same as in choosing a brood bitch. Keep in mind that you are breeding the *whole* inheritance of a sire, not just his phenotype (what you see), regardless how extraordinary he himself may be.

If you are unsure about a young or unproven male that looks exceptional, you may want to go back to the fountainhead and breed to his sire, which would give you at least one-half brothers bloodwise for all practical purposes with which to continue.

Breeding is not an exact science. There is no one formula that will insure success to every breeder, and

Strong family traits, a consistency of type passed through the sire line. Left to right all sired by George's Red Rustler: Maggie of Copper Canyon (out of Faxon's Jamie), Champion Bright Future of Windermere (out of Wilson's Little Annie UD), "George's Red Rustler" (Ginter's Rusty ex Ginthers Red Velvet), Champion Copper Canyon Caligari CD (out of Quaglino's Miss Pooh), De Rose's Blue Velvet (out of De Rose's Sally), Hoyt's Dago Moreno UD (out of Faxon's Donnagal).

Courtesy George

no two dogs are alike. It is often said that serious breeding is an art. The combined instincts of the breeder to cross certain individuals, lines, and types become subject, knowingly or unknowingly, to a medium of genetics. Genetics is correctly defined as an unexacting science.

On the far left is Champion Coles Buttons of Talkook STD-csd (Coles Bandit ex Coles Cajun Queen) pictured winning the Brood Bitch class at the 1981 ASCA National Specialty with her progeny by Champion Poudre Silver Sage of Coppertone (Heard's Salt of Flintridge ex Ch Shanks' Ginks).
Courtesy Cole

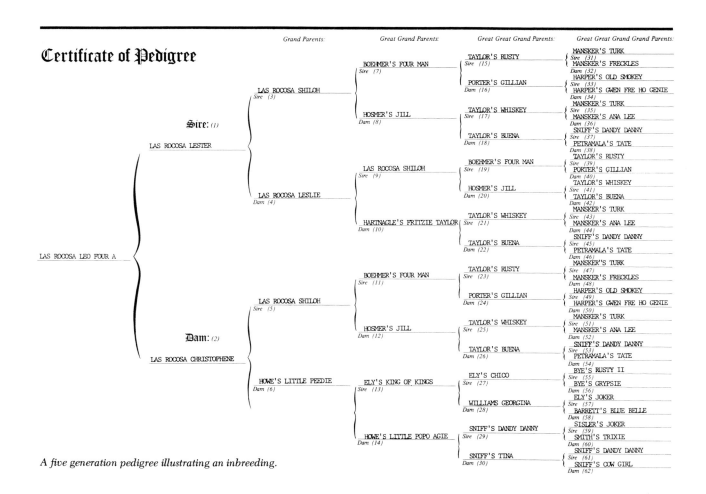

Certificate of Pedigree

A five generation pedigree illustrating an inbreeding.

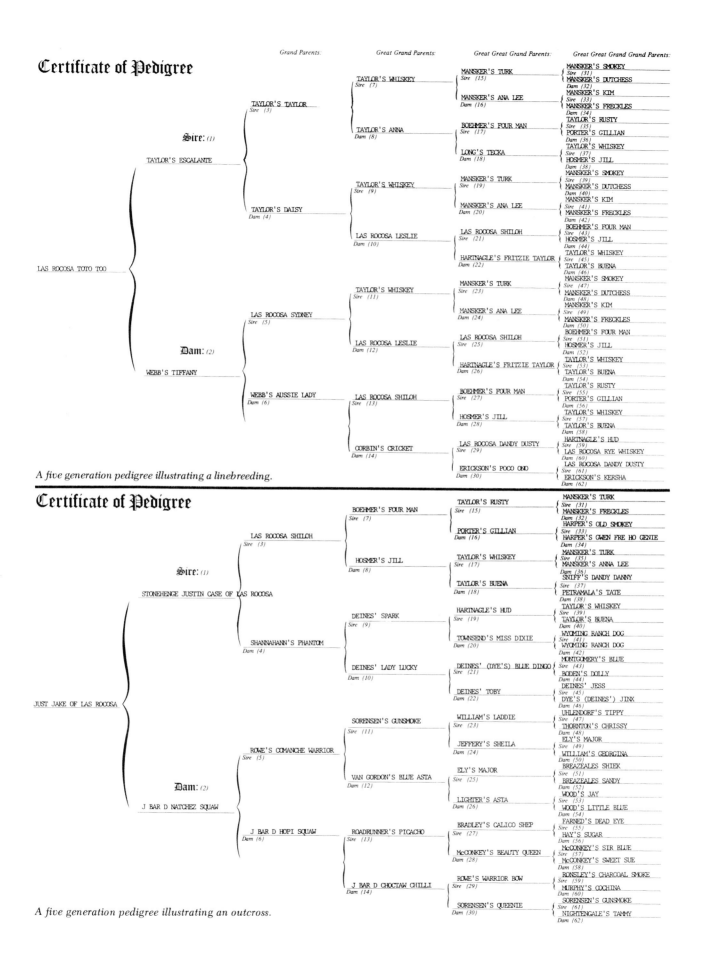

Certificate of Pedigree

	Grand Parents:	Great Grand Parents:	Great Great Grand Parents:	Great Great Grand Grand Parents:

Sire: (1)
TAYLOR'S ESCALANTE

Dam: (2)
WEBB'S TIFFANY

LAS ROCOSA TOTO TOO

TAYLOR'S TAYLOR — Sire (3)
TAYLOR'S DAISY — Dam (4)
LAS ROCOSA SYDNEY — Sire (5)
WEBB'S AUSSIE LADY — Dam (6)

TAYLOR'S WHISKEY — Sire (7)
TAYLOR'S ANNA — Dam (8)
TAYLOR'S WHISKEY — Sire (9)
LAS ROCOSA LESLIE — Dam (10)
TAYLOR'S WHISKEY — Sire (11)
LAS ROCOSA LESLIE — Dam (12)
LAS ROCOSA SHILOH — Sire (13)
CORBIN'S CRICKET — Dam (14)

MANSKER'S TURK — Sire (15)
MANSKER'S ANA LEE — Dam (16)
BOEHMER'S FOUR MAN — Sire (17)
LONG'S TECKA — Dam (18)
MANSKER'S TURK — Sire (19)
MANSKER'S ANA LEE — Dam (20)
LAS ROCOSA SHILOH — Sire (21)
HARTNAGLE'S FRITZIE TAYLOR — Dam (22)
MANSKER'S TURK — Sire (23)
MANSKER'S ANA LEE — Dam (24)
LAS ROCOSA SHILOH — Sire (25)
HARTNAGLE'S FRITZIE TAYLOR — Dam (26)
BOEHMER'S FOUR MAN — Sire (27)
HOSMER'S JILL — Dam (28)
LAS ROCOSA DANDY DUSTY — Sire (29)
ERICKSON'S POCO ONO — Dam (30)

MANSKER'S SMOKEY — Sire (31)
MANSKER'S DUTCHESS — Dam (32)
MANSKER'S KIM — Sire (33)
MANSKER'S FRECKLES — Dam (34)
TAYLOR'S RUSTY — Sire (35)
PORTER'S GILLIAN — Dam (36)
TAYLOR'S WHISKEY — Sire (37)
HOSMER'S JILL — Dam (38)
MANSKER'S SMOKEY — Sire (39)
MANSKER'S DUTCHESS — Dam (40)
MANSKER'S KIM — Sire (41)
MANSKER'S FRECKLES — Dam (42)
BOEHMER'S FOUR MAN — Sire (43)
HOSMER'S JILL — Dam (44)
TAYLOR'S WHISKEY — Sire (45)
TAYLOR'S BUENA — Dam (46)
MANSKER'S SMOKEY — Sire (47)
MANSKER'S DUTCHESS — Dam (48)
MANSKER'S KIM — Sire (49)
MANSKER'S FRECKLES — Dam (50)
BOEHMER'S FOUR MAN — Sire (51)
HOSMER'S JILL — Dam (52)
TAYLOR'S WHISKEY — Sire (53)
TAYLOR'S BUENA — Dam (54)
TAYLOR'S RUSTY — Sire (55)
PORTER'S GILLIAN — Dam (56)
TAYLOR'S WHISKEY — Sire (57)
TAYLOR'S BUENA — Dam (58)
HARTNAGLE'S HUD — Sire (59)
LAS ROCOSA RYE WHISKEY — Dam (60)
LAS ROCOSA DANDY DUSTY — Sire (61)
ERICKSON'S KERSHA — Dam (62)

A five generation pedigree illustrating a linebreeding.

Certificate of Pedigree

	Grand Parents:	Great Grand Parents:	Great Great Grand Parents:	Great Great Grand Grand Parents:

Sire: (1)
STONEHENGE JUSTIN CASE OF LAS ROCOSA

Dam: (2)
J BAR D NATCHEZ SQUAW

JUST JAKE OF LAS ROCOSA

LAS ROCOSA SHILOH — Sire (3)
SHANNAHANN'S PHANTOM — Dam (4)
ROWE'S COMANCHE WARRIOR — Sire (5)
J BAR D HOPI SQUAW — Dam (6)

BOEHMER'S FOUR MAN — Sire (7)
HOSMER'S JILL — Dam (8)
DEINES' SPARK — Sire (9)
DEINES' LADY LUCKY — Dam (10)
SORENSEN'S GUNSMOKE — Sire (11)
VAN GORDON'S BLUE ASTA — Sire (12)
ROADRUNNER'S PICACHO — Sire (13)
J BAR D CHOCTAW CHILLI — Dam (14)

TAYLOR'S RUSTY — Sire (15)
PORTER'S GILLIAN — Dam (16)
TAYLOR'S WHISKEY — Sire (17)
TAYLOR'S BUENA — Dam (18)
HARTNAGLE'S HUD — Sire (19)
TOWNSEND'S MISS DIXIE — Dam (20)
DEINES' (DYE'S) BLUE DINGO — Sire (21)
DEINES' TOBY — Dam (22)
WILLIAM'S LADDIE — Sire (23)
JEFFERY'S SHEILA — Dam (24)
ELY'S MAJOR — Sire (25)
LIGHTER'S ASTA — Dam (26)
BRADLEY'S CALICO SHEP — Sire (27)
McCONKEY'S BEAUTY QUEEN — Dam (28)
ROWE'S WARRIOR BOW — Sire (29)
SORENSEN'S QUEENIE — Dam (30)

MANSKER'S TURK — Sire (31)
MANSKER'S FRECKLES — Dam (32)
HARPER'S OLD SMOKEY — Sire (33)
HARPER'S GWEN FRE HO GENIE — Dam (34)
MANSKER'S TURK — Sire (35)
MANSKER'S ANNA LEE — Dam (36)
SNIFF'S DANDY DANNY — Sire (37)
PETRAMALA'S TATE — Dam (38)
TAYLOR'S WHISKEY — Sire (39)
TAYLOR'S BUENA — Dam (40)
WYOMING RANCH DOG — Sire (41)
WYOMING RANCH DOG — Dam (42)
MONTGOMERY'S BLUE — Sire (43)
BODEN'S DOLLY — Dam (44)
DEINES' JESS — Sire (45)
DYE'S (DEINES') JINX — Dam (46)
UHLENDORF'S TIPPY — Sire (47)
THORNTON'S CHRISSY — Dam (48)
ELY'S MAJOR — Sire (49)
WILLIAM'S GEORGINA — Dam (50)
BREAZEALES SHIEK — Sire (51)
BREAZEALES SANDY — Dam (52)
WOOD'S JAY — Sire (53)
WOOD'S LITTLE BLUE — Dam (54)
FARNED'S DEAD EYE — Sire (55)
HAY'S SUGAR — Dam (56)
McCONKEY'S SIR BLUE — Sire (57)
McCONKEY'S SWEET SUE — Dam (58)
RONSLEY'S CHARCOAL SMOKE — Sire (59)
MURPHY'S COCHINA — Dam (60)
SORENSEN'S GUNSMOKE — Sire (61)
NIGHTENGALE'S TAMMY — Dam (62)

A five generation pedigree illustrating an outcross.

Champion Windermere's Sunshine of Bonnie Blu CDX (Ch Wildhagen's Dutchman of Flintridge CDX ex Wildhagen's Thistle of Flintridge) with the "Sunshine boys," both out of Blue Heather of Windermere.
Courtesy Williams

14
REPRODUCTION

The science of reproduction is directly responsible for the development of any species or breed. Reproductive cells with inheritant factors are passed down through generations. The female produces ova (eggs). When united with the male's reproductive cells (sperm), and if fertilized, life will be initiated—another generation to carry on the inherited genetic makeup.

THE BROOD BITCH

The reproductive tract in the female consists of two ovaries (which are the source of estrogen, the hormone responsible for female characteristics), two oviducts, and two uterine horns (the womb, a "Y"-shaped structure) which form a muscular ring called the cervix. The cervix is tightly closed except during estrus and whelping. The cervix at the neck of the uterus separates the uterus from the vagina. The vagina is the passage that leads from the uterus to the vulva (it is also a urinary outlet).

The canine female reaches puberty (sexual maturity) generally between six and fourteen months. The female is monestrus, meaning that she will have only one heat cycle per breeding season. She may cycle at any time during the year, usually twice a year. The reproductive cycle is broken into four distinct phases: proestrus, estrus, metestrus, and anestrus. These stages vary slightly between individuals.

Proestrus

The ovaries are the essential reproductive organs in the female. The ova (eggs) are contained within tiny sacs called follicles. While under the influence of follicular stimulation hormone (FSH), the follicles develop on the ovaries. The ova are minute, but as they reach maturity they increase in size. Maturing ova produce the estrogen hormone, which induces the blood-tinged discharge (uterine lining) and the swelling of the external genitalia (vulva). This marks the beginning of the heat cycle. The female will usually drink more water during proestrus and will therefore urinate more frequently. Males are attracted to the female through the scent of pheromone in the vaginal secretions and urine. The odor creates the hormonal stimulation in the male.

The bitch will be playful with dogs of both sexes, but when the male tests her receptivity by trying to mount her, she will swing away, snap, and growl at him. During the courtship, the female becomes aloof and coquettish, while the male becomes a show-off, and sometimes a clown. He will usually parade around and try to impress her. The female will not allow copulation until she reaches estrus.

Estrus

As the female approaches estrus, the period of receptivity (while she is in a "standing" heat), you will observe a pronounced genital swelling due to the high levels of estrogen. The pink, blood-tinged discharge will begin to "clear," or you may notice a yellowish straw color.

When she is ready to be bred, the female's attitude toward the male will change drastically from hostile to receptive. She will "flag" her tail and lift it toward the side. She will arch her back and swing her hindquarters toward the male. When the male mounts her, she will stand to be bred. The swelling of the external genitals may be less pronounced than in the previous day. It is generally agreed that the first day of estrus occurs when the bitch will accept the male for copulation. The duration of estrus is generally between six and fourteen days, with the average being around nine or ten days.

The female will shed her eggs one to three days from the first point of estrus (receptivity). The female may continue to accept mating for close to a week.

Metestrus

Metestrus is the short period between three to five days after the ova are released. During metestrus, the follicular cavities in the ovaries secrete progesterone, the pregnancy hormone.

Diestrus

Diestrus is the fourth stage of the reproductive cycle and can occur about six days after ovulation. It marks the end of the heat cycle. It varies with each individual, but most bitches will be completely out of heat between the eighteenth and twenty-third day, with the average being twenty-one days.

During the next two months, the progesterone level will remain high in her system, whether or not she has been bred. Diestrus is characterized by the refusal to mate. The outward signs of proestrus, such as flirting, are more or less absent. Physical signs, such as swelling of the external genitals, are diminished, and there is a decline in the vaginal discharge. The female may display hostility toward an advancing male.

Mammary Glands

The mammary glands are not directly concerned with reproductive processes, but they are dependent upon the ovaries for their growth and functioning. These glands are made up of milk-secreting tissues that communicate with the exterior by a teat. The milk secreted by one gland cannot transfer to another, but the milk from each may be reabsorbed and pass into the blood.

Pseudo-Pregnancy (False Pregnancy)

When the ova do not become fertilized, the body may behave as though the female is bred. The breasts start to develop and secrete milk. One may see all the signs of a normal pregnancy. In rare cases, the bitch

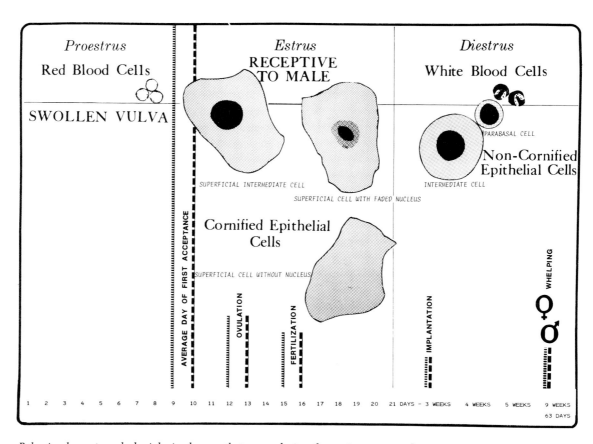

Behavioral events and physiologic changes that occur during the canine estrus cycle.

may also exhibit symptoms of labor. Pseudo-pregnancy is the period when the body will function as though it were in actuality pregnant, although in reality it is not.

Anestrus

Anestrus is the resting stage for the reproductive cycle, and hormonal secretions are very low. Anestrus may last from three to nine months, depending upon the individual, her age, and the environment.

VAGINAL SMEARS

Vaginal smears are microscopic examinations of the cell formations within the vaginal tract. The smear will map out hormonal patterns for bitches with "silent heats" (estrus cycles with little visible indication) and indicate optimum breeding times during artificial insemination.

A small quantity of vaginal material is collected from the vaginal wall and then swabbed onto a slide. The slide is treated with a stain solution and then a distilled water bath. When the slide is dry, the contents are examined under a microscope to reveal cell formations and to record the changes as hormonal activity progresses.

During proestrus, there is an accumulation of red blood cells with an insignificant amount of white blood cells. An abnormally high percentage of white blood cells indicates that an infection is present. As

Ely's Blue (1950, Heavron's Bob ex Young's Bitchie) the Legendary "Ghost Dog" on the old gold National Stock Dog Registration (IESR) Certificates. "Old Blue" was a full sister to Sisler's Queen and a major contributor of many foundation offspring including Hartnagle's Badger. Sisler's Panda, one of Jay Sisler's trick dogs, was a daughter of Ely's Blue. Courtesy Juanita Ely

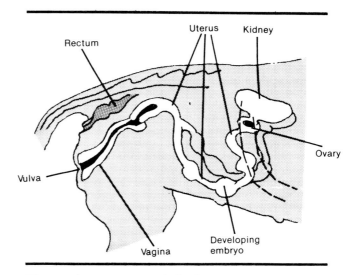

The reproductive system in the bitch.

the cycle progresses and estrogen levels rise, the epithelium tissue (vaginal lining) increases in density. The cells are then shed from the surface of the lining and discarded in the discharge. Epithelial cells are easily distinguished from blood cells. They are larger, and the nucleus of the cell structure is enveloped in a translucent rim.

The number of blood cells will decrease as the heat cycle progresses. The epithelial cells continue to transform toward what is known as the "cornified" stage, at which point they change from a regular to an irregular shape. In the cornified stage, the nucleus (yolk) will be barely visible, if present at all. The rim of the cell will begin to curl up. When all cells are in the cornified stage, actual estrus begins, accompanied by the visible signs during the acceptance period. Ovulation will occur three days later. The ova will take approximately three days to mature, at which point the eggs will be fertilized (about six days following the first incidence of the fully cornified stage). The cells should remain cornified from ten to fourteen days. At the beginning of diestrus, the cells sharply progress back to the noncornified state.

If, while examining vaginal smears over an entire cycle period, the cells never become cornified, then you can be sure that ovulation has not occurred. Even if bred, the female may not conceive.

THE STUD DOG

Once the tissues of the body reach a certain stage of growth and body development begins to decrease, the reproductive cells (the sperm in the male and the ova in the female) begin to ripen. Normal sexual activities of the male generally occur when the dog is eight months old.

When the male reaches sexual maturity, the testicles are descended into the scrotum. They are present around weaning age. The scrotum is a double sac situated outside the body itself, under the tail and anus. The testes are responsible for producing semen, which is composed of spermatozoa and other fluid secretions. Spermatozoa originate from the seminiferous tubules. The testes not only produce the reproductive or germ cells—the sperm—but they contain Leydig cells from which testosterone—the male hormone—is secreted. Testosterone is also necessary for spermatozoa to mature and become fertile.

The testicles are subdivided into coiled seminiferous tubules. They straighten out at the top of the testes and join to form a combined tract, or one tubule known as the epididymis. After leaving the testicles, the spermatozoa travel through the epididymis, where the sperm become motile and fertile.

The remainder of the semen is produced by fluid secretions from the prostate gland, located at the beginning of the urethra. It surrounds the neck of the bladder. Semen is passed in three fractions. It is during the transferring of the last, or third fraction, that the actual "tie" occurs.

Champion Wildhagen's Dutchman of Flintridge CDX (The Herdsman of Flintridge ex Heard's Savor of Flintridge). "Dusty" was the first ASCA breed Champion of record.
Courtesy Wildhagen

The first fraction contains a minute amount of fluid secreted from the urethral glands. It is devoid of spermatozoa. The second phase is the sperm-bearing fraction. During this sperm-rich stage, conception can take place. The third and final stage is comprised of prostatic secretions that are free from sperm.

The penis is made up of the urethra and muscle tissue called the glans penis. Together, they facilitate

Left to right: Heard's Blue Spice of Flintridge (Harper's Old Smokey ex Smedra's Blue Mistingo), Heard's Chili of Flintridge (Harper's Old Smokey ex Heard's Blue Spice of Flintridge), Heard's Salt of Flintridge (Harper's Old Smokey ex Heard's Blue Spice of Flintridge). Foundation dogs of the Weldon T. Heard DVM's Flintridge line.
Courtesy Hartnagle

entry into the female's vaginal opening without full erection. The female's "muscular ring," which contracts, causes a thrusting reflex. As soon as the bulbus glandis swells, completing the penile erection, ejaculation occurs. The full swelling of the bulbus glandis "locks" the male's penis within the female's vagina. When the male rotates his body backward and dismounts, the penis is reflected backward 180 degrees. The penis is bent back behind the bulbus glandis, which will constrict the veins so that the blood does not return to the body. The erection remains while ejaculation continues to drive the sperm into the oviduct (where fertilization takes place) during the third fraction of ejaculate. The breeding "tie" may last anywhere from five minutes to an hour (sixty minutes), but generally it will last between fifteen to thirty minutes.

It should be noted, however, that conception may take place without a tie.

SEMEN EVALUATION

It is imperative for the semen to be properly collected and handled in order to give an accurate evaluation. Temperature shocks, contamination, and urine can give inaccurate results.

Several factors are considered in such an evaluation. Sperm are observed for motility (locomotion), which should indicate the ability to travel swiftly in direct lines to fertilize an ovum. The genetic material is contained in the head of the sperm, while the tail enables the sperm to reach the ova. Morphology is observed to determine if normalities exceed abnormalities of sperm formation. Abnormalities can include misshaped heads, kinked or bent midpieces, coiled tails, detached heads, and so forth.

The above information is used to determine the fertility or lack of it in a stud dog. In cases where infertility is suspected, information such as protoplasmic droplets and bent tails can be directed toward improper maturation in the epididymis (possibly an indication of disease or infection of the epididymis).

If poor results are attained on one evaluation, especially if the male has not been bred recently, then the evaluation should be repeated.

EXERCISE

Every Australian Shepherd should receive proper exercise throughout his life. A regular exercise program is especially important for breeding animals. Regular exercise stimulates circulation, which is responsible for supplying oxygen and vital nutrients to the tissue cells. It is imperative to build and maintain the cardiovascular system. It is too often forgotten that the heart is a muscle and must be maintained to withstand stress and shock. Exercise is the natural aphrodisiac for stud dogs. It maintains a healthy appetite, helps alleviate boredom, and keeps the mind active and alert.

Swimming, daily brisk walks, retrieving games (such as Frisbee) and actual herding work and/or training are all ways to keep your Aussies physically fit. It is important that you use good judgment regarding the age and physical capabilities and limitations of your dog. Consistency and regularity are important. Irregular spurts of activity may result in muscle strain and exertion and lend a susceptibility toward injury. A walk around the house or kennel is not sufficient exercise to maintain an animal in adequate muscle tone.

DIET

There is no single factor more responsible for excellent health than diet. Poor nutrition is a big factor in reproductive failure.

WHEN TO BREED

Excessive breeding demands placed upon sires and dams should be avoided before the dog reaches maturity. The vigor from a certain degree of maturity is essential for the highest reproductive efficiency.

This, however, is often in conflict with man's desire for early and late financial returns from his breeding animals. Though young animals are frequently violated in breeding practices, it is not uncommon for a dog to be bred almost to the point of senility. The results are often unsatisfactory, such as the stud's inability to settle the bitch or the bitch's inability to conceive. Abortion, retained afterbirth, and weak offspring are not uncommon under those circumstances.

Ideally, the sire should not be used before one year of age, although he is generally capable of reproduction at eight months of age. The bitch may come into estrus as young as six months and be capable of reproduction. Even though she can conceive, she will not be physically mature enough until she is

Las Rocosa Lester, noted for his intense working progeny.

nearly two years old. By this time the individuals have developed mentally and physically, which enables them to deal with the excessive demands of reproduction. When bred younger than this, the individual may be robbed of the chance to attain mental and physical development—so important for a solid foundation.

THE MATING

Generally speaking, it is ideal to breed an inexperienced male to a proven, cooperative bitch, especially the first time. However, some maiden bitches, if receptive toward the young stud, are a wiser choice than a veteran bitch with an alligator-type of response. This inexperienced bitch should be bred ultimately to an experienced "veteran" stud, if possible.

Prior to the actual time of mating, it is assumed that both the stud dog and brood bitch have been checked by a veterinarian for reproductive soundness. All contracts and financial arrangements should be agreed upon before the actual mating takes place.

The external areas surrounding both the female's vulva and the male's sheath should be cleansed to prevent contamination. Take great caution to use a mild shampoo. Avoid any soap or shampoo that may be harsh and cause irritation. Rinse the areas well with clear water. NEVER apply any agent (especially ones with spermicidal characteristics) to the genitals, primarily to the internal folds, unless advised to do so by your veterinarian.

The actual mating can be best accomplished in an area devoid of outside distractions. No more than two people should be present to lessen possible confusion.

The ground or floor surface should have good footing, such as broom-finish concrete, rubber matting, carpeting, or grass. Avoid slick flooring.

When the stud and bitch are first introduced, there will generally be a period of courtship before copulation. Mating can often take place without direct assistance, but someone should always be present to help if necessary.

When the timing is correct, it is quite obvious (especially with a cooperative female). Occasionally, the bitch will allow the stud to mount her, but when the penis touches her vulva, she may yelp and pull away. If this occurs several times, you may need to wait until the following day. The experienced stud dog, however, is a better judge of such matters than any chart, especially if the bitch is going through an unusual heat cycle.

The bitch in a standing heat during the period of receptivity will swing her hindquarters toward the stud and "flag" her tail. The bitch's vulva may contract when the male's nose or tongue touch it. When the male mounts, he will grasp the female's flanks with his forelegs. The stud will thrust his pelvis several times before he gains entrance to the vaginal opening. He will step on alternate hind legs and increase the pelvic thrusting to seek intromission to the vaginal opening. Once intromission occurs, the glandis bulbus passes through a muscular ring, which then contracts, and the glandis bulbus engorges with blood to initiate the "tie." The male may then pause and attempt to swing one hind leg over to one or the other side and turn 180 degrees around after dismounting. The pair will then remain in a tail-to-tail position for the duration of the "tie."

The male may need assistance in swinging his hind leg over the female's back. Some females will act aggressive toward the stud even though they are in the period of receptivity. A vaginal smear can be taken to confirm the stage of her heat cycle. One assistant should take charge of the female's head if she acts aggressive toward the male or tries to bite him. If she tries to bite him, apply an emergency muzzle (described in the first aid chapter). If a bitch becomes frightened, she may snap at anything, including you.

If the bitch tries to jump around or lie down especially during the tie, you must intervene. Place your arm under her stomach to keep her on her feet. Give her reassurance by speaking to her in calm tones. Do not allow her to drag the male around once they are tied. The other assistant should hold the male's collar if necessary to prevent him from dragging the female around.

One tie appropriately timed is sufficient to produce a nice litter. It is a common practice to breed on the first or second day of estrus, then to skip a day and breed again on the third or fourth day (approximately forty-eight hours apart). The period of receptivity for each female is different. One female will stand for a stud on the tenth day of her cycle, while another will not be ready until the fourteenth day.

Five generations from the left to right: McCorkle's Young's Buzzy (Russell's Scott ex Mehryn's Cotton), McCorkle's Blue Tule, Fog (McCorkle's Young's Buzzy ex Palmer's (Young's) Shadow), Ch. Sweet Seasons of Heatherhill (Ch Wildhagen's Dutchman of Bonnie-Blu CDX ex McCorkle's Blue Tule Fog), Heavenly Sunshine (Ch Windermere's Sunshine of Bonnie-Blu CDX ex Ch Sweet Seasons of Heatherhill), Half Heaven Half Heartach (Ch Pay the Piper of Aberdare CD ex Heavenly Sunshine.)   *Photo by Dai Rubin*

The stud should not be bred every day. It takes forty-eight hours for the spermatozoa to regenerate for maximum fertility. There is no advantage whatsoever to breeding a female every day even though she will accept the stud. In fact, overuse can be detrimental to the stud.

IF BREEDING INDIVIDUALS, ESPECIALLY A BITCH, CANNOT BE BRED NATURALLY, THEN THEY SHOULD NOT BE BRED OR USED FOR BREEDING PURPOSES.

Silvertone's foundation sire Champion Las Rocosa Ricky Taylor (Ch Las Rocosa Shiloh ex Hartnagle's Fritzie Taylor).
Courtesy Allee

CONCEPTION

Fertilization, or conception, takes place when live sperm are present in the oviduct and the ova are ripe (mature). Fertilization cannot take place until the ova have matured, even though both sperm and ova may be present in the oviduct. The sperm remain motile in the oviduct for several days.

Fertilized ova will leave the oviduct and enter the uterine horn between eight and twelve days after conception. Implantation—when the ova become attached to the uterine wall—occurs about eighteen days after ovulation. After implantation, placental tissue will form around the fetus. These fetal membranes nourish the puppies with nutrients from the dam's maternal blood and then circulate fetal waste back to the dam for removal in her own excretion.

Dual Mating

Cases have been reported in which a female will have been bred by more than one male. During the receptivity period, a female may permit one or more males to mount and copulate with her. Once each ovum has been fertilized by a sperm, it becomes impenetrable. Therefore, while each puppy can have only one sire, a litter may be comprised of one or more sires.

If the female is bred to a specific stud and accidently becomes bred to another male, it is possible that some of the ova will be fertilized by one male, and one or more of the ova will be fertilized by another male.

The litter sired by more than one sire will have half-brothers and sisters. If both sires are purebred, then the puppies are purebred but not registrable. If one sire is purebred and the other sire of a different breed or a mongrel, then only the portion sired by the purebred male will be purebred but not registrable.

It is a fact that there is *no foolproof method of proving* who sired what; therefore, puppies produced from a dual mating cannot be registered because there is always a 50 percent chance that the offspring may have been sired by the other male. It is the breeder's responsibility to safeguard a female in heat from being exposed to any male other than the one to whom she is to be bred. If you plan not to breed her, then she should be kept away from all males capable of reproduction, including her immediate relatives. Contrary to popular belief, a female in heat does not discriminate between brothers and fathers, even though raised side by side. When a female is in heat, reproduction is governed by hormones, not emotion (although on occasion a female may gain fondness for one certain mate and be difficult to breed to any other than that particular individual).

REPRODUCTIVE SOUNDNESS

Nutrition, genetics, general management, and health all play primary roles in breeding soundness. Many factors determine reproductive soundness in both the male (stud) and the female (bitch). Sterility in either is defined as unproductiveness, or the inability to reproduce. In other words, it is a condition in which a normal mating of apparently healthy dogs is not followed by conception. Sterility may result from any one or more of a large number of conditions including age, environment, stress, diet, disease, lack of proper exercise, overwork, irregular work and/or exercise, underfeeding, or nutritional deficiencies. Some of these factors result in permanent sterility, while others are more temporary. Reproduction cannot take place if the genitals are diseased. For example, to continue to subject a female with an abnormal discharge to repeated services (matings) in hope that she will settle is basing expectations on false premises. Healthy puppies cannot be incubated within, or produced from, sexually diseased parents.

Breeding unsoundness is always a cause for rejection of Aussies intended to be included in a breeding program, although this unsoundness may not impair the individual's ability to function in other capacities. Breeding unsoundness includes malformation of the genitals and of the birth passageway, cryptorchidism, monorchidism, scrotal rupture, and other abnormalities.

Hereditary unsoundness is the most serious because of the possibility of transmission to the offspring. Other unsound characteristics caused by injury (such as a broken pelvis) do not pass to the offspring but may cause death in the female. When either an injury or hereditary unsoundness is subjected to the strain of reproduction, especially labor while whelping, the female may die.

GENITAL INFECTIONS/DISEASES

Brucellosis

Brucellosis is an infection caused by bacteria from the genus *Brucella*, which includes four principle species: *Brucella canis*, *Brucella melitensis*, *Brucella abortus*, and *Brucella suis*. The latter three, although rare in canines, have been reported to affect dogs that are more closely associated with infected herds of domestic livestock. A newly described organism, *Brucella canis*, became more prevalent in dogs and was recognized in the 1960s. The disease can be identified by positive cultural or serologic results.

The symptoms of brucellosis are rather inconstant and indefinite. Abortion is probably the most characteristic occurrence in the female. To a lesser degree, "orchitis," infections of the accessory sex glands, and other systematic malfunctions occur in both the male and female. Infertility is prevalent in both sexes. Other symptoms include conception fail-

Hartnagle's Fritzie Taylor (Taylor's Whiskey ex Taylor's Buena), one of the grand dams of the breed, making the ASCA Honor Roll as a leading producer of Champions of Record along with Certified Working Dogs.

ures, neonatal deaths, and stillbirths. Repeated abortions all point toward brucellosis. The organism is present in the blood, urine, milk, and semen of infected dogs.

Brucellosis is venereal or congenital. Brucellosis may be transmitted during copulation or from ingestion of placental tissue and/or vaginal secretions. Infection can occur via contact with contaminated surfaces.

Brucellosis is characterized by an enlargement of the lymph nodes. Individuals affected with the disease may be more fatigued.

Management plays an important role in controlling the spread of the disease. Isolation and/or elimination of diseased individuals is imperative. Surrounding areas of the housing and kennel runs should be disinfected. Presently, there is no cure for brucellosis. Treatment includes neutering or spaying followed by antibiotic therapy.

Vaginitis

Vaginitis is an inflammation of the vagina. The condition is often characterized by a discharge. Before reaching sexual maturity (puberty), "adolescent" bitches may develop a type of vaginitis. Males seem to be excited by the odor of the discharge. This will generally disappear with the first estrus.

Champion Slash V Little Rock CD (Ch Slash V Rocky Top ex Myrup's Gabby), a well known champion and sire of working dogs.
Courtesy of Dahly

Inflammations and infections of the vagina and/or vulva may result from an injury (trauma) during the actual breeding or whelping (parturition). Contamination of the perineal area (the area in front of the anus extending to the external margin of the vulva) may result in an ascending infection. Foreign bodies and bacteria are the most common causes.

Abnormal heat cycles, spayed females, and older bitches can be affected by vaginitis. Bladder infections sometimes can accompany the condition. Vaginitis that often affects older bitches is noted by a heavier discharge that causes them to clean the vulva constantly unless too ill to tend to themselves properly. The mucous membranes may be irritated and reddened.

It is best to seek the professional assistance of your veterinarian if a discharge is noticed. A visual examination does not always determine the actual source of infection. Blood-tinged and/or pus-filled discharge may develop into a far more serious condition such as metritis or pyometra. Both require professional care.

Proper hygiene, such as bathing the perineal area with a mild, nonirritating germicidal and clipping the hair away from the perineal area, will help alleviate the chances of contamination.

Acute Metritis (Postpartum Disease)

Metritis is an inflammation of the uterus. It commonly results from a bacterial infection acquired during parturition (whelping), sometimes during

Champion Flashback of Windermere CD ATD-d OTD-s (Ch Sun's Mark of Windermere CD ex Westwind's Miss Moon Glow CD ATDsd). *Courtesy Williams*

estrus, and during breeding. Dead fetuses, retained placenta, and trauma to the mucous membranes of the uterus and vagina all provide a suitable environment for bacteria to gain entry into the uterus through the open cervix. Abortion greatly magnifies the chances for a bitch to acquire metritis.

Infections can occur by the careless use of A.I. instruments that contaminate and/or injure the uterine wall or vagina. They may also be introduced by the stud dog or through careless attempts to dilate a smaller vagina (which should never be attempted).

Bitches affected with acute metritis are depressed. There is a brownish or blood-stained, foul-smelling discharge. Fever, loss of appetite, vomiting, tenderness in the uterine region, and a swelling and congestion of the vulva occur. If the bitch has a litter, she may be neglectant. The condition requires antibiotics with immediate veterinarian attention. Treatment may also necessitate surgery. The mortality rate increases with advanced stages of the disease.

Pyometra

Pyometra (hyperplastic endometritis) is an accumulation of pus in the uterus. It is extremely serious and can prove fatal unless treated immediately. It will appear more frequently in females over five years of age. While metritis is more commonly associated with a bacterial infection, pyometra appears to be more of an endocrine (hormonal) problem. It is attributed to an ovarian dysfunction with an increased progesterone secretion. When the cervix contracts under the influence of progesterone, pus fills the infected uterus, with no outlet for drainage. A lack of appetite (anorexia) is usually followed by depression. The respiratory rate increases and the temperature falls, then elevates again. As the condition progresses, the temperature will fall and become subnormal. There is generally a continuous, purulent discharge accompanied by a sickly sweet odor. The vulva may be enlarged, and occasionally, persistent diarrhea may accompany the disease. The abdomen is enlarged, and pain may be present upon touch. Other symptoms include progressive weakness and extreme thinness. There may be vomiting following the intake of water. Due to elevated temperatures, the female will want to drink large amounts of water.

The problem becomes obvious three to six weeks following estrus, when the glandular secretions provide a foundation for the multiplication of organisims. The bitch will become extremely ill if not treated. Professional help must be sought immediately, or death will soon follow. Since the disease does not respond well to drugs, surgical removal of the uterus may be imperative unless it can be treated by cleansing under the influence of certain hormones in coordination with antibiotics. The latter is successful only in selected cases.

REPRODUCTIVE PROBLEMS

The Brood Bitch

Abortion and Resorption of Whelps - External and internal influences may create an environment inadequate to sustain life of the developing whelps, in which case death will occur and the female's system will either resorb or expel the litter. Substances that may produce an irritant to a newly developing whelp may have little or no effect once the whelps have become established.

Hormonal imbalances, severe illness, high fever, disease, bacterial and viral infections, fatigue due to exertion, trauma, kicks and/or blows over the abdomen, shock, certain chemical substances and drugs such as worming medications, poisons, surgical shock, exposure to the elements, malnutrition, and nutritionally inadequate diets are all recognized as direct and indirect causes of abortion and resorption of the whelps. A progesterone deficiency also causes an inability to maintain pregnancy.

Bacterial contamination introduced to the uterus through the use of unsanitary instruments (such as the pipette used during artificial insemination) and non-hygienic natural breeding practices also cause abortion and resorption of whelps. The number of instances can be minimized by employing better management practices. Stricter sanitary measures, such

as a gentle cleansing of the area surrounding both the male's and female's external genitals with a mild germicidal, followed by a thorough rinsing with clean, lukewarm water before breeding, are necessary steps.

REPRODUCTIVE SOUNDNESS

The Brood Bitch

Before Breeding - The bitch has to be in peak condition, which is the result of continual effort. Not only must she be free from parasitic agents and current on all innoculations *prior* to breeding (to assure maximum protection and immunity to the puppies), but she must be maintained on a high-quality diet.

Your bitch should be given an annual health checkup. Prior to breeding, she should be given a reproductive soundness examination. Her overall condition should be checked, including temperature, respiration, urinary functions, weight, skin (hydration/condition), and dental condition. She should be at optimum weight before breeding. If she is too heavy, she may have problems developing milk for the puppies once whelped. Vaginal cultures should be obtained to identify the presence of bacteria or infections such as brucellosis. A vaginal examination should be done to detect possible vaginal strictures.

Sterility is a condition of infertility. Whatever the cause, there are no "cure-alls" for the condition. Rather, each case requires careful diagnosis and specific treatment.

Thyroid imbalances such as hyperthyroidism (an overactive thyroid) and hypothyroidism (deficient

Champion Rising Sun of Windemere (Ch. Windermere's Sunshine of Bonnie-Blu CDX ex Fisher's Blue Heather of Windemere).
Courtesy Smith

Briarbrook's top stud Champion Fieldmaster's Three Ring Circus (Ch Fieldmaster of Flintridge ex Whispering Pines of Flintridge) is one of the best known "Fieldmaster" sons.   Courtesy Wilson

thyroid secretions) can totally alter the metabolism. Discharges and infections within the reproductive tract (usually in the cervix, uterus, or fallopian tubes) and some types of physiological imbalances—cystic ovaries, failure to ovulate, retained afterbirth, neonatal death, abortions, resorptions, genetics, obesity, and specific diseases—can all lead to reproductive failure. If sterility is suspected, then blood work should be done to check the thyroid levels also. A bitch should never be bred when an infection is present, because the condition could spread.

The Stud Dog

The stud must be in optimum condition. He must be kept free from parasitic agents and be current on all innoculations. He should be maintained on a regular exercise program and a top-quality diet. He should be checked periodically for brucellosis and other infections. A sperm evaluation should be made when the reproductive soundness examination is performed. At this time, your veterinarian could also determine which problems may or may not be hereditary.

The prepuce (the fold of skin that covers the head of the penis) should be checked for inflammation, lacerations, and persistent frenulum (a condition in which a fold or membrane restricts the mobility of the prepuce). The penis should be checked for abnormal discharge or inflammation, lacerations, and tumors.

The testicles should be carefully palpated and evaluated for size and consistency. Palpation should also reveal abnormalities (if present) and pain, tumors, or hernias. One testis may be slightly larger than the other, but a great degree in size variation is not normal. Testes lacking a moderate amount of firmness may indicate testicular degeneration and atrophy. Swollen or enlarged testes may indicate infections.

Until the testes descend into the scrotum, the stud will remain infertile, because while the testes are retained in the abdomen—their position in fetal life—the sperm, being very susceptible to high temperatures, cannot develop. The scrotum, then, is a device for keeping the testes at a lower-than-body temperature.

It sometimes happens that only one testis will descend into the scrotum. This condition is known as monorchidism. In other cases, neither testis may descend, and this is known as cryptorchidism. In cases where just one descends, the male may be fully fertile but should *never* be bred, because this condition is a serious hereditary fault. Failure of the testes to descend may be due to improper functioning of the anterior pituitary gland.

The prostate should be palpated for size and shape, which should help reveal any prostatic diseases

The legendary Champion Las Rocosa Rojo Hombre CD (Ch Las Rocosa Shiloh ex Hartnagle's Fritzie Taylor).
Courtesy Watts

and tumors. These conditions can greatly alter semen and reduce fertility.

Decreased concentrations of testosterone may occur in a male if there is a hormonal cause for lack of libido (sex drive). Males with a history of previous inflammatory diseases may have temporary infertility secondary to elevated body temperatures during the febrile episodes.

Diseases of the epididymis can also cause infertility in the stud dog. A direct cause of infertility can be due to the thyroid function, which can totally alter the state of metabolism.

Following a period of inactivity as a stud, a male should be bred twice to a bitch to ensure live sperm in the semen.

If there is a question regarding fertility, thyroid activity should be checked by a blood test. Medications and X-rays can temporarily alter the male's ability to produce live sperm, so be sure to guard against this when breeding. Consult your veterinarian.

Casa Buena Kameo CDX, OTD (Ch Fairoaks Stormy Streaker ex Lingle's Foxie) shows natural retrieving instincts at eight weeks of age.   *Courtesy Middleton*

ARTIFICIAL INSEMINATION

Artificial insemination (A.I.) is a process of artificial breeding. It refers to the artificial or manual introduction of the sperm (through the use of fresh or frozen semen) into the female's genitals. It is therefore distinguished from a natural mating. A.I. is not intended to replace natural breeding, but it is an effective measure to help prevent the transmission of venereal diseases and infections that may on occasion occur from natural breeding.

Artificial insemination with either fresh or frozen semen can offer a supplemental method for a breeding

program. A.I. with fresh semen is a very effective step toward breeding a female to a superior stud that may be temporarily incapable of naturally covering the bitch due to an acquired injury, such as a broken leg.

Frozen semen helps cut prohibitive shipping expenses, possibilities of loss, exposure to injury, death, disease, infection, or trauma that may occur during shipment. Artificial insemination is a step toward preventing the overuse of a prominent sire. Frozen semen banks offer a solid foundation toward maintaining genetic material from superior sires, especially if a stud was lost prematurely due to disease or disaster.

Each species or breed can only progress through the progeny of great sires and dams, and then through their offspring. One must not lose sight of the future and overlook present, great individuals however, while trying to recreate the past.

The Bitch

The bitch must be in the correct stage of her estrus cycle, which can be diagnosed and confirmed by examining a vaginal smear microscopically and/or by observing her reactions while in the presence of a "teaser" male. Ovulation usually occurs between twenty-four and seventy-two hours after the onset of estrus.

Due to the longevity of the male's sperm in the reproductive tract, it is suggested that insemination within the first few days of estrus would allow sperm to be present in the oviduct to fertilize the ova as they mature.

It is essential that only sterile equipment be used and that it be maintained at body temperature. In-

Champion Fieldmaster's Cast The Die (Ch Little Abner of Flintridge ex Ch Briarpatch of Bonnie-Blu) one of Briarbrook's sires.   *Courtesy Wilson*

semination is best handled by a veterinarian or by an experienced veterinarian technician due to the dangers of incorrect insertion of the pipette. The techniques of insemination are as essential as the methods employed for collecting and handling semen.

The one great disadvantage to artificially inseminating bitches that are unable to breed naturally is that one may easily introduce a hereditary weakness and reproductive complications into a line that would have been eliminated had it been left up to nature.

Erin George with her well-known champion, Copper Canyon's Caligari (George's Red Rustler ex Quaglino's Miss Pooh).
Courtesy George

The Stud

The techniques of A.I. include collecting semen from the male and examining it microscopically for the absence of foreign material. Volume is measured, Ph (ranges from 5.5 to 6.5, averaging 6.0) determined, the color noted, and motility, density, and morphology observed.

Semen must be properly collected and handled if correct results are to be obtained. Adverse effects on the quality of semen can result if factors are introduced such as exposure to cold or heat shock (incorrect temperatures), contamination to chemical agents, disinfectants, soaps, alcohol, spermicidals, urine, or excessive quantities of water.

Champion Fieldmaster's Blue Isle Barnstormer (Ch Fieldmaster's Three Ring Circus ex Fieldmaster's Lodi) BOB winner at the 1983 ASCA National Specialty.
Courtesy Magazzine

Pretty as a picture. Mistretta's Misty Shadow (Ch Mistretta's Ballou Pirate ex Van-B's Misty Blue) with her litter sired by Champion Hilltop Apollo L.R. (Ch Sharp's Ragnar ex Robertson's Cindy).
Courtesy Mistretta

15

GESTATION AND WHELPING

Puppies are born approximately nine weeks, or sixty-three days, from the time of conception. A variation of a few days is not uncommon. Pregnancy can be diagnosed by feeling puppies through the abdominal wall. It is also possible to diagnose pregnancy as early as twenty-nine days with the use of an instrument that can detect heartbeats.

About the third week of pregnancy, it may be possible to feel the whelps in the uterus, which has naturally become enlarged. The whelp may feel like a lump the size of a ping-pong ball. You can gently palpate (feel) the external area along the abdomen down toward the rib cage. Careless probing, however, will only cause irritation and discomfort to your bitch. There is no way that you can determine how many fetuses the bitch is carrying, because some of the embryos will be located higher up in the uterine horn. Around the fifth week (thirty-fourth to thirty-sixth day), the embryos will be engulfed by fluids, and it may be more difficult to discern their presence.

No noticeable outward physical signs of pregnancy will occur in the bitch until the fifth week after conception. At that time, you may notice an enlargement of the abdomen and loin area, high up behind the ribs. The teats may be enlarged with a pinkish coloration.

MANAGEMENT

During the first five weeks of gestation, feed your bitch the same quality diet, and maintain the same routine to which she was accustomed prior to conception. You must employ common sense. She should not be coddled, but nor should she be allowed to engage in violent activity. She should continue the type of play and exercise that she is used to. Running, herding, jumping, chasing balls, Frisbee, and play are all acceptable, providing that she is not allowed to do overly strenuous activities. Lack of exercise and obesity can cause whelping problems. Controlled exercise should always be part of the daily routine.

It may be wise to keep her away from flying hooves from the middle to the latter stages of pregnancy to avoid possible injury to the abdominal area. During the latter stages of pregnancy, she may not feel like getting a great deal of exercise. She should be encouraged, however, to take daily walks, which will help to keep her fit. This is especially important for the house companion that may or may not be used to a great deal of exercise. During the hot summer months, walks during the cool mornings and evenings are more pleasant than ones during the heat of the day. It is unwise to let her play with overly rough companions, but a familiar playmate will encourage free exercise.

During the last four weeks of gestation, your bitch will require an increased food intake. Her body will demand more nutrients balanced by appropriate levels of energy. Adjust her food consumption as she requires it. Water should be available at all times. By the time she whelps, she will require a 15 to 20 percent increase. Self-feeding programs are well-suited, as they allow the bitch to take in nutrients as her body requires. If you feed predetermined portions, then feed your bitch according to her body weight. You must be constant in keeping track of her daily weight changes and feed accordingly. Feed your bitch the same amount of ration per pound of body weight. From the time of conception to the time of whelping, she will be eating 15 to 20 percent more food. The predetermined portions should then be divided into two or three feedings throughout each day. This will avoid undue pressure from the intestinal tract on the enlarged uterus.

A diet designed specifically for lactation is ideal for the bitch during gestation. The diet should contain at least 25 percent protein on a dry matter basis. If the protein content of the ration is below that, feed a "complete" all-meat supplemental commercial canned ration as 15 to 25 percent of the total. However, do not oversupplement with any one ingredient. All ingredients must be balanced or the diet becomes deficient. If is far more beneficial and less expensive over the long run to invest in a diet designed to meet the nutritional needs of your bitch. A cheap diet may take fifty dollars worth of supplements to be adequate. Incorrectly supplementing vitamins and minerals or oversupplementing with fat can lead to a deficient diet and create serious imbalances. It can also increase the mortality rate in your puppies. It can never be stressed enough that if the diet being fed is a quality, well-balanced, "complete" diet, vitamin and mineral supplementations are not necessary and can prove more detrimental if an imbalance is created. It is therefore most economical to invest in a top-quality professional diet. Consult your veterinarian.

Your bitch may have lapses in her house training, in that there will be a greater amount of pressure on her bladder (created from growing puppies). It would be wise to take her out before retiring and then again first thing in the morning upon rising.

Any signs of illness, abnormal odorous discharges (bloody, greenish, or blackish), elevated temperature, vomiting, diarrhea, or listlessness should be immediately reported to your veterinarian. Infections indicate that some complication may occur.

From a week to several days before whelping (parturition), the bitch may have a sagging appearance in the loin. She will have shortness of breath due to the whelp pressing upon the vital organs. The sunken-in look is acquired due to the puppies "dropping down." Her breasts will turn pink to reddish in color and become enlarged.

During the entire gestation period, the bitch's body undergoes elaborate preparations for the final event. The placenta has generated enough surplus hormones to prepare the breasts. The breasts contain a treelike structure of milk ducts, with the nipples representing the tree trunks. Under pressure of increased hormone production, these structures become enormously enlarged, shooting out thousands of new branches and twigs.

Everything is in a state of readiness to provide food for the new life. Actual milk production, however, will not start until the pituitary gland at the base of the bitch's brain gives the word.

A bundle of joy. A six week old litter of Glacier-Crest puppies.

Courtesy Kline

WHELPING BOX

At least one week prior to whelping, the bitch should be moved to her whelping box. This will accustom her to new surroundings. If the litter arrives a few days early, then you will be prepared.

The whelping box (or house) should be large enough to accommodate the bitch with her rapidly growing puppies and, if necessary, to provide adequate shelter until the litter is weaned. If the whelping box has high sides, like a house with a roof or lid, the top should be removable or built with hinges to allow easy access. The box should be constructed with material that can be cleaned and disinfected easily to discourage viral, bacterial, and parasitic infections.

The box should be well ventilated but never drafty, so that the bitch and puppies do not become overheated. The box can be built slightly off the ground (one to three inches) to prevent dampness and cold from seeping inside. Some designs include a railing that is placed three to four inches from the floor bottom and the same distance from each side. This margin may help prevent the bitch from pinning and crushing the newborns against the side walls. Whether indoors or out, the box should have one side lower or an opening to enable the bitch to get away from the puppies when necessary.

The Bedding

Except during the actual whelping, the bedding should consist of larger carpet pieces. Indoor-outdoor carpeting is excellent because it can be hosed off and disinfected. Thick towels, blankets, and mattress pads will allow the puppies traction while nursing and moving around and are easily removable. Terry cloth should not be used, because the puppies' toenails can get caught in it.

Cedar wood shavings, fresh hay or straw, or shredded computer tape can also be used. However, it is best to reserve this type of bedding for older puppies nearing weaning age. Never use any loose, deep, or flimsy material that can suffocate or bury the puppies.

When using fresh hay or straw, guard against rodent or parasite contamination. Use only cedar wood shavings that have not been treated with chemicals to eliminate the chance of poisoning.

Bedding During Whelping - The actual bedding should consist of clean newspapers that can be disposed of when soiled and dampened. After the puppies are born, other types of bedding can then be used.

PREPARING FOR THE WHELPING

Supplies that should be on hand when preparing for the whelping include several paper sacks or plastic garbage bags, towels, dental floss, sterilized scissors, germicidal, iodine, oxytocin (or calcium), brandy, milk, eggs, honey, a heating pad, a hair dryer, and in an emergency, a good hot water bottle. An emergency number for your veterinarian should be on hand. You should also have bitchs' milk replacer, a ten-to-fifty milliliter (preferably plastic) syringe, a number five or number ten catheter, adhesive tape, disinfectant, a pencil, and a pad.

THE ONCOMING LABOR

Several days before the onset of labor, your bitch may begin nesting. She may try to locate a place other than the one that you have designated for her, which is why it is important to choose a secluded place away from traffic and activity. She will probably decrease her food intake, but the most reliable clue toward approaching labor is the drop in body temperature. Several days prior to whelping, her temperature may drop several degrees from the normal temperature of 101.5 F. to 102 F. down to 100 degrees F. She will probably be panting more heavily because of her discomfort. The bitch may lie first on one side and then on the other. She may even squat. She may appear to be more restless and pant more frequently for several days, especially if this is her first litter. The older, more experienced brood bitches may have better developed mammary glands than the young bitches, but this varies with each individual.

LABOR

Your bitch may begin "nesting" by vigorously shredding up her bedding, scratching and digging around her bedding, and at the carpet to prepare a comfortable whelping spot. This may occur off and on for twenty-four to thirty-six hours, or for as little as two hours. She may even try desperately to find a new location under the house, barn, or in some favorite secluded resting spot around the yard under the shrubs and bushes. Keep an eye on her, especially during the cold months, in case she begins to whelp. She could possibly drop one on the ground or escape to some secluded spot at the last minute to give birth. When she goes out for her daily exercise or to relieve herself, you should supervise and restrain her activities.

Her natural instincts are to seek solitude in which to protect herself and her puppies. Other animals (even her playmates) and people may be a threat. It is wise to keep all other animals away, even her constant companions. This is not the time to invite the children and neighbors in for a look. Your bitch may go into a state of hysterical excitement, delay the whelping, try to hide, or even become aggressive toward them—and rightfully so! If your bitch feels threatened, she may injure the puppies while whelping or try to hide them once they have been whelped.

BATHING YOUR BITCH

In preparation for the upcoming labor, you will need to cleanse your bitch's hindquarters, stomach, and teats with a mild, nontoxic antiseptic or germicidal. If you bathe her entirely, do it a week prior to the due date (especially in case the bitch will be early in whelping) before her temperature drops. Use lukewarm water to avoid any drastic temperature shock that could upset her system. You can use her regular shampoo, but also apply a mild disinfectant to her stomach and hindquarters. Be sure to rinse her well and dry her completely to avoid chilling. If there is excessive feathering that could become entangled with the birthing of the litter, it should be thinned out and clipped away from the area around the vulva. This will help the bitch keep herself cleaner during the following weeks. Comb the hair away from the bitch's nipples. If there is excessive hair around them, it may be wise to clip it away. This will make suckling easier and cleaner for the puppies.

IMMINENT LABOR

During this stage, the bitch may appear more restless than the previous few days. She now pants continually and will lick her hindquarters intermittently. Periodically, she may fall asleep in her whelping box awaiting the time of delivery.

Contractions will begin lightly during this prelabor period but will eventually increase in both frequency and severity. The first-time expectant mother may appear extremely curious as to the activity taking place within her body. She may be a bit more nervous than the proven bitch, but if everything is going along normally, her instinct will guide her through the entire process.

It will serve as a valuable reference point to note when the prelabor began, because if the bitch does not begin whelping during the next twenty-four to thirty-six hours, something may be wrong that will require veterinarian assistance. Extreme pain, trembling, shivering, vulvular bleeding, collapse, vomiting, foul and odorous discharges, and straining for over two to three hours are all reasons to get her to your veterinarian. Consult your veterinarian if the female does not whelp by the sixty-fifth day and immediately if any of the above symptoms occur.

For the most part, the Australian Shepherd is an extremely healthy breed with minimal whelping complications. This is due to the fact that the majority of foundation bitches used in breeding programs were healthy and sound breeders, which passed down through the generations.

WHAT BEGINS LABOR?

One theory is that the vastly enlarged uterus has been stretched beyond its endurance, and that the uterine horn expresses itself by contracting in an effort to expel the irritant—the puppies. The theory most accepted is that just before the whelping process begins, there is a dramatically sharp decline in the amount of sex hormones circulating in the bloodstream. The placenta has become senile and is no longer able to produce hormones that have made the uterus lie quiet for months. In any case, this rapid decline of hormones in the bloodstream is a signal that labor is about to begin. The uterus, which is made up almost entirely of muscular tissue, starts to contract.

Just prior to the onset of actual labor, the bitch's temperature will drop sharply to 97 or 98 degrees F. You may notice that the mucous membranes have become pale. There may be a thick mucous discharge from the vulva which should be free from color and foul odors. The bitch will clean the external genitals because the contractions will cause a vaginal discharge.

Internally, the whelping process has already begun. The cervix will begin to "relax." It dilates during the first stage of labor, and the puppies rotate so as to be in the correct position for their journey down the uterine horn. Canine fetuses lie in two tubes—the uterine horns—which are shaped like a short-stemmed "Y". Puppies are generally carried on both sides but may be all in one horn or the other. The puppies are packed in tightly at the time of birth. Each puppy born has a 50 percent chance of being presented for delivery hind end first (breech). If the head is born first, the birth is easier because the shape of the head is more suited for forcing its passage through the pelvis. A tail or foot does not bring pressure to open the passageway. There is no way to turn a puppy inside the mother, because the area is too cramped after the uterus has contracted around the fetus during labor.

Each puppy is propelled by contractions of the uterus and the fluid pressure in its own bag. The fluid is the dilating and distending medium when the uterus relaxes in front of it and contracts behind it. The bitch may have contractions that will make her hind legs stiffen and push. Take note of when the bitch exhibits the first straining pain. This may be violent enough to cause her to grunt or to cry out. Most people think that dogs deliver their young in short order, without pain or trouble. This is far from the truth. The bitch does not exhibit pain as much or give a lot of voice to her pain.

THE WHELPING

The actual whelping usually begins with this pain. The bitch may rest a few moments. Involuntary contractions of the uterus combined with voluntary abdominal muscles push upon the whelp. The final labor period lasts from the time the bitch has regular contractions until the birth of the first puppy. It should not last any longer than an hour before the birth of the first puppy. The bitch may walk around and drink water between labor pains. If she needs to go outside, she may squat and strain a little after relieving herself. Just bring her calmly back to her whelping box.

A gush of water should follow the first straining pain or major contraction. As the sac containing the placenta becomes dislodged, it releases the surrounding fluids, which flush out the birth canal and serve as a lubricant. You may notice wet spots or wet papers in the whelping box. A black, water-filled sac will appear at the vulva. This is the bag of amniotic fluid which precedes the birth of each puppy.

Sometimes the sac breaks during the course of delivery, in which case you may only see a rush of a black-greenish fluid. Normally the bitch will tear the sac by licking or biting at it. In the case of a maiden bitch the sac may appear and retract once or twice at the entrance to the vulva. The puppy should soon be expelled. If it is not after several times, you may need to assist. The bitch may be crouching or lying and sometimes even standing for the final ex-

pulsion. Some bitches like to brace themselves against the side of the whelping box to get better leverage.

Each puppy is completely enclosed in a sac, which is a thick grayish, membranous bag filled with liquid. The puppy gets its oxygen (and nutrition) before birth from the bitch. The placenta (afterbirth) is attached to the mother's uterus. The whelp in the sac is connected to the placenta by the umbilical cord. At the time of birth, the uterus begins to contract, pushing the puppy downward for its entrance into the world. At that time, the placenta detaches from the uterine wall, leaving the puppy "on its own."

There is still enough oxygen left in the blood of the placenta to supply the puppy during the birth process, but if the birth is delayed too long, the puppy will smother. The bitch should turn to tear the sac away by licking it away from the face. She will bite the umbilical cord, crushing it with her teeth to keep it from bleeding.

Wait for a moment to see if the bitch will do this on her own. If she does not do this quickly, do it yourself by tearing the membrane away from the face, nostrils, and mouth, and then wipe the puppy's face with a cloth. Use a baby's nose tube to clear the mouth. If the puppy remains in the bag, it could get amniotic fluid into its lungs, causing pneumonia or suffocation. Give the puppy back to its mother. Some maiden bitches are frightened of their newborn pups, and the maternal instincts may not be very evident until the delivery of a few puppies.

It is very important to be a nonobvious observer. Do not interfere if the bitch appears to be in control. Your interference may cause the bitch to be nervous, in which case she may react in an irrational manner. She may even resort to cannibalism if she feels threatened and may try to eat the "endangered" puppies.

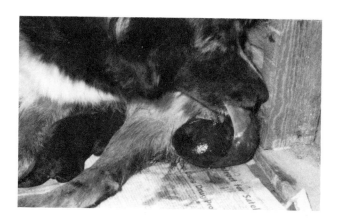

A black water-filled sac containing the puppy will appear at the vulva. The wet spots on the papers in the whelping box are from fluids called "water" that lubricate the birth canal.

Photo by Jerry Rowe
Courtesy Sharon Rowe & Sue Dennis, authors of "Pups N' Stuff"

The bitch will tear the sac (a thick greyish membranous bag) away from the puppy in order that it may breathe. She will lick it away from the face, nostrils and mouth.

Photo by Jerry Rowe
Courtesy Sharon Rowe & Sue Dennis

It is best to resist your impulse to help unless there is an immediate danger to the bitch or puppies. A normal, healthy bitch is capable of having her puppies easily with no assistance unless a complication arises. Your job as the observer is to be there in case a problem does occur.

The bitch washes and tumbles each puppy about very vigorously as soon as they are born, for several reasons. The hard washing makes the puppy complain loudly, which gets air into its lungs. It also stimulates circulation and dries the wet coat. If necessary, you can accomplish the same thing by rubbing the puppy briskly, head held down (to allow possible fluid to drain) with a turkish towel.

REMOVING FLUID FROM THE LUNGS

A puppy may need to have fluid removed from its lungs. Hold the puppy in your hand with its back and the back of its head and neck against the palm of one hand. Place its face down lower than the rest of the body between the first two fingers of your other hand. Hold the puppy's head, neck, and body firmly. Place your thumb and fingers around the tiny body. Then, in a sharp motion, swing your hands downward. Never swing the puppy by its legs. The puppy should gasp, taking in air, and gravity should help pull the fluid and mucous out of the lungs. Wipe it off as it appears. Repeat the shaking process until the puppy's breathing is free of fluid. Hold the puppy close to your ear and listen for rasping or rattling noises, which mean that fluid is present. Check the tongue to see if the puppy is getting enough oxygen—a blue tongue indicates that the puppy is *not* receiving enough oxygen.

The shaking and brisk rubbing with a towel can be alternated and repeated to get a weak puppy breathing normally. Get the puppy dry, and keep it warm.

SEVERING THE CORD

The bitch severs the cord by crushing it so that it does not continue to bleed. She will crush the cord either before or after expelling the placenta. The cord seals adequately when the bitch cuts it with her teeth, and there is little need to worry about bleeding. She will then clean the puppy, while the puppy makes its way to nurse. Healthy, strong puppies will begin sucking vigorously.

If the bitch does not cut the cord, you must do so. Tie dental floss about two inches from the puppy's body (loop it around twice and knot), clip the cord with a pair of dull (sterile) scissors, and swab it with iodine. Never pull the cord from the puppy. The pressure placed on the navel could cause a hernia. When the cord dries up, the excess will drop off. For the moment, however, it is best only to clip away any thread ends that the bitch may be able to rip away, because this could also cause a hernia.

EATING THE PLACENTA

A bitch's purpose in eating the placenta is to provide her with nourishment and liquid complete with protein, vitamins, and hormone substances that her body needs. In the wild state, a bitch would be unable to hunt for food, and the placental nourishment would sustain her during the first few days after whelping. Keep track of the number of placentas expelled. If there wasn't one for each puppy, you will need to contact your veterinarian. A retained placenta can cause serious complications, such as uterine infections, pyometra, or metritis. Sometimes the placenta will not be expelled directly after each birth, but it should be expelled with the birth of the following puppy.

Rather than waiting for her contractions to expel the placenta, the bitch is pulling it out on her own.
Photo by Jerry Rowe
Courtesy Sharon Rowe & Sue Dennis, authors of "Pups N' Stuff"

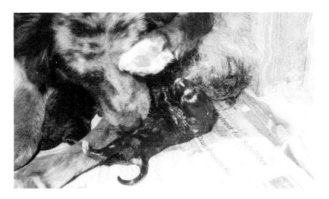

The mother will detach the puppies from the placenta by "cutting the cord."
Photo by Jerry Rowe
Courtesy Sharon Rowe & Sue Dennis

After the bitch has whelped the litter she requires sufficient time to rest while the puppies quietly nurse.
Photo by Jerry Rowe
Courtesy Sharon Rowe & Sue Dennis

Some mothers will pick up their puppies to move them from one place to another.
Photo by Charles Anderson
Courtesy Sharon Rowe & Sue Dennis, authors of "Pups N' Stuff."

BREECH BIRTHS

When a puppy is whelped breech the hind legs appear first, or the buttocks may come first with the hind legs folded back. The puppy could even be presented upside down. When this occurs, the hind legs will appear first, or the buttocks may come first with the hind legs folded back. Very often during a breech presentation, the puppy will arrive safely and easily. But occasionally a problem may arise. If the puppy remains stuck, or if it appears and then disappears back several times, you may need to step in and help.

Grasp the puppy gently with a sterile terry cloth. Use a gentle, steady, firm pull timed with the bitch's own effort to expel the whelp. If you jerk or roughly grasp the head, tail (never grasp the tail), or legs, you may cause permanent damage. A lubricant such as Vaseline may help. Never pull straight out or upward. Always pull firmly and slightly down toward the bitch's stomach. You may need to pull gently to one side and then to the other. If the puppy is upside down, you may try to gently rotate the body so that its own backbone is parallel to that of the bitch. If during a breech presentation only one leg is out, you will need to use a sterile, gloved finger to locate the other leg and guide it out. If after several attempts you have no success, call your veterinarian. Too long of a delay may put the bitch and the other puppies in immediate danger.

Unlike normal puppies that cry out when the mother begins washing them, puppies that have been placed under stress during the whelping procedure may be limp and quiet. These puppies require immediate assistance, because it is possible that the oxygen supply has been cut off. These puppies may lack the strong pink-reddish tones of good circulation and may appear blue. Even the lifeless-appearing puppy may be able to be saved if you begin supportive measures at once. If the puppy is bloodstained or stained with a green fluid, you can be sure that it is in a critical state.

Make sure that all of the membrane is removed from the puppy's mouth and nostrils. If the puppy fails to breathe immediately, give artificial respiration. First suck any contents from the nose. Place your lips over the puppy's nose and mouth and blow. Use small, short breaths so that you don't rupture the lungs.

Use a towel to briskly rub the body as the mother would when she begins to clean the puppies. You may even have to use your index finger and lightly tap the puppy's back, which should make the puppy gasp for breath. Once the puppy begins breathing normally and its color is normal, you can attend to the navel cord. Grasp it several inches away from the puppy's body between your thumb and forefinger. Gently milk the remaining nutriment into the puppy once or twice. Make sure that you do not place any pressure on the cord. With the cord pinched between your fingers, you can either cut or tear the cord. Be sure to keep the puppy from becoming chilled.

Now place the puppy on one of its mother's teats so that it may intake some colostrum. It is imperative for the puppy to receive milk within the first twenty-four hours of life. Colostrum contains antibiotic substances that give the puppy temporary immunity against infectious diseases. It helps get the puppy off to a healthy start in life.

You may have to gently open the puppy's mouth and place it on one of its mother's teats. The puppy should start sucking. If not, *gently* apply pressure to the bitch's teat to express milk, and then gently apply enough pressure on the puppy's lower jaw to open the mouth.

HARD LABOR

When the bitch has been in hard labor for two hours with no puppies arriving, or the labor has completely ceased and you think that there may be more puppies inside, either call your veterinarian or take the bitch there yourself. She probably needs professional help. If you are in doubt, consult him about the situation immediately.

The uterus of some females does not have the required "tone," or push power, to expel the puppies. This may be the result of improper exercise, of a lengthy labor, or of the birth of a large litter. The bitch generally becomes weary, a condition called uterine inertia. She is incapable of having contractions sufficient to move the puppies downward and out.

You may give the female two to three teaspoons of brandy in a bowl of milk and honey (or sugar) with an egg yolk or two, calcium may be beneficial, combined with a small rest, to help revive her strength. Take the bitch out on lead during intervals of whelping to relieve herself. Make sure that you carry a towel in case she whelps while on "break." The short walks will introduce fresh air into her lungs and help improve her circulation.

Your veterinarian may recommend a hormone injection (oxytoxin). Due to the nature of oxytoxin, a dose can be given intramuscularly to stimulate contractions of the smooth muscle of the uterus. This type of injection may be repeated at intervals. Directions must be followed explicitly, and oxytoxin must never be given until the cervix and birth canal are completely dilated. Oxytoxin is usually given after whelping, or at least after the whelping of one pup. It is also used to "clean out" any remaining uterine contents. Consult your veterinarian. He may prescribe a limited amount of oxytoxin to keep on hand if at his discretion he feels you would have the ability to use it to the letter as recommended.

PROBLEM WHELPING

Sometimes the head or the puppy itself may be too large to pass through the pelvis. If professional help is not given in time, the puppy will die along with others of the litter. A dead puppy is a source of possible infection to the bitch. If untreated, she may die or be unable to have any more litters. Never wait for your bitch to collapse. More than two hours after delivering a puppy or three hours at the onset of labor is a signal to respond.

If the bitch is in labor a long time trying to deliver a dead puppy, and surgery is required, she may be too weak from the pain and effort to survive the anesthetic. Further, if the bitch has become poisoned from the presence of one or more dead puppies in the uterus, she is an extremely poor risk for surgery.

There are two possible solutions to problem whelping. Your veterinarian will have to decide upon the best method. His primary concern is for the life and well being of the bitch, which should be your concern, too.

Forceps

If the puppy is dead, an experienced veterinarian may remove the puppy with forceps. He will carefully have to extract it little by little. Puppies usually cannot survive a forceps delivery. This method is seldom used if more than two puppies are present in the uterus.

Cesarean Section

A Cesarean section can be performed, and is always indicated, if any of the puppies have a chance of being alive (considering that you've taken adequate care and have not waited too long) and the mother is in good condition.

This type of surgery is necessary if the pelvic bone and muscle structure are too rigid to permit sufficient separation to allow the passage of a puppy. Some females have male-type pelvic construction. This can also happen if a female is too old before having her first litter. Whelping complications can also occur from injuries such as fractured pelvic bones, etc. An experienced veterinarian can help diagnose this continuing complication when the first Cesarean is done. It is not advisable to breed a female if she is unable to have a litter naturally.

The female who has had an anesthetic for delivery is not herself until at least a half day to an entire day after delivery. Provisions have to be made for feeding and care of the puppies. If you place the puppies with her before she has completely recovered from the anesthetic, they might hurt her and she might bite them, not fully realizing what is going on.

A side, or flank, incision for Cesareans is more satisfactory. The bitch can lie comfortably on one side and not have a sore spot near any nipple. Offer the bitch a drink of warm milk, chicken or beef broth, or plain water. Allow her a few hours of rest, then give the puppies an opportunity to nurse.

CARE AFTER WHELPING

Only after the mother has had sufficient time to clean the puppies and to regain her strength will you want to go over the puppies. Note identifying markings, and weigh each puppy. Examine each puppy for defects and/or unsoundness.

Make sure that the bitch gets a chance to exercise. Initially, she will be reluctant to leave her puppies. Make sure that no other animals or people will make her feel threatened for her litter. Allow the bitch to take short breaks to relieve herself. After the first three days, she should not be so reluctant to leave her puppies. The bitch will not be very hungry, but you should have food and water available at all times.

The first twenty-four hours are crucial to the newborn puppy. It is during this time that they will gain their mother's colostrum.
Courtesy Smith

You will probably notice a discharge for several weeks after the whelping. A darker red discharge clearing to a pinkish color is a healthy sign, as it usually means that all afterbirths have been expelled. A bright red discharge can indicate hemorrhage that requires immediate professional attention. A greenish-colored or purulent discharge often occurring within the forty-eight to seventy-two-hour period after whelping generally indicates an infection, which will require immediate attention from your veterinarian.

The female's temperature will return to normal if everything is normal. If the temperature rises above 102.5, it is a signal for concern. Any unusual or odorous discharges or obvious bleeding should be reason enough to consult your veterinarian.

You will want to call your veterinarian as a courtesy to let him know that all is well, at which time it is ideal to schedule a visit for the following day. Within twelve hours, and no later than twenty-four hours, she should receive a general checkup and possibly oxytoxin to insure proper "clean-out."

MILK SUPPLY

The breasts should feel full to the touch when milk is sufficient. Sometimes a bitch's milk doesn't "come down" normally. This can be noticed if the puppies appear restless and if after nursing the puppies lack a full, well-rounded appearance. Gently press the nipple between two fingers. A drop of milk should readily form. If not, it will be necessary for you to get the bitch to the veterinarian. Occasionally, an injection of oxytoxin during the first twenty-four hours following whelping will help to induce the milk flow. This also helps to rid the uterus of any possible retained debris. If this is not taken care of, the puppies will not receive the vital colostrum.

If the bitch is ill or has had a lengthy whelping, you may need to temporarily assist with her duties and care for the puppies until her milk comes down.

ECLAMPSIA (PUERPERAL TETANY)

Eclampsia is a disease of nursing bitches and is occasionally observed during the final stages of pregnancy. If not treated immediately, it can cause death. The condition is due to a calcium imbalance, which may be due to the bitch's inability to utilize the calcium and phosphorus in her system. It is also caused by strain placed on the bitch while nursing a large litter. The disease is marked by nervousness, convulsions, excitability, stiffness, and staggering.

The attacks appear suddenly and can resemble heat prostration. The affected bitch may be unable to stand. She may stagger around, her muscles becoming rigid and exhibiting a stilted gait. The temperature rises; the respiration is rapid, and pulse is accelerated. You will probably notice panting, excitement, and restlessness followed by convulsive spasms; the bitch will fall to her side and kick violently. The muscles become tense, and mucous membranes are congested, and there is an increased flow of saliva. The bitch will remain conscious during an attack. The duration and severity of an attack vary, but affected animals should receive immediate treatment. This is an *emergency* situation, and veterinarian care is imperative for the survival of the bitch.

Some breeders will supply a calcium and phosphorus supplement in a ratio balance of 1.2:1. Bone meal is natural and probably one of the safer calcium/phosphorus supplements available. If you are feeding a professional diet designed for the lactating bitch, then it probably won't be necessary. Consult your veterinarian.

MASTITIS

Sometimes a litter (expecially a large one) will place undue stress on the bitch while nursing. The strain traumatizes the mammary glands. The needle-sharp nails of the puppies can scratch and bruise the bitch's breasts, creating further trauma.

Mastitis is inflammation of the breasts. It is a condition that results principally from infection with microorganisms. A wide variety of bacteria, as well as some yeasts, are capable of producing mastitis.

The affected breast or breasts may be hot, hard, tense, and tender. The milk may be watery and straw-colored and on occasion blood-tinged and may be stringy. The milk secretion is greatly or completely suspended. There is a general systemic disturbance, such as depression, and a rise in temperature accompanied by a loss of appetite.

The breast must be protected from injury as much as possible. Once the bacteria enter the opening in the teat, they may establish themselves in the milk cistern.

If the condition progresses, mastitis may be noticed when the affected breast(s) abscess and "burst," which may look as if the breast has been ripped, forming a jagged and gaping wound.

Hot and cold compresses and antibiotic treatment are imperative. Call your veterinarian for diagnosis and treatment. This condition may be complicated with other problems such as metritis.

Chronic mastitis is not easily recognized. Although inflammation occurs, only small areas of tissue are involved, and the milk will appear normal. However, the chemical properties of the milk change from the inflammation, and bacterial activity increases. Occasionally, chronic mastitis will develop into acute mastitis. When this occurs, the milk will have clots and a watery appearance.

If the puppies seem ill, or cry, it may be due to a colicky condition caused from "bad milk." Depending upon the severity of the condition, the puppies may have to be entirely weaned and handfed. If not weaned and handfed, the sucklings may die from the affected milk. Regardless of the form of mastitis, the bitch will need to undergo antibiotic treatment and will require veterinary care. Providing the bitch's condition is not toxic, the puppies may continue to nurse. The affected breast(s) should be isolated and protected. Your veterinarian may be able to tape the affected teat with gauze. Keep the puppies' nails trimmed down to minimize injury to the breasts.

THE BITCH'S TEMPERAMENT

It is natural for the even-tempered bitch to become protective for her puppies in the presence of strangers, family, friends, and neighbors. Recent reports indicate that 500 milligrams of vitamin C may help alleviate a disgruntled attitude, although it will not alter her protective instincts.

Looking at the world with the security of her mother at her side.

Date bred	Date due to whelp	Date bred	Date due to whelp	Date bred	Date due to whelp	Date bred	Date due to whelp	Date bred	Date due to whelp	Date bred	Date due to whelp	Date bred	Date due to whelp	Date bred	Date due to whelp	Date bred	Date due to whelp	Date bred	Date due to whelp	Date bred	Date due to whelp	Date bred	Date due to whelp
January	March	February	April	March	May	April	June	May	July	June	August	July	September	August	October	September	November	October	December	November	January	December	February
1	5	1	5	1	3	1	3	1	3	1	3	1	2	1	3	1	3	1	3	1	3	1	2
2	6	2	6	2	4	2	4	2	4	2	4	2	3	2	4	2	4	2	4	2	4	2	3
3	7	3	7	3	5	3	5	3	5	3	5	3	4	3	5	3	5	3	5	3	5	3	4
4	8	4	8	4	6	4	6	4	6	4	6	4	5	4	6	4	6	4	6	4	6	4	5
5	9	5	9	5	7	5	7	5	7	5	7	5	6	5	7	5	7	5	7	5	7	5	6
6	10	6	10	6	8	6	8	6	8	6	8	6	7	6	8	6	8	6	8	6	8	6	7
7	11	7	11	7	9	7	9	7	9	7	9	7	8	7	9	7	9	7	9	7	9	7	8
8	12	8	12	8	10	8	10	8	10	8	10	8	9	8	10	8	10	8	10	8	10	8	9
9	13	9	13	9	11	9	11	9	11	9	11	9	10	9	11	9	11	9	11	9	11	9	10
10	14	10	14	10	12	10	12	10	12	10	12	10	11	10	12	10	12	10	12	10	12	10	11
11	15	11	15	11	13	11	13	11	13	11	13	11	12	11	13	11	13	11	13	11	13	11	12
12	16	12	16	12	14	12	14	12	14	12	14	12	13	12	14	12	14	12	14	12	14	12	13
13	17	13	17	13	15	13	15	13	15	13	15	13	14	13	15	13	15	13	15	13	15	13	14
14	18	14	18	14	16	14	16	14	16	14	16	14	15	14	16	14	16	14	16	14	16	14	15
15	19	15	19	15	17	15	17	15	17	15	17	15	16	15	17	15	17	15	17	15	17	15	16
16	20	16	20	16	18	16	18	16	18	16	18	16	17	16	18	16	18	16	18	16	18	16	17
17	21	17	21	17	19	17	19	17	19	17	19	17	18	17	19	17	19	17	19	17	19	17	18
18	22	18	22	18	20	18	20	18	20	18	20	18	19	18	20	18	20	18	20	18	20	18	19
19	23	19	23	19	21	19	21	19	21	19	21	19	20	19	21	19	21	19	21	19	21	19	20
20	24	20	24	20	22	20	22	20	22	20	22	20	21	20	22	20	22	20	22	20	22	20	21
21	25	21	25	21	23	21	23	21	23	21	23	21	22	21	23	21	23	21	23	21	23	21	22
22	26	22	26	22	24	22	24	22	24	22	24	22	23	22	24	22	24	22	24	22	24	22	23
23	27	23	27	23	25	23	25	23	25	23	25	23	24	23	25	23	25	23	25	23	25	23	24
24	28	24	28	24	26	24	26	24	26	24	26	24	25	24	26	24	26	24	26	24	26	24	25
25	29	25	29	25	27	25	27	25	27	25	27	25	26	25	27	25	27	25	27	25	27	25	26
26	30	26	30	26	28	26	28	26	28	26	28	26	27	26	28	26	28	26	28	26	28	26	27
27	31	27	May 1	27	29	27	29	27	29	27	29	27	28	27	29	27	29	27	29	27	29	27	28
28	Apr. 1	28	2	28	30	28	30	28	30	28	30	28	29	28	30	28	30	28	30	28	30	28	Mar. 1
29	2			29	31	29	July 1	29	31	29	31	29	30	29	31	29	Dec. 1	29	31	29	31	29	2
30	3			30	June 1	30	2	30	Aug. 1	30	Sep. 1	30	Oct. 1	30	Nov. 1	30	2	30	Jan. 1	30	Feb. 1	30	3
31	4			31	2			31	2			31	2	31	2			31	2			31	4

Whelping chart, courtesy of Gaines.

Lois George with her friends.

Photo by Thom Carter

16
RAISING PUPPIES

CARING FOR THE NEWBORN

The first twenty-four hours are crucial to the newborn puppy. Puppies must be able to nurse within this time to obtain the bitch's colostrum—the milk that is secreted by the bitch just after parturition. Colostrum is more concentrated than ordinary milk, and it contains higher levels of protein and vitamin A. Through the colostrum, the puppies are able to gain initial passive immunity against disease during the first few weeks.

Regular bowel movements in puppies are very important. Two common problems are constipation and diarrhea. Impaction of meconium—the excrement accumulated prior to birth—may prove fatal. Meconium is passed naturally when the mother licks the newborn puppies for stimulation. The blackish substance is passed with the first bowel movement. The puppy depends upon the cleaning and licking to pass bladder and bowel wastes, which the bitch will clean up and consume.

VITAL SIGNS

The average suckling's temperature during the first two weeks is 94 to 97 degrees F. and rises to 99 degrees F. By the fifth week, the temperature should be nearing the adult body temperature, which is between 101 and 102.5 F.

During the first twenty-four hours of life, healthy newborn sucklings have a cardiac rate that accelerates from 120 to 150 heartbeats per minute up to 220 beats per minute through the first five weeks. The respiratory rate is eight to eighteen breaths per minute during the first twenty-four hours and fifteen to thirty-five breaths per minute during the following five weeks. The adult Australian Shepherd has an average respiration rate of seventeen to eighteen breaths per minute but can vary from ten to thirty breaths per minute, and a heartbeat of eighty to one hundred and forty beats per minute.

The first few weeks of life are devoted to eating and sleeping. During this period of "activated sleep," the puppies develop muscles through twitching and involuntary body movements. Newborn puppies make a sort of content humming sound when everything is alright. Crying, moaning, wailing, or restlessness (crawling) are danger signals. Chilling, overheating, hunger, and disease can all cause discomfort and even death to sucklings. Handling should be kept to a minimum during this time.

Newborn sucklings do not have a shivering reflex (thermoregulatory mechanism) until after the sixth day of life, nor do they have the ability to maintain their own body temperature. They depend on their mother's or littermates' warmth, or they get warmth from external sources such as heating lamps or heating pads.

The environmental temperature for sucklings during the first two weeks should be 85 degrees F. During cool weather, puppies are susceptible to hypothermia, which can cause death. However, a room temperature higher than 90 degrees F. can cause dehydration and death, because newborn puppies cannot pant to help regulate body temperature. The temperature of the whelping box can be reduced by five degrees weekly after the puppies' first seven days of life until it reaches 70 degrees F. by the time the puppies are between six to eight weeks old.

When the puppies near the eighteenth day, they will begin to walk, further stimulating the ability to maintain their own body heat.

The puppies should be identified by recording specific and unique markings or by painting the toenails with different brilliant colors of poodle nail polish. They should be weighed daily for the first week of life and then every two to three days until they are four weeks old. A consistent weight gain and normal stools will give you the most accurate reflection of the puppies' state of health. The newborns should gain weight from the first day of life and gain steadily until they reach adulthood.

Following along in his mother's footsteps. Puppies learn as they tag along doing daily chores. Take special care not to expose them to rough stock until they are able to take care of themselves (somewhere between six months and one year of age).

The sucklings should gain one to two grams per day, per pound of approximated adult weight. For example, a puppy expected to weigh forty pounds at maturity should gain forty to eighty grams, which can also be computed to one and a half to two and a half ounces (1 ounce = 28 grams) per day during the first six months. Most Aussies continue to grow at a steady rate until they are approximately six to nine months of age, at which time they will begin to slow down. If there is not a constant growth pattern (which can be confirmed by weighing every week), then you will need to adjust and/or supplement the puppies accordingly.

EXAMINATION OF WHELPS

Within the first twenty-four hours, you will need to examine each puppy for abnormalities that can occur due to improper development of the embryo. The Australian Shepherd is primarily a sound breed. Only a few abnormalities found in newborn puppies will be of immediate interest to the breeder.

Abnormalities can be due to some genetic factor or may be congenital caused by a foreign substance that crossed the placental barrier such as medications, vaccines, viruses etc.

Defective White Factor

The Australian Shepherd Breed Standard will guide you in determining audio and/or visual impairments, or blindness and/or deafness. These problems can affect them anywhere between the age of five weeks and two years. These puppies must be culled at birth due to the heartache they will bring when the unsoundness becomes apparent.

Eyes - The pupil will be perfectly positioned in the normal sound eye. Eyes can be checked and confirmed for soundness by a certified ophthalmologist. Eye problems are more thoroughly discussed in "Genetics." A few of the more easily recognized problems include offset pupils, which are evidenced by incorrect placement and shape of the iris; small pupils; sunburst pupils, in which the pupil appears fuzzy; and unformed eyes. Visual impairments in puppies may not be readily noticed in familiar environments because the puppies may possess minimal vision during the first month or so. If the sight diminishes, affected individuals may have familiarized themselves with their immediate surroundings. These puppies may go undetected until placed in an unfamiliar environment or until the furniture gets moved from its original place. The problem will first be noticed when these puppies are observed bumping into things.

Unformed Eyes - Occasionally, the eyes will have faulty development in the embryo stage. The iris and pupil may be present but generally faded. There is an apparent lack of muscular control characterized by a wandering eye. In severe cases, the eye can float out of sight when the puppy turns its head. The unformed eye may appear cloudy white, which should not be confused with the blue color of normal eyes the first few days after opening. Brown eyes are a darker blue, while the blue eyes are a few shades lighter. The normal eye color will richen as the puppy grows toward weaning stages.

Ears - Puppies that possess normal or only slightly impaired hearing will generally startle at loud or sudden noises, at the age of three weeks, once the ears open. This may be difficult to detect, because if two puppies are lying together and they hear a sudden noise, the normal puppy will react first, while the deaf or impaired puppy may react to the normal puppy, rather than to the noise. Your veterinarian can more easily recognize audio problems, so if you suspect a hearing impairment, consult a trained professional.

Cleft Palate

A cleft palate is evidenced by the presence of milk bubbling from the nostrils. A cleft palate occurs when there is a gap or opening in the roof of the mouth which leads directly to the sinus. The gap can vary in size from a slight pinhole to a large slit extending the length of the palate. In severe cases, a bilateral cleft will reach from the upper lip through the premaxilla and along the length of the hard palate. This fault interferes with the puppies' ability to nurse, and they often die of starvation.

A normal palate has thin ridges slightly raised which run from the center line of the palate to the outer edges. The roof of the mouth is firm to the touch. Cleft palates in the Australian Shepherd are rather isolated instances.

Harelip

The harelip, a split in the upper portion of the lip extending into the nostril, is due to improper formation of the muzzle. I know of no documented cases in the Australian Shepherd.

Hernia

The umbilical hernia has been known to affect the Australian Shepherd and is due to trauma placed upon the navel during the severing of the umbilical cord. Other hernia problems are rare in the Australian Shepherd.

Internal Disorders

A puppy or an entire litter may be affected by some internal disorder. One problem that may be mistaken for the cleft palate is that of an underdeveloped esophagus. In sucklings, the milk is forced out through the nostrils, restricting the passage of food. Puppies generally die when they begin consuming a more solid diet. This is *not* common with the Australian Shepherd.

Intestines Outside of the Body

This condition occurs when the walls of the stomach do not knit together properly in the middle before birth. It is believed to be a fault in the development of the embryo.

CULLING

Culling is not a pleasant subject, but it is one of the grave responsibilities in breeding Australian Shepherds. Culling takes place when some factor becomes apparent that will affect the mental and physical welfare of the prospective owner, the Australian Shepherd breed, and the individual Aussie. Euthanasia (humane death) can be arranged when you take your bitch in for her postwhelping examination.

TAIL DOCKING AND DEWCLAWS

Tail docking is traditional with the Australian Shepherd. Herding or driving dogs were exempt from taxes, and the tails were docked to prove their status and occupation.

Docking and dewclaw removal should be done between the third and fourth day. Some breeders will dock within the first twenty-four or forty-eight hours after birth. This extra twenty-four hours gives the puppy an opportunity to stabilize his system through the first three days of nursing.

There are many methods of removing tails, and it is wise to have an experienced breeder or your veterinarian show you the correct way the first few times. IN ANY CASE, THE DOCKED TAIL SHOULD COVER THE ANUS. It has also been expressed by certain breeders that cutting too close may damage certain nerve endings and affect the mobility of the hindquarter. The specific purpose of the tail is to show expression, but most important to wisk away debris and to provide a balancing factor. In specific cases, it is more difficult for an individual to maintain cleanliness without at least one or more joints.

Each joint can be estimated as an inch in length at adulthood. The Breed Standard allows up to four inches in length to accommodate the natural bobtail, AN IDENTIFYING CHARACTERISTIC OF THE AUSTRALIAN SHEPHERD. However, it is more widely accepted for show dogs to be docked between the first and second joint at birth or shortly thereafter.

Back dewclaws are not always present in the Australian Shepherd, but the front ones are. Occasionally, there may be one hind dewclaw. These should always be removed, and this can be done easily when the tail is docked. Even after removal, regrowth may occur. The front dewclaws may or may not be removed, according to your personal preference. Removal lends a clean appearance to the foreleg and eliminates the possibility of getting hung up and ripped on dense thicket. Because the front dewclaws are more tightly attached to the bones of the leg, removal is a bit more crucial. Your veterinarian or an experienced breeder can show you how, but *NEVER* use any type of hot iron to sear or cauterize. The intense degree of heat has been known to stunt the bone, causing improper development of the toes.

TOENAILS

Within a few days after birth, your puppies will need to have the tiny hooks trimmed from their razor-sharp toenails. This practice keeps the puppies from tearing up their dam's breasts, which can make her reluctant to feed her litter. It also begins to establish early minimal socialization and handling.

RAISING ORPHAN AND FOSTER PUPPIES

If you have orphan puppies, try to find another mother who will take them. Survival is greatly increased with a canine foster mother. Many females will accept orphans if you rub the scent of her own puppies on the newcomer(s). Always offer the puppy bottom first—rarely will a bitch with strong mothering instincts ignore a bottom to clean! If no substitute bitch is available, if the bitch will not accept the puppies, or if she does not have an adequate supply of milk for her own litter, then you must take over the job. If another animal around the house wants to be a "foster" parent, do not discourage it. The attention and warmth will be beneficial.

The main need of newborn puppies is to be dried thoroughly and be kept at a constant temperature. In the case of an emergency, put the puppies inside clean socks or sweater sleeves. Keep the heads and noses out. A heating pad covered with a waterproof material and set on a very low temperature can also be used. Place one-half of the pad on the floor of the box, and the other half up on the side wall. This way, the puppies can get close to the warmth if they are cold, or get away if they are too warm. If a hot water bottle is used, continually check for constant temperature to prevent the bottle from cooling. A drop in temperature can initiate hypothermia by chilling the puppies. Hot water bottles should probably be covered with a blanket or towel to prevent burning the neonatal puppies. Keep orphan puppies in a sturdy box large enough to accommodate the puppies but small enough for them to maintain their own body heat. Use material that the puppies' nails cannot get caught in. Newspaper is unsuitable for maintaining the puppies' temperature.

Keep the box in a draft-free area in your house. Do not leave the puppies in the sun or on the damp ground or other surfaces. Keeping them in the house will allow you easy access and observation. If something is wrong, you will be alarmed by their crying or by the feel of their body temperature.

Young children should be taught to sit on the floor while holding puppies. Sara Pasek and "Pokey."   *Courtesy Potter*

Orphan puppies can either be bottle-fed or tube-fed. The latter is the most efficient method if there are more than a couple of orphans, but bottle feeding is advantageous and imperative in developing the natural "sucking reflexes."

Many puppies have been lost from overanxious feeding. A tiny puppy is unable to pass urine or move the bowels without stimulus. This occurs naturally when the bitch licks and cleans her puppies during the first two weeks. This stimulus must now be done with a damp, warm cloth or a piece of damp, warm gauze or cotton. Gently massage the stomach and the urinary and anal orifices with the damp material after each feeding. Keep stroking until elimination discontinues.

Bottle feeding is beneficial to orphans in that it allows the puppies to develop their natural "sucking" reflexes. When the puppies are newly whelped, instincts direct the neonatals to their mother's teats, which they grasp with their tongue and mouth. The strong suction induces the milk flow. The puppies use their paws to "knead" their mother's breasts, further stimulating milk production. It is also important to give the puppies a natural nursing position—lying on the stomach with the head raised slightly. Never feed puppies on their backs, as they will choke easily.

The natural bobtail.

The proper formula is designed specifically to simulate the characteristics of the bitch's milk. These fall under several brand names, such as *Esbilac®*, *Vetalac®*, and *Unilac®*. Dennis F. Lawler, D.V.M. (Purina Labs) recommends a laboratory-tested emergency home-formulated milk replacer: One cup of milk (eight ounces), three egg yolks (no albumin), one tablespoon corn oil, one drop high-quality oral multiple vitamin (preferably baby vitamins), and a tiny pinch of salt. This should be blended uniformly and warmed to 95 to 100 degrees F. When tested on the human wrist, the temperature should be very near your own (it should feel warm, not hot).

Use a baby bottle (i.e. Playtex Nurser) with a firm nipple. If the milk will not readily form droplets on your wrists, you will have to use the tip of a heated needle to prick the tip. Test it again. The milk shouldn't flow out, but seep. Too much milk flow could choke the puppy. Squeeze a small amount of milk into the tip of the nipple and place it in the puppy's mouth.

Feed the puppy five to six evenly spaced intervals throughout the day and night during the first week, four to five intervals throughout the second and third weeks, and three to four intervals during the fourth and fifth weeks. A regular schedule should be kept to avoid the possibility of colic. *Pepto Bismol®* may help relieve digestive disturbances. Some breeders will occasionally use a drop or two of whiskey mixed with warm water. If this does not seem to do the trick, then you will want to feed at more frequent intervals and possibly adjust the amount of formula. The puppies will indicate their needs by the amounts of food that they accept and by their level of contentment after consuming it. Hand-fed puppies must be burped in the same manner as a human baby after feeding.

Mix only enough formula for immediate feedings. The bottles and nipples should be thoroughly disinfected between feedings to prevent contamination.

When the puppies begin to walk, introduce them to solid food. The gruel made for orphan puppies can consist of their own formula blended with food designed to meet the needs of "growth." If this causes diarrhea, use water or vegetable broth with the diet. Continue to supplement the formula until the puppies are at least four or five weeks old. At this point, the puppies should be eating solid food quite well.

The correct feeding position.

Photo by Jerry Rowe
Courtesy Sharon Rowe, "Pups N' Stuff"

Tube Feeding

Tube feeding employs a method of "injecting" the formula into the puppy's stomach. This is a valuable aid in supplying nutrients to neonatal puppies, and it can be done with ease, since the puppies do not develop the gag reflex until about the twelfth day. Tube feeding can help to get puppies off to a good start, but once the puppies seem to "pick up," you should switch to bottle feeding.

Tube feeding involves considerably less time as compared to bottle feeding. If the chore of caring for orphan puppies becomes too great with a larger litter, perhaps a friend will share the burden.

For tube feeding, you will need a ten (ml or cc) to fifty (ml or cc) plastic syringe. The tubing should consist of some sort of semirigid rubber that can be passed down into the puppies' stomachs. A number five catheter tube (similar to the ones used for premature human neonatals) is ideal for the newborn puppy.

To determine the correct length for the tube, hold the puppy so that its head will be extended forward (not up). Place a tube along the side of each puppy. The tip of the tube should NOT extend past the last rib, from the tip of the nose. Mark the tube. This will allow the tube to extend into each puppy's stomach. It must not go beyond the mark, because it could cause pressure or perforate the stomach. Constantly recheck this length, and remark it as each puppy grows. Before using, boil the syringe and tube. After each use, disinfect to prevent contamination.

Heat the formula to 95 or 100 degrees F., near your own body temperature. Double-check the puppy's position, and if necessary, readjust it. If you have no success, seek professional assistance. Your veterinarian can demonstrate the correct ways of tube feeding.

Fill the syringe with the already warmed bitch's milk replacer, then attach the premeasured catheter tube. Expel the air from within the syringe by injecting the plunger just until the formula begins to drip from the tip of the tube. Place each puppy (one at a time) horizontally in the natural nursing position. While on the stomach on either a flat surface or in the palm of one of your hands, gently extend the puppy's head forward, neither up nor down. Lubricate the catheter with several drops of formula. Open the mouth partially, and carefully slip the tube over the tongue. The puppy should begin to swallow the tube. As this happens gently insert the tube no farther than the predetermined mark (identified with adhesive tape). If there is any resistance, withdraw the catheter. Any difficulty may alert a danger signal.

Once you are confident that the tube is in the stomach, inject the fluid slowly. The administration should gradually take place over a period of two to two and one-half minutes. When the puppy has been fed the correct amount, the stomach should appear round and full, but not hard and distended.

After you have fed the puppies, you will need to clean them to stimulate excretion. This must be done during the first few weeks of life. You will be able to recognize when the puppies are capable of eliminating on their own without the need of external stimulus. However, you will still need to keep the puppies cleaned meticulously as the mother would.

Generally, you can administer two ounces of bitch's milk replacer per pound of body weight in a twenty-four-hour period during the first weeks. This will yield sixty to seventy calories per pound of body weight every twenty-four hours. The second week the puppy will require approximately two and one-half ounces of bitch's milk replacer per pound of body weight every twenty-four hours. Three ounces of the formula given during the third week should provide an estimated eighty to ninety calories per pound of body weight every twenty-four hours. During the third or fourth week, you will begin to introduce the puppies to a gruel. The puppy's system may now require 100 to 110 calories per pound of body weight each day.

CARE OF THE EYES

Puppies' eyes begin to open between the seventh and the fourteenth day. The lids first open at the inner corner and gradually extend toward the outside. The tissue around the eyes may become swollen when the eyes begin to open. Soak a gauze or cotton pad in a solution of lukewarm water or in a mixture of boric acid, and gently swab the eyes clean. Pus may secrete from the slightest pressure. Keep the eyes cleaned with each scheduled feeding.

Consult your veterinarian, as any infection can spread and cause complications. Neglect or improper handling may result in loss or impairment of the eye(s) for life. Also, the infection may respond best to the application of certain ophthalmic ointments that your veterinarian may want to prescribe.

If eyes become puffy or swollen before they are open, you will need the assistance of your veterinarian. Do not attempt to pry open the eye tissue. The eyes are very sensitive, and you could cause permanent damage.

BOWEL MOVEMENTS

The puppy should have three to six bowel movements during a twenty-four hour period. The stool should be firm and yellowish. If diarrhea occurs, administer a few drops of *Kaopectate®*, or *Milk of Magnesia®*. If the excretia appears curdled, the pup-

py is being overfed, and more than likely he will look bloated.

Give plenty of TLC.

PUPPY AILMENTS

Healthy neonatal sucklings feel warm to the touch. They nurse vigorously, and when stimulated by their mother, they should demonstrate vitality versus a lifelessness. Many factors can affect the newborn puppy, and the puppy in return has a very limited ability to react to the environment and to disease processes.

Dehydration

Besides lacking the shivering reflex for the first six days, newborns have a minute amount of subcutaneous fat (fat lying directly beneath the skin). Until the puppy's main energy supply is replenished through several days of nursing, his energy source—glycogen (blood sugar that is stored in the liver before birth)—becomes rapidly depleted. Dehydration is apparent when the skin looks loose and nonelastic. It will remain "pinched" rather than immediately springing back to its original state. This is an extremely serious condition. Generally, puppies require sixty-five to ninety ml of water per pound of body weight every day. If the puppy appears to be only mildly dehydrated but is nursing vigorously, then keep an eye on him. However, it is best to consult your veterinarian, because what may look like a mild case of dehydration could be accompanied by complications.

If the puppies are being kept in a warm environment, the chances for your puppies' survival are very good.

Chilling and Hypothermia

Chilling results in hypothermia, which becomes complicated by hypoglycemia. The vicious cycle may begin when the mother refuses to nurse the puppy and pushes him away from the others, or when a puppy is accidently removed from the whelping box.

A hypothermic puppy will feel cool to the touch. Care must be taken not to raise the body temperature too quickly, inducing shock. Bring circulation to the puppy by gently rubbing the puppy between your hands or with a towel. Place the puppy underneath your armpit or your shirt, jacket, or coat. Severely chilled puppies may be revived by immersing the pup up to its neck in a pan of luke warm water, then thoroughly drying it to prevent chilling. Heating pads set at low temperatures are used *ONLY* when the puppy has regained normal body temperature.

Do not feed any formulas until the puppy's body temperature normalizes. Administer glucose only for the first feeding, and this only when the puppy feels warm again. The digestive system is unable to sufficiently digest formula until the body temperature is normal. *Gatorade®* has been used under emergency circumstances as a fluid replacer until veterinarian assistance can be sought. One teaspoon of honey or corn syrup (forms of glucose) in an ounce of warm water can also be substituted. This can be administered by an eye dropper every fifteen to thirty minutes. If necessary, minute amounts can be administered with a tube. Do not introduce milk replacer formulas if the body temperature is below 94 degrees F.

Diarrhea

Diarrhea is a common occurrence in puppies and may be caused by any one of several conditions, including bad milk from the mother, parasites, infections, varying formula preparations, overfeeding and/or overeating, colic, etc. Diarrhea can easily lead to dehydration.

Two to four drops (up to eight) of *Kaopectate®* every few hours may help correct the situation. *Milk of Magnesia®* may also be helpful. Rice water has been known to be an effective remedy against diarrhea in certain circumstances. If the situation is not corrected within the first twelve hours, consult your veterinarian. Administer all forms of glucose at only one-half teaspoon to one ounce of water, and feed only small amounts. Hand-fed puppies should temporarily be taken off formula. If the puppy volunteers to nurse the mother, then allow him to do so. Saline solutions, some containing electrolytes, can be administered subcutaneously in the case of dehydration caused by diarrhea.

Overheating

Guard against overheating, which will be symptomized by crying, screaming, and general restlessness. The puppy may hyperventilate. Dehydration may also accompany the condition. Immediately remove the puppy away from the heat back into a normal temperature, which is about 85 degrees F. during the first six days.

If a puppy cries and whimpers while being kept in the correct temperature, then something else may be wrong. Consult your veterinarian.

Constipation

Constipation causes toxemia. The puppy may appear normal in general appearance, but it will not nurse or demonstrate vitality. The puppy may squeal and whimper. Use a damp, warm cloth to gently massage the stomach. If this does not produce results and relief for the puppy, take it to the veterinarian.

Canine Herpes Virus (CHV)

Herpes virus is a fatal infection causing sudden death. It is acquired between the time of whelping to one month of age, generally between three days to three weeks of age. The incubation period is three to eight days.

CHV is responsible for vaginitis in adult bitches. It may be manifested in adults by a nasal discharge or an upper respiratory tract infection. CHV growth is greatly inhibited at 102.2 degrees F. The virus flourishes between 95 and 98.6 degrees F., which is the average temperature range of puppies through the first month of life. At about five weeks of age, puppies are nearing their adult temperature, which is why the virus does not develop to an acute degree in adult dogs.

Bitches that have been infected with CHV develop immunity. Subsequently, puppies whelped after an infected litter generally will not be overtaken by the virus.

Cases of tracheobronchitis, commonly called "kennel cough" (a respiratory tract infection), may be an adult expression of herpes virus. Individuals with the symptoms should be isolated.

Presently, there is no vaccine for CHV. The initial symptoms are similar to those found in distemper, hepatitis, and viral pneumonia. The puppies become hypothermic, they stop nursing, they are listless, and they have runny noses, labored respiration, and congestion. Cyanosis (blue skin coloration) of the nose leather, lips, feet, and tongue is due to unoxygenated blood. Agonized crying and screaming lasts for hours until death. The lungs are generally affected with pneumonia. Death usually occurs within twenty-four hours after the onset of symptoms.

If you suspect any of the above symptoms, get to the veterinarian. You will be unable to save the litter, but a diagnosis is imperative to correctly determine the virus.

SOCIALIZATION

From the time the puppies begin to walk, you will want to introduce them to various household noises—children talking, laughing, television noises, radio programs, pots and pans. The interaction with everyday activities will make an immense difference.

Handling

Until the puppies begin to walk, all handling should be at a minimum. They especially need this time to sleep and eat. The most important period is between three and twelve weeks. The puppies should receive an overabundance of loving care. They should receive actual human contact when you pet or brush the puppy, and when you trim the toenails, etc.

Temptation of Windermere with a six-hour old lamb.

Courtesy Williams

It is excellent when the puppies can spend several hours each day with the family during the various daily routines. This contact is extremely important for all puppies. You can never hope to build a confident individual without this early handling.

A short ride in the car will accustom the puppies to riding, and this provides one more situation in which to "handle" the puppies. Socialization prepares each puppy for a well-rounded future as a superior companion, working dog, and obedience competitor.

RECOMMENDED VACCINATION SCHEDULE

Puppies should receive their first vaccinations at eight weeks of age, followed by revaccinations (sometimes called booster shots) at twelve and sixteen weeks, or according to your veterinarian's recommendations. ANNUAL boosters are required.

PUPPY EVALUATION

At birth and during the first couple of weeks, blocky heads and firm neck attachments are desired features that express adequate substance. The bodies should feel well-rounded and solid. A healthy puppy should show strength in its movements. Beware of a puppy that appears to be limp or that feels weak.

Ideally, the litter should be as uniform in size and shape as possible. Often there is one that is slightly

Exposure to all things is necessary to develop a well-rounded disposition.

larger and one that is slightly smaller than the other puppies in the same litter. This is no need for concern as long as the difference is not extreme. It has been said that this may be attributed to matings that take place throughout the fertile cycle. A true "runt" is not necessarily the smallest puppy in a litter. A runt will have stunted physical characteristics exhibiting dwarflike traits.

As the eyes and ears begin to open, you will notice continuing developmental changes in the head. As the eyes open, they will be deep blue. The adult eye color will become apparent at eight weeks.

By the third and fourth weeks of age, the head is beginning to shape into proper proportion. The ear muscles are taking charge by five weeks of age. The ears will begin to take shape and go through many stages by lifting up and/or dropping down. At this

Proper handling and socialization is imperative to developing a sound mind and body.

age, the puppies are also very active. You will want to observe them jumping, running, and playing. Observant alert puppies are desirable. If you have one that seems to hang back away from the activities, you will first want to observe it for good health. Between seven and nine weeks you will notice the pecking order establish. The dominant puppy may change from day to day. If a puppy has been bullied or "beat down" it may be wise to separate the litter into two or three groups allowing each equal time away from the others. This is especially important if the puppies will be going into separate homes. This is a good time to start minimal crate training and car riding experience. Grooming and other such tasks will enable you to initiate the human/dog relationship while building confidence.

Between eight to twelve weeks of age, each puppy should look like it will as an adult but in miniature. Puppies that trot as the main gait are said to be in balance with themselves. Testicles should be present in males at this age.

During rapid growth, the hindquarters may appear to be higher than the forequarters. The topline may appear to sag while the legs go in different directions. In evaluating puppies during this adolescent stage, breeders prefer to see different traits. In some lines, a puppy that "toes out" slightly is more likely to correct itself even as late as three or four years of age when the dog has filled out and is fully matured. Certain developmental stages are more bloodline specific, and the experienced breeder will be able to guide you through these periods.

The ears will usually go through a variety of changes during teething. One ear may stand straight up while the other hangs down on the other side. If the ears are small in size and stand "pricked" or semipricked during this stage, some breeders will "weight" the ears to cosmetically correct them for show purposes. They will roll up wetproof adhesive tape placed on the inside tops of the ears and then "set" the ears to fold at one-fourth to one-half above the base. In cold weather, these ears may stand up more than during warm weather. You can gently massage ear leather to make ears more pliable and willing to lie down. Products such as vitamin ointments, bag balms, and neatsfoot oil will also soften ear leather. Caution should be taken during cold weather to prevent frostbite damage caused by restricted circulation to the ears when taped or glued.

Between twelve weeks and twenty weeks, the puppy coat will shed out, and the adult guard hairs will begin growing in. They will first appear down the back and across the shoulders. The feathers and ruff will become more profuse. It is also during this period that the bite may "shift" as the muzzle lengthens and the jaw grows into adult proportions.

Dispositions are entirely individual. Most Australian Shepherds will go through an insecure adolescent period between six and nine months of age. This is a very critical mental developmental stage. Socialization and handling are imperative to build confidence.

Pigmentation on the nose leather is a concern for many Aussie owners. Pink spots on the nose, especially those that are surrounded by pigment, will usually fill in with age. Pink spots *in* the nose should not cause concern. The dudley nose (one without pigmentation) is a concern due to direct sun exposure. The sun can cause irritation to the unpigmented area; therefore, it is more susceptible to sunburn and solar dermatitis. Although the butterfly nose is faulted after one year of age, some Aussies may take two to three years for the nose to become fully pigmented. This is due to the breed's tendency for coat coloring to darken with age. Some deep-colored merles will appear almost solid in color as these individuals approach their twilight years.

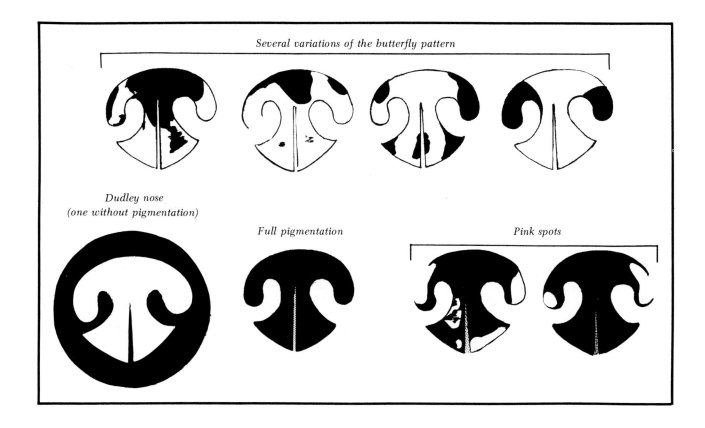

Several variations of the butterfly pattern

Dudley nose
(one without pigmentation)

Full pigmentation

Pink spots

MATURITY

Some bloodlines are quick to mature. In early developing lines, individuals may appear fully matured by twelve months of age. By two and one-half to three years of age, these individuals may appear to be "overdone," thereby lacking athletic ability.

Early maturity has given youngsters the disadvantage of being "pushed" to finish their championships, obedience titles, stock dog titles, and so forth, before they have reached the mental maturity to accept the pressures of competitive preparation and training.

In slower maturing lines, individuals will be physically "balanced" but will not fully "blossom" or "fill out" until two and one-half to three or even four years of age. These individuals often look exceptional at six and seven years of age. The Australian Shepherd possesses longevity because of slow maturation. Maturity is a quality that must be observed to fully understand the changes manifested during growth. When your dog reaches this point, he will look more like the individual that you pictured when you acquired a puppy from a certain cross and/or bloodline.

Due to the varying degrees of developmental differences between bloodlines, it is wise to observe not only the parents, grandparents, brothers and sisters, but also the progeny of the aforementioned to gain a keener insight about the pattern of development in related individuals. This should tell you a lot about your puppy. Remember, however, that each dog is an individual. There are many physiological changes that take place from puppyhood into adulthood. Generally speaking, all individuals will go through "stages" where they are not "together" and in certain instances will appear to "fall apart" during the teenage stage. This of course, will vary with each individual. They will begin to regain physical balance somewhere between nine and eighteen months.

End Notes

Dennis F. Lawler. D.V.M., *Tube-feeding Puppies* (St. Louis, Missouri: Ralston Purina Company, 1980).

L.D. Lewis, D.V.M., Ph. D, *Feeding and Care of the Dog*, From Notes presented at the Animal Reproduction Laboratory, Fort Collins, Colorado, Colorado State University, 1980.

The same male at different stages of development. Upper Left: twelve weeks old. Upper Right: four months old. Lower Left: at one year old the individual is skeletally proportioned but the muscles have yet to "fill out." At this stage the adult guard hair and undercoat have fully replaced the puppy coat. Lower Right: two and one-half years old.

The very typical expression that identifies Australian Shepherds.

Courtesy Mary Welch

17
GENERAL CARE

While cleanliness is imperative, fancy operations with expensive, made-to-order houses, chain-link fencing, cement runs, and stainless steel pans are impressive. Just remember that a show place does not guarantee the health, care, or welfare of its occupants. Nor does it guarantee the knowledge of the owner. The most important feature to any kennel is the care of the dogs through commonsense management.

No matter how impressive or modest the layout, a few basic features must be considered. Your plans need not be expensive or complex. With a little imagination, you may be able to convert existing buildings into an adequate setup. You must also consider local zoning regulations. State, city, and county departments should be consulted for specific requirements. Some research facilities or other breeders can provide blueprints or share their ideas with you.

Suitable and necessary features in your dog shelter include smooth, impervious walls to avoid breeding areas for germs and parasites and to facilitate effective cleansing and disinfecting. The housing should be placed so the drainage is good, sloping away from the shelter. Kennels should *not* be located near bodies of stagnant water or swamps.

There is a well-founded belief that the best layout is with the long axis in a north-south direction, which means an easterly exposure. A northern exposure is cold and, because of a lack of direct sunlight, is frequently damp, though it does offer the advantage of coolness during the hot months. A southern exposure is hot and more likely to subject the dogs to pesty insects. An eastern exposure at least compromises many of the disadvantages of either northern or southern exposures. Ideally, the layout should offer relief from the sun in the summer and allow maximum sun exposure during the coldest months. An overhang of corrugated tin or fiberglass can provide shade along with trees, shrubs, and nontoxic vines.

A kennel should be a sound, waterproof structure in good repair. A good, reasonably high foundation and double walls or walls of porous material (with impervious inner surfaces) afford the best insulation. Floors with a broom-finished cement, though more difficult to clean, give each dog better footing. The coldness of cement floors may be largely prevented by insulating them with a thick layer of cinders or with hollow tile or brick under the concrete. Or you may place loose, properly fitted wooden platforms on top of the cement floor. Floors should also have drains to carry away liquid waste. This does not necessarily involve an extensive system, as it may be attained by shallow gutters directed toward a common channel. Floors should be sloped to provide proper drainage.

All wooden, cinder, or concrete surfaces should be sealed with a coat of epoxy paint (or similar substances such as lacquer paints) to further protect against parasitic infestations and disease.

VENTILATION

Oxygen is obtained from fresh air; therefore, proper ventilation is necessary. Screened, louvered windows and sunroofs (with or without a screen) can all provide fresh air and light.

NATURAL LIGHT

There must be an adequate source of natural sunlight either directly or through light-pervious material other than ordinary glass (ordinary glass does not permit ultraviolet radiation). Sunlight is a source of germ "control," (sunlight filtered through ordinary glass is not destructive to germs) and plays a vital role in enabling animals to absorb nutrients such as calcium from food.

SLEEPING QUARTERS

Each sleeping compartment should be large enough to accommodate your Aussie while stretched out without the dog being limited in length or width. Measurements are generally taken on the mature Aussie. The compartment should be tall enough to allow your dog to stand naturally with the head elevated so that he is not forced to be restricted or made to "duck."

The entrance should be large enough to accommodate your dog. A flap hung over the door will allow easy access. Many variations can be made with a little imagination, and there are also commercial options available.

BEDDING

To provide comfort, your facilities must either be adequately heated and/or bedded with appropriate material. Dogs can contract bone and muscle ailments when improperly and insufficiently bedded on cold cement or hard surfaces and floors. A variety of materials make good bedding. Washable blankets and rugs are ideal, but fresh, clean hay, straw, cedar shavings, leaves, or sawdust are adequate. All of these substances absorb a relatively high amount of moisture, which is desirable. The shorter materials are best used when an individual is sick or for the very young because their feet will not become entangled. Soiled bedding should be removed and replaced frequently.

RUNS AND EXERCISE

All indoor/outdoor facilities should have connecting outdoor runs to ensure adequate exercise, fresh air, and natural light. The more confined the dog, the more exercise will be required to maintain mental health and muscle tone. The Australian Shepherd is an active working breed. It goes without saying that each individual needs sufficient room to exercise regularly.

Each dog needs a yard or run in which to exercise safely. Running at large, unsupervised, is not only dangerous, but it is irresponsible on the part of the owner. At the other extreme, you see dogs chained up to any type contraption which is thoughtless and certainly not recommended.

If you have only one or two dogs, then a securely fenced yard is probably sufficient. Even with only one or two dogs, it is wise to have a secure run, especially for females in estrus or when you are unable to be with your dogs to supervise.

Any and all runs should be securely fenced with dog-proof wire and equipped with secure latches and hooks. To be safe, you must be positive that the entire area is free from broken glass, sharp objects, and edges such as rusty metal, torn and broken wire, and holes. The area should be at least six feet high. Aussies have been known to dig out from under a secure fence, climb, and/or even jump. If in doubt, an overhang or top can be installed. The perimeter of dog areas should be securely fenced. Six feet will maintain most individuals.

A platform should be available, especially to allow mothers to get away from their babies on occasion and when weaning. A jungle gym, crate, or large wooden box are wonderful for dogs of all ages. Rubber tires also make excellent objects to stand on and jump across. Rubber balls, plastic milk jugs, old tennis shoes, rubber thongs, and slippers make good "chew" toys to carry around.

Play and exercise areas should also have shade during the summer months that will lend protection

First snow.

from the elements. The platform, if constructed properly, can serve this purpose somewhat, but a corrugated tin or fiberglass overhang above it will work well. The main objective is to provide a secure, safe area for your dogs to "romp" without the threat of danger.

Ideally, runs should be six feet wide by thirty feet long. The longer the better. The thought behind the length is that it gives each dog the opportunity to "run" without "running in circles." A solid stockade-type fence between six and eight feet high of wood, cinder blocks or similar materials, as well as trees, shrubs, and vines around the perimeter of the kennel, will help muffle sound and may form a screen to help block airborne disease. Soothing music from a radio will also have a calming effect on dogs to further eliminate disturbance.

SANITATION

You should have an adequate service room for cleaning your equipment, washing water bowls etc. There should be no accumulation of debris and/or excretia. Soiled gravel and sand should be replaced

Youngsters in their play yard.

frequently, and there should be adequate disposal for such wastes.

If there is any problem with insects or rodents, professional help should be sought (often county extension agents are available) to prevent contamination and disease.

A good pair of Dooling sticks will aid in quick cleanup. There are also several varieties of "mini" septic tanks—systems that use live organisms (enzymes) to dissolve excretia. The liquefied material then "leaches" into the ground through its miniature leaching field (bed) to make disposal sanitary and manageable.

Sanitation is a constant concern for the dog owner. If you live in the city and must use a confined area, or especially if you must use a park or other public facilities, it is imperative to clean up after your dog.

FOOD AND WATER

To prevent contamination, all food must be stored in a sanitary manner. Rodent and insect-proof containers are a good investment. You must be able to provide a safe and sanitary water supply for your animals. Potable water should be available to your dogs at all times. The addition of 2 ounces of apple cider, vinegar or lemon juice to 1 gallon of water will help balance the pH for the intestinal tract.

SICK ANIMALS

You must be able to provide an adequate place that isolates sick individuals from the others until veterinary care is available.

WHEN YOU HAVE LIMITED SPACE

If space is limited and you are unable to provide a proper exercise area or fenced yard, portable exercise pens may be of aid. Several rolls of snow fence may also prove adequate. They can be attached to almost anything (several stakes can be used for stabilization), including your house. When not in use, they can be rolled up, yet in only minutes serve as an ingenious setup enabling your dog to be out in the fresh air without being "on the loose."

Trolley System

Although it is never recommended that you "chain" or "tie up" your dog, the use of a trolley system (used only with a thick, wide leather or nylon collar—NEVER USE WITH THIN OR TRAINING OR "CHOKE" COLLARS) equipped with a shock-absorber system may be a helpful device to provide outdoor exercise if you are unable to supervise.

TATTOOING

The use of collars for temporary identification is ineffective in the case of stolen, stray, and often lost individuals. The role of positive identification afforded through tattooing is limitless. It affords protection for valuable breeding stock, champions, working dogs, and faithful companions. Positive identification is often necessary during litigation regarding stolen dogs, as well as for other transactions including artificial insemination and sale transfers. With each individual that is sold, a transfer slip should accompany each dog to the new owner. Nose and paw prints, freeze-branding, and tattooing are all methods of permanent identification. Tattooing is the only absolute proof of ownership in a court of law.

The abdomen or inside right thigh are the safest areas to tattoo that cannot be easily mutilated through amputation. Positive identification consists of tattooing an owner's social security number on this area. For a minimal one-time fee this number can be registered for a lifetime with the National Dog Registry

(NDR). Once the initial fee is paid, there is generally a tattooing fee of a few dollars for each additional dog. Tattoo clinics are often available in conjunction with local shows and matches and through your veterinarian. Once registered with the NDR, the identity of a missing or stolen dog can be verified and confirmed.

Tattooing is a quick (it usually involves no more than a few minutes), painless procedure. A vibrator unit is used to permanently apply the numbers, then tattoo pigment (ink or paste) is applied for easy identification. Numbers on the thigh should be made readily visible by clipping the hair. Tattoos on the abdomen are often more visible than anywhere else.

TO OBTAIN FURTHER INFORMATION AND REGISTRATION FORMS, WRITE OR CALL: THE NATIONAL DOG REGISTRY (A TWENTY-FOUR-HOUR AGENCY),
227 STEBBINS ROAD
CARMEL, NEW YORK 10512
PHONE NUMBER—(914) 277-4485.

SPAYING AND NEUTERING

Unless you intend to breed your female or male or exhibit in the conformation ring, you may want to consider having your female spayed and/or your male neutered. Spaying is not a painful operation, and it is conducted while the patient is under anesthesia. There is no major danger involved, but there is always risk when any patient undergoes major abdominal surgery. However, there is a far greater risk that an unspayed bitch will develop life-threatening uterine infections and/or mammary tumors (a common malignancy in the bitch). The probability of breast cancer decreases when spaying is performed prior to two and one-half years of age, and especially prior to the first heat cycle.

Although there is the possibility that one out of a thousand females will end up dribbling urine after being spayed, the condition can be controlled by periodic doses of medication. Your veterinarian would be able to tell you the estimated figures regarding the probability of incidence and cost of medication.

The expense of spaying will vary with the location and economy of the area and with the age, size, and physical condition of the bitch. Often veterinarians offer their services at a reasonable fee to prevent unwanted puppies.

Spaying will not in any way affect the intelligence or disposition of your dog. The problems of overweight females often attributed to spaying can more often result from an improper diet and inadequate exercise.

Leading the way.   *Courtesy Weaver*

It is not advisable or necessary to allow the bitch to have one litter before being altered. Nor is it recommended that a female be bred just for the sake of having the litter so that the children can learn about the miracle of life. This knowledge can be better obtained through a visit to a local farm or zoo.

There are alternatives to spaying. Although the surgical procedure and anesthesia are basically the same as for spaying, tubal ligation only prevents conception from taking place. Contraceptive drugs are available to prevent estrus in the bitch but only provide a temporary alternative method. The use of these drugs is recommended only while under the supervision of your veterinarian, and only if you do not intend to breed the bitch at a future time.

Reproductive control of unaltered females involves constantly supervising the bitch throughout the twenty-three-day estrus cycle twice a year. The owner must take full responsibility for providing a secure enclosure that is inaccessible to other dogs. If you do not have a secure area, then you will have to keep her with you and take her out to exercise on lead, never leaving her unattended even for one minute. You may decide to place your female in a reliable boarding kennel during this time to eliminate the chance of an unwanted litter and also to discourage stray male dogs from creating a nuisance.

Neutering is the surgical removal of the testicles (castration). It can be performed at any age on the healthy male. Ideally, males should be neutered prior to maturity of the sex organs before male behavioral traits begin to develop at about six months of age. The neutered male will be less likely to stray. Neutering also prevents testicular tumors and helps to decrease and prevent other conditions such as prostatic disease, perineal tumors, and hernias.

The only surgical alternative to neutering is a vasectomy. The procedure and anesthesia are basically the same as for neutering. Vasectomies only prevent reproduction, but do not eliminate behavioral or medical problems related to intact sexuality.

SHIPPING BY AIR

Air shipment is the quickest, most reliable way of getting your Aussie from one point to another, both nationally and internationally. It is also the most commonly used mode of transportation upon the sale or purchase of a puppy.

For whatever reason you will be shipping, it is the responsibility of the shipper to see that the individual is routed safely to his destination.

Health Certificate

Prior to shipping, a health certificate must be issued by a licensed veterinarian. There are time limitations on health certificates governed specifically by each state. If your veterinarian does not have this information, contact your state health board.

Age

No individual should be shipped prior to eight weeks of age due to the tremendous stress factors involved, including susceptibility to infections.

Shipping

Contact the airline for specific information regarding flight numbers and departure and arrival times. Always try to get a direct, nonstop flight to avoid long layovers in terminals. This is not always possible, however, and a connecting flight may have to be used. Try to coordinate sufficient time for transfer between carriers. Contact the buyer by phone the night before shipping to relay flight information. If the dog is to accompany you while in flight, you should also make prior arrangements with the airline. You will be able to take your dog along as excess baggage with an accompanying fee. Reservations made well in advance are imperative, because airlines will only accept a limited number of "live" cargo during any one flight.

Most airlines require that animals be checked in at least two hours prior to the scheduled takeoff time, but no more than three hours prior to shipping, unless by previous arrangement, and only under special circumstances.

Secure your copy of the air bill. Be sure to list the declared value and insure the dog. Ask that the airline also include NOTIFY ON ARRIVAL (NOA) on the air bill. Two phone numbers should be listed for the receiver, if possible, so that he may be easily reached.

Your dog will be placed in the air kennel and weighed. You should be available either at the airport or at a given phone number in the event that something would prevent the shipment of your dog or the flight from taking off.

Shipping charges are categorized as prepaid (paid for in advance) by the shipper or collect (shipping fees paid for upon receipt). The method of payment should be agreed upon by both parties in advance.

Exploring the world together.

Time out!

Sedation is not recommended unless advised by your veterinarian, and only then if tested prior to the time of shipping. Exercise and water your dog before shipping him.

Weather

It is critical that your dog be acclimated to the temperatures in which he will be shipped. It is best not to ship during temperature extremes, such as weather that is below zero and over eighty degrees. If the individual is maintained indoors in a temperature-controlled environment, then temperatures less than 45 degrees F. or above 75 degrees F. may be considered extreme. During cold months, ship during the middle part of the day. If it is necessary to ship during the hot months, then schedule late evening and night or early morning flights. Take into consideration when the flight is due to arrive at its destination, and estimate the temperatures expected at that time and place.

A good dog is a best friend. Jeremy King with Hoyt's Dago Moreno UD (George's Red Rustler ex Faxon's Donnagal).
Courtesy Warren

Shipping Kennel (Crate)

Your dog will need an appropriate shipping kennel. It can be constructed of metal, wood, or heavy plastic and must be sturdy. Many commercial travel crates meet the necessary requirements while providing a safe means of sheltering your dog. Wire kennels are susceptible to being crushed and are drafty. Metal kennels may conduct heat and cold more rapidly than those made of wood. If well-ventilated, fiberglass kennels are widely used. Regardless of the material, the kennel must have solid flooring lined with sheets of newspaper and covered by plenty of shredded newspaper to absorb moisture. A carpet square cut large enough to cover the floor surface is also excellent. This can be topped with shredded newspaper. Whatever material is used to line the inside of the kennel, make sure that it is nontoxic.

The air kennel must be large enough so that the individual may sit and stand erect without restriction, as well as turn around and lie down in a natural position without being cramped. It should not be so large that the individual might be tossed around inside.

Many commercial travel kennels comply with the regulations for sufficient ventilation. There must be at least a minimal surface area designed to provide ventilation whenever two solid walls are constructed opposite of each other. If the crate is designed with three solid walls, then at least half of the entire surface must provide adequate ventilation.

Be sure that the ventilation holes are small enough to keep the paws, nose, or even bobtail from slipping through and becoming crushed.

The doors of many commercial travel kennels are designed to provide at least 90 percent ventilation on the front surface. Most doors have wire or metal bars.

It is generally required that the exterior of the kennel contain necessary documents, including health certificates and the air bill. The label should clearly contain pertinent information about the shipper and the consignee's address and phone number. The destination should also be listed, especially if it is different than the consignee's address. Use sturdy strapping tape to securely attach necessary labels to the crate. *LIVE DOG IN TRANSIT* should appear in letters not less than one inch high in at least two places. *DO NOT PLACE NEAR DRY ICE* should also appear near the first one. Dry ice is used for perishable cargo, and the fumes can easily kill a dog. If you need to send accompanying information, place it in an envelope and put it under the label or separately attach it in the same manner. There should be arrows pointing to the top of the crate/cage on at least two sides of the kennel. Many commercial crates will already have this.

A dish or container should be secured in the air kennel so that an attendant can provide water without opening the door. Do not leave loose objects inside the kennel. Your dog should be watered and exercised by you before being placed in the travel com-partment and being shipped. The dog should receive additional water at least every twelve hours as required by law while in transit. If the weather is considerably warm or cold, you might want to instruct the airline to offer water more frequently during layovers and upon arrival. This information must appear on a label on top of the kennel. Puppies less than sixteen weeks of age should be given food every twelve hours, and puppies more than sixteen weeks of age should be fed every twenty-four hours while in transit. Consult your airline agent.

It is advised that only one dog be shipped per crate. A dam is allowed to be shipped with her puppies in the event that they are less than eight weeks old, but it is not advisable to ship prior to weaning. Check with your airline for regulations.

The person receiving the individual should notify the shipper by telephone after receipt of the dog. If upon arrival the dog appears to be in obvious distress, a veterinarian should be immediately contacted. Since a health certificate accompanies each individual, it can be reasonably assumed that if the dog appears to be shy, quiet, listless, or frightened, he may be suffering from a simple case of "jet lag." It may take two to three days to make the total transition. On or after the third day, the dog should be taken to the new owner's or agent's veterinarian to establish a record.

Not to be mistaken for snarling, "grinning" is a characteristic of some Australian Shepherds.

So typically Aussie in the splendor of a New England snow Champion Wildhagen's Dutchman CDX (The Herdsman of Flintridge ex Heard's Savor of Flintridge) and Wildhagen's Thistle of Flintridge (Sisler's John ex Heard's Chilie of Flintridge) are pictured in front of the historic Mary Martha Church.   Courtesy Wildhagen

18
NUTRITION

Nutrition is the single greatest factor responsible for enabling each Australian Shepherd to realize his full inherited potential. Your dog's system is a complex myriad of functions. To operate smoothly, the system requires energy that comes from proteins, fats, and carbohydrates. Before these nutrients can be utilized by the system to provide energy, they must undergo a chemical change called *metabolism*. Metabolism consists of two basic activities: (1) *anabolism*: the building process in which the absorbed nutrients and complex chemical compounds that have been stored in the system are used in the formation or repair of cells, which form body tissue; and (2) *catabolism*: the decomposition of nutrients under the influence of hormones, enzymes, and the nervous impulses are oxidized for the production of heat and work.

In order for metabolism to be most effective, it must be governed by enzymes that require vitamins and minerals for performance of regulatory tasks. The lack of one can totally upset various biochemical processes.

There are six basic elements to nutrition: (1) water; (2) protein; (3) carbohydrates; (4) fats; (5) vitamins; and (6) minerals.

WATER

Next to oxygen, water is the most crucial substance for all plant and animal life. The need for water in the canine individual is regulated by thirst, and the amounts required by each individual depend on gestation, lactation, growth, stress, environment, activity, age, and temperament.

Water aids in temperature control. It acts as the media in which blood carries nutrition to the cells and removes waste products from the system. The need for water is often overlooked and neglected. An abundant supply of fresh, clean drinking water should be available at all times.

PROTEIN

Protein is essential for the repair and wear of all body tissue, as well as hormones, enzymes, and antibodies. It is needed for the development of stronger muscles, ligaments, organs, bones, teeth, and coat.

Proteins are complex organic compounds made up chiefly of amino acids. The amino acids may therefore be called "building blocks" from which proteins are made. The quality of protein is determined by its profile and balance of essential amino acids and availability of digestible material within food substances. A shortage of one single amino acid will limit the utilization of all others and therefore reduce and limit tissue repair and growth and break down the resistance to infection. Any shortage will also contribute to a lack of stamina and loss of condition.

CARBOHYDRATES

Carbohydrates are made by plants in the process of photosynthesis. They are energy foods often called the "protein-sparing" nutrients, and they consist mainly of sugars, starches, and cellulose.

Unlike protein, unused carbohydrates are stored in the body as converted fat and as glycogen in the muscles and liver. Starches and sugars provide the most readily available source of energy. In the absence of carbohydrates, the dog's system is able to employ fat and protein in terms of energy. Although fat and protein can supply these needs, they are less expendable. Protein provided primarily as an energy source can cause severe stress on the liver.

Cellulose forms fiber and governs the resorption of water. This, in turn, aids the body in the proper formation and elimination of wastes.

Certain sugars and starches, such as large amounts of lactose found in cow's milk, are often difficult for the dog's system to digest and absorb—many times causing diarrhea. Uncooked starches, such as found in cereal grains and various other food products, must be properly cooked and processed before they can contribute any nutritional value and avoid causing diarrhea.

FATS

Fats are the most concentrated source of energy. When the glycogen stores are used up, fat comes into play. The fuel value is about twice as great per ounce as the fuel of carbohydrates. Fat increases the palatability of the diet. It helps maintain and alleviate dry coats and scaly skin and conveys fat-soluble vitamins within the system. Rancid fats, however, destroy valuable fat-soluble vitamins and should be guarded against.

VITAMINS

Vitamins yield no energy, yet they play an integral role in maintaining anabolic and catabolic functions. Certain vitamins are dependent on one another. One cannot be substituted or replaced by another. Vitamins fall into two categories: (1) *water-soluble vitamins:* B-complex and C, which must be replenished on a regular basis; and (2) *fat-soluble vitamins:* A, D, E, and K. These vitamins are absorbed and stored within the system.

MINERALS

Minerals are not sources of energy. They regulate the system's dynamic balance. An intricate relationship between minerals and other dietary constituents can be affected by a change only in one. Minerals must be supplied in adequate amounts and in proper ratio in order to maintain the dynamic balance.

DIET

In order for any diet to be adequate, it must be complete *and* balanced. To be "complete," it must contain all necessary ingredients vital to nutritional needs. A diet is "balanced" only if all vital nutrients are in proportion with energy (calories) to provide needed "fuel" that will enable utilization of proteins in the body-building processes.

Metabolism is crucially dependent on certain quantities of individual nutrients. The lack of a single ingredient can halt or diminish the metabolic "chain of events," while an overdose of an ingredient or nutrient can mask the properties of the nutrients that are so necessary to complete vital chemical interrelations.

Initially, the pup depends on its mother for a balanced diet ... later, the owner will be responsible for good nutrition.

Champion Briarbrook's Lena Jo (Ch Fieldmaster's Three Ring Circus ex Ch Patch-Work Quilt).   *Courtesy of Wilson*

At the watering hole. Patch-Work Drum STD-d (Ch Fieldmaster of Flintridge ex Ch Windsongs Foggi Notion). Courtesy Pierson

HOMEMADE DIET

A homemade diet including the finest cuts of meat and fresh vegetables, combined with necessary vitamins and minerals, may or may not be totally balanced. If the homemade diet is formulated by a nutritionist, it can be excellent.

COMMERCIAL DIET

Commercial diets are by far the most practical and are usually less expensive. These diets are available in dry, semimoist, and canned varieties. The major dog food manufacturers maintain research facilities to control, maintain, and regulate proper rations of nutrients including vitamins and minerals. There is a constant effort to utilize the latest knowledge of nutrients and canine-nutrient requirements to improve existing products.

METHODS OF FEEDING

You can provide your Aussie's diet in either one of two ways: (1) portion feeding; and (2) free feeding or self-feeding.

Portion Feeding

The portion feeding method requires hand feeding a premeasured amount of food on a regular schedule. The amounts fed can be controlled or adjusted according to individual requirements: weight loss, weight gain, or for weight maintenance. Portion feeding may help regulate the metabolic changes for inactive, spayed, neutered, or elderly individuals that may retain large appetites by adjusting the amount to meet actual physical requirements. With this method, dogs should be fed at regular intervals to maintain steady appetites, proper digestion, and regular elimination. Fresh, clean drinking water should be provided and made available at all times.

Free Feeding

Free feeding, commonly known as self-feeding, has many advantages. By consuming small amounts of food on a frequent basis, the level of nutrients in the bloodstream remains more constant. Free feeding has a quieting effect on dogs, since there is no before-feeding excitement. Food is always available to nibble on, which helps prevent boredom and discourages the investigation and eating of stools. If more than one dog is present, free feeding assures meeker or more submissive dogs of getting sufficient quantities of food.

There are containers designed for free feeding. Individual pails or dishes can be chosen to hold one or several day's ration of a dry or semimoist diet. Semimoist diets must be replenished more frequently. Since moist or canned diets easily spoil, they should *never* be fed by this method.

Converting individuals from portioned feedings to the self-feeding method should be done gradually over a period of several days. Feed the regular ration, then place the free-feeding container out. Eventually discontinue the scheduled rations. An ample supply of fresh drinking water should be available at all times.

VARIETIES OF DIET

Commercial diets are available in three general forms: dry, semimoist, and canned.

Dry

The dry foods can be broken into three types: *kibble, meal,* and *expanded.*

Kibble - Kibble and biscuit varieties are a baked dough prepared from soybean flour, wheat flour mixed with meat meals, milk products, yeast, vitamins, and minerals. The heat process in baking cooks starch granules, which make carbohydrates in these biscuit-type foods readily available to your dog's system.

Meal - Meals consist of dry ingredients either as a blend of granular powders or as flakes mixed together to form a ration.

Expanded - Expanded nuggets and pellets are homogenized foods that are made by blending ingredients such as cereal grains, meat meals, vegetable products, fish meals, fat, and milk products along with vitamins and minerals. The blend is then cooked and formed into pellets or expanded into nuggets of varying shapes and sizes. The stability of the mixture is improved through cooking, which makes nutrients more readily available to your dog. Prior to packaging, fat is sprayed onto the food.

Of the available commercial diets, dry foods are the least expensive per pound of dry content. Dry diets are easily stored and can be free-fed. They provide good exercise for teeth and gums and help prevent accumulation of tartar on the teeth.

Generally speaking, meat products contain a higher-quality protein than cereal products. Dry foods *may* contain a lower-quality protein. However, protein quality depends on the ingredients used by the manufacturer, not on the form of diet.

Because manufacturers are limited in their choice of ingredients that can successfully be used in the dry food process, essential fatty acids may or may not be present. The lack of fat also limits the caloric density of food. A dry, dull hair coat with scaly skin can be one of the first signs of a fatty acid-deficient diet. One or two teaspoons of a vegetable oil may be added per cup of dry diet fed. Vegetable oil contains more essential fatty acid content than pork, poultry, beef, or butterfat. Vegetable oils are usually a better choice than wheat germ oils high in vitamins D and E, fish liver oils high in vitamin D, or the commercial oil supplements with vitamins and minerals. The addition of these nutrients to an otherwise balanced diet may cause an imbalance that in turn may create an overall deficient diet through vitamin overdose.

The addition of at least one teaspoon of vegetable oil per cup of dry food (four teaspoons per pound of food) and no more than two teaspoons per cup (or eight teaspoons per pound) of dry food will also increase the energy content.

Without supplementation, most dry dog food contains approximately 1,350 to 1,700 calories per pound of food—or 300 to 350 calories per cup. The digestible energy ranges from 65 to 75 percent. Dry foods contain approximately 8 to 12 percent water and 88 to 92 percent food solids.

Semimoist

Semimoist foods have a fairly long shelf life and require no refrigeration. Semimoist foods cost about the same as canned diets when purchased in individual premeasured packages. Semimoist diets purchased in ten- or twenty-five-pound bags will slightly lower the cost per feeding.

This form of diet provides the highest digestible energy due to the sugars used to preserve the food. An advantage to a semimoist diet is that a greater variety of ingredients, such as fresh and frozen meats, can be used. Semimoist diets contain about 1,350 calories per pound, or 500 calories per each six-ounce package. They contain about 30 percent water and 70 percent food solids.

Canned

All forms of ingredients may be utilized in the formation of canned rations. These diets generally contain more fat per pound of dry matter than any other form of diet, and therefore yield more energy per pound. Complete and balanced canned rations can meet the needs of lactating bitches whose higher caloric demands require an easily available energy source. A disadvantage to the canned and semimoist diets is that they are more expensive.

Canned Meat - Some of the more expensive canned products are compositions of meat by-products either alone or supplemented with vitamins and minerals. While the palatability is extremely high and the protein quality very good, your Aussie is forced to use protein as his main energy source, which puts undue stress on the system. These products can be used to increase palatability to a dry diet when added at 10 to 25 percent.

SUPPLEMENTATION

Supplementation to a professional-quality, "complete and balanced" ration is not recommended in most cases. To do so may upset the balance and therefore create an inadequate, nutritionally deficient diet. On a dry matter basis, an acceptable diet should consist of at least 25 percent protein, 10 percent fat, and at least 1,400 calories, but more acceptably 1,600 to 1,800 calories per pound of dry matter. The addition of selected ingredients may be necessary if you are feeding a grocery store variety diet as compared to a professional mix. Fat is the most expensive ingredient, and a quality diet can be determined by the percentage of fat included.

It is possible to supplement 10 to 25 percent (no more than 25 percent, however) without affecting the overall balance of a good dry diet. The best choice to *increase food acceptance and available energy* is through the addition of two teaspoons of a cold-pressed vegetable oil per cup of dry food (eight teaspoons of oil per pound of dry food).

Butter, margarine, animal fats (meat fats), lard, and tallow are saturated fats as compared to unsaturated fats such as vegetable and fish oils. Margarine is a solidified vegetable oil that is generally fortified with vitamin A and is therefore nutritionally similar to butter. Margarine is recommended over butter due to its higher unsaturated fatty acid content.

Although a vegetable oil, coconut and palm oils used in some nondairy products are high in saturated fats.

Vegetable and meat broths and even water drained from cooked pasta (such as macaroni) are ideal to increase the palatability of a good dry diet.

Vegetables and Vegetable Juices

Vegetables are composed mainly of carbohydrates and water but contain very little protein. Vegetables and vegetable juices are an excellent source of vitamins and minerals. Juices are easily digested, and vegetables provide necessary bulk to a diet. Vegetables are usually available in fresh, frozen, canned, and dried varieties. Fresh vegetables must be thoroughly rinsed to remove chemical residues and dirt. Vegetables quick-frozen are comparable in nutrient content to fresh vegetables. Drying, on the other hand, tends to decrease nutritional value. Whenever possible, vegetable skins should be left on because of the nutrients found in the skins.

Light green vegetables provide a great deal of carbohydrate cellulose, vitamins, and minerals, while the richest source of nutrients is found in the greener varieties. Vitamin A is contained in both yellow and dark green types. Potatoes provide good sources of vitamin A, vitamin C, and some of the B vitamins, as well as protein.

Meats

Liver when fed raw is especially nutritious, although dogs generally prefer it cooked. The supplementation of fresh liver at least once or twice a week will provide protein, fat, carbohydrates, minerals, and vitamins. Liver also helps to combat iron deficiency anemia due to its high iron and B-12 content. Liver is also available in tablet or powdered form called "desiccated" liver.

Although raw meat is considered nutritious, it should always be well cooked to avoid the transmission of parasites. This is especially important in the case of pork and wild game. Lamb, beef, and pork are also good sources of the B-complex vitamins and certain minerals including phosphorus and iron. Organ meats, including the liver, tongue, kidneys, heart, brains, and sweetbreads (glands of lambs or calves), are generally richer in vitamins and minerals than the muscle meats. The leaner the meat, the more protein available per pound.

Poultry

Poultry also contains the B-complex vitamins as well as iron and phosphorus while providing a good source of protein. White poultry meats contain less connective tissue and fat than the dark meat and therefore are easier to digest. However, the dark

poultry meats are richest in vitamins B-1 (thiamine) and B-2 (riboflavin). Poultry must be thoroughly cooked to prevent food poisoning.

Fish

Fish provides an excellent source of high-quality protein. Fish is rich in polyunsaturated fatty acids and minerals, including iodine and potassium. Fish is available in fresh, frozen, canned, dried, salted (not recommended), and smoked varieties. Due to possible bacterial infections, fresh fish and shellfish should be carefully stored, wrapped, and cooked. Fish, as with the varieties of meat, should be well-cooked to prevent parasite transmission. In either case, bones must be completely removed. Canned fish are nutritionally balanced and are highly palatable to most dogs. Freshwater fish provide minerals, including phosphorus and iron. Saltwater and shellfish lend rich iodine sources. The unsaturated fat levels fluctuate with the season and species. Shellfish are relatively high in cholesterol content but are low in fatty acids. Salmon, halibut, mackerel, and other fatty-type fish provide good sources of the fat-soluble vitamins A and D.

Dairy Products

Dairy products boast the best protein/calorie ratio without disturbing the calcium-phosphorus ratio of the diet. The supplementation of dairy products such as cottage cheese is most naturally balanced, although cheeses, yogurt, and milk can be used. Many dairy products also come in powdered and canned varieties. Dairy products are excellent sources of complete protein, and they provide one of the safest supplements in regard to the calcium/phosphorus ratio. Milk must be pasteurized in order to kill bacteria. Homogenized milk is more easily digested than unhomogenized milk due to the blending of the fats within the milk itself.

Whole milk contains between 3 to 4 percent fat. When the fat is removed, the milk is classified as "skim." Two-percent milk contains 2 percent fat. Milk is often fortified with fat-soluble vitamins A and D. Skim milk and nonfat dry or powdered milk must be fortified in order to contain these fat-soluble vitamins. Skim milk and nonfat dry milk are still rich in protein and calcium. When one-half of the water content is removed from whole milk, the milk is classified as "evaporated." When the water is removed and sugar added, it is classified as "condensed milk."

Although yogurt is made from milk that is fermented, it contains a greater percentage of A and D and B-complex vitamins than milk and is high in pro-

Two of a kind.

tein. Yogurt has been reported to improve the intestinal flora and is especially beneficial in restoring intestinal flora after the use of antibiotics. Yogurt is also easily digested, and it has been reported to aid in yeast infections in the bitch.

Buttermilk is the by-product of churning butter, but it is generally cultured. Cultured buttermilk results when specific bacteria are added to skim or churned buttermilk. Buttermilk is an excellent source of the bacteria that aid digestion in the intestinal tract. Powdered buttermilk is also an economical supplement and is easier to store than fresh buttermilk.

Butter itself contains a high percentage of saturated fat as well as the fat-soluble vitamins A and D.

Once milk solids are separated from the water, a variety of cheeses are produced. Regardless of flavor and texture, cheeses contain protein, fat, calcium, and phosphorus.

Milk has been known to cause diarrhea, especially if given in too large of a quantity and should either be decreased, varied, or eliminated from the diet if the condition persists after the third day of supplementation. Goat's milk is an excellent substitution because it is highly digestible. Dairy-vegetable blends can also be used.

Eggs are an ideal source of protein because they contain all of the essential amino acids and iron. Eggs must be cooked. If fed raw, they will "tie up" necessary biotin (a B-vitamin) in the canine body system. The egg yolk also provides lecithin, which helps break up fats and aids in digestion.

Lecithin

Lecithin is available in granule, capsule, and liquid forms. Although high in phosphorus, lecithin unites with iron, calcium, and iodine to aid in the digestion and absorption of fats. Lecithin has been reported to help increase immunity against viral infections. There are no toxic levels for lecithin.

Molasses

Regular molasses is rich in iron, calcium, phosphorus, and other minerals and vitamins. One tablespoon of regular molasses can also be dissolved in one cup warm liquid (water, vegetable broth or milk) and added over a dry diet to increase palatability.

Brewers Yeast

Brewer's yeast can be obtained in powder, tablet, and flake forms. Brewer's yeast helps to increase the nutritional value of foods. It is a natural source of protein, as well as the B-vitamins and minerals, including phosphorus. Due to the high levels of phosphorus in relation to the calcium, it is necessary to supplement four tablespoons of dry powdered milk or the equivalent of eight ounces of skim milk for every tablespoon of brewer's yeast. Brewer's yeast is nonleavening and cannot be substituted by regular yeast. Brewer's yeast has also been reported as a possible protection against vitamin D toxicity that occurs through incorrect supplementation. It may even increase a dog's resistance to flea infestations.

Wheat Germ and Wheat Germ Oil

Wheat germ is an excellent source of protein, vitamin E, and the B-complex vitamins and minerals, including iron. Wheat germ also contains calcium and phosphorus. As with brewer's yeast, wheat germ must be supplemented with either four tablespoons of dry milk powder or the equivalent of eight ounces of skim milk to every tablespoon of wheat germ. Wheat germ must be properly stored and refrigerated. The wheat germ oil extracted from wheat germ is one of the richest sources of vitamin E, a fat-soluble vitamin.

Bone Meal

Bone meal is one of the safest calcium/phosphorus supplements available. A tablespoon per day will aid in bone, teeth, and tissue development. Bone meal is especially beneficial to individuals on a limited milk intake. Bone meal is difficult to overdose. A source of vitamin D, such as in egg yolks, milk, and fish liver oils, is necessary to regulate the absorption of calcium/ phosphorus and then to distribute the minerals to the bones and teeth.

Kelp

A natural source of iodine, kelp has been reported to produce a calming effect. It also helps to induce a richer skin pigmentation in nose and eye leather. Kelp is rich in B-complex vitamins, D, E, and vitamin K, as well as calcium and magnesium. As with all seaweed, sea plants are rich in all minerals.

Apple Cider Vinegar

Apple cider vinegar has been reported to be beneficial when one tablespoon is given daily either in the food or two ounces (one-fourth cup) per gallon in water. Ideally it should be supplemented with iodine. This will reportedly produce an environment unsuitable for flea infestations.

When given with dairy products, apple cider vinegar has been reported to decrease the chance of digestive, urinary, and reproductive tract problems.

Gatorade®

Gatorade® in water can be extremely beneficial for hardworking individuals or those under stress.

SUMMARY

During periods of physical and/or mental stress, your dog will require a larger caloric intake without added bulk. Hot climates decrease the desire to eat, yet increase the energy needed for cooling, whereas cold climates increase the calories expended for warmth or heat.

A top-quality professional feed should be used to eliminate unnecessary supplementation. It is always best to consult your veterinarian before supplementing your dog's diet, especially with vitamins

and minerals. The fat-soluble vitamins are quite easy to overdose, causing nutritional imbalances. Generally, more nutritional deficiencies are due to unnecessary supplementation with improper quantities. Never supplement over 25 percent of any diet.

You can judge the quality of any diet by the vim and vigor of your dog. You should be able to run your hand alongside and feel his ribs, but not the concave between the ribs. The coat should have a healthy glow.

PERFORMANCE

The only avenue to an accurate evaluation of any diet is through results obtained in feeding trials. To evaluate particular diets, feed a maintenance level for six days. During this time, standardize your dog's daily activities, and determine maintenance amounts accordingly. You must also consider your dog's stage of life.

Avoid diets that cause diarrhea after the first two days. On the third, fourth, fifth, and sixth days, weigh the total amount of diet consumed. Collect the excreted feces and place them in a plastic bag. Label the package, stating the contents (so that there will be no confusion!). Weigh the stools to determine an acceptable ration, and divide the weight of the stool by the weight consumed to produce it. The diet is an acceptable ration if the stool weight is less than 25 percent of a canned diet, 70 percent of a semimoist diet, or 90 percent of a dry diet.

If water is normally added to the dry diet, then mix one part dry food with three parts water BY WEIGHT. The stool should weigh no more than 25 percent of dry food intake.

The quality of diet is directly reflected by what is able to be digested and absorbed by your dog. Poor-quality rations contain ingredients unable to be utilized by your dog; therefore, a larger volume of undigested, unabsorbed material passes into the feces as waste material.

An easy test can be done by feeding an adult as per the instructions on the package daily for three weeks. Maintain and structure daily activity as evenly as possible. Take a beginning weight and an ending weight. Weigh your dog at the same time before each feeding. Avoid all diets that are unable to maintain a normal weight evidenced by the fact that your dog loses weight.

A test can be done by comparing your litter's growth to a standard growth curve. When you wean your litter of puppies, "free-feed" them and then make comparisons, keeping in mind that there will be slight differences between breeds of similar developmental patterns and even between individual lines within the Australian Shepherd breed. However, any food that fails to support a constant growth rate during the first nine months should not be considered adequate.

QUANTITIES TO FEED

Feeding instructions offer a guideline. The actual amounts required are determined by individual needs and environmental conditions. Individuals with the same weight, genetic background, general environment, and activity can have as much as 100 percent variation in daily food intake. One individual may actually require twice as much food as an extremely similar individual.

MAINTENANCE

Maintenance diets are for Aussies that have reached physical maturity and are engaged in normal activity. This type of diet should provide adequate quantities of nutrients to support a mature individual with a steady, consistent body weight and to help promote general health.

REPRODUCTION

Gestation and lactation severely alter nutritional needs due to additional stress on the female. The female's body depends on previously stored nutrients obtained from a highly digestible, balanced ration. Females deprived of an adequate diet will not have sufficient levels of energy, amino acids, vitamins, and minerals, resulting in low conception rates, abnormal fetuses, and a reduction in milk production. During the fourth week of gestation and until parturition to weaning, the female will require a higher caloric density.

Lactation

Lactation is the most taxing element in a female's life. Not only must she meet her own energy and maintenance needs, but those of her rapidly growing litter. A high-quality diet is *imperative*. Your female will require three and one-half times more food than during her maintenance stages. Many diets based on requirements for growth may not have sufficient nutrient density to meet the needs of a bitch nursing a large litter.

If a top-quality, well-balanced ration is being provided, no supplementation is necessary. A complete, all-meat supplementation between 15 and 25 percent (not to exceed 25 percent) of the overall diet can be given. The addition of vegetable oil is acceptable in increasing caloric density but should add up to eight tablespoons per pound of the total diet.

Reproductive Problems Related to Nutrition

Diarrhea can occur during lactation caused by excessive food consumption. Since the low-calorie diet is incapable of providing sufficient energy, the bitch is forced to consume larger amounts in an attempt to meet essential nutrient and energy needs. It is a progressive problem because the diarrhea further minimizes the availability of the diet.

When a bitch is deprived of an adequate diet, dehydration can take place. There will be a lack of muscle tone (atrophy). A loss of body weight will be evident after whelping and especially after weaning. Other symptoms related to diet deficiencies are the "Fading Puppy Syndrome" (agalactia—a condition where the mammary glands fail to produce milk), acid milk (bacterial mastitis changes the pH (7.1) of the bitch's milk from a more neutral pH to a more alkaline pH), anemia, and toxic milk (toxic fluids caused by decomposing tissue and fluids from the placenta created in the uterus).

Portion Feeding

For portion feeding, you can use the following guideline to help calculate the appropriate amounts to feed. Weigh the entire litter when they are about three or four days old. Multiply the total litter weight figure by 100 calories per pound of body weight, plus the normal maintenance level (caloric density). This will help determine appropriate quantites to feed. The caloric or energy needs will increase until the litter is weaned.

Free Feeding

Free feeding helps supply and distribute the nutrient levels as required and self-regulated by the bitch. A top-quality diet designed to meet nutritional needs of a lactating bitch is the most economical and, by far, the wisest choice.

If necessary, a ration containing a larger amount of calories per pound of dry matter can be supplemented with vegetable oil or bacon grease to boost the energy level. There is no substitute for quality ingredients presented in a form available to the canine system.

GROWTH

Growth requires twice as much energy than other stages of life. Youngsters employ the accelerated energy levels to enable their systems to utilize essential nutrients for body building and the building of the skeleton (bones), muscles, and vital organs. The system begins to establish and build a resistance to disease during this time. A diet designed specifically for growth should be fed during this active stage.

WORKING AND PERFORMANCE

You get back exactly what you invest. The hardworking Aussie can require between two to four times the energy levels than during maintenance periods. Temperature also plays a role. In cold environments, your Aussie will not only require energy while working, but will demand sufficient energy in order to maintain adequate body heat.

For active, working Aussies, it may be necessary to feed a light meal two to three hours before working and then give the remainder of the diet after they have relaxed or cooled off. Depending on the environmental temperature, Aussies worked for long sessions or during heavy periods may show signs of *ataxia* and/or *fatigue*. They may suffer from *hypoglycemia*, and in such instances, convulsions would not be uncommon. A snack and water, if fed at least once or twice during a day and periodically during a heavy day, will help sustain him until he can consume the bulk of his meal.

A drink of water periodically throughout the day will boost energy levels approximately 75 percent in the working Australian Shepherd. Water is essential for hard-working dogs in all stages of life.

Semimoist diets make an excellent "pickup" during times of stress because of the high levels of digestible energy. Dry diets are advantageous for energetic, active, and hard-working Aussies due to the greater number of calories per pound of dry matter. There are professional diets designed to meet the needs of active Aussies. These dry-type diets specifically contain increased nutrient amounts in addition to the boosted energy levels. Unlike many products designed for the average pet, these concentrated products do not contain bulky filler. These diets allow your Aussie to consume boosted energy levels in smaller quantities due to their denser characteristics.

GERIATRICS

The metabolic rate in older Aussies is reduced. They require an easily digestible diet due to internal changes in the intestinal tract, liver, and pancreas. Extreme levels of protein are hard on the liver and kidneys. Unsaturated fats help maintain the skin and hair coat in a healthy condition, but diets rich in excessive fat are not easily digested by older Aussies.

Worn-down and missing teeth make it difficult for older dogs to consume diets of hard biscuits and bones. There are many good-quality diets available in dry, semimoist, and canned varieties that are easily consumed by older Aussies and that at the same time meet the needs of aging dogs. Liquids such as water and meat or vegetable broth can be added to moisten dry foods and make them easier to eat.

Due to differences in the aging process between individuals, it is best to consult your veterinarian. Your veterinarian can help you determine the specific needs of your Aussie. Through proper management, you can prolong an enjoyable life!

CONCLUSION

There is *no* substitute for a good diet. The choice between a top-quality diet over a bargain or generic brand has sound economic reasoning behind it. The initial investment may be a few more dollars, but when you consider that it takes a smaller quantity of a superior product to satisfy the needs of your Aussie versus the larger amount it will take of a bargain brand—plus supplementation—it only makes good sense.

There is no guarantee that if your dog is allowed to eat as much as he can of an inferior product— even with the supplementation of the finest quality ingredients— he will receive adequate levels of balanced nutrition. Often inferior products contain poor-quality ingredients unable to be digested, absorbed, and/or utilized by the dog's system. This may be compared to the old saying of: "You can't make a silk purse out of a sow's ear."

Nutrition is the single greatest factor that enables your Aussie to reach his maximum inherited potential. It is the very factor that boosts performance levels whether on the range or in the whelping box.

Diseases such as skeletal disorders and allergies can in many cases be avoided or prevented with a proper diet. Essential nutrients are responsible for all bodily functions. They aid in building the body's defense against disease and help develop a resistance to infectious agents. It is less expensive to invest in a good diet than the time and costly medication to try curing and correcting the problems incurred thereof.

Some people believe that they can take a cheaper product, supplement it with scraps and other goodies, and come out boosting its quality. The unfortunate problem here is that when a dog's body requires a certain amount of energy and the diet is highest in bulk—not energy—he will have to consume two to three times as much of the inferior product without any guarantee of being able to satisfy his needs. More than likely, he will not be able to take in adequate energy levels due to the extra bulk and will suffer the consequences—by lacking sufficient "staying power" (if he is in a working situation) or losing weight. Or, in the case unique to females, by not being able to maintain her own body condition let alone nurse a litter of puppies.

There is *no* substitution for a good diet.

The look of Eagles. Green's Boots OTD-s ATD-cd (Auten's K.C. Dan ex Auten's Candy). *Photo by Kris Green*

19
GROOMING

Grooming is a complex behavior displayed by domestic dogs and their ancient ancestors. In general, grooming is hygiene. Dogs practice grooming by licking, rubbing, rolling, scooting, scratching, and shaking debris from their coats. Dogs care for their eyes, nose, and nostrils by rubbing their faces with their paws and forelegs.

In the wild, the wolf can be observed rubbing against bushes and brush to remove dead hair—in essence, a form of brushing. He may roll on his back, twisting his body from side to side to improve stimulation. He cleans and moisturizes his coat and skin by licking.

During illness, wolves and dogs alike lack the desire and capability to care for themselves. Because the cells of the skin and coat are subject to rapid turnover, disease states are soon reflected in them. Also, lack of general attention can cause deterioration of the coat and body. Grooming keeps the skin functioning naturally and lessens the chance for the skin to become diseased. It also improves the overall condition and muscle tone.

HAIR COAT

Length, strength, density, texture, and condition of the hair coat depend on genetic makeup, nutrition, environment, proper care, and health of your Aussie. A straight coat will appear to grow faster and will look slightly longer than a wavy coat because the shortest distance between two points is a straight line. The typical Aussie coat varies between being straight and wavy.

The hair root determines coat texture and shape because it lies in the *follicle*—a tubelike depression or pocket encasing the hair root. Straight hair grows from a straight hair root and is round in cross-section. Wavy hair is oval in cross-section and grown from a slightly curved hair root.

Each strand of hair has three distinct layers, none of which contains blood vessels or nerves. The first layer, the *cuticle*, surrounds and protects the underlying two layers. The *cortex*, in the middle, gives the coat elasticity and strength and contains the pigment that designates coat color. The center core, called the *medulla*, resembles marrow in a bone. The *papilla*, lying beneath the hair root, supplies blood and nerves that contribute to the growth and regeneration of the hair.

Coat activity is divided into three distinct stages: (1) *anagen*—an active growing stage; (2) *telogen*—a resting stage; and (3) *catagen*—the transition between the first two stages. It is during the latter stage that shedding takes place; new hair pushes out the old hair as it surfaces.

Results achieved through proper care are determined by the limits of genetic makeup. The quality of inherited coat texture can be enhanced through a maximum state of health but can never be changed.

The Aussie's coat is a mirror reflection of his body. Coat condition accurately reflects his state of health. A dry, lackluster coat may indicate that some factor is out of balance. Such symptoms can be the result of an internal illness, infestation of parasites, or a diet inadequate for individual requirements.

A glossy coat with a lively resilience begins inside. The coat is nourished only after all the vital organs and body have been fed.

GROOMING TABLE TRAINING

Grooming establishes a healthy rapport between you and your Aussie when it is done in a kind manner. Harsh handling only builds a resentment toward this necessary chore. Grooming can have a calming effect which can build a very strong foundation for future handling. Providing a puppy is managed properly from his earlier stages, he should be a pleasure to teach.

Set a grooming routine. Begin his first few grooming periods while you both sit together on the floor. Teach him to accept brushing while standing up and lying down. Keep each session short to hold your puppy's interest.

An active youngster will easily learn to submit to this type of restraint while his mind is flexible and his body small. You will want to eventually graduate to the grooming table. The "table" allows you to work easily without stooping or bending. Yet, any dog crate, bench, or flat surface will serve the purpose if it is sturdy and of adequate size and height. Place a rubber mat, thick rug, or towel on it to give your dog secure footing. A grooming "noose" may be helpful by giving the dog additional security and aiding in restraint.

Combine short sessions on the table with a soothing voice and hands. Your dog may be frightened or unsure at first, but kind, patient handling will give him confidence. Initially, do not be concerned if he does not lie or stand perfectly still. Perfection comes

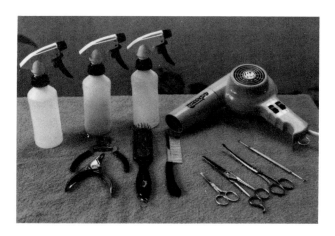

Common grooming tools.

with practice. Make each session a pleasurable experience. A few minutes every day will familiarize him with handling.

Always lift a youngster on and off the table. If young dogs are allowed to develop a habit of jumping off the table, injuries may result. As he gets older, he can be taught to jump up. *Never* leave him unattended or tied on the table without supervision. Keep one hand on him to prevent him from leaping off. This will also reassure him.

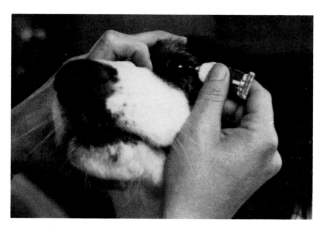

Placing ointment ALONG the eye NOT inward.

EYES

Eyes require regular attention and should be checked daily. Any brownish matter in the corners of the eyes should be wiped away with a gauze pad. Avoid using any type of cotton (balls, rolled, etc.), as the fibers may stray and irritate the eyes. You can bathe the eye(s) with warm water or a commercially prepared eyewash, then dry them with a fresh piece of gauze or gauze pad. If and when the eye is irritat-

Table training begins early for this youngster pictured with his papa. Courtesy Smith

ed, keep matter from spreading across the eye by wiping from the corner of the eye outward. Never wipe across the entire eye.

If a persistent discharge or inflammation of eye tissue are present consult your veterinarian. Runny, weepy eyes can be a sign of serious illness.

EARS

Examine ears frequently. Wipe away any visible dirt with either a gauze pad or cotton. Clean the inside ear leather only, and *do not* probe or push beyond what you can see. Check ears for wax, ear mites, and any irritations often referred to as "cankers."

Veterinarian assistance is required if your dog displays any of the following: continuous scratching at the ears; shaking the head in an unusual fashion; holding the head to either side; or emitting any foul or offensive odors from the ear(s).

To clean the ears, apply a commercially prepared ear wash, witch hazel, vinegar, or a mild antiseptic on either a cotton or gauze pad. After cleaning, gently dry the ear(s) with a fresh gauze pad or piece of cotton. They can be lightly dusted with an ear powder to absorb excessive moisture. Be cautious when applying any substance to the ear, avoiding those that would irritate sensitive ear tissue.

TEETH

The teeth, mouth, and gums should be examined daily. A large, raw beef knuckle or soup bone given at least once a week will keep your dog's gums tight and the teeth free of tarter. Dog food fed dry will also help.

Light cases of tartar can be removed with an ordinary toothbrush, a fine emery board, a charcoal pencil, or a tooth scaler. Teeth should be scaled from the gums to the tip of the tooth. Have them cleaned by your veterinarian occasionally. Tarter can be the cause of bad breath and receeding gums. Should bad breath continue, have your dog examined by your veterinarian for the possibility of internal parasites, a mouth disorder, or an upset stomach.

Teeth discolored or pitted can be the result of systemic problems at a time when the teeth were forming, such as distemper or certain chemicals, or can even be the result of current disease. If in doubt, consult your veterinarian.

The back molars often accumulate the greater amount of tartar... scale from the gums to the tip of the tooth.

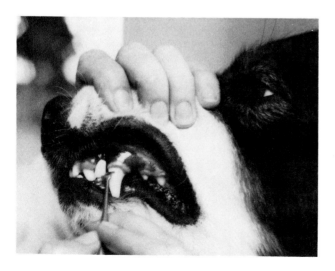

Teeth should be scaled from the gums to the tip of the tooth.

Showing off those pearly whites.   *Courtesy Wilson*

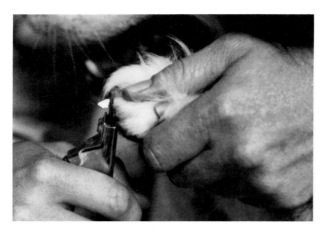

Using guillotene nail clippers.

Using a nail grinder.

TOENAILS

The practice of pedicuring should begin at a very early age. You must nip small bits in the beginning to build your dog's confidence in allowing you to work with his feet. Too few dogs have occupations in which their nails are worn down naturally. Most dogs must have their nails maintained by artificial means.

Nails can be trimmed with one of several varieties of nail trimmers or grinders. A nail file, emery board, or jeweler's file may be used to smooth the rough edges of the nail. Nails left untrimmed and allowed to grow long put undue stress on the paw by forcing the weight on the back of the pads. This condition tends to spread and break down the foot. Regular attention to the nails will help maintain the proper length. The "quick" (vein) will recede with regular and frequent trimming. Correctly trimmed nails should not touch the ground, allowing the individual to stand squarely and compactly on the pads. Nails left long can get torn off or snagged and can also scratch furniture.

It is easier to differentiate the quick from the nail when the nails are white, as opposed to liver or black. The quick appears to be a "pink vein" and travels approximately three-fourths of the way through the nail. In actuality, the quick is living tissue that gives rise to the nails.

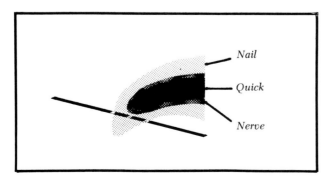

Begin by trimming off the "hook" of the nail. Then take off the remaining dead nail in smaller bits, Should you nick the quick, drawing blood, dab an alum powder, styptic powder, or styptic pencil on it. Cold water or cornstarch may also be used, but you should follow up with iodine, Mercurochrome® , or a similar antiseptic. Your dog may be nervous and not want you to continue, yet you should do so as if nothing happened. Continue with patience and a little more caution. Do a few nails at a time, and break it up with intervals of brushing until all nails are completed. If your Aussie has front dewclaws located on the inner legs above the paws, trim these. Untrimmed dewclaws will curl inward and pierce into the foreleg, causing considerable pain, possible infection, and perhaps abscessing.

ANUS

Check the anal area for cleanliness. If the area is soiled, brush any dry substance away. Wash and dry the area.

An active, healthy Aussie rarely has any problem whatsoever with the anal glands. The anal glands, located at either side of the anus, contain a lubricant which aids in the elimination of feces. Occasionally, these glands can become compacted. One indication is a persistent scooting, licking, or chewing at the perineum.

Anal glands must be evacuated at times. Should this become necessary, consult your veterinarian.

SHEDDING

Shedding is a natural process that is governed by the length of daylight more than by temperature changes. Old hair is sloughed off before the new growth matures. Daily brushing can stimulate blood circulation to encourage new growth. Exercise is also important in stimulating blood circulation.

Artificial light conditions confuse the house dog's system; consequently, these dogs shed lightly all year. If the home is overheated, there may be excessive shedding as well as dry skin during the winter.

When the female weans a litter, there will no longer be a demand for the milk, causing her milk flow to "dry up." The bitch's body will undergo hormonal changes that will trigger the shedding process. The bitch will appear almost bald when the coat is completely shed. This can take place during any season. The new coat will grow back during the following several months.

BRUSHING

One object of brushing is to distribute natural oils throughout the coat, thus improving the elasticity of the hair and giving the coat body and strength. Brushing your dog's coat cleans it and brings out shine and natural luster. It also dislodges loose hair and whisks away surface dirt, debris, and the daily accumulation of dust and lint.

Effective brushing begins with using the correct brushes. The best choice for general purposes is a quality "pin" brush—one that has large, blunt pins set on a rubber cushion base. Incorrect brushing or poor grooming tools can cause considerable damage to the coat and skin. Brushing by dragging an implement across the coat will break, split, and uproot the hair. Bristles shaped at a sharp angle will scratch the skin, cause irritation, and cause the dog to become reluctant when being brushed.

Daily brushing is far superior to any other routine, but a thorough brushing several times a week will maintain most Aussies in good condition. The chore of getting a neglected coat back into shape can be quite an ordeal if a regular schedule is ignored.

The proper way to brush is from the skin out to the ends of the coat. This stimulates circulation, aids in removing dead cells, and distributes natural oils. As you brush from the skin out, brush with the direction of growth, or the "grain." After the coat has been brushed out in this fashion, brush the hair *against* the grain to promote better circulation from blood to skin. Now work it back in the direction of the regular growth.

Some individuals prefer starting at the head and working back to the hindquarters. Others prefer to work from the feet up. Choose whatever process works best for you and your dog.

Natural shine is encouraged by using a natural bristle brush. Natural bristles have imbrications remarkably similar to canine hair, unlike smooth plastic, nylon, or wire bristles. This leads to absorption and greater distribution of natural oils.

Inherited coat texture will dictate the appropriate textured brush—softer bristles for finer hair, stronger bristles for a coarser coat. For the average Aussie, you will need to choose a medium-textured bristle brush for medium coarseness.

BATHING

If you keep your dog in a clean environment and brush him on a regular schedule, baths can be held to a minimum of one or two a year. Bathing too frequently will remove natural substances that give protection to the skin and coat unless steps are taken to condition the coat after bathing.

Left: The correct way to hold grooming scissors. Note the position of fingers and thumb. Right: Incorrect. The fingers and thumb can be easily strained. Always keep scissors well sharpened for easier handling.

However, bathe your Aussie whenever necessary. Necessary means when your regular brushing no longer does the trick or if he has acquired a "doggie" odor. Providing your Aussie is in good health, the odor should be eliminated with a bath. If it is not, consult your veterinarian, as the cause may be medical.

Before bathing, brush the coat thoroughly. Pay special attention to the fine hair behind the ears and the long hair on the legs and hindquarters—referred to as "feathers." Remove any mats before bathing. With the help of a wide-tooth comb, *gently* work mats out with your fingers. A drop of oil may help. *Do not* rip the mat(s) out, because the ears are extremely sensitive and your dog will not respond favorably. If there are large mats that do not work out with this method, make several lengthwise cuts through the mats, then work them out gently. If possible, try to avoid cutting off the entire mat—it will appear "chopped." *Do* place a comb next to the skin under the mat to protect the skin from an accidental nick.

If it is necessary to cut the mat, place your blunt-nose scissors just under the mat and over the comb, slowly snip the mat. Never point the scissors toward the body, head or eyes.

For secure footing in the tub, you may want to place a rubber mat in the bottom. Fill the tub with lukewarm water, making sure that the water is comfortable to touch.

Place a large cotton pad or ball in each ear to keep water out. You can even place a drop of mineral oil or a general eye ointment in each eye to prevent eye irritation should any shampoo suds get into eyes. Wet your dog, making sure to avoid getting water in the ear canals. Pour a small amount of shampoo in the palm of your hand. Rub palms together to work up a lather, then work it through the coat with your fingers. Never pour shampoo directly on the coat—it can often be difficult to remove. A plastic applicator can be used to apply shampoo diluted by half with water (ratio 1:1). Many commercial shampoos are based on harsh detergents that damage the coat by indiscriminately stripping it of natural oils and penetrating far into the hair shaft and skin. The best solution is to use a mild shampoo that is pH balanced to leave the coat and skin in a neutral state. Chemists measure the state of dog's hair coat, like skin, on a pH scale from 1 to 14. A healthy coat is considered to be 4.0 to 5.0, which is slightly acidic. There are many excellent human and dog shampoos with a complimentary pH balance. A good shampoo will clean the coat, yet not strip it of natural oils.

Many groomers use a small amount of bluing in the water to bring out the sparkle in white trim. The bluing "burns" out yellow stains, returning white to a white state. No amount of scrubbing will achieve this, and, in fact, scrubbing may cause skin irritation and damage white hair—which is not as strong as colored hair. Shampoo the white areas with a sponge or a gentle bath brush, using only a mild shampoo. The face may be washed with a washcloth or sponge and clean water. Be sure to rinse *thoroughly* all shampoo from the skin and coat with lukewarm water. Soap residue will not only leave a film that dulls the coat, but it can also irritate the skin.

A dry coat and skin will benefit from a good conditioner and a quality intensive-conditioning treatment. Conditioners improperly used or not thoroughly rinsed out can weaken the hair by coating the hair shaft with an oil residue, thus clogging the hair follicle and attracting oils and dust. You may even try adding two tablespoons of apple cider vinegar to a quart of warm water for the next to last rinse (after conditioning).

After bathing, place a towel over the head, ears and neck to prevent your dog from shaking water all over the house.

Throughout the entire bath, until the time your dog is completely dry, protect him from any and all drafts. Dogs can suffer upper respiratory problems if they get chilled while wet.

If possible, allow your dog to shake off excess water. Gently towel dry. A leather chamois works well on the coat, and a blow dryer will be helpful. Start drying at a higher setting, then switch to a lower one when the coat is still somewhat damp. Always hold the dryer at least six inches away from the coat, and keep the dryer in motion. Excessive heat is not only damaging to the coat, but you can burn your dog's skin. Use a warm—not hot—setting initially, then switch to a cool setting to finish.

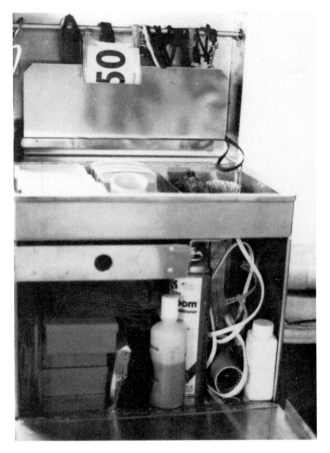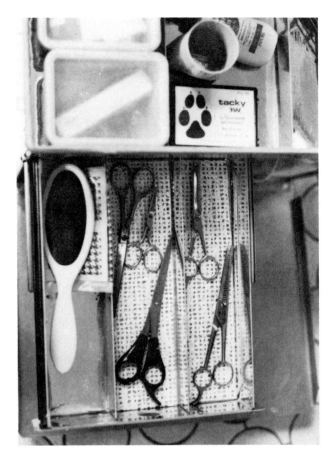

Left: A well organized tack, show, or grooming case is an asset to any owner or exhibitor. Right: Each item has a place.

You can use the blow dryer to get the appearance of more volume by brushing the coat against the growth pattern. For a smoother appearance, brush the coat with the grain. After bathing, be sure to remove the cotton from your dog's ears.

DRY CLEANING

Dry cleaning should be used whenever there is a possibility of chilling. Aging dogs, young puppies, ill or recovering dogs, and bitches nearing the last stage of pregnancy should be guarded against becoming entirely wet. Dry cleaning can also be used when your dog needs just a simple "freshening up."

You can wash the feet off in either a bucket or tub. Take a damp cloth and work it over the coat, paying special attention to the dingy areas. Do not use a wet or sopping cloth, and dry thoroughly.

Several commercial dry shampoos are available expressly for this purpose. One of the best dry-cleaning agents, however, is baby powder. Cornmeal, cornstarch, fuller's earth, or cedar sawdust can also be used. Should any dry-cleaning agent be applied to your dog, make certain that you avoid the eyes.

The coat must be completely dry before you sprinkle the dry cleaner into the coat. For better penetration, you can brush the coat against the grain of growth, then rub the dry cleaner into it. Allow the dry cleaner to remain in the coat long enough to absorb odors. Then, brush all remains out. If any dry cleaner is left in the coat, it will dry it out and absorb essential natural oils. Use a leather chamois or a natural bristle brush to brighten the darker colors and distribute these natural oils back through the entire hair coat. Let your dog shake afterwards to loosen any cleaner left in his coat.

TRIMMING

The Aussie is a utilitarian and should be exhibited in a near to natural state. A certain amount of trimming is necessary, however. The friction created during movement naturally wears down toenails and hair from around pads, showing off a tight, compact foot. Therefore, scissoring is justified to enhance an outline that would be naturally worn away if each individual were in a situation to do so. Trim away from and around pads with a pair of blunt-nose scissors.

Some exhibitors believe that trimming is a tool to create illusions that camouflage faults. Such tricks will never make a poor Aussie into a good one, fool the eye of a knowledgeable judge, or alter genetic makeup. However, judicious trimming can aid in making a neater presentation.

Authoritative brushing can intensify the most complimentary lines for each individual. Brushing technique can also make a slight difference between two Aussies of similar quality—it creates visual impact without altering protective covering.

To accentuate a feature such as stifle angulation, brush hair against the grain. To minimize a feature, brush the hair in the direction of growth. Knowledgeable brushing can also prevent the coat from indicating a fault that does not exist.

stock. The whiskers are used as "feelers" to gauge the position of the dog's head when in close contact with stock. To trim the whiskers on a working dog would risk serious injury to the dog from being kicked.

EXHIBITION PREPARATION

Preparing for show competition should begin at least one month prior to the show. Concentrate on brushing every day, trimming the toenails weekly, and tending to all other regular chores of exercise and management.

Bathe from either one day to one week ahead of the show. Some Aussies will benefit from recent bathing, while others will need a few days to adjust natural texture and oil distribution.

One week prior to the show, trim hair around the pads and neaten hair on the back of the hocks and the pasterns.

Left to Right: Trim hair on perimeter of pads and remove stray hairs by "rounding off" perimeter from topside view.

Fortunately, the Australian Shepherd's protective covering does not interfere with his work. Any excessive scissoring or trimming of the protective covering itself can leave the dog more susceptible to skin injuries, insects, heat, cold, rain, snow and/or to be nicked by flying hooves and horns.

Sparse, stray, and straggly hairs should be removed to neaten the outline; however, this practice should not be used in an attempt to alter the coat. The long hairs that sometimes grow on docked and natural bobtails may be distracting from the total outline, and therefore may be removed to neaten the overall appearance. The feathering on a female may be thinned for purposes of cleanliness and prevention of entanglement during whelping.

Whiskers may or may not be trimmed, depending on personal preference. However, whiskers should never be trimmed on an Aussie used to work rough

Keeping this regimen, all you should have to do is brush your dog on the day of the show.

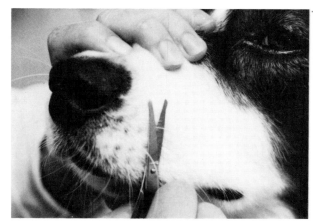

Use only blunt nosed scissors around the eyes and face when trimming whiskers. Never cut or point scissors towards the eyes.

Left: Hair on pasterns should be trimmed between heel and digital. Right: The right foot is neat and compact while the foot on the left has a few stray hairs that need trimming.

Left: Removing sparse, stray hairs. Right: The finished product. Hock and foot are neat and trim.

Because of their inherent ability with working stock, Aussies make superb assistants for rodeo clowns. Rodeo clown Bunky Hall is pictured here with his aide, Dally.

20
INFECTIOUS DISEASES

Germs, viruses, parasites (internal and external), chemicals, poisons, inadequate nutrition, and injuries are all considered to be disease-producing agents, and disease may be defined as any abnormal condition of the body tissues.

Whatever causes disease, and wherever it may be located in the body, its activities result in an inflammation of the affected part. The suffix "itis" means "inflammation of," and when attached to the root of the name of an anatomical part, it means an inflammation of that specific part. Any injury results in the destruction of tissues and cells, and the inflammatory reaction that follows is an effort on the part of the body to repair the injury. This effort is manifested by increased circulation to the part affected and seepage of serum and other blood elements into the tissues to remove the damaged tissue.

Infections that cause disease are the result of invasion of the tissues by viruses or bacteria (microorganisms). These agents can enter through the respiratory system, the digestive tract, the genitals, and the skin, and then they multiply and attack the tissues, producing a disease condition. The bodily forces engage efforts to repel invaders. The mechanisms of infection and resistance are quite complex.

In order for an infecting agent to invade the tissues of your dog successfully, it must have the ability to overcome the body's defenses and establish itself within the host's body. Then it must be able to multiply actively, producing a disease process, or to survive the carrier stage until conditions are right for multiplication. The host, on the other hand, is protected within limits by immunity or resistance.

Immunity may be built up by natural contact with limited amounts of infection in the field that do not produce an outright expression of the disease, and by artificial procedures such as vaccination. Colostrum from the dam's milk provides puppies with temporary immunity called passive immunity. The maternal antibodies are received from vaccination given prior to breeding. These antibodies protect the puppies against disease early in life but can entirely block and/or interfere with active immunization (i.e. vaccination).

Many factors influence or interfere with vaccination immunity. Some include age, nutrition, maternal antibodies, and the nature of the vaccine. Certain vaccines gain a better immune response when injected intramuscularly (into the muscles), while other vaccines respond most effectively when given subcutaneously (under the skin).

Colostral antibody interference during the critical period of susceptibility (nine to sixteen weeks) can affect active immunization differently in puppies of different dams. Litters of puppies whelped from bitches with high antibody titers (the amount of antibody in the blood) receive immunization when colostral antibodies drop to low levels. This may occur as late as between fourteen to sixteen weeks following whelping.

There are many reasons why it is best to entrust immunization to your veterinarian. Factors that may influence and affect the entire vaccination process itself are often unrecognizable by an untrained eye. Pregnancy, age, fever, and nutritional status are all points to be considered when administering vaccines.

Legal ramifications tied to rabies as well as potential human deaths related to improperly handled rabies vaccinations are major reasons for veterinarian assistance.

Puppies should receive their first vaccination at eight weeks of age followed by revaccination (sometimes called booster shots) at twelve and sixteen weeks, or according to your veterinarian's recommendation. *ANNUAL BOOSTERS ARE RECOMMENDED.*

VIRAL DISEASES

Canine Distemper Virus

Distemper (CDV) in dogs is caused by a virus. Distemper is the most common infectious viral disease of the dog and occurs throughout the world. It is a primary cause of illness and death in unvaccinated dogs. No dog is exempt from susceptibility to the disease. Very few non-immunized dogs will reach one year of age without having contracted some degree of distemper. The disease rarely occurs in unweaned puppies from vaccinated mothers, as the puppies are still under passive immunity from their dam.

Dogs may begin to show signs six to nine days after exposure. Predictive signs may or may not be apparent until two or three weeks after exposure. The eyes become sensitive to light, as shown by squinting. There is a watery discharge from the eyes (conjunctivitis) and often from the nose (rhinitis). The rectal temperature usually rises to about 103 to 105 degrees F. Swelling can often be detected at that time in the lymph nodes of the throat. Tonsillitis may also be present, and the mucosa of the pharynx may be reddened. Death can occur during convulsions as a result of the virus attacking the nervous system.

Five to seven days after the onset of the fever, it usually reaches a peak. It then begins to drop to nearly normal until the seventh or tenth day. It then begins to rise again. Throughout the rest of the disease, the temperature is irregular. The secondary stage occurs about ten to fourteen days later.

The catarrhal form of distemper is very common. Catarrhal inflammation of the mucous membranes of the body is accompanied by nervous symptoms and pustular eruptions of the skin. Catarrh of the respiratory tract is manifested by sneezing and occasional coughing accompanied by rhinitis. The nasal discharge becomes purulent and is sometimes streaked with blood. It may develop a greenish-yellow coloration. The affected animal may rub his nose with his forepaws to relieve irritation. The discharge can clog the nasal openings, which may force the dog to breathe through his mouth. There is a noticeable inflammation of the eyes along with a tendency to avoid light.

Digestive symptoms begin early with the onset of the virus. The intestinal form produces signs such as a loss of appetite, vomiting, constipation, diarrhea, extreme thirst, dehydration, and coating of the tongue.

Epileptiform fits are a manifestation of early nervous system difficulties. Partial paralysis usually begins in the hind limbs and progresses forward. In the final stages, the affected animal is unable to get around, and paralysis of the respiratory muscles and diaphragm eventually leads to death.

The exanthematic form is characterized by skin eruptions which begin in a pustular rash that can later become encrusted and emit a repulsive odor. The rash is especially evident on the skin of the stomach and on inner surfaces of the thighs. The urine may contain bile pigment, indican, acetone, and albumen. Significant changes generally occur in the white blood cells. The disease usually lasts from ten days to six weeks.

Exposure to cold, parasite infestation, malnutrition, and/or inadequate diet and unhygienic conditions are believed to make dogs more susceptible to distemper. Thirty to 80 percent of the dogs that develop distemper die.

Distemper virus may be transmitted through contaminated objects, urine, stools, saliva, and nasal discharges or through aerosol droplets created by breathing. The virus can be transmitted in the air. It can be destroyed by heat and by many disinfectants in several hours, but it is resistant to drying and low temperatures for days. The virus is able to survive freezing temperatures for months.

As is true of most viral diseases, present-day supportive measures such as antibiotics and drugs are limited in their ability to alter the course of the disease once it has become well-established. Careful nursing by a trained specialist is imperative. Any dog afflicted with an infectious disease should be under the strict supervision of your veterinarian.

While still nursing, puppies are protected while under the immunity received through their mother's milk. Bitches that contract distemper during pregnancy may have a miscarriage. Indications of the virus contracted during teething stages are brownish, pitted teeth, caused by lack of enamel formation when distemper occurs in the developing stages.

Pregnant bitches should be vaccinated prior to breeding to guarantee maximum immunity of the litter. Due to damage that may occur to developing embryos, pregnant bitches should never be vaccinated during gestation.

over the abdominal area. A common symptom in the late stages of hepatitis is inflammation of the cornea, which gives the eye a bluish appearance called "hepatitis blue eye." "Blue eye" has been recorded to occur as a reaction to inferior quality vaccines but is less common with quality vaccines.

One cycle of this disease lends a solid immunity, but because the virus may be shed in the urine, even recovered animals should be considered carriers for six months or longer.

Vaccinations are the most effective means of prevention, aided by sanitation (strict rodent control), parasitic freedom, and good nutrition.

Infectious Canine Hepatitis

ICH (Canine Adenovirus Type 1, CAV-1) is an inflammation of the liver. It is one of the most common contagious diseases known to dogs. ICH affects primarily the liver and endothelial cells. Distemper and hepatitis can occur at the same time. Canine hepatitis is caused by a different virus than human hepatitis.

The virus is generally passed in the urine. It can also be shed in other body secretions such as the saliva and feces of healthy carriers and nonclinical cases. Transmission can occur between dogs or from rats to dogs. It may also be hand-carried and transmitted indirectly through contaminated objects and even on clothing. Incubation is three to five days.

At 4 degrees F. the virus is stable. It is capable of withstanding severe temperature changes up to 130 degrees F. and can stand continual freezing and thawing.

Early signs are similar to those seen in distemper, such as a serous discharge, but the main difference between hepatitis and distemper is the appetite. With distemper the appetite may seem to be lost, but it is maintained by individuals affected with hepatitis.

The temperature rises above 104 degrees F. at the onset, usually accompanied by intense thirst. The fever lasts from one to six days. Susceptible individuals may develop severe enteritis (internal inflammation), which may be accompanied by rectal bleeding. Bleeding and bruising are signs of ICH. The white blood count may drop. After the initial temperature rise, the fever may drop to subnormal. A coma may occur, but death generally follows within the first twenty-four hours. The cornea may become opaque.

In milder cases, ICH may run a slight course for approximately two weeks. Symptoms may occur between the fourth and sixth days after exposure. There may be a slight hemorrhage or lesions of the mucous membranes, bloodshot eyes, and running eyes and nose. Tonsillitis may develop, and jaundice can occur. Due to swelling of the gallbladder, there is soreness

Canine Parvovirus

Canine parvovirus—CPV—is manifested by intestinal inflammation (severe enteritis) accompanied by diarrhea and possibly vomiting. The virus is highly contagious. The intestinal lining, the heart, the lymphoid tissues, and the bone marrow are all prime targets for parvovirus invasion.

Canine parvovirus is manifested in two forms, cardiac and intestinal. The cardiac form generally occurs in puppies less than eight weeks of age and is manifested by sudden death, crying, difficult breathing, gasping for breath, listlessness, cessation of nursing, and an irregular heartbeat. Myocarditis (inflammation of the heart muscle) can occur without enteritis. Presently there is no effective treatment for myocarditis.

In the intestinal form the virus can affect dogs of any age, but generally it occurs in the very young and the aged. When parvovirus invades the intestinal tract or lymphoid tissues enteritis results. The initial symptoms are depression and a lack of appetite. This is followed by vomiting, diarrhea, and a temperature between 104 and 106 degrees F. The stool is fluid and may contain blood. The odor is distinct (one of bloody diarrhea). Dehydration and a decreased white blood count occur, and inflammation of the mouth membranes may be visible. Depending upon the age and general health of the individual, supportive therapy including fluid and electrolyte replacement, combined with medications and antibiotics to control the vomiting and diarrhea, may or may not be successful. The administration of *Gatorade®* has been used to help the rapid onset of dehydration only until professional assistance can be sought. A shock-type death can occur as little as two days after the initial onset of symptoms. Parvo is often fatal, and affected individuals should be placed under the supervision of your veterinarian.

Vaccination is imperative for control of the disease. Since its first appearance (1978), reliable, safe vaccines have been formulated. Several are now available in combination forms, including other viral and bacterial agents.

Immunized individuals may contract parvovirus during the "critical period"—a point at which the maternal antibodies interfere with or block active immunization from taking place. Those individuals then become susceptible to the disease. They can become infected if exposed, because the vaccine is not yet able to function.

An antibody titer can be taken to measure the degree of antibody in the dam's blood (and subsequently the amount within the puppy's system). From this information your veterinarian can determine the most effective schedule to begin vaccinating. A second method is to vaccinate puppies on a frequent schedule—at eight weeks, at twelve weeks, and again at sixteen weeks followed by an annual booster innoculation. During periods of outbreaks or in areas of high incidence, your veterinarian may want to alter the schedule in order to lend a blanket protection. Your veterinarian is constantly receiving updated information about disease agents and methods of control; therefore, it is always best to follow his advice.

Canine parvovirus is a hardy organism. It is resistant to extremes in temperature and is not affected by common disinfectants, detergents, and alcohols. It can be transmitted via inanimate objects as well as people. The virus can remain inactive for long periods but is extremely contagious during what is known as the "shedding" stage. Transmission occurs mainly through the fecal wastes of infected dogs. It may also be present in the urine and saliva. Once the virus is ingested, the incubation period is three to four days.

The virus particles "shed" in the feces are especially concentrated. Try to prevent contact by removal of all fecal wastes. Strict sanitation measures will not eliminate the virus but will help control its availability to your dogs and prevent it from harboring on the surfaces of the surrounding area. The most effective disinfectant is one part of sodium hypochlorite (*Clorox®*) diluted in thirty parts of water.

Canine Tracheobronchitis

Commonly called "kennel cough," or pneumonia, these respiratory tract infections can be caused by many different viral and/or bacterial agents such as Bordetella bronchiseptica, Canine parainfluenza (CPI), Canine adenovirus type 2 (CAV-2), and Canine adenovirus type 1 (CAV-1). These airborne, highly contagious disease agents induce inflammation of the trachea, bronchi, and lungs. The disease produces mild to severe symptoms manifested by a dry, forceful, harsh, hacking cough, which may cause a gagging reflex during coughing spasms. When there is more lung involvement, the coughing will be wet and blowing and will cause a gagging reflex. These symptoms can become complicated by pneumonia that develops as a result of secondary bacterial invasions.

Canine tracheobronchitis, like the human cold, must run its course. Individuals afflicted with "kennel cough" should be kept relatively quiet. On occasion, stubborn forms will linger for several months. Certain cough suppressants may be effective in helping the symptoms, but your veterinarian may want to prescribe a specific antibiotic. Due to the nature of the disease, it is best to isolate affected individuals.

Immunization is gained through vaccination.

Rabies

Rabies is a filterable virus that affects the central nervous system. Rabies can occur in all warm-blooded animals (mammals), including wild carnivores, skunks, foxes, raccoons, bats, farm animals, and domestic dogs and cats. The virus is transmitted through contact with infected saliva either by a bite from an infected animal or human or through contact via a cut or break in the skin. Although the virus concentrates in the central nervous system, it can also occur in the blood and rarely in the milk.

Symptoms may appear in as few as ten days up to as much as several months. The individual may become restless, and his disposition may completely reverse. The dog may be unusually affectionate or withdrawn and more curt. He may disappear and wander for several days, or he may hide in some dark place or corner. You may even notice a change in the individual's voice marked by a dismal howl or bark.

Depending upon which part of the nervous system is affected by the virus, each individual will exhibit one of the two forms of the disease. In the "furious" form, the disease is typified by the classical "mad-dog syndrome." In this irrational state of mind, the affected individual may roam for quite a distance. He may be viciously aggressive and may snap or bite at anything in the way—infecting the victim(s) with the fatal virus. Noise can provoke attack. Affected individuals will lose their instinctive fear of natural enemies. The pupils will become dilated while the expression exhibits anxiety. The affected dog will probably appear to be frothing at the mouth, which is a classic symptom of rabies. The excessive saliva is due to the difficulty in swallowing caused by paralysis. If confined, the affected animal may snap at, bite, and chew at the surrounding wire, bars, chain, and frame of his confines. Sometimes the force and vigor of this attempt will result in broken teeth. Foreign objects are often swallowed. Death will occur within three to seven days. The victim will lapse into a paralytic state and die due to the progressive paralysis.

Because of legal ramifications, it is advisable to have your veterinarian administer rabies innoculations.

In the preliminary stages, rabies can be confused with other diseases. If you suspect rabies, confine the dog, but do not destroy him. Contact your veterinarian immediately. He will be able to differentiate rabbies from other illnesses.

If you or your dog is attacked by a rabid animal. *irrigate the wound with profuse quantities of running*

In the "dumb" or paralytic form, the disease is characterized by paralysis of the muscles. The muscles of the lower jaw usually become paralyzed and the mouth remains open. Salivation is profuse combined with an inability to swallow. This symptom is often mistaken for a bone or other foreign object lodged in the back of the mouth or throat. However, when an object is lodged, the individual will generally make an attempt to remove it with his paws, unlike the rabid animal, who will not. The individual affected with the paralytic form is not vicious or aggressive. Progressive paralysis will usually overcome the entire body, followed by a state of coma and death.

Rabies can be prevented through vaccination on a program determined by your local rabies control laws. Because of the potential human fatalities associated with rabies, it is imperative to comply with state laws.

warm water, and thoroughly cleanse the area with soap and a germicidal disinfectant. An antirabies vaccination will be administered for humans, but generally dogs bitten by a rabid animal will have to be destroyed. This may be prevented *only* if your dog has current rabies vaccinations. It is recommended that your dog receive his first rabies shot between twelve and sixteen weeks of age.

BACTERIAL DISEASES

Leptospirosis

Leptospirosis is an infection caused by spirochete, a bacterial organism that divides and multiplies in the system. Three types are known to affect dogs. In one type, rats are the most common carrier. The second type is associated mainly with the canine species, and a third type is less common. Contaminated water, especially stagnant water, is a common source. The spirochetes are shed in the urine of infected animals.

The incubation period is five to fifteen days. The first signs include yellowish-bile vomitus and darkened urine. Other signs are lameness in the hindquarter accompanied by muscular stiffness. Tenderness surrounds the abdominal, groin, and kidney regions. Appetite diminishes and is accompanied by vomiting and an elevated temperature of 103 to 106 degrees F. This may last one day to three weeks. Depression, jaundice of the mucous membranes and eyes, and/or internal bleeding are among the more common symptoms, along with increased thirst, prostration, vomiting, diarrhea with or without blood (which would indicate hemorrhagic gastroenteritis) and congested eyes. The temperature may drop to normal or subnormal. Dehydration is generally apparent.

In severe cases, individuals may die within five to ten days, or recovery may begin during the second week, extending into the sixth week.

Most of the tissues are actively affected, including the liver and lymph nodes. Generally, the kidneys are affected by varying degrees of nephritis (an inflammation of the kidneys) and are subject to most of the damage.

Immunization is available and is often contained in a combination with distemper and hepatitis vaccines. Annual boosters are recommended.

Salmonellosis

Salmonellosis is considered a secondary infective agent which becomes active in the dog's body after physiological stress has taken place, such as a viral infection, exposure to temperature extremes, surgery, or exhaustion. It seems to be more common in young or old individuals that are in a debilitated state. In an acute state, the infection may induce "fatal septicemia" followed by death in approximately forty-eight hours.

Salmonellosis is caused by the salmonella bacteria, which are consumed in contaminated feed and water and usually shed in the feces. The organisms may survive for months in wet, warm places. Salmonella bacteria thrive at temperatures between 40 and 140 degrees F. The bacteria are readily destroyed by normal cooking temperatures of 165 degrees F. and are unable to grow under freezing temperatures. However, once the temperature is warmed to 40 degrees F., the bacteria will begin to grow again.

When infected with salmonellosis, the digestive tract is especially affected. Sudden onset of diarrhea or chronic diarrhea (with or without an elevated temperature), loss of appetite, depression, and vomiting are common symptoms.

Adequate sanitation, including disinfecting watering and feeding utensils, will help minimize exposure. Individuals affected with gastrointestinal symptoms should be isolated. At the first signs of disturbance, seek professional medical care.

Tetanus

Tetanus is not rare, but its occurrence is not commonplace among the canine species. Tetanus is caused by a powerful toxemia infection, or poison, formed in the body by a specific germ. Symptoms of tetanus appear in the majority of cases between ten to fourteen days but can appear from a few days up to several weeks after the germs gain entrance into the body. The tetanus germs and spores remain localized where they enter the body at the place of a wound. The toxins formed by the germ are absorbed by the blood and circulated throughout the body.

The term "lockjaw" stems characteristically from the initial symptoms manifested in the disease, including spasms of the temporal and jaw muscles. It is very difficult for an affected individual to chew, and swallowing is inhibited by the spasms that progress to other muscles. Stiffness in the muscles is especially evident in the "sawhorse" straddling type of gait. The Aussie's bobtail will be elevated and stiff. Due to the temporal muscle spasms, the ears will be drawn together and in some cases be held erect. Between intervals of relaxation, the muscles will contract instantly at the slightest stimulus such as noise, touch, or even a stream of light.

Constipation commonly occurs, and respiration is rapid and labored. Cardiac function may or may not increase due to the disturbances of the circulatory and respiratory systems.

Generally, death is due to dysfunctioning or exhaustion of the vital organs. The temperature generally remains just slightly above normal during the course of the infection but may elevate to 108 or 110 degrees F. following a fatal attack. Death generally comes between seven and ten days following the onset of symptoms.

Debris, feces, and soil may contain the spores of the bacillus. Due to the nature of tetanus, which thrives in the absence of air, it is imperative to employ cleanliness. The germ becomes especially active and dangerous when a wound is not thoroughly cleansed and irrigated with proper germicidals to prevent spores from germinating in the wound tissue. Improperly applied dressings of wounds that prevent air from circulating around the injury provide an ideal breeding ground.

If there is evidence of tetanus, muscle spasms, or stiffness, veterinarian assistance should be sought immediately to improve chances of recovery and to relieve the painful muscle contractions.

End Notes

Carmichael, Leland, D.V.M., Ph.D. *Herpes Virus, Canis: Aspect of Pathogenesis and Immune Response.* Journal of Veterinary Medicine Vol. 156-June 1970.

Carmichael, Leland E. D.V.M., Ph.D. and Pollock, Roy V.H., D.V.M. *Newer Knowledge About Canine Parvovirus* - 30th Gaines Veterinary Symposium at the School of Medicine, Oregon State University January 27, 1981, Cornell University.

Christoph, Horst-Joachin *Diseases of Dogs*, Oxford: Pergamon Press LTD. 1975 ISBN 0-08-15800-5.

Huxsoll, David L. D.V.M. Ph.D. and Hemelt, Irene E. A.B. *Clinical Observations of Canine Herpes Virus.* Journal of Veterinary Medicine Vol 156-June 1970.

The Merck Veterinary Manual, Rahway, New Jersey U.S.A.: Merck and Company, 1973, ISBN 911910-51-4.

Playing peek-a-boo.   *Photo by Hubert Green*

21
PARASITES

INTERNAL PARASITES

Parasite control in dogs is of two general types—preventative and medicinal. Medicinal control is totally dependent on the preventative measures taken against reinfestation. Medicinal control is also controversial. In many cases, overworming and indiscriminate worming are greater detriments to the dog than the parasites themselves. An appropriate dosage for a healthy dog can be deadly for the rundown or sick individual.

Preventative measures include establishing sanitary conditions, controlling food habits, and maintaining control of your dog's whereabouts. Medicinal control involves the administration of chemical agents to parasitized animals, which should be attempted only while under your veterinarian's supervision.

Preventing parasite infections hinges on a thorough knowledge of the sources of infection, the modes of transmission, the life cycles of particular parasites, and the resistance of the preparasitic stages to physical and chemical agents.

One of the main sources of infection is an environment contaminated with feces or other excrement that contains parasite eggs or larvae. Your dog can become parasitic when he swallows the parasite in its infective state with food or water or when the larval worm burrows through the skin and tissue. Strict sanitation is important. Apply chemicals to the soil that can destroy parasite eggs and larvae. Dogs can acquire other parasites, particularly tapeworms, by eating inadequately cooked meat or fish, discarded intestines, or animal carcasses.

A few internal parasites are transmitted by fleas, flies, lice, ticks, and mosquitoes. Control in this situation involves eradicating the intermediate host or preventing the dogs from being bitten. This may be accomplished by judicious use of suitable chemical agents and by limiting the freedom of the animals to run at large.

Parasitic infestation may also be avoided by grooming your dog regularly, by providing dry, comfortable sleeping quarters free from drafts, and by maintaining the animals on a balanced diet. The importance of diet has been demonstrated in dogs that have shown a greater susceptibility to hookworm when on an inadequate diet.

The symptoms exhibited by parasitic animals are seldom distinctive and are easily confused with those of other diseases. Therefore, many pets die each year when proper treatment is not given or is unduly delayed. The owner must be able to recognize the need for medical attention, but it is equally important for him to realize that improper treatment will delay recovery. Subsequently, a prompt, accurate diagnosis is imperative. Fecal samples should be checked to determine involvement of parasitic agents. Appropriate medicine can then be prescribed. The drugs used for removing parasites are poisonous to a certain degree, and the dosages must be determined individually on the basis of age, weight, and general condition of the dog. To avoid injury and damage by improper worming, it is advisable in all cases to entrust the medication to your veterinarian.

THE PARASITES

Nematodes (Roundworms)

Roundworms (Ascarids) are some of the most common and injurious parasites in the canine species especially to weanlings. Ascarids are white and yellowish, are two to eight inches in length and resemble thin spaghetti. They are occasionally passed in large numbers in the feces or vomitus of puppies. While alive, they have a tendency to coil in a spiral.

Numerous eggs of the ascarids are passed in the feces of the dog and become infective within a few days under favorable conditions. The infective eggs are swallowed in contaminated feed or water and hatch in the small intestine. After penetrating the intestinal wall, the young worms pass to the lungs via the liver and heart. They escape from the blood vessels to the air passages and are either coughed up or crawl up the trachea. They are swallowed and develop to maturity in the small intestine within a few weeks. Ascarid larvae, like those of the hookworms, may pass from the circulatory system of the pregnant female to the developing embryos.

The most common symptoms of ascarid infection in puppies are marked enlargement of the abdomen, lethargy, and digestive disturbances. Large numbers of worms may be eliminated in the feces or vomitus when the infections are heavy. Coughing may be noted when larvae are passing through the lungs. Pneumonia commonly follows massive invasion of the lungs.

To prevent ascarid infections, you must be aware of the two main modes of infection, namely, the swallowing of eggs and the passage of migrating infective larvae to developing offspring through the placenta. To this end, large roundworms in the intestine of the dam should be removed by an appropriate medication before breeding. The female should be kept under conditions that diminish exposure to embryonated eggs of this parasite until after the young are weaned. This may be best accomplished by housing the bitch in an area not previously occupied by other dogs.

Before the female is moved to clean quarters, all accumulations of dirt and feces on the hair coat and on the skin, particularly around the mammary glands, should be thoroughly removed. To prevent prenatal infections, it is imperative that the dam not be exposed to embryonated eggs. It is of little use to keep the dam free of these worms by medication if she is constantly exposed to new sources of infection. The larvae that hatch from embryonated eggs in the body of the dam and migrate through her bloodstream may be incapable of developing to maturity in her intestine because of an acquired immunity, but they are fully capable of passing through the placenta to the unborn young and, indeed, may have a greater tendency to do so in a mature, resistant animal.

During the suckling period, the feces of lactating bitches should be gathered and disposed of. Frequent grooming by brushing the coat and washing the pads and feet in an attempt to remove adherent eggs will lend great support in controlling ascarid infections.

Children should be supervised while around lactating bitches and young puppies until the ascarid infection is under control and eliminated. Like the larvae of hookworms, those of canine ascarids may invade the body tissues of people and present a public health problem.

Hookworms

Hookworms are white or grayish roundworms about one-half to three-fourths inch long and about as thick as an ordinary straight pin. The front is slightly bent upward to give a hooklike appearance, and the mouth has teeth or cutting plates. Hookworms generally are firmly attached to the lining of the small intestine, but in heavy infestations they may occur also in the cecum, colon, and rectum.

Hookworms have the same life cycles as ascarids. The adult females produce many eggs, which are eliminated with the fecal material of the dog. When temperature and moisture are favorable, wormlike larvae hatch from the egg within a few days. In a week or so, the young larvae are transformed into the infective stage. Susceptible animals become parasitized when the infective larvae are swallowed in contaminated feed or water or when they are brought into contact with the mouth on rubber bones, balls, or other objects. Infective hookworm larvae may also penetrate the skin of susceptible hosts. In pregnant females, they may pass by way of the circulatory system to developing young.

Larvae that penetrate the skin are carried with the blood to the lungs, where they escape to the air passages. They are eventually coughed up and swallowed and are then passed to the intestine, where they develop to maturity. Infective larvae that are swallowed with contaminated feed and water pass directly to the intestine without going through the lungs.

Hookworm eggs first appear in the feces three to six weeks after the larvae reach the intestine, the worms generally maturing more rapidly in young animals. In prenatal infections, however, eggs may be found in the feces as early as twelve days after birth. In the absence of reinfection, hookworms may persist in the intestine of the dog for as long as two years, although most of them are eliminated within six months.

Because these parasites are voracious bloodsuckers, the principle symptoms of hookworm disease are associated with chronic hemorrhage. There is a pronounced anemia, manifested by extremely pale mucous membranes, marked depression, a reluctance to move about, weight loss, and death.

The dog may have persistent diarrhea in the early stages of the disease, and the feces may be streaked with blood. As the condition advances, the feces contain progressively larger amounts of blood and mucous. Shortly before death, the bowel movements may consist almost entirely of blood. Since the bitch generally keeps the puppies and bedding free of fecal material during the first few weeks, prenatal infections may end fatally before hookworm disease is suspected. Black, tarry stools can be present before the worms are old enough to produce eggs.

Australian Shepherd

It has been approximated that forty hookworms may withdraw as much as an ounce of blood during a twenty-four-hour period. Iron deficiencies can result due to the large loss of blood. Infections of several hundred worms are not uncommon, even in nursing puppies. But that is only part of the blood loss—the worms have a tendency to migrate to new areas, and the abandoned sites continue to bleed for some time after the worms have moved.

Shaded earthen runs provide a favorable environment for hookworm larvae during warm weather. Spring and fall are the most likely times for hookworm infection because hookworms cannot withstand extreme temperatures. Hookworms are the most dangerous internal parasites to dogs. Blood transfusions may be necessary to build up affected individuals before worming.

Infective hookworm larvae may also penetrate the skin of the host and become established in the intestine after migrating through the bloodstream and lungs. Unlike the thick-shelled, embryonated eggs of the ascarid, however, infective hookworm larvae are subject to destruction by chemical agents and thus afford a vulnerable point for control.

It is more difficult to control hookworm infections in temperate zones. Hookworm larvae on hard surfaces or on bare dirt runs in kennels may be destroyed with a saturating solution. The interval between treatments is governed by the amount and frequency of rainfall.

How often you treat the soil depends on also the degree of infestation of the dogs and the type of soil. Heavy clay requires fewer applications than sandy loam. Applications should be repeated more frequently during the spring and summer in the northern part of the country and on a year-round basis in warmer climates. Chemicals can become ingested and harm your dog, other livestock and the vegetation, therefore should not be applied to lawns, flowerbeds, or other cultivated plots. Your veterinarian will be able to suggest the best choice for your unique situation.

Whipworm

The whipworm found in dogs is a white or gray worm that generally occurs in the cecum, or blind gut. It is two to three inches long when mature and resembles a small whip. The life cycle of the whipworm is direct—that is, infection occurs when susceptible animals swallow embryonated eggs in contaminated feed or water. The eggs hatch in the small intestine, and the young worms reach maturity in the cecum about three months later.

The damage produced by the whipworm is not well understood, although a variety of symptoms have been associated with heavy infestations. Symptoms commonly attributed to whipworm infection are abdominal pain, lethargy, chronic diarrhea, and anemia, or alternate periods of diarrhea and constipation. In extreme cases, this may cause death. In many cases, however, the worms appear to do little harm.

The whipworm is hard to remove successfully with medicinal agents because of its sheltered location. Prevention depends primarily on prompt, thorough disposal of feces and the use of clean utensils for feed and water. The thick, impervious eggshell of this parasite, like that of the ascarid, does not permit destruction by chemical agents.

Nematodes of the Circulatory System

Heartworm - The heartworm is primarily a parasite of the canine. It is encountered in all parts of the United States but occurs more frequently in the southern states and along the eastern seaboard in dense mosquito populations. The worms are long, slender, and whitish. The males and females are, respectively, about six and twelve inches long. Heartworms are generally located in the right ventricle and pulmonary artery but may occur under the skin, between muscles, and in other places.

The life history of the heartworm differs materially from that of the intestinal roundworms. The adult female does not lay eggs, but she deposits living larvae, called microfilariae, directly into the bloodstream. The microfilariae are removed from the blood by bloodsucking arthropods such as fleas and mosquitoes. Experimental findings suggest that fleas may be one of the most important vectors in the transmission of heartworms.

After a period of growth and development in the body of the intermediate hosts, the larvae become infective and capable of becoming established in susceptible dogs. The transmission of infective larve occurs while the vectors are feeding on the host. The young worms undergo development in various extravascular tissues before migrating to the heart and adjacent vessels. It takes approximately four months for the worms to reach maturity.

down and gasp or collapse completely, but after a short rest he recovers and is apparently normal for a while. Sometimes the dog will develop a distinctive cough that fails to respond to medication. Abdominal dropsy and swelling in the legs and other parts of the body may be seen in long-standing cases because of poor circulation.

Positive diagnosis of heartworm infection can only be made by finding the active microfilariae in the blood. It should be recognized, however, that microfilariae may persist in the blood for as long as two years after the adult worms are dead and that adult worms may occur in locations other than the heart and adjacent vessels. It is possible, therefore, that adult worms may not always be found in the heart of animals that show microfilariae in the circulating blood.

Trematodes (Flukes)

Salmon Poisoning - The trematodes, or flukes, that parasitize carnivores are generally small, unsegmented, flat worms that require two intermediate hosts in order to complete their life cycles. The first

Australian Shepherd

The heartworm is a serious menace among active working dogs. Heartworm infection is prevented through the administration of a heartworm preventative on a regular basis. Also, insofar as is practical, try to protect your dogs from the bites of fleas and mosquitoes. This is difficult for working dogs, but the use of mosquito repellents (flea shampoos) may help.

Symptoms associated with heartworm infections are generally observed during or after vigorous exercise, although some heavily infested dogs may show no symptoms whatsoever. Probably the most characteristic symptom is rapid fatigue. The animal may lie

of these is a snail. The second is usually a fish or some other aquatic animal, although in a few instances other animals may serve as the second host. Only one trematode, the salmon-poisoning fluke, is of major importance in the United States. This parasite is limited primarily to regions of the Pacific Northwest where it is associated with a fatal disease of dogs, foxes, and coyotes. The parasites are hardly visible to the naked eye and are generally deeply embedded in the lining of the small intestine.

The eggs of the fluke are passed in the feces and hatch after several weeks of development in water.

The liberated larvae eventually penetrate a freshwater snail in which certain developmental changes occur. They emerge later as tadpolelike larvae penetrate the body of fish of the salmon family, and encyst in the muscles and other organs at the infective stages. The definite host becomes infested after eating raw or improperly cooked fish. The flukes reach maturity in a week or ten days.

So called salmon poisoning is caused by a rickettsialike organism, which is transmitted by the fluke. The rickettsia occur in the blood and lymph tissue of infected animals, and the infection can be transmitted by injecting those substances into susceptible dogs. Dogs that recover spontaneously or because of treatment with established remedial agents are immune to the disease, although the flukes may become established in their intestinal tract.

The symptoms of salmon poisoning develop seven to ten days after the infected fish are ingested by susceptible hosts. At first there is an elevated temperature, marked depression, loss of appetite, and increased thirst. Vomiting and diarrhea begin after a few days. The feces are mucoid and watery, but in time they become blood-tinged and are nearly all blood in the final stages of the disease. Death usually occurs within a week or ten days if the patient is not treated. Treatment of salmon poisoning is directed against the rickettsia rather than the flukes for which there is no effective treatment.

Rickettsial Diseases

Rickettsia are any one of several bacteria-like microorganisms. Ticks are generally the vector that transmits the disease. Rickettsia is infective in all of its stages, including the egg.

Canine ehrlichiosis - is an infectious disease that may be fatal to young dogs and has been found to be a chronic ailment in old dogs. It is known to affect all closely related canidae. The brown dog tick is the most common tick known to carry canine ehrlichiosis.

Recurrent fever, pus-filled mucus discharge from the eyes and the nose, odorous breath, emaciation, convulsions, hysteria, paralysis, and gastroenteritis are all symptoms of the disease. If veterinary care is not sought, death will result. The disease is often complicated by concurrent infections.

Cestodes of dogs

Tapeworm - There are at least fourteen varieties of tapeworms known to infest dogs in the United States. Some species occur only rarely and may be limited to certain geographical areas where suitable hosts exist.

The injury that tapeworms produce is not well understood, although digestive disturbances, abdominal pain, nervousness, poor external appearance, diarrhea, excessive gas production, vomiting, and scooting have been associated with heavy infestations. However, the chief importance of canine tapeworms concerns their transmission to man and livestock. Also, segments of tapeworms may be passed involuntarily by infested animals and may soil rugs, furniture, and bedding.

The double-pored tapeworm - occurs commonly in dogs. The adult worm is twelve to sixteen inches long. The segments are shaped like melon seeds and resemble grains of rice when dried. Infection is established when the dog swallows fleas or lice in which the larval stages are found.

This tapeworm may be transmitted to people, particularly children, as a result of accidental swallowing of the intermediate host.

Controlling and Preventing Tapeworm - Satisfactory medication against tapeworms is difficult because some remedial agents frequently fail to remove the scolex (head) of the parasite, but produce only a "shearing" action on the strobila, or chain of segments. In that event, another complete strobila develops from the undisturbed scolex, and in time (depending on the particular species of tapeworm involved), ripe segments again are eliminated with the bowel movements.

A variety of medicinal products are available for removing tapeworms. None is effective against all species, and selection of the appropriate drug depends on an accurate determination of the particular tapeworm involved.

Prevention of tapeworms in dogs is especially difficult because their intermediate or infective stages occur in natural foodstuffs and in such common external parasites as fleas and lice. Nevertheless, every effort should be made to prevent the animals from ingesting infective material, a recommendation that necessitates the control of fleas and lice, proper disposal of viscera on the farm, and restriction of the animal's freedom to roam at large under conditions that permit it to kill and eat mice, rabbits, squirrels, and other intermediate hosts.

House companions and dogs raised in kennels have little chance to acquire tapeworms other than the common double-pored species that is transmitted by fleas and lice. For dogs, therefore, prevention of tapeworms may be achieved largely by applying insecticides that will remove pests from the host (dog), his bedding, and his premises. Preventing infection in dogs on the farm that are permitted to roam at large is virtually impossible. Control under these conditions consists largely of removing worms from the infested animal with the appropriate medicinal agents, as well as closer supervision.

Protozoan Diseases

The Protozoa, a minute, one-celled organism, is responsible for several diseases of dogs that are of importance in the United States. Two common diseases, coccidia and giardia, involve the intestinal tract. The other, canine babesiases (piroplasmosis), leishmaniasis, and toxoplasmosis, are parasites of the blood and associated organs.

Coccidia - Coccidiosis is widespread throughout the country but is particularly prevalent in the warmer areas of the South. Two species of coccidia, are commonly found in dogs. These parasites invade the cells of the small intestine, where they multiply rapidly and destroy considerable tissue. The organisms eventually give rise to resistant egglike forms— oocysts—which are eliminated in the feces. Under favorable conditions, the oocysts become infective in a few days and are transmitted to susceptible hosts in contaminated feed and water.

This disease is marked by severe diarrhea, in which the feces are mucoid and contain large amounts of blood depending on the severity of the infection. Coccidiosis is usually a disease of young dogs. Marked depression, loss of appetite, general weakness, anemia, and dehydration also are noted. Heavy infections can result in death. Coccidiosis is induced by physiological stress. Shipping, weaning, diet changes, cold and damp weather, overcrowding and fatigue are several forms of stress.

The control of coccidiosis consists of providing and maintaining strict sanitary conditions, proper nutrition, and the use of coccidiostatic drugs as prescribed by your veterinarian.

Giardia - Giardiasis, an intestinal infection of dogs, is caused by the protozoan, Giardia canis. This disease occurs mainly in young animals but can occur in adult dogs and humans. The disease is characterized by soft, light-colored stools, dysentery and diarrhea, and in heavy infections, the feces are bloody and mucoid and generally have an offensive odor.

The parasites live in the small intestine and pass through two stages. The parasitic stage, called a trophozoite, is pear-shaped and active. It may be seen in fluid or semifluid feces when the feces are examined under a microscope. The oval-shaped, inactive cystic stage is found only in formed stools. It is this stage that is transmitted from one host to another. It is commonly passed in the feces of the beaver. A dog may contract the disease by drinking from infected streams and waters. It has been often referred to as "backpackers" disease.

Giardia presents a major public health problem. Filtered water systems are not totally effective against giardia, and therefore untested water should be boiled before drinking. Dogs infected with giardia have been reported to respond to the administration of Flagyl (metronidazole). Treatment of giardia infection is largely preventative.

Canine Piroplasmosis

This disease is caused by an organism known as Babesia canis and is transmitted by ticks. The pear-shaped parasites are found in red blood cells. In the United States, the brown dog tick, is considered to be a chief vector.

The disease may occur in either an acute or chronic form. Dogs affected with an acute form are off feed but generally show an increased thirst. The pulse and respiration rates are increased, and the dogs commonly have an elevated temperature. The mucous membranes of the mouth and eyelids often are reddened in the early stages but may become yellowish as the condition progresses, an indication of jaundice. The acute cases frequently terminate in death. The symptoms in the chronic form are less pronounced. There may be an intermittent fever, diminished appetite, and loss of weight. The dogs are generally anemic and become weak and indifferent to their surroundings. Death may be delayed for several days or weeks; sometimes the animals recover.

Treatment generally requires several days. The dosage of similar drugs must be calculated carefully on the basis of age, weight, and general physical conditions.

Prevention of the infection depends largely on tick control. This may be accomplished by dipping or washing your dog with suitable insecticidal preparations recommended by your veterinarian and applying residual insecticidal sprays to dwellings and runs occupied by the dogs.

Toxoplasmosis - Toxoplasmosis is a parasite that invades rapidly multiplying cells. The cells eventually "burst," freeing the toxoplasmas, which spread and infect the cells throughout the system. The parasite can be contracted or transmitted by infected mothers in utero to their fetuses or acquired through feces, urine, nasal secretions, or by ingestion of infected raw meat. Distemper decreases the dog's ability to resist toxoplasmosis.

Now under the classification of coccidium, toxoplasmosis occurs throughout the world under a variety of climatic conditions. It can be transmitted from various species of affected animals to man.

Symptoms include nervous disturbances that may be apparent due to "tremors," enteritis, emaciation, fever, jaundice, apathy, uncoordination, paralysis, and even gastrointestinal ulcers. Toxoplasmosis may be suspected when dogs are under a year of age or if the symptoms occur following an infectious disease such as distemper or even hepatitis.

Whenever you suspect that your dog's health is being affected by illness, get him to the veterinarian immediately. Proper diagnosis is imperative for successful treatment. In the case of toxoplasmosis, a positive diagnosis cannot be made without serological tests.

EXTERNAL PARASITES

Fleas

The fleas that commonly infest dogs are the dog flea, and the cat flea which is even more common to the dog. Fleas are wingless, bloodsucking insects with powerful legs. The latin term "ctenocephalides" for flea means "comb head," which is an identifying characteristic of the flea. Adults of both species are small insects with brown compact bodies.

All fleas pass through four stages—the egg, the larva, the pupa, and the adult flea. Eggs are laid on the dog and drop to the ground, where they hatch several days later into wormlike larvae. Larvae are not parasites; rather, they live on organic matter in the dust or soil. The debris and dust in sleeping quarters of heavily infested animals contain dried blood that was passed in the feces of the adult fleas, which makes food for the larvae.

In several weeks the larvae is full grown and spins a tiny cocoon in which it transforms from the larva to the pupa. The pupa changes to an adult flea in about a week. The adult fleas may not emerge for some time unless disturbed by a vibration.

For any treatment to be effective, you must first control the fleas. Fleas are prevalent in areas of high humidity, and they flourish in the damp, cool surfaces of sand, concrete, and dirt floors. Cracks and crevices offer places for development, as well as rugs, curtains, furniture, and your dog's bedding.

Many good commercial preparations are available for controlling fleas ranging from shampoos to sprays to powders. But it is best to first consult your veterinarian because some products may cause toxic symptoms in nursing puppies, create allergic reactions, or cause secondary infections.

Lice

Several species of lice may be found on dogs. Lice fall into two categories—the sucking louse and the biting louse. Sucking lice have piercing mechanisms which can be retracted up into the body. Blood is their food source. An allergic reaction is not uncommon due to the bites and/or the feces of lice. They also transmit disease agents. Chewing lice are equipped with parts resembling nippers that enable them to nibble at the hair and skin debris of their host. Some will pierce through the skin and take blood.

The sucking and biting lice are quite different in structure and feeding habits, but their life histories are similar. All lice pass through the egg stage, several nymphal stages, and the adult phase. The eggs (ova), called "nits," are fastened to the hair of the host. The nymphs are similar to the adults in appearance except for the size and the lack of sexual organs.

Lice are wingless insects with "dorsoventrally" flattened bodies. Unlike fleas, lice are host- and nutritive-specific and cannot meet ther nutritional requirements on any other host. In large numbers, lice can cause death associated with anemia, more common in the young or debilitated. It is less of a problem in well-nourished, mature dogs in their prime. Chewing lice are intermediate hosts of the tapeworm.

Heavy infestations can lower the dog's resistance and make him susceptible to other diseases. They also can lead the way to secondary bacterial infections and/or fly infestations due to the small wounds that are created. A rough, dry coat with or without matts can be due to lice.

Even though the life of lice depends on their host, it is a good idea to clean grooming equipment and bedding. There are several excellent medicated shampoos available that can be used to bathe your dog with a minor case of lice infestation. Severe cases however should be treated by your veterinarian.

Mites

Mange is an unsightly and painful skin condition caused by the burrowing or feeding of mites,

Australian Shepherd

several species of which attack dogs. Mites are related to both spiders and ticks. Many are barely visible to the naked eye, and the others are microscopic in size. The condition is contagious and is spread by contact with infested animals.

The sarcoptic mange of dogs is related to the human infection called scabies. The female mite burrows into the upper layers of the skin, where she will lay twenty to forty eggs. After three to seven days, the eggs will hatch and produce larvae—tiny mites with three pairs of legs. The larvae grow to nymphs by molting, and the nymphs grow to adults in the same way. The nymphs and adults have four pairs of legs, but the nymphs are sexually immature. The entire life cycle requires two to three weeks. The larvae, nymphs, and males do not burrow into the skin but live under crusts or scales on the surface.

Sarcoptic mange may occur on any part of the body, but usually it appears first on the head. It spreads rapidly. Red spots appear and develop into small blisters. The scratching of the animal causes the reddish area to spread.

The burrowing of the female causes the skin to exude serum, which dries in crusts or scabs. The infected part of the skin becomes dry and covered with crust, the hair may come out, and the skin may thicken and become wrinkled. Itching is intense. The scratching may give rise to secondary bacterial infections and sores. Bacterial action in the scabs and sores causes an unpleasant odor. If the infection is not checked, digestion and other body functions become impaired, and death may result.

This species of mite can live for a time on people. Unnecessary handling of infected dogs should be avoided.

Demodectic, or red, mange of dogs is caused by a long, wormlike mite which lives principally in the hair follicles of the skin. It has also been found in certain lymph glands and in the liver, spleen, lungs, and other internal organs. In typical cases, the mites appear in great numbers in association with bacteria, which cause the most unpleasant symptoms of the infection.

The first evidence of demodectic mange is the appearance of bald, reddened areas. After invasion by the bacteria, the infection becomes pustular, the skin becomes thicker, poisons formed by the bacteria affect the general health of the animal, and a disagreeable odor is produced. The infection may last for several years. It usually causes death if unchecked.

Ear mange of dogs is caused by mites. The mites do not burrow in the skin but live deep in the ear canal, near the eardrum, and feed through the delicate skin. Irritation results, and the ear canal becomes congested. The dog scratches and rubs his ears and shakes his head in an attempt to relieve the itching, or he may run in circles or show other evidence of nervous disturbances.

Mange may sometimes be confused with other skin conditions. It can be diagnosed positively only by microscopic examination of scrapings from the diseased parts.

A well-balanced diet is extremely important in preventing mange. Dry, clean quarters with protection from debilitating effects of internal parasites and regular, thorough grooming will promote overall good health, which, in turn, will increase the dog's resistance to skin diseases of all kinds. Above all, the dog should *never* be permitted to associate with mangy animals or to frequent premises occupied by them, since they are the main sources of infection.

Rational treatment is contingent upon prompt, accurate diagnosis, because the various types of mange differ in their response to remedial measures. Improper treatment is costly and may cause injury to the patient or permit the condition to reach an incurable state.

Ear mange will generally respond promptly to one or two weeks application of an appropriate commercial product.

Ticks

Approximately six of the nearly four hundred worldwide varieties of ticks present a threat to dog owners. With the exception of the spinose ear tick, the species of ticks known to infest dogs are varieties of "hard ticks" commonly called wood ticks. The spinose ear tick is of the "soft tick" family.

Wooded areas, sandy beaches, and overgrown fields attract tick infestations. Ticks are transferred when the dog rubs against grasses, bushes, and shrubs, or they drop off as the dog passes underneath trees.

Ticks impose a major threat by transporting diseases and causing severe anemia and an overall breakdown of the system's defenses. They can create open abscesses and sores that make targets for screwworms and maggot infestations.

The brown dog tick feeds almost entirely on the canine. This type of tick is difficult to get rid of because it easily adapts to life in the relatively dry environments of kennels, houses, and apartments. Yards and homes in southern states can be infested. Your dog can pick up these ticks from infested premises and in turn infest his own living quarters.

Adult ticks are reddish brown, flat, and about one-eighth inch long when unfed. Both females and males feed on dogs, and mating even takes place on the dogs.

Unlike the males, the females engorge with blood. They turn dark gray and become almost one-half inch long. This process takes approximately six days, at which time the females drop off and seek a hiding place. They lay one thousand to three thousand eggs, which will hatch in three to eight weeks. The light brown, six-legged larvae, or seed ticks, are approximately one-fiftieth inch long before feeding. When they feed on dogs, they become slate gray and approximately one-twentieth inch long. Feeding requires three to six days, after which they drop off, seek hiding, and molt to mature, eight-legged males and females.

Ticks will crawl over floors, walls, and furniture in heavily infested homes searching for a host. They will rarely bite people. Their mere presence is annoying, however. Heavy, continuous infestations of your dog will create irritations and a noticeable loss of condition. Open wounds may result when pulling the ticks off and may become infected.

You should always examine your dogs after they have been playing or working in tick-infested areas such as in the woods or overgrown fields. Removal should be done very carefully. Ticks should be grasped as near to the skin as possible with forceps and touched with a hot needle or match stick. Be sure that the burrowed head is out, and be careful not to break the head or mouth parts. If this happens, you must also remove the broken parts. The bite should be disinfected in the same manner as a small cut. Never handle the tick with ungloved hands, since the infectious organism (disease of spotted fever) can easily spread to humans.

Tick control not only requires treatment of dogs, but of the infested area itself. Information regarding tick control can be obtained from state and county extension offices and pest control centers.

Spinose ear ticks - are commonly found in both semiarid and arid regions. The spinose ear tick spends between one and seven months developing from the larvae stage to the nymphal stage. It then drops from the ears and crawls up trees, fences, or structured buildings, molts into the adult stage, and lays its eggs.

Infestation of the spinose ear tick is evident when dogs hold their heads in an atypical position and rub at their ears trying to remove the ticks. The ticks bury themselves in the waxy secretions and debris. There is often a foul-smelling mixture of tick debris and wax. The ears should be checked and cleaned frequently with weekly grooming. If any ticks are found present they should be removed. Heavy infestations are best handled by a veterinarian.

Fungal (Mycotic) Diseases

Fungus is an unsightly disease caused by specific spores that may be transmitted through contaminated dust and soil. A fungal disease can be discovered, if present, at an early stage during the daily grooming period. It appears as a small round spot devoid of hair which will emit a fluid secretion. The serum will ooze out from under the scab, or scaly skin, causing more hair to fall out, thus increasing the size of the lesion. The hair, dandruff, the serum itself, or fleas may carry the spore to infect other places and dogs. Some of the fungus diseases are contagious to humans.

Disinfectants and iodine medications can be applied directly to fungus lesions. Medicated baths given at regular intervals may also be prescribed in addition to certain medications. There are many types of fungal diseases, some of which are specific to certain regions throughout the country. Professional assistance is imperative for proper diagnosis and effective treatment.

Fungal Pneumonias - Contamination may occur when a dog or person comes into contact directly with the infection. It may also be contracted by breathing, which can result in what is known as fungal pneumonia. There are many types of fungal pneumonias, several of which are region-specific. These are generally characterized by a persistent cough. Unlike bacterial pneumonias, fungal pneumonias have a poor response to treatment, including administration of antibiotics.

Ringworm - Ringworm is not a worm at all but a fungus infection. It is a contagious disease of the skin that can take on the characteristic form of small circular bare or scaly patches. It may also look like fine gray cigarette ash at the roots of the hairs, or even appear to have brownish-yellow crusts. A raw, bleeding surface may appear when the crusts are removed by scratching or rubbing to relieve itching, although not all cases are accompanied by intense itching.

It is extremely difficult to diagnose, but ringworm often shows up in a luminous form under ultraviolet light.

The disease is caused by specific fungi that are somewhat similar to certain ordinary molds. It is best to seek your veterinarian's expert diagnosis, which is necessary for proper treatment. Different types of fungi respond to different types of medication.

In a world all their own. Jick Taylor with "Just Jake."

22

FIRST AID

Since accidents often occur at unexpected times far from a place where you can get immediate help, you must be able to act quickly and effectively in order to save your Aussie's life or to prevent further complications of an injury until you are able to get professional medical help.

When an accident occurs, it is important to keep in mind the five principles of first aid, which are (1) to restrain the patient to prevent futher injury and to prevent injury to the handler; (2) to maintain open air passages and respiration; (3) to maintain cardiac function; (4) to control bleeding; and (5) to prevent or treat for shock.

CARING FOR AN INJURED DOG

Administering Medication

Pills are most effectively given by opening the jaw and placing the tablet or capsule on the back of the tongue with two fingers. Then close the mouth, holding it firmly with one hand while you stroke your dog's throat with the other hand. This should cause him to swallow. Be sure that the pill is far enough on the back base of the tongue for easy swallowing, but not so far that the windpipe is endangered. Another method is to place your hand over your dog's muzzle with your fingers on one side of the upper jaw and your thumb on the other side. Firmly press his lips against and under his teeth. Use your other hand simultaneously to pull his lower jaw away in order to drop the pill at the back base of his tongue. Then with your index and middle fingers, slip it toward his

throat. Quickly close his mouth and hold it shut until he swallows. Lubricating the pill with butter or margarine or concealing the tablet inside a small bite of hamburger may be helpful.

Liquid medications can be given by using the "cheek pouch." Hold the muzzle closed while you gently put your fingers in the side of your dog's mouth to pull his lower lip up and out to form a pouch. Then pour or spoon liquid into the funnel, which will direct the medication backward through the teeth. Release your grip on the muzzle enough to permit easy swallowing. Do not let your dog shake or drop his head until he has consumed the medicine. Do not hold his head too high, because liquid may pass into his lungs. An unbreakable syringe without the needle, an eyedropper, a spoon, plastic vials dispensed by a druggist, or even a basting utensil are ideal for giving liquids. Only administer medication on the advice of your veterinarian.

Applying an Emergency Muzzle

Even the most trustworthy Australian Shepherd can become frightened or panic-stricken when injured and in pain. You may need to restrain him from biting while you are trying to help him. A cloth muzzle is the most effective way to prevent this. You may use a length of gauze bandage, nylon stocking, a strip of cloth, a necktie, a cloth belt, a leash, a soft cord, or a piece of rope approximately two feet long. Make a double half hitch by wrapping the bandage twice around the muzzle of the dog and securing it with a knot under the chin. Tie the ends together behind his ears at the back of the head to keep it from slipping off. Be alert for signs of vomiting. Should this happen, remove the muzzle immediately to prevent choking or suffocation. Do not leave the dog unattended with the muzzle on.

Artificial Respiration

When breathing has stopped, administer artificial respiration by lying the dog on his side. Quickly check inside the mouth to be sure that no object is blocking the air passage. Pull the tongue forward, and extend the head and neck forward to establish an open air passage to the lungs. The most effective method of artificial respiration is by "mouth to nose." Place your mouth over the dog's muzzle. Cup your hands over the entirety (nose and mouth), forming an airtight seal, and begin to blow air into the lungs. Care should be taken to observe the chest and stomach of the patient to insure that the lungs are being inflated and not the stomach. Continue this until he begins breathing strongly on his own. For administering artificial respiration, one deep ventilation every five seconds is sufficient. The normal respiratory rate for your Australian Shepherd is approximately eighteen to twenty-two breaths per minute but can vary from ten to thirty breaths per minute.

Another method is "chest compression." The lungs are located against rib walls in the thorax or rib section. Push down on the rib cage in a firm and rhythmic manner, releasing the pressure every two to five seconds until normal breathing is restored.

Cardiopulmonary Resuscitation (CPR)

A dog can sustain life approximately two and one-half to three minutes after the heart has stopped beating. Signs indicating cardiac arrest are: no detectable heartbeat, absence of the arterial pulse, a gray discoloration of the mucous membranes, dilated pupils, and respiratory failure.

When the heart has stopped beating, it can be stimulated by external cardiac compression. Place the palms of your hands on the dog's chest (with the dog lying on his side) directly over the heart, compress the chest with a force appropriate to the size of the victim, then release. The motion should not be jerky, and it is advisable to hold the compression briefly before release. The compressions should be done at the rate of sixty per minute. Continue to compress and release at this rate until the heart begins to beat. Normal heart rates for your Australian Shepherd range between 70 to 100 in an adult and 90 to 140 in the smaller and younger dogs. To check the pulse, palpate, or feel, the femoral artery located in the mid third inner aspect of the thigh.

When both breathing and pulse have stopped, administer supportive measures. After every fifth compression at the rate of sixty compressions per minute (or one compression per second), give one breath. If two persons are at the scene, one can perform cardiac compressions at the rate of sixty per minute, while the other performs artificial respiration, interposing one breath after every fifth compression.

Carrying an Injured Dog

If you need to transport an injured Aussie, a solid, flat surface such as a door, a broad board, or several boards fastened together make an ideal stretcher. However, since most accidents occur where these items are not available, you must improvise. You can make use of a blanket, rain slicker, shirt, coat, puptent, or any other available item. Any strong cloth can serve as a stretcher. Tie knots in each corner, and insert a strong branch or pole in the knots in each side or through the sleeves of a shirt, jacket, or slicker to form a sling.

ABDOMINAL INJURY

Should your dog sustain blunt trauma to the abdominal region, internal hemorrhage is possible. In a rare occurrence, a dog may sustain a tremendous force or penetrating injury to the abdominal area, rupturing the abdominal wall and spilling the intestines. Do *not* attempt to wash off or replace the organs in the abdominal cavity, because it will become contaminated. *Do* prevent the dog from licking or chewing at the organs. Use plastic wrap or a thermal "space blanket" to wrap the organs to retain moisture. Then place towels and blankets over this dressing to keep the organs warm. Treat for shock. The dog may also vomit blood. If this happens, lie the dog on his side, with his head slightly lowered, so that the blood will not be sucked back into the lungs, especially if the dog is unconscious. Get immediate professional assistance.

ANIMAL BITES

Bites normally come in the form of puncture wounds. Because all animals harbor bacteria in their mouths, contamination can result which may lead to infection. It is best to consult with a veterinarian regarding a puncture wound. He or she will be able to determine whether systemic antibiotics may be indicated.

BLEEDING

Bleeding from superficial wounds caused by minor injuries is stopped by the natural clotting of blood upon contact with air. If this does not stop bleeding, apply direct pressure over the bleeding point

The flash to grab your attention with the quality to hold it. Champion Jay Hawk of Coppertone (Ch Blue Jasper of Coppertone ex Ch Shanks' Ginger Blue of Coppertone). Courtesy Kline

with your finger or thumb. Your hands should be clean, or you should place a piece of clean, preferably sterile material over the wound before the pressure is applied. If the injury is on a limb, elevate the injured leg while applying direct pressure on the wound. Pressure can also be applied above the artery that serves the injured limb. For example, to control hemorrhage for a lower hind leg injury, apply pressure to the femoral artery on the inside of the dog's thigh. Continue the pressure until the bleeding has stopped.

You can also cover the wound with a compress bandage of sterile gauze, and wrap it tightly over the injured area; however, the direct pressure method is better. It is difficult to apply a pressure bandage to the trunk without restricting breathing, so be especially careful. On a limb, a compression bandage should include all areas distal (toward the foot) to the wound, with the wrapping beginning at the toes and working up the leg with *even* pressure so that circulation to the foot is not cut off.

Profuse arterial bleeding is dangerous because blood in an artery is under direct pressure from the heart. If the artery is severed or torn, the blood will be bright red and will flow out irregularly in spurts, timed with the heartbeat. To stop bleeding from an artery, apply pressure between the heart and the wound.

If the wound is gaping or jagged, put gauze over it and hold the gauze in place with adhesive tape until you can get the patient to a veterinarian. Never place cotton directly on the wound because it leaves fibers that are difficult to remove.

Internal Bleeding

Even if there is no apparent injury after an accident, your Australian Shepherd may be hemorrhaging internally. If he is weak or prostrate, if mucous membranes (gums, tissue surrounding the eyes) are pale, or if you notice distention of the abdomen, he may have been injured internally. Internal bleeding induces shock. Wounds of the chest or abdomen may cut or tear large veins, causing severe internal hemorrhage. This situation requires immediate professional attention. If there is bleeding from the nose, mouth, or ears with no apparent damage to those areas, it may indicate a head injury. Treat the condition by keeping the patient as quiet and immobile as possible. Carry the patient on an improvised stretcher and get to a veterinarian immediately. Treat for shock.

BRAIN INJURY

A brain concussion can occur as the result of any trauma to the head. Other types of brain injury may appear similar. Signs of possible brain injury are: shallow respiration, feeble pulse, dilated or pinpoint pupils, or pupils of uneven size. If conscious, the dog may carry his head cocked to one side or become uncoordinated. The patient can demonstrate partial or total unconsciousness. Blood appearing from the ears or nose may indicate brain hemorrhage. Vomiting may occur. Be careful to observe that vomitus does not get sucked back into the lungs, especially if the patient is unconscious. As with any type of severe injury, treat for shock. Do not give any stimulants. Keep the patient quiet to avoid further trauma. Seek professional assistance as soon as possible, because swelling of the brain can lead to additional damage.

BROKEN TEETH

Tooth dislocations and fractures in a working breed like the Australian Shepherd are not uncommon. Injuries range from teeth being jarred loose, chipped, or broken to being totally uprooted. Teeth can be driven into the nasal cavity, lip, cheek, or tongue. Hemorrhage is usually present, and the movement of the tongue will slow clotting.

If the wound is minor and hemorrhage at a minimum, apply an ice pack to control bleeding. Bleeding from a single cavity can also be controlled by applying direct pressure. Your veterinarian may have to suture large lacerations and use a form of immobilization such as pinning and wiring to heal fractures of the teeth and the jaw assembly. In certain cases, a dislocated tooth with a root can be replaced in its cavity and remain functional with proper dentistry. If the tooth is not too dirty, rinse it with cold water.

Preserve all gum fibers still clinging to the tooth. If the tooth is excessively soiled, rinse it with eight ounces (or one cup) of ice water mixed with one quarter ounce (two tablespoons) of salt. In both cases, seek professional medical care immediately.

BRUISES

Bruises accompany many types of injuries. Apply a cold pack to prevent swelling of a new injury. Use a warm compress to improve circulation on an already swollen injury.

BURNS

Burns damage and destroy the protective layers of skin and tissue that guard against infection. Burns are a result of contact with corrosive chemicals, friction, heat, and/or electricity. Burns are extremely painful and prone to infection. Serious burns can lead to shock. If the area is larger than a small spot, prevent contamination and get professional help immediately. Treat for shock if indicated.

Alkali Burns

For a minor alkali burn, wash the involved area liberally with cold water before applying vinegar or lemon juice, diluted in cold water.

Acid Burns

For minor acid burns, apply a solution of sodium bicarbonate, such as baking soda in water.

Friction Burns

Treat friction burns with a protective coating such as an antibiotic ointment or petroleum jelly.

Kerosene, Turpentine, and Gasoline Burns

For minor burns caused by kerosene, turpentine, or gasoline, use a mild oil over the affected area, then wash gently with soap and water. Keep the area from becoming contaminated, and get professional help.

Thermal Burns

Burns caused from scalding by hot or boiling water, grease, or from contact with hot objects should be irrigated immediately with cold water or strong, cold tea. Then apply a simple protective coating like an antibiotic ointment or petroleum jelly. For serious thermal burns, contact your veterinarian immediately.

Unknown Chemicals

For minor burns caused by unknown chemicals, wash the area liberally with cold water and saturate it with a solution of sodium bicarbonate in water. In the case of chemical burns, avoid the use of petroleum jelly, oils, or ointments.

CONSTIPATION

Constipation is a condition of the bowels in which defecation is difficult and irregular. It is characterized by recurrent attempts to defecate and is sometimes accompanied by a whimper of sharp pain. Sometimes the feces will be blood-streaked or hard and dry.

Dogs confined for long periods of time without proper exercise and debilitated individuals are prone to constipation. A poor diet can result in constipation. The condition can also be caused by an obstruction, a hernia, a tumor of the colon, a swollen prostate gland, parasites, abscesses, or a foreign object. Consult your veterinarian to determine the cause.

Treatment

Simple first aid for mild cases of constipation consists of applying warm soapy water to the exter-

Friendships between a boy and his dog are like none other.

nal area and anus in the case that dry feces have formed an external block. A teaspoon of vegetable oil on your dog's feed may help to soften the feces. You may also want to reevaluate your dog's exercise program. If your dog is constipated after two days or is showing any other symptoms, do not hesitate to call your veterinarian.

CONVULSIONS

Convulsions are not a disease, but a symptom of another disorder. Seizures can be caused by epilepsy, viral infections, internal parasites, distemper, high fever, an accidental injury, or tumors.

Seizures can be localized or generalized. They occur suddenly with uncontrollable muscular twitching and may be accompanied by frothing at the mouth, loss of bladder and bowel functions, and vomiting. The dog may fall to his side, kicking rigidly, or he may begin running wildly, staggering into objects.

If your dog experiences a convulsion, clear the area of any objects on which he may injure himself. Because of his lack of control over his actions, keep fingers and hands away from his mouth so that he does not accidently bite down. If breathing has stopped, administer artifical respiration when the convulsion has stopped. (See Artificial Respiration.) Lie the dog on his side to allow excess saliva to drain from his mouth. If the dog has vomited, make sure that he doesn't breathe it into his lungs. After the convulsion has passed, get the patient to the veterinarian as soon as possible. Never administer any medication to a dog that has seizures without veterinarian approval and guidance.

CUTS AND WOUNDS

There are several types of wounds: lacerations, punctures, incisions, abrasions, and bruises. Lacerations are common and may occur upon the impact of a kick, a vehicle collison, a dog fight, or a snag from a piece of wire or a branch. It is an irregular-shaped wound that is caused by a ripping effect. Puncture wounds may result from a dog fight or porcupine

Harper's Old Smokey (1957-1972) Tucson's Joe ex Tucson's Sis. Foundation sire of the breed.

quills and occur when a sharp object penetrates deeply into the tissue. An incision is caused when a sharp object such as glass makes a clean slicing cut. Abrasions are made upon contact with a surface that scrapes the skin and tissue. Bruises can accompany many types of injuries but most commonly happen upon impact with an object not sharp enough to penetrate the skin.

Cuts and wounds should be covered with a clean, preferably sterile, dressing to prevent further contamination and be examined by a veterinarian. If the wound is jagged or gaping, place a strip of adhesive tape over the dressing until treatment can be administered. A cold compress will help to control swelling and pain. A hot compress improves circulation of an already swollen wound. If necessary, control hemorrhage.

For very minor, superficial wounds you can first remove any foreign objects such as glass or slivers. Cleanse the area with soap and water and apply a mild antiseptic such as 3 percent hydrogen peroxide mixed with equal parts water. A mouthwash such as *Listerine®* can also be used.

In the case of the puncture wound (i.e., a superficial bite, etc.), pour 3 percent peroxide into the wound. Wash the surrounding area with germicidal soap or a mild antiseptic. Puncture wounds heal the best from the inside out. Shave or trim the hair surrounding the wound. Do not allow the skin to quickly heal over the top. Wash the wound several times a day, then apply peroxide and insert an antibiotic ointment. As with any healing wound, observe closely for signs of infection, such as redness, swelling, or the feeling of heat over the involved area. Contact your veterinarian if these symptoms become apparent.

DIARRHEA

Diarrhea is an intestinal disorder in which the bowel movement is characterized by fluidity and frequency. As with vomiting and convulsions, it is not a disease itself, but a symptom of another disorder. It can occur from allergies, infectious diseases, metabolic disease, parasites, foreign bodies, an unclean feeding utensil, overfeeding, or a change in diet. Lactose found in milk is a common cause of loose or watery stools. Check your dog's stool regularly for indications of a possible problem.

Normal feces vary in color depending on the individual and his diet. Normal color usually ranges from light brown to dark or ruddy brown. Black feces may result from a diet high in meat content, while grayish white stools may indicate the presence of large amounts of bone. Nursing puppies or dogs on a diet high in milk or cereal grain will exhibit a light brown or tan stool.

Any blood, mucous, or foreign substances in the stool or abnormal color and consistency should be brought to the attention of your veterinarian.

Treatment

Mild cases of diarrhea can be treated by administering one tablespoon of *Kaopectate®* (or *Pepto Bismol®*) per twenty pounds of body weight three times a day. It will help if you feed your dog an easily digested diet containing a cooked starch such as rice and/or rice water. You may give the dog as much as he will consume in the way of oral fluids to replace losses. *Gatorade®* can be administered. Chicken broth is excellent. Hard-cooked eggs and creamed cottage cheese may also be fed. Persistent diarrhea may be an indication of something far more serious than a mild upset stomach. If it continues for more than twenty-four hours or is accompanied by vomiting or other symptoms, seek professional assistance.

DISLOCATIONS

Dislocations, fractures, and sprains can be caused by any strong impact. A dislocation is a displacement of a bone that is entering into a joint. Joints in the shoulder, hip, jaw, knee, toes, and pasterns are all susceptible to dislocation. The affected limb is, in essence, out of joint and will be held in an abnormal position. Reluctance to bear weight and swelling will occur.

Apply a cold compress to relieve pain and minimize swelling. Do not try to readjust the dislocation,

Fieldmaster's Cota CDX (Ch Fieldmaster of Flintridge ex Glacier Crest Naughty Pine), as an eight-week-old puppy.

Courtesy Young

because you may further damage the tissue and nerves surrounding the bone. Keep the dog quiet and immobilize the limb to prevent further injury. Take the patient to the veterinarian to reposition the joint. Prolonged delay may add complications and make it impossible to reset the joint by manipulation.

ELECTRIC SHOCK

Electric shock can be transmitted by electrical cords, power lines, and lightning. Death usually results from respiratory failure and/or cardiac arrest.

If your dog is in contact with the current, do not touch him. If he has urinated, be cautious not to step in any moisture when you touch him. Try to turn off the current by unplugging the cord from the outlet, or by switching off the circuit breaker. If you are unsuccessful, get assistance. Do not put your own life in jeopardy.

Once the dog can be safely approached, begin supportive measures if the heart or breathing has stopped. Treat for burns and/or shock, if necessary, and seek professional medical attention.

EYE INJURY

The correct eye placement in the Australian Shepherd allows protection from traumatic blows (such as flying hooves) as well as from scratches and lacerations. Sometimes, however, the eye may become injured. Injuries resulting in varied pupil sizes between the right and left eye, unresponsive pupils to light, and/or greying of the cornea are all EMERGENCY SIGNALS that require immediate veterinarian attention.

A severe blow can cause the eye to become dislocated from its socket. This is a true emergency and requires immediate professional care. Do *not* attempt any cleansing or manipulation of the eye, because you could damage it further.

Any foreign bodies in the eye that cannot be washed away by irrigating the eye with a *gentle* stream of lukewarm water should be treated by a veterinarian only. Do not attempt any manipulation of an eye with a penetrating foreign body. If a superficial foreign body is removed by irrigation, continue to observe the eye for irritation or pain, which indicates that professional attention is required.

FISH HOOKS

Fish hooks can be caught in the mouth or feet. Cut the barb off the end of the hook with a pair of wire-cutting pliers or similar tool so that the remaining end can be pulled through. If possible, cut off the

Hartnagle's Badger (1954-1969). (Christiansen's Buster ex Ely's Blue) foundation sire of the early Hartnagle line of Australian Shepherds.

eye so that you will not have to pull the barbed end back through. Clean the wound and apply an antiseptic. Observe for signs of infection.

FOREIGN BODY

Objects can become lodged behind back teeth, wedged across the roof of the mouth (hard palate) between the teeth and cheeks, and sometimes driven into soft tissue. This usually causes your dog to panic. He may paw frantically at his muzzle or shake his head, choke, or cough. Sometimes the jaw cannot be closed. You may notice unusual salivation, difficulty in swallowing, lack of appetite, weight loss, and depression. The symptoms vary due to the location of the foreign object and the length of time it has remained.

Examine the dog's tongue on both the top side and underneath. Examine gums, teeth, and the hard palate. If the dog is extremely agitated, seek professional help to avoid the possibility of being bitten. To examine the throat, place a handkerchief over the dog's tongue for a better grip. Pull the tongue out to view the throat. Sometimes thread becomes looped and imbedded around the tongue. The dog may show signs of retching, gulping, salivation, and decreased or no appetite. In cases of imbedded thread, there is linear reddening that can be seen on and underneath the tongue.

If on examination the object is not too deeply imbedded, it may be removed with a pair of tweezers or dental forceps. If the object is in close proximity to the throat, do not attempt to remove it yourself. Also, if the object is deep or is not easily dislodged, have it removed by your veterinarian.

Food gulped down without the dog chewing it first can result in vomiting or retching of a mucous substance. If you can see the object, it may be possible to grasp it and remove it with forceps. If it is not easily removed, leave the job to a trained specialist. You may cause complications and force the object farther down. Some foreign objects must be located by methods such as radiography.

When a foreign body is present in the intestines, there will be attempts to vomit, abdominal pain, sensitivity to touch in the abdominal area, constipation, retching, excessive salivation, and possible diarrhea.

Never attempt to induce a dog to vomit in the case of a foreign body. This is a job for your veterinarian. If the object is rough or sharp, you may cause considerable damage, lacerations, and even perforation, which can induce death.

Foreign objects in the rectum can cause symptoms similar to those of constipation and constipation itself. If you suspect a rectal foreign body, contact your veterinarian.

FRACTURES

Although the Australian Shepherd is a sturdy working dog, a blow or other abnormal force on the skeletal structure can fracture bones and cause considerable damage.

A fracture is a broken bone indicated by the inability to bear weight on or use a leg or jaw. Another symptom is swelling or abnormal alignment of the injured structure. Fractures can occur in several different forms. When a bone has been fractured in one place with no other damage, it is referred to as a simple closed fracture. When damage such as torn or perforated muscle tissue and skin accompanies a broken bone, it is termed an open fracture. A comminuted fracture describes a bone that has been fractured in more than one place. Some types of fractures are more serious than others, but all need attention.

Do not try to set the fracture. In a compound fracture where the bone protrudes through the skin, a sterile dressing is required to prevent further contamination. Keep the broken limb immobilized. The use of a temporary splint will help prevent sharp edges of the bone from cutting a blood vessel or puncturing a vital organ. However, if excessive manipulation is required to apply the splint, it is best not to attempt it. Tie the limb gently and loosely with bandages or cloth to a pillow, board, stick, or any similar item. Some fractures, such as the skull and shoulder assembly, cannot be splinted. Keep your patient as immobile as possible during transport. Treat for shock if necessary.

FROSTBITE

Frostbite is a rare occurrence in animals that are healthy and well-nourished. However, if frostbite should occur, bring the victim into a warm area and allow him to thaw out gradually. If shelter is unavailable, gently warm or massage areas with your hands or with a soft material. Never rub or massage a frozen area such as the ears with snow, ice, or a coarse material, because it can induce gangrene and easily bruise, tear, and irritate frozen tissue. Instead, soak affected areas in luke-warm water. Vinegar may also be added to the luke-warm water to help thaw the tissue.

Cover your dog with a blanket, sweater, or coat to help maintain his body heat, and get him to a warm shelter as soon as possible. With severe cases of frostbite, as seen in physically injured or trapped animals, no home treatment should be attempted. Take the patient directly to a veterinarian.

HEATSTRESS

Overweight individuals, puppies, and geriatric dogs are more vulnerable to heatstress than dogs in good condition and excellent health.

Heatstroke

Heatstroke is the most frequent type of heatstress. It is most commonly due to exposure to high temperatures, high humidity, and inadequate ventilation.

Initially, heatstroke is characterized by panting, bright red mucous membranes, an increased heart rate, and elevated body temperature. This is followed by a stuporous state, pale mucosa (because of the onset of shock), the extremities are hot to the touch, and the dog may exhibit a watery diarrhea. Final stages of heatstroke are coma and respiratory arrest.

The onset of heatstroke is rapid. Your dog can withstand fevers of 105 degrees F. and above for only a few minutes before permanent damage to the brain and central nervous system occurs. If death is to be avoided, get the dog to a cool, shaded place and, if possible, immerse him in cool water. Otherwise, cool him off by applying cold water to his body any way you can. Do not use ice cold water, as the shock may result in death. Ice packs, however, may be applied to the head and neck. If the dog is conscious and not suffering extreme symptoms, allow him to lick ice cubes. Recovery depends on prompt treatment. Get professional help as soon as possible. Make every attempt to *prevent* heatstroke by keeping your dog in a shaded, well-ventilated area with constant access to fresh, cool water during warm (hot) weather.

Heat Cramps

Heat cramps are painful and are caused chiefly by the loss of salt from the system and by extreme exertion in hot weather. Heat cramps do not commonly occur in dogs; however, the Australian Shepherd may be affected if he is working in the intense heat. As with the other forms of heatstress, ACTION WITHOUT DELAY is imperative to prevent death. Always take your dog to your veterinarian for heat-related injuries.

Heat Exhaustion

Heat exhaustion can occur when a dog has been exposed to intense heat and heavy exercise, has worked hard without adequate water, or when there is a lack of salt in the dog's system. Symptoms are fatigue, muscular weakness, and circulatory collapse. See Heatstroke for treatment. This is an emergency situation that requires immediate action and professional assistance.

HYPOTHERMIA

Hypothermia is a severe lowering of the body temperature that occurs when a dog gets wet and is exposed to cold weather and wind. Hypothermia is seldom seen in a healthy dog that can seek shelter. It is more commonly seen in old or unconscious animals that are injured or diseased, when exposed to cold.

Hypothermia is characterized by violent shivering, drowsiness, slow or absent pulse, dilated pupils, and shallow, infrequent respiration. As the temperature drops below 90 degrees F., shivering will be absent, and the body will be stiff due to increased muscle tone.

The patient should be brought into a warm place and be allowed to warm slowly to normal temperature. Cover the patient with blankets to aid in heat retention. A light massage of the limbs may be helpful. Administer cardiopulmonary resuscitation if necessary. Treat the patient for shock, and seek professional assistance.

INSECT BITES AND STINGS

Insect stings are usually minor, but an allergic reaction can occur. For simple bites and stings, you may apply a cold compress to relieve the pain and swelling. In the case of a bee sting, remove the stinger first. Insect sting treatments are also helpful.

Observe all stings and bites for severe reactions. Symptoms can vary from pain, local swelling, burning, and itching to excruciating pain, muscle cramps, fever, nausea, abdominal pains, convulsions, severe swelling, blisters, shallow respiration, and unconsciousness. Respiratory difficulty is one of the main symptoms for an allergic reaction.

At the first sign of a systemic reaction, get the patient to a veterinarian immediately. If breathing stops, administer artificial respiration. Avoid unnecessary movement, keeping the patient quiet.

LUNG INJURY

Any blow to the chest or inhalation of certain chemicals can cause lung damage. A fractured rib may puncture the lung. There may or may not be external, visible hemorrhaging. Very likely bleeding may occur in the chest cavity. Labored breathing and/or irregular breathing are accompanied by pain in the chest and coughing of foamlike, brilliant, crimson blood.

There is little you can do until professional help is available except to protect visible wounds. More than likely, the victim will try to choose a position that gives him the greatest relief from pain. Allow him to do so. Be careful when moving him to avoid further damage, especially if a fractured rib is involved. Treat for shock. Do not administer any liquids.

NEAR-DROWNING

The Australian Shepherd is an instinctive swimmer. However, even the strongest swimmer can become exhausted and drown. If your dog has sustained an injury, he may be incapable of swimming well enough to keep from drowning. If the dog can be rescued safely and is conscious, cover him with a blanket or coat to prevent chilling, and dry him thoroughly. If he is willing to drink, a warm liquid may be helpful. Watch for signs of shock. It is advisable to have him examined by a veterinarian for possible complications or undetected injuries.

If the dog is unconscious, wrap him in a coat or blanket. Administer artificial respiration if he is not breathing. If vomiting occurs, do not allow vomitus to be sucked back into the dog's lungs. Get the patient to a veterinarian immediately.

NOSE INJURY

A blow or trauma to the nose can cause pain, bleeding, and swelling. Apply an ice pack or cold compress to the nose—this should curb swelling and stop the bleeding. Observe for indications that the dog is having difficulty in breathing. Consult your veterinarian if bleeding continues or breathing difficulty is apparent.

POISONING (TOXICOLOGY)

Any substance (solid, liquid, or gaseous) that is capable of producing a harmful or deadly effect can be considered a poison. Poisoning can occur from ingestion, inhalation, injection, skin contact, or bites. If you discover that your Australian Shepherd has been a victim of poisoning, speed is imperative. PROFESSIONAL MEDICAL HELP SHOULD BE SOUGHT IMMEDIATELY. Dogs can be poisoned with anything from insecticides, rodent bait, and ordinary household cleaning agents to even the smallest amount of antifreeze licked from the ground. Poisoning is usually caused by carelessness, but on occasion dogs have been subject to deliberate poisoning.

Symptoms of poisoning will vary with the posion, but they include trembling, shivering, vomiting pain, paralysis, panting, salivation, convulsions, coma, dizziness, staggering, difficulty in breathing, shallow breathing, diarrhea, loss of appetite, weakness, depression, and sometimes vision difficulties. These symptoms can also be indicative of other dis-

In essence the Breed Ring winner should be able to go out and function in the real world where soundness and conformation are measured by the yardstick of performance. Champion Las Rocosa Little Wolf.

eases or conditions. PROMPT ATTENTION BY A VETERINARIAN IS THE SAFEST AND MOST CERTAIN WAY TO ASSURE PROPER DIAGNOSIS AND TREATMENT. Your ability to identify the exact source and type of poison will give your veterinarian vital life-saving information. If the package containing the poison lists an antidote (a substance to neutralize the poison), report that information to your veterinarian, or take the package or container with you. If you are not sure of the source, it may be helpful to take a small sample of vomitus (if the victim has been vomiting) in a clear plastic bag or container along with the dog to the veterinarian. However, do not delay unnecessarily.

A *Toxicology Hotline* is available to all dog owners without charge twenty-four hours a day, seven days a week. The service was established in 1978 by the University of Illinois College of Veterinary Medicine. Aussie owners are urged to add this Hotline number to their other emergency numbers: (217) 333-3611. If you have a local poison control center, enter that number in the space provided _____ so that you will have it in the event of an emergency.

To eliminate the influence of poison before great harm or death occurs, give the dog milk (or water) to help dilute the poison. Under *no* circumstances, administer anything by mouth if the victim is convulsing, depressed, partially conscious or unconscious. After consultation with your veterinarian by phone, he may or may not recommend to induce vomiting, depending upon the type of poison and apparent symptoms.

An emetic is a substance to induce vomiting. In the case of poisoning, it can be helpful to eliminate some of the toxins and to reduce the absorption of the poison. An emetic should *never* be given in the case of a corrosive poison, such as an acid or alkalai substance.

There are prepared emetics, such as syrup of ipecac, or you may use a solution of peroxide and water or a strong salt solution. To mix a peroxide emetic, mix equal parts of peroxide (3 percent) and water and administer one ounce of the mixture or two tablespoons for every ten pounds of body weight. To mix a strong salt solution, use three quarters of an ounce to one ounce (four to six teaspoons) of salt or mustard powder added to eight ounces (one cup) of warm water, making sure not to get the solution into the dog's windpipe. Keep in mind that puppies will need slightly less than an adult. Repeat if necessary. Consult your veterinarian.

The "universal antidote" is also good to keep on hand in case of emergencies and may be helpful in the event that professional medical attention is not immediately available. However, there is no substitute for professional care. The universal antidote is prepared by mixing two parts (two tablespoons) powdered or crumbled burnt toast (activated charcoal), one part (one tablespoon) of *Milk of Magnesia®*, and one part strong tea. The carbon in the toast helps absorb poisons, the magnesium has a soothing effect on the mucous membranes of the stomach and a laxative action that may also neutralize acid poisons, and the tannic acid in the tea tends to neutralize caustic alkaline materials.

Champion Hilltop L.R. Apollo (Ch Sharp's Ragnar ex Robertson's Cindy), the senior sire of Hilltop.   *Courtesy Robertson*

Acid

Acids include hydrochloric, nitric, sulphuric and battery acids, bleach, and toilet bowl cleaners. Symptoms are: burning sensations in the mouth, throat, and stomach; obvious abdominal pain (sensitive to touch); cramps; disorientation; bloody diarrhea; possible vomiting; and difficulty in breathing.

If you think that your Aussie has sustained acid poisoning, contact your veterinarian immediately. Watch for signs of shock. If acid has come into contact with the skin, wash the affected area with a solution of sodium bicarbonate (baking soda) in cool water. If acid has had contact with the eyes, flush gently with cool water and consult your veterinarian.

To treat acid poisoning, DO NOT INDUCE VOMITING. Neutralize the poison with an alkali, such as sodium bicarbonate in water, *Milk of Magnesia®*, *Pepto Bismol®*. Then administer a demulcent such as milk, olive oil, or egg whites. Get to your veterinarian immediately.

Alkali

Common alkalies are lye, ammonia, drain cleaners, potash, washing powders, and paint removers. Symptoms are similar to those for acid poisoning.

Because of the corrosive nature of alkalies, DO NOT INDUCE VOMITING. Seek professional assistance immediately. Watch for signs of shock. If alkali has come into contact with the eyes, flush gently with cool water and consult your veterinarian. For contact with the skin, rinse the area with a mild acidic solution such as diluted vinegar or lemon juice in water. Diluted vinegar or lemon juice administered may help counteract the alkalai poisoning enroute to your veterinarian.

Carbon Monoxide

Carbon monoxide is a colorless, odorless gas that is commonly produced from the exhaust of automobiles. It may develop when charcoal, gas, kerosene, coal, or oil is burned in areas with inadequate ventilation. The gas invades the bloodstream through the lungs. It unites with hemoglobin in the red corpuscles and restricts oxygen from being carried to cells throughout the body. This causes asphyxiation. Early symptoms include nausea, dizziness, sleepiness, and gasping breathing, followed by unconsciousness.

Get the victim into fresh air immediately. If the victim is gasping for air or breathing has stopped, initiate artificial respiration.

Coumarin, Pindone, and Warfarin

These substances are contained in a variety of rat poisons. Chemicals contained within these cause anticoagulation of blood, and death is caused by massive hemorrhage beneath the skin. Symptoms are: severe shock, bleeding from the nose, blood in vomitus and/or feces, mucous membranes are pale, pulse is rapid and feeble, general body weakness, and the body feels cold.

There is no effective first aid treatment for this type of poisoning. Get immediate professional help. Your veterinarian may administer drugs to induce coagulation.

If you see your dog ingesting an item containing this type of poison, induce vomiting before the poison has an opportunity to reach the intestines.

Petroleum

Gasoline, kerosene, and coal oil, as well as distillates such as lighter fluid, benzene, and furniture

Sometimes the Aussie's natural curiosity gets him in trouble...but not this time.

polish, are petroleum products. Poisoning symptoms include burning, irritated coughing and a possible coma. Seek immediate professional attention. In the meantime, you may dilute the toxin by giving plenty of milk, milk and raw egg whites, *Milk of Magnesia®*, or bread soaked in milk, but only if the patient is conscious and not showing signs of depression.

Strychnine

Strychnine is a frequent cause of poisoning. Increased respiration combined with anxiety may be the first signs. Reflex irritability is greatly increased so that the slightest stimulation by touch or sound may cause extreme reflex activity. Convulsions are sudden, as in epilepsy, and the entire body may become rigid. Spasms last from three to four minutes, accompanied by intervals of complete relaxation. There is no effective first aid treatment for strychnine poisoning. Get immediate veterinary attention.

If you see your dog ingesting poison that you suspect is strychnine, induce vomiting immediately; if not, DO NOT administer an emetic. Consult your veterinarian at once.

TEEP, Pestox III, Parathion, and Malathion (Pyrophosphates)

Any area that is contaminated by a poison must be washed with plenty of water. Contact with insecticides is characterized by muscular twitching, respiratory spasms, pinpoint pupils, heavy salivation, and cramping. If your dog has been contaminated by absorption through the skin, he must be bathed immediately with soap and water to prevent further contamination. Consult a veterinarian immediately.

As a final note, it should be emphasized that PREVENTION is the best cure. Keep all hazardous substances out of the reach of your pet, and be especially cautious with a curious puppy in the household.

PORCUPINE QUILLS

Armed with a bristling coat of approximately thirty thousand barbed quills, the porcupine can drive his well-aimed tail at his enemy, leaving barbed spears in the victim. Quills are extremely painful. They can vary in length from one to four inches. Each quill is needle-sharp with fine barbs that flare in opposition. Quills should be worked out gently, not yanked. It is very painful for the dog and in some cases may require veterinary assistance. If you are alone, grip your dog between your legs. Each movement he makes can work the spears deeper. Using pliers or forceps, slowly twist out each quill. Start with those in the chest area behind and under the shoulder. These may work their way through the skin into the vital organs. Next pull out the quills in the face and legs. After the quills are removed, apply an antiseptic over the wounds. If there are many quills, your veterinarian may have to administer an anesthetic. Check the throat and mouth carefully for quills. Cactus may be removed in a similar fashion. Treat for puncture wounds.

SHOCK

A state of shock can occur following severe stress or trauma, such as hemorrhage, cardiac failure, injury, or disease. Shock is a collapse of the circulatory system, weakening the heart and diminishing the blood flow. If treatment is delayed, shock can result in death.

Signs of shock can be variable. Look for the following: eyes appear dull, lackluster; pupils may be dilated; rapid and weak pulse; rapid, irregular, labored breathing; cold extremities; anxiety; prostration; pale mucous membranes; and thirst.

Treatment

Get the patient to a veterinarian as soon as possible. The administration of intravenous fluids and certain drugs may mean the difference between life and death. During transport, maintain, but do not raise, the body temperature. If the weather is cold or damp, place blankets or extra clothing over and under the victim. Provide shade if the weather is hot. A light massage of the limbs may be helpful. Do not give food or liquid, but if the patient is conscious and thirsty, you may offer an ice cube for him to lick. Assure adequate breathing and control any bleeding. Keep the patient very quiet enroute to professional help.

SKUNKS

Skunks are fitted with a pair of perineal glands from which a pungent, offensive-smelling secretion is sprayed when the animal is startled. If your dog encounters a skunk, wash his eyes liberally with cool, clear water and give him a bath with tomato juice, followed by a bath with soap and water. Diluted lemon juice, vinegar, or mouthwash also helps to neutralize the odor.

SNAKEBITES

Poisoning by snakebite is not uncommon in the working dog. The most common types of snakebites in the United States are the rattlesnake, copperhead, and water moccasin, all of which affect the circulatory system; the bite from a coral snake affects the nervous system. Lethal doses of venom are based on the quantity of poison injected, which is quite variable. Many bites may not be venomizing, and species of snakes will vary in venom potency.

Speed is essential. Most bites will occur on the head, shoulders, thighs, and legs. The bites from pit vipers puncture the skin. Though often difficult to locate, there are two tiny puncture wounds where the fangs have entered the tissue. Painful swelling develops around the wound and rapidly spreads to adjacent tissues. This may be accompanied by accelerated heart rate, vomiting, nausea, faint pulse, difficult respiration (especially if strikes occur on the head and neck), salivation, diarrhea, impaired vision, convulsions, paralysis, shock, and muscular weakness, followed by collapse and death. In the case of the coral snake, the bite may not produce pain and local swelling, but the other signs are more pronounced: difficulty in swallowing, depression, insensitivity of the limbs, and skeletal and respiratory paralysis.

If your dog has been working or exercising, it will increase the speed of absorption into the system, and if the wound is located in a vascular area, death can occur within a matter of five to ten minutes. Subdue the animal and keep the patient immobilized to minimize the uptake of venom while you transport him (DO NOT allow him to walk). You can carry him across your shoulders if necessary. Immediate medical attention is essential.

In case there is a delay in getting the dog to a veterinarian, the following treatment may be of help. Lie the dog down and keep him immobilized. If possible, clip the hair from the wound. If the bite is on a limb, place a wide, flat tourniquet two inches above the wound, between the heart and the wound. Do not place the tourniquet so tight that you cut off circulation of the arteries. You should be able to insert a finger beneath the band. Check the dog's pulse below the wound. If you are unable to feel it, loosen the tourniquet until you are able to feel a pulse. Clean the wound with soap and water and apply an antiseptic, if available. Sterilize a knife or razor blade over an open flame or with an antiseptic. Enlarge the fang wounds with shallow, linelike incisions about one-half inch long that are parallel to the blood supply. You need to cut to the depth of the muscle, but DO NOT cut vital structures (tendons, nerves, vessels), and do not crisscross incisions. Draw the venom from the wound by applying suction to the incisions with the use of a small suction cup that is available in snakebite kits. Mouth suction is not recommended, because two lives might be lost. Maintain suction for thirty minutes. If swelling reaches the band, leave the band in place and apply a second one two inches above the first one. Administer artificial respiration if necessary, and prevent shock. Keep the wound area free of contamination, and get to a veterinarian as soon as possible. In areas that have a large snake population, and where veterinarian care is not readily accessible, your veterinarian may prescribe a dose of antivenom for use in an emergency, to be followed by professional medical attention.

In the event of a snakebite with neither immediate veterinary care nor the necessary equipment to incise the fang wounds and apply suction, keep ice on the affected area and apply a wide, flat tourniquet as described above. Follow up with immediate professional help.

SPRAINS

Sprains and other injuries to ligaments and muscles are often difficult to distinguish from fractures. The injury occurs when there is torque on a joint that elongates the ligament. The affected area is swollen and tender. Keep your dog quiet, and if necessary apply a temporary splint (see Fractures). If you are unsure of the kind and extent of the injury, treat it as a fracture.

THROAT INJURY

A blow to the throat can damage and injure the larynx and is manifested by labored breathing, pain, and swelling. Severe injury and swelling can even lead to suffocation. If the larynx is penetrated, you will hear air leaking out with blood seeping from the wound.

Apply a cold pack to the wound. Do not cleanse the area with liquid because you might get moisture into the air passage and possibly the lung, which will cause further complications. Get your dog to the veterinarian immediately.

VEHICLE COLLISION

An automobile collision can cause considerable physical damage from bruises, abrasions, and broken bones to abdominal injury and skeletal damage. Control hemorrhage. Administer artificial respiration and/or external heart massage. Treat for shock. Get professional help without delay.

VOMITING

Persistent vomiting often indicates a more serious disorder. It can be caused by poisoning, infectious diseases, or foreign bodies and can easily lead to dehydration, which is life-threatening. Treat for fluid losses. Gatorade® and similar fluids are necessary to replace electrolytes. If vomiting is persistent, recurrent, or accompanied by other symptoms, or if vomitus contains blood or abnormal material, a veterinarian should be consulted without delay.

Occasionally your dog will suffer from a simple upset stomach. He may vomit after eating grass, if he gets extremely excited or nervous, or if he gulps down food or water quickly. This type of vomiting is not alarming and is (or should be) followed by normal behavior. If you know your dog and his normal behavior and attitudes, you can easily determine if he is ill or depressed.

"Cooling off."   *MacSpadden Photo*

Proud parents. Left to right: Beauwood's Whispering Pine (Ch Yankee Clipper of Wingmont ex Beauwood's Paprika), Sakonnet Times, and Sakonnet's American Revolution CD (Sorensen's Red Man ex Taylor's Blue Prissy).   *Photo by L.M. Gray*

23
THE AGING AUSSIE

Because of the "willing" Aussie attitude, aging is hardly apparent. The older Aussie is still an excellent companion. He has adapted to your routine and life-style so well over the years that he has become an important member of the family. The aging Aussie plays a vital role in any home. He will be nonetheless eager to please. He will guard the flock, home, and heart with as much courage and devotion as he displayed in his younger years. He may be your self-appointed public relations chairman.

The older, experienced Australian Shepherd may play an active part in teaching young, inexperienced dogs the "ropes," but he will maintain dignity and sometimes a degree of aloofness toward the youngsters' antics. The older Aussie will often surprise you and join in on the fun and games with the vitality of puppyhood.

You will have to make it a point not to take your old friend for granted and put him on a shelf. There will be special times ahead for you both. Keep in mind your dog's physical and mental well-being. Do not allow or ask him to engage in activities beyond his physical capabilities, but simple jobs around the farm or ranch, a little swimming, or a game of ball or frisbee, if not exerting, are excellent. A peaceful walk will give you and your dog pleasure and will provide exercise that is not too taxing in the older years. Your old dog may not understand having to share your time and attention with the youngsters. He will be indignant to think of another taking his place while he is left at home to "hold down the fort." He will nevertheless anxiously await his turn.

Grooming and handling are enjoyed immensely by the Aussie. The well-kept individual is testimony to the health and longevity represented in your breeding stock. For the breeder, there is no greater honor than to be able to "show off" the veterans of the breed, especially those grand foundation sires and dams.

MANAGEMENT

Caring for the aging Aussie should not only prolong life, but it should prolong an enjoyable life right up to the end. The average Australian Shepherd lives to be twelve years of age.

Periodic visits to your veterinarian will be invaluable in diagnosing existing and potential problems. Aging is manifested in a variety of physical changes.

Obesity can be a problem with some aging dogs due to the decreased energy requirements. It may become necessary to adjust the caloric density by providing a low-fat diet. An appropriate ration containing a high-quality protein balanced in smaller amounts may also help alleviate additional stress on the urinary functions (kidneys and bladder). Overfeeding can hasten internal organ degeneration. On the other hand, weight loss and harsh, dry coats in certain individuals can result from the inability of the intestinal tract to absorb and utilize nutrients efficiently. A higher caloric density (energy) diet fed in smaller quantities at more frequent intervals (such as two or three times a day) may be beneficial. With age, the senses are not nearly as keen, and the ability to smell decreases. It is therefore sometimes necessary to provide a diet that contains a strong fish and/or meat aroma and to warm the ration. Supplementation of the B complex (especially B-12) vitamins has been reported to aid in appetite and food assimilation. Also, due to worn down and lost teeth, it may become necessary to moisten dry diets or provide a semimoist or canned variety.

Adding bulk to the diet will help regulate bowel movements and alleviate constipation. Fresh or cooked vegetables, or several tablespoons of vegetables formulated for infants' diets are excellent.

Giving vitamin C has been reported to benefit the arthritic dog. Consult your veterinarian about special diets, including prescription diets.

The older dog is more susceptible to disease, and tissue repair and recovery from disease, illness, and surgery are slower. Dehydration can more commonly occur due to reduced water intake.

Wildhagen's Thistle (Sisler's John ex Heard's Chilie of Flintridge) at the 1982 National Specialty as a twelve-year-old.
Courtesy Smith

Martin's Josie (Taylor's Whiskey ex Taylor's Buena), taking it easy as an aging thirteen-year-old in 1982.   Photo by Patsy Carson

Champion Las Rocosa Leslie CSD (Ch Las Rocosa Shiloh ex Hartnagle's Fritzie Taylor) an active working dog pictured at eleven years of age.

Since his ability to adjust to environmental temperatures (thermoregulation) lessens with old age, the Aussie deserves special consideration for all of his years of devotion. He should be maintained where he may be cooler in the summer and warmer in the winter. He must be kept from lying in drafty places and on the cold, damp ground. In the summer, he must be kept from lying in the hot sun or in a hot vehicle. As outdoor temperatures near seventy-five to eighty degrees, the inside of a vehicle can approach well over one hundred degrees within minutes. Lack of ventilation and water easily lead to heat stroke, which can also occur even though you may have opened each window an inch or two. Although not recommended, if you absolutely must take your dog with you during summer months, make sure that you provide plenty of fresh, cool water and that you check on him every half hour.

GROOMING

Daily brushing is important. (See the chapter on grooming.) Grooming provides an opportunity to check for tumors, cuts, and any other abnormality. Keep the coat in good condition to improve circulation and skin tone and, to a slight degree, help maintain subcutaneous muscle tone. The skin loses its youthful elasticity and often becomes dry during the aging process. The hair coat thins out and the natural oils are reduced. Due to activity of the sebaceous glands, fatty secretions sometimes develop into little cysts on the skin. These are harmless.

Oral hygiene is part of daily grooming. Provide rawhide chew toys. Due to sensitivity of the gums and loss of teeth, the large bones that were formerly enjoyed may not be able to be utilized. A moistened toothbrush dipped in baking soda and salt, or a mild toothpaste can be used to brush the teeth. If the teeth contain slimy tartar, extensive plaque, gingivitis, or evidence of peridontal disease, paint the teeth and gums with 2 percent tincture of iodine on a cotton stick. Do not use enough so that it can be swallowed. Consult the veterinarian for special care. Evidence of oral ulcers may also result from insufficient food consumption.

Muscle tone atrophies in old age. The bones are more subject to fracture due to their brittle nature. Respiratory and cardiovascular functions also begin to lessen with age. The endocrine system (hormones) becomes deficient as well. Mammary gland nodules and tumors on the testicles are frequently seen. Tumors (neoplasms) may or may not cause damage. Sometimes due to their location and size, they eventually disrupt the capacity of specific organ functions. Whenever you suspect any type of tumor, take your dog to the veterinarian.

The aging process also affects the nervous system, which indirectly affects the senses, including audiovisual characteristics and memory responses. You may not notice any difference until you take your dog outside of his familiar surroundings. When vision begins to fail, he can be taught to respond to sound and vibration. The Aussie that is hard of hearing can be trained (even at an older age) to respond to hand signals. Irritability and disorientation are also attributed to the aging process of the nervous responses. You will notice, too, that your old friend requires more sleep.

WORKING THE AGING AUSSIE

As long as your Aussie has the will to work and is physically capable, he can work right up to the end. Because of the will to please, these dogs will do anything asked of them. Don't push your dog beyond his capabilities. Situations such as deep sand can be taxing, and a dog may easily overexert himself. Remember that he may not have the stamina that he once had. Back off when your dog is getting tired and learn to recognize those signals. The older dog may not be able to get in and away from flying hooves and horns with youthful ease. The aging, experienced dog is often aware of his own limitations and will calculate carefully before he moves in to take hold. Since the old bones do not heal as well as young ones, avoid sending your dog into tight, vulnerable places or letting him become fatigued.

The old stock dog will still be a valuable hand on the operation. Younger dogs can carry out the strenuous tasks, while the older dog is there to oversee a job and even bark out a few commands. Simple jobs will make him feel like a useful hand. This dedicated

dog has learned his jobs well and is a pleasure to handle. He can also help your promising youngsters get a solid start in their careers. The older dog's smooth style is calming to inconsistent stock dogs. The presence of the older dog will give the youngster confidence but will not "wind him up" as does the presence of the fiery young dog.

How long you can work a dog depends largely on what he is conditioned to do. In any event, do not work him as hard as before. Muscle soreness can affect the older working dog and usually comes from exertion. When you see that your dog is stiff after working, a warm massage or even warm packs will tend to ease soreness. One or two tablets of *Bufferin®* may also be effective to relieve muscular discomfort. Consult your veterinarian for an exact dosage.

Arthritis

The hip, shoulder, and leg action can become slowed by different types of arthritis. Stiffness and limping are often indicative of other problems as well including injury and neurological disorders. Your veterinarian can best diagnose and advise correct treatment and/or necessary medication to relieve pain.

SAYING GOODBYE

There may come a time when your dog is not able to enjoy life. As an old dog, he may suffer with pain and discomfort. As your dog's best friend, you owe him the blessing that only you can grant. While in the comfort of your arms, you can let him go painlessly in seconds without further suffering.

Lamar's (Mansker's) Turk (Mansker's Smokey ex Mansker's Duchess), the sire from which a dynasty grew pictured at fifteen years of age. Courtesy Cornwell

Bibliography

Altamira, Rafael. *The History of Spain*. Van Nostrano Co. Inc., 1949.

Bailey, E. Murl D.V.M. *Emergency and General Treatment of Poisonings*, College Station, Texas.

Bowen, R.A. D.V.M. *Breeding Soundness Examination of the Male*. Colorado State University, Animal Reproduction Laboratory, Ft. Collins, Co, 1980.

Bowen, R.A. D.V.M. *Outline of Reproductive Anatomy*. Colorado State University, Animal Reproduction Laboratory, Ft. Collins, Co, 1980.

Bowen, R.A. D.V.M. *Reproductive Diseases in the Male*. Colorado State University, Animal Reproduction Laboratory, Ft. Collins, Co, 1980.

Bowen, R.A. D.V.M. *Reproductive Physiology of the Dog*. Colorado State University, Animal Reproduction Laboratory, Ft. Collins, Co, 1980.

Bowen, R.A. D.V.M. *Seminal Evaluation*. Colorado State University, Animal Reproduction Laboratory, Ft. Collins, Co, 1980.

Burnham, Patricia Gail. *Playtraining Your Dog*. New York: St. Martins Press, 1980.

Carmichael, L.E. D.V.M. *Canine Brucellosis: The Silent Threat*. James A. Baker Institute For Animal Health, Cornell University, 1984.

Crow, John A. *Spain: The Root and the Flower*. New York: Harper and Row, 1975.

Defourneaux, Marcelin. *Daily Life in Spain in the Golden Age*. Translated by Newton Branch. England: George Allen and Unwin Ltd, 1970.

Evans, C.D., D.V.M. *Heat Stress: Warm Weather Hazard to Dogs*. Purina Kennel News, Vol. 3, Kansas City, MO, 1976.

Faulkner, L.C. D.V.M. *Reproduction in Dogs*. Colorado State University, Animal Reproduction Laboratory, Ft. Collins, Co, 1980.

First Aid and Emergency Care Workbook, Third Edition.

Fox, Dr. Michael W. *Understanding Your Dog*. New York: Coward, McCann and Geoghegan, Inc., 1972.

Hafen, LeRoy R., and Rister, Carol Coke. *Western America*. Prentice-Hall Inc., 1941.

Haskins, Steve C. D.V.M. M.S. *Cardio-pulmonary Resuscitation*. 170 Vol. 4, #2 February Continuing Education Article #6. Department of Surgery, School of Veterinary Medicine, University of California, Davis, California.

Hippolyte-Mariejol, Jean. *The Spain of Ferdinand and Isabella*. Translated by Benjamin Keen. Rutgers, New Jersey: The State University, 1961.

Holmes, John. *The Farmer's Dog*. London: Popular Dogs Publishing Co, Ltd., 1973.

Holst, P.A. D.V.M. *Breeding Management*. Colorado State University, Animal Reproduction Laboratory, Ft. Collins, Co, 1980.

Holst, P.A. D.V.M. *Vaginal Cytology*. Colorado State University, Animal Reproduction Laboratory, Ft. Collins, Co, 1980.

Hoskins, Johnny D. D.V.M. *Diarrhea*. Ralston Purina Company, 1975. Hoskins, Johnny D. D.V.M., Veterinary Clinic Sciences, Small Animal Hospital, Iowa State University, Ames, Iowa.

How to Be Your Dog's Best Friend. Boston-Toronto: Little Brown and Company, Ltd., 1978.

Kamen, Henry. *The Concise History of Spain*. London: Thames and Hudson Ltd., 1973.

Lamar, Howard R. *The American West - The Reader's Encyclopedia Of*. Harper and Row Publishers, Inc., 1977.

Longton, Tim and Hart, Edward. *The Sheepdog: It's Work and Training*. London: David and Charles, Ltd., 1979.

Lopez, Barry Holstun. *Of Wolves and Men*. New York: Charles Scribner's Sons, 1978.

Managing the Sheep Dog. South Australia: Department of Agriculture Extension Bulletin No. 20.75.

The Merck Veterinary Manual. Rahway, New Jersey: Merck and Company 1973.

Mills, A.F., McIntyre, W.V. and Herbert, S.F. *Dogs and Stock, a Practical Guide to Handling*. Wellington, Auckland, Sydney, Melbourne: A.H. and A.W. Reed Ltd., 1971.

McKendrick, Melveena. *The Horizon Concise History of Spain*. American Heritage Publishing Co., Inc., 1972.

Olson, P.N. D.V.M. *A Method for Collection of Semen in the Dog*. Colorado State University, Animal Reproduction Laboratory, Ft. Collins, Co, 1980.

Olson, P.N. D.V.M. *Artificial Insemination of the Bitch*. Colorado State University, Animal Reproduction Laboratory, Ft. Collins, Co, 1980.

Olson, P.N. D.V.M. *Clinical Approach to Reproductive Failure in the Dog*. Colorado State University, Animal Reproduction Laboratory, Ft. Collins, Co, 1980.

Olson, P.N. D.V.M. *Reproductive Patterns in the Bitch*. Colorado State University, Animal Reproduction Laboratory, Ft. Collins, Co, 1980.

Olson, P.N. D.V.M. *Reproductive Patterns in the Male*. Colorado State University, Animal Reproduction Laboratory, Ft. Collins, Co, 1980

Osweicer, Gary D., D.V.M. *Common Poisonings in Small Animal Practice.* Columbia, Missouri.

Paul, Virginia. *This Was Sheep Ranching Yesterday and Today.* Seattle, Washington: Superior Publishing Co.

Pickett, B.W. D.V.M. *Seminal Handling for Maximum Reproduction Efficiency.* Colorado State University, Animal Reproduction Laboratory, Ft. Collins, Co, 1980.

Rearing and Training a Working Dog. New Zealand: Department of Agriculture Bulletin No 308.

Stockner, P.K. D.V.M. *Reproductive Diseases of the Female.* Colorado State University, Animal Reproduction Laboratory, Ft. Collins, Co, 1980.

Stockner, P.K. D.V.M. *Reproductive Soundness Examination.* Colorado State University, Animal Reproduction Laboratory, Ft. Collins, Co, 1980.

Thorne, Martha Covington. *Handling Your Own Dog.* New York: Doubleday and Company, Inc., 1979.

Wallach, S.J.R. D.V.M. *Sexual Behavior of the Male and Female Dog.* Colorado State University, Animal Reproduction Laboratory, Ft. Collins, Co, 1980.

Wellman, Paul I. *The Trampling Herd.* Quinn and Boden Co, Inc., 1939.

Whitney, Leon F. D.V.M. *Dog Psychology.* New York: Howell Book House, 1978.

JUST A STOCKDOG STORY
by Gary Bogy

Do you remember when I was just a little tyke,
and you bought that hot new colt named Ike.
He was the colour of new fallen snow,
I ran right down to say hello.
Then he kicked a mighty blow,
he nearly hit me, but I ducked low.

I got mad and heeled him hard,
we fought all over the yard.
And when the storm's end was near,
you were pullin' on my ear.
Then I knew I done wrong,
and sang out a sad song.

You said it would be all right,
it was just a kid fight.
Back then you were just a boss,
to a young pup and a green broke hoss.
We made the rounds the three of us,
gathered stock and lots of dust.

That was how it all began,
we all became working friends.
Remember that steer we penned out West,
his horns were longer than the rest.
He was aiming to run me thru,
if it had not been for Ike and you.

Dropped a loop around his neck,
then I really gave him heck.
Then you met that darned old girl,
left me and Ike in a swirl.
We could not find you for a while,
then you brought her home with a smile.

She was really neat,
I loved to lay there by her feet.
One day we got a place of our own,
you and her called it a home.
You remember that brindle bull named Prince,
he had you pinned against the fence.

I told him to let you go and bit him very hard,
he must have kicked me from the yard.
Now I found a place to rest,
like those mountain meadows out West.
But the flowers here stay year-round,
and nobody ever mentions a dog pound.

All the animals here are friends,
it's the way it should have always been.
I sure missed you there at first,
and knew it could not have been worse.
They say it never, never ends,
and I keep making more good friends.

I wanted you to know I am okay,
And I hope to see you here someday.

Index

Jeanne Joy and Little Wolf

Jeanne Joy Hartnagle has been associated with Australian Shepherds for her entire life. In her book, *All About Aussies*, she presents the dogs as she has grown to know them.

From her kindergarten years, when she helped her uncles with the sheep at lambing time, to the times that she spent with the round-up at the Taylor Ranch in Moab, Utah, Jeanne Joy has seen the Aussie in the environment for which he was originally bred and used—as a herding dog par excellence, yet versatile enough to do any other task that is asked of him.

Jeanne Joy has successfully shown Australian Shepherds in conformation, obedience, and working trials since she was fourteen. She also trains and coor-

dinates performing trick dogs. Presently she is an accredited Australian Shepherd Club of America conformation and stock dog judge.

As an author, she is a member of the Rocky Mountain Writers Guild. Jeanne Joy has written articles for *Cattleman Magazine*, among other publications and is on the editorial staff of the *Aussie Times*, the official publiction of the Australian Shepherd Club of America, Inc.

Ms. Hartnagle is currently writing a book on the American bullfighter and rodeo clown with co-author Rick Chatman, one of the leading clowns and the 1984 champion bullfighter on the Wrangler Pro Tour in the Professional Rodeo Cowboys Association.